Integrating Psychological and Pharmacological Treatments for Addictive Disorders

Integrating Psychological and Pharmacological Treatments for Addictive Disorders distills the complex literature on addiction, offering a curated toolbox of integrated pharmacological and psychotherapeutic treatments in chapters authored by leading experts. Introductory chapters on the epidemiology, etiology, and fundamentals of addiction treatment provide a concise overview of the state of the field. Subsequent chapters then focus on the treatment of specific substance use disorders and on gambling disorder. Finally, a chapter on the treatment of addiction in primary care addresses the opportunities for clinical care in nonspecialist outpatient settings. Physicians, psychologists, social workers, and other mental health professionals will come away from the book with an essential understanding of evidence-based practice in treating addiction and the scientific foundations of those approaches.

James MacKillop, PhD, is the Peter Boris Chair in Addictions Research, director of the Peter Boris Centre for Addictions Research, and a professor of psychiatry and behavioural neurosciences at the Michael G. DeGroote School of Medicine at McMaster University/St. Joseph's Healthcare Hamilton. He is also a senior scientist at the Homewood Research Institute and holds courtesy faculty appointments at the University of Georgia and Brown University. He conducts translational research using basic behavioral science, cognitive neuroscience, behavioral genetics, and clinical science to advance the understanding and treatment of addiction.

George A. Kenna, PhD, RPh, is an assistant professor of psychiatry (research) at Brown University, where he performs clinical trials for the treatment of alcohol use disorder. He is a clinical pharmacist at Westerly Hospital, Westerly, Rhode Island, and is also an adjunct assistant professor at the University of Rhode Island.

Lorenzo Leggio, MD, PhD, MSc, is a physician-scientist who conducts clinical research on medication development and the role of neuroendocrine signaling in addictions. His clinical and research training took place between the Catholic University of Rome and Brown University. Throughout his career, he has worked at Brown University and National Institutes of Health.

Lara A. Ray, PhD, is a professor of psychology, co-director of the Addiction and Behavioral Medicine Clinic, and a faculty member in the department of psychiatry and biobehavioral sciences and Brain Research Institute at the University of California, Los Angeles.

Clinical Topics in Psychology and Psychiatry
Bret A. Moore, PsyD, Series Editor

For a complete list of all books in this series, please visit the series page at: www.routledge.com/Clinical-Topics-in-Psychology-and-Psychiatry/book-series/TFSE00310

Practical Psychopharmacology
Basic to Advanced Principles
by Thomas L. Schwartz

Women's Mental Health Across the Lifespan
Challenges, Vulnerabilities, and Strengths
edited by Kathleen A. Kendall-Tackett and Lesia M. Ruglass

Treating Disruptive Disorders
A Guide to Psychological, Pharmacological, and Combined Therapies
edited by George M. Kapalka

Cognitive Behavioral Therapy for Preventing Suicide Attempts
A Guide to Brief Treatments Across Clinical Settings
edited by Craig J. Bryan

Trial-Based Cognitive Therapy
A Handbook for Clinicians
by Irismar Reis de Oliveira

Integrating Psychotherapy and Psychopharmacology
A Handbook for Clinicians
edited by Irismar Reis de Oliveira, Thomas Schwartz, and Stephen M. Stahl

Anxiety Disorders
A Guide for Integrating Psychopharmacology and Psychotherapy
edited by Stephen M. Stahl and Bret A. Moore

Integrating Psychological and Pharmacological Treatments for Addictive Disorders

An Evidence-Based Guide

Edited by
James MacKillop,
George A. Kenna,
Lorenzo Leggio, and
Lara A. Ray

NEW YORK AND LONDON

First edition published 2018
by Routledge
711 Third Avenue, New York, NY 10017

and by Routledge
2 Park Square, Milton Park, Abingdon, Oxon, OX14 4RN

Routledge is an imprint of the Taylor & Francis Group, an informa business

© 2018 James MacKillop, George A. Kenna, Lorenzo Leggio, and Lara A. Ray

The right of the editors to be identified as the authors of the editorial material, and of the authors for their individual chapters, has been asserted in accordance with sections 77 and 78 of the Copyright, Designs and Patents Act 1988.

All rights reserved. No part of this book may be reprinted or reproduced or utilized in any form or by any electronic, mechanical, or other means, now known or hereafter invented, including photocopying and recording, or in any information storage or retrieval system, without permission in writing from the publishers.

Trademark notice: Product or corporate names may be trademarks or registered trademarks, and are used only for identification and explanation without intent to infringe.

Library of Congress Cataloging-in-Publication Data
Names: MacKillop, James, 1975– editor. | Kenna, George A., editor. | Leggio, Lorenzo, editor. | Ray, Lara, editor.
Title: Integrating psychological and pharmacological treatments for addictive disorders : an evidence-based guide / edited by James Mackillop, George A. Kenna, Lorenzo Leggio, and Lara Ray.
Description: New York, NY : Routledge, 2017. |
Series: Clinical topics in psychology and psychiatry |
Includes bibliographical references and index.
Identifiers: LCCN 2017002445| ISBN 9781138919099 (hbk : alk. paper) | ISBN 9781138919105 (pbk : alk. paper) | ISBN 9781315683331 (ebk)
Subjects: LCSH: Compulsive behavior—Treatment. | Compulsive behavior—Chemotherapy.
Classification: LCC RC533 .I58 2017 | DDC 616.85/227—dc23
LC record available at https://lccn.loc.gov/2017002445

ISBN: 978-1-138-91909-9 (hbk)
ISBN: 978-1-138-91910-5 (pbk)
ISBN: 978-1-315-68333-1 (ebk)

Typeset in Bembo and Gill Sans
by Florence Production Ltd, Stoodleigh, Devon, UK

This volume is dedicated to the courageous patients seeking to break the vicious cycle of addiction and the committed mental health professionals working to provide them with the tools to do so.

James MacKillop, George A. Kenna,
Lorenzo Leggio, and Lara A. Ray

To Emily, Annabelle, and Cael

James MacKillop

To the tireless efforts of all the past, present, and future researchers, staff and support personnel at the Brown University Center for Alcohol and Addiction Studies

George A. Kenna

To Dave S., for his tireless and uncompromising devotion to patients with addictive disorders

Lorenzo Leggio

To my husband, Kyle, and my three beautiful daughters, Carmen, Piper, and Gabriela

Lara A. Ray

Contents

List of Figures	ix
List of Tables	x
Notes on Contributors	xi
Series Editor's Foreword	xiv
Acknowledgments	xvi

PART I
Epidemiology, Etiology, and Treatment of Addictive Disorders   1

1   The Epidemiology and Public Health Burden of Addictive Disorders   3
    KEVIN D. SHIELD, SAMEER IMTIAZ
    CHARLOTTE PROBST, AND JÜRGEN REHM

2   The Etiology of Addiction: A Contemporary Biopsychosocial Approach   32
    JAMES MACKILLOP AND LARA A. RAY

3   Evidence-Based Treatment of Addictive Disorders: An Overview   54
    JOHN F. KELLY, BRANDON G. BERGMAN,
    AND CRISTI L. O'CONNOR

PART II
Integrated Treatment for Specific Addictive Disorders   75

4   Alcohol Use Disorder   77
    GEORGE A. KENNA AND LORENZO LEGGIO

5	**Tobacco Use Disorder** JAMES MACKILLOP, JOSHUA C. GRAY, MAX M. OWENS, JENNIFER LAUDE, AND SEAN DAVID	99
6	**Opioid Use Disorder** MONICA BAWOR, BRITTANY DENNIS, JAMES MACKILLOP, AND ZAINAB SAMAAN	124
7	**Cannabis Use Disorder** JANE METRIK AND DIVYA RAMESH	150
8	**Stimulant Use Disorder** ALLISON M. DAURIO AND MARY R. LEE	172
9	**Gambling Disorder** JON E. GRANT AND SAMUEL R. CHAMBERLAIN	205
10	**Addiction Treatment in Primary Care** MEGAN M. YARDLEY, STEVEN J. SHOPTAW, KEITH G. HEINZERLING, AND LARA A. RAY	221

Index 230

Figures

1.1	Prevalence of alcohol use disorders (AUDs) by WHO region and the world, 2010	6
1.2	Percentage of the total burden of disease attributable to alcohol consumption in 2010	9
1.3	Deaths per 100,000 by age group attributable to alcohol use disorders (AUDs) globally in 2010	10
1.4	Age-standardized disability adjusted life years (DALYs) lost attributable to alcohol consumption globally in 2010 per 100,000 people	11
1.5	Age-standardized prevalence of daily tobacco use in 2012 by country	13
1.6	Age-standardized deaths attributable to tobacco smoking globally in 2010 per 100,000 people	16
1.7	Age-standardized disability adjusted life years (DALYs) lost attributable to tobacco smoking globally in 2010 per 100,000 people	17
1.8	Prevalence of opioid, cannabis, cocaine, and amphetamine dependence by sex in 2010	20
1.9	Burden of disease attributable to opioids, cannabis, and stimulants (cocaine and amphetamine) by age in 2010	23
1.10	Age-standardized disability adjusted life years (DALYs) lost attributable to drug dependence globally in 2010 per 100,000 people	23

Tables

1.1	Conditions causally associated with alcohol use and corresponding ICD-10 codes	7
1.2	Diseases that are causally related to tobacco use	15
1.3	Burden of disease attributable to opioids, cannabis, stimulants (cocaine and amphetamine), and other drug dependence in 2010	22
1.4	Additional burden of disease attributable to opioid and stimulant (cocaine and amphetamine) dependence as risk factors for suicide in 2010	22
3.1	The Bradford Hill criteria for evaluating causal and effect relations	56
3.2	Phase model of treatment research for pharmacological and behavioral treatments	59
3.3	Summary of evidence-based treatment criteria and definitions	61
3.4	The steps of the Quality Enhancement Research Initiative to help improve patients' outcomes by helping clinical programs adopt, implement, and sustain EBPs	68
4.1	Summary table	93
5.1	Assessment instruments for a multidimensional pretreatment smoking profile	110
5.2	Summary table	113
6.1	Summary table	139
7.1	Summary table	161
8.1	Studies on psychosocial treatments	174
8.2	Studies on pharmacological treatments	181
8.3	Studies on combined psychosocial and pharmacological treatments	187
8.4	Summary table	194
9.1	Summary table	216
10.1	Summary table	227

Contributors

Monica Bawor, PhD, Peter Boris Centre for Addiction Research, Department of Psychiatry and Behavioural Neurosciences, McMaster University

Brandon G. Bergman, PhD, Department of Psychiatry, Massachusetts General Hospital, Harvard Medical School

Samuel R. Chamberlain, MB/BChir, PhD, MRCPsych, Department of Psychiatry, University of Cambridge

Allison M. Daurio, BS, Section on Clinical Psychoneuroendocrinology and Neuropsychopharmacology, National Institute on Alcohol Abuse and Alcoholism; and National Institute on Drug Abuse, Bethesda, Maryland

Sean David, MD, SM, DPhil, Department of Medicine, Stanford University, Palo Alto, California

Brittany Dennis, PhD, Peter Boris Centre for Addiction Research, Department of Psychiatry and Behavioural Neurosciences, McMaster University

Jon E. Grant, JD, MD, MPH, Department of Psychiatry and Behavioral Neuroscience, University of Chicago

Joshua C. Gray, MS, Department of Psychology, University of Georgia, Athens, Georgia; and Department of Psychiatry and Human Behavior, Brown University, Providence, Rhode Island

Keith G. Heinzerling, MD, MPH, Department of Family Medicine, University of California, Los Angeles

Sameer Imtiaz, MSc, Centre for Addiction and Mental Health (CAMH), Toronto, Canada; and Institute of Medical Science (IMS), University of Toronto, Canada

John F. Kelly, PhD, Recovery Research Institute, Addiction Recovery Management Service; and Center for Addiction Medicine, Massachusetts General Hospital, Harvard Medical School

George A. Kenna, PhD, RPh, Brown University; Westerly Hospital, Westerly, Rhode Island; and University of Rhode Island

Jennifer Laude, PhD, Department of Psychology, University of Kentucky

Mary R. Lee, MD, Section on Clinical Psychoneuroendocrinology and Neuropsychopharmacology, National Institute on Alcohol Abuse and Alcoholism; and National Institute on Drug Abuse, Bethesda, Maryland

Lorenzo Leggio, MD, PhD, MSc, Bethesda, Maryland

James MacKillop, PhD, Peter Boris Centre for Addictions Research, Department of Psychiatry and Behavioural Neurosciences, McMaster University; and Homewood Research Institute, Homewood Health Centre

Jane Metrik, PhD, Department of Behavioral and Social Sciences Center for Alcohol and Addiction Studies, Brown University School of Public Health; and Substance Abuse Treatment Program, Mental Health and Behavioral Sciences Service, Providence Veteran's Administration Medical Center

Cristi L. O'Connor, MHS, Department of Psychiatry, Massachusetts General Hospital, Harvard Medical School

Max M. Owens, MS, Department of Psychology, University of Georgia, Athens, Georgia

Charlotte Probst, MS, Centre for Addiction and Mental Health (CAMH), Toronto, Canada; and Institute for Clinical Psychology and Psychotherapy, TU Dresden, Germany

Divya Ramesh, PhD, Department of Behavioral and Social Sciences, Center for Alcohol and Addiction Studies, Brown University School of Public Health

Lara A. Ray, PhD, Department of Psychology and Department of Psychiatry and Biobehavioral Sciences, University of California, Los Angeles

Jürgen Rehm, PhD, Centre for Addiction and Mental Health, Toronto, Canada; Institute of Medical Science, University of Toronto, Canada; Institute for Clinical Psychology and Psychotherapy, TU Dresden, Germany; Campbell Family Mental Health Research Institute, Toronto, Canada; Department of Psychiatry, University of Toronto, Canada; and Dalla Lana School of Public Health, University of Toronto, Canada

Zainab Samaan, MBChB, DMMD, MSc, PhD, MRCPsych, Peter Boris Centre for Addiction Research, Department of Psychiatry and Behavioural Neurosciences, McMaster University

Kevin D. Shield, PhD, Centre for Addiction and Mental Health, Toronto, Canada; Institute of Medical Science, University of Toronto, Canada; and International Agency for Research on Cancer, Lyon, France

Steven J. Shoptaw, PhD, Department of Family Medicine, University of California, Los Angeles

Megan M. Yardley, PhD, Department of Psychology, University of California, Los Angeles

Series Editor's Foreword

Integrating Psychological and Pharmacological Treatments for Addictive Disorders: An Evidence-Based Guide is the fifth book in one of Routledge's newest series, Clinical Topics in Psychology and Psychiatry (CTPP). The overarching goal of CTPP is to provide mental health practitioners with practical information that is both comprehensive and relatively easy to integrate into day-to-day clinical practice. It is multidisciplinary in that it covers topics relevant to the fields of psychology and psychiatry, and appeals to the student, early career, and senior clinician. Books chosen for the series are authored or edited by national and international experts in their respective areas, and contributors are also highly respected clinicians. The current volume exemplifies the intent, scope, and aims of the CTPP series.

Editors James MacKillop, George A. Kenna, Lorenzo Leggio, and Lara A. Ray bring together some of the world's top scholars and clinicians and provide a comprehensive review of evidence-based treatments for addictive disorders. Unlike many books that focus on either psychosocial or pharmacological interventions, the editors highlight the latest and most salient research that guides effective integrative clinical practice. A thorough review of the epidemiological data surrounding alcohol, tobacco, and prescription and illicit drugs sets the stage for a thoughtful discussion about the biopsychosocial explanation for the development of addictive disorders. The subsequent seven chapters break down what we currently know about effective pharmacological and psychosocial treatments for the most common addictive disorders, including opioids and gambling. The final chapter discusses the application of these interventions in the setting that most frequently sees these disorders – primary care.

The clinician will likely find all chapters equally important and beneficial – a relatively uncommon experience with edited books. Of particular importance and excellence is the chapter on opioid use disorders. As the abuse and dependence rates of prescription narcotics continue to rise and reach epidemic proportions, the fields of addiction psychology, psychiatry, and medicine struggle to effectively combat the ill effects of this cotemporary social disease. In addition to reviewing the latest evidence for popular medications such as buprenorphine, naloxone, and naltrexone, the authors give equally important attention to the latest support for using cognitive, behavioral, and family therapies.

Another important component of the current volume is its focus on delivering effective interventions in the primary care setting. Not unlike psychiatric disorders, primary care practitioners see the lion's share of addictive disorders. The authors discuss evidenced-based means for assessing and treating these disorders, understanding limitations of time and resources. They also review a means for better integration addiction treatment into primary care clinics, which treats the problem where it is often first diagnosed. This is similar to what is being done for psychiatric disorders in primary care clinics.

In an area of clinical practice that has posed some of the most significant challenges for healthcare providers over the past few decades, it is refreshing to see a volume of this quality. It is also surprising that we are just now seeing such a comprehensive, focused, and clearly written book on the topic. MacKillop, Kenna, Leggio, and Ray have done the field a great service by producing such an excellent resource. Researchers and clinicians of all stripes will find this volume worth its weight in gold.

Bret A. Moore, PsyD, ABPP
Series Editor
Clinical Topics in Psychology and Psychiatry

Acknowledgments

The development of this volume was supported, in part, by the Peter Boris Chair in Addictions Research, the Homewood Research Institute, and grants from the Canadian Institutes for Health Research (365297; JM) and the National Institutes of Health (DA041226, LAR; P30 DA027827, JM; AA021744, LAR; AA022752, LAR; AA023669, LAR, JM; AA024930, JM; and AA022214, LAR). The authors have no conflicts of interest to declare.

Part I

Epidemiology, Etiology, and Treatment of Addictive Disorders

Chapter 1

The Epidemiology and Public Health Burden of Addictive Disorders

Kevin D. Shield, Sameer Imtiaz, Charlotte Probst, and Jürgen Rehm

Competing interests: The authors have declared that no competing interests exist

Scope of the Chapter

The use of addictive substances and engagement in addictive behaviors have taken place since the beginning of recorded history, are postulated to have contributed to human evolution [1], and occur worldwide. Furthermore, compulsive and addictive behaviors that are characterized by an impulse, drive, or temptation to perform the behaviors are also hypothesized to be the result of evolutionary pressures [2]. It is theorized that people engage in the use of addictive substances and in addictive behaviors for pleasure, to feel better, as a social lubricant, out of curiosity, and "because others are doing it" [3]. After initiating substance use or engaging in an addictive behavior, an individual's vulnerability to becoming addicted to the substance or behavior is dependent on numerous complex and interacting genetic and environmental factors [4]. The harms caused by the use of addictive substances are dependent on the substance used, as well as the amount and patterns of substance use [5, 6].

The following chapter provides an overview of the epidemiology (mainly prevalence) and burden of disease associated with the use of alcohol, tobacco, and illicit drugs, and the use disorders associated with these substances. Current medical definitions of addictive behaviors (see the Diagnostic and Statistical Manual of Mental Disorders (DSM) 5 [7]) include gambling and consider Internet/gaming addictions as potentially addictive behaviors. Specifically, in the DSM-III, pathological gambling was introduced as a disorder of impulse control [8], suggesting an intrapersonal difficulty in controlling one's actions. In the DSM-IV, similarities to the phenomena of substance use disorders were discussed [9], namely similarities in the neurological activation of the reward system [10], genetic similarities [11], and similarities of specific symptoms such as craving and tolerance [12]. These discussions led to the inclusion of gambling disorders in the category of substance-related and addictive disorders in the DSM-5 [13]. In addition, in the DSM-5 [7], Internet Gaming Disorder was identified as a condition warranting more clinical research and experience before being formally included in the DSM as a disorder.

Data are scarce on the epidemiology and burden of addictive behaviors such as gambling or gaming disorders. For example, ALICE RAP (Addiction and Lifestyles in Contemporary Europe Reframing Addictions Project; www.alicerap.eu) aimed to provide such data for countries in the European Union (EU), but did not find data on the prevalence of gambling disorders for these generally data-rich high-income countries.

This chapter also provides an overview of the various definitions of addictive disorders. Although there are medical (psychiatric) definitions found in the DSM-5 and in the tenth revision of the International Classification of Diseases (ICD) [14], these definitions are rarely used in fields other than medicine. For example, in the case of tobacco, medical classifications of tobacco use disorders are not used in the field of epidemiology, and are not included in the burden of disease classifications. With respect to illicit drug use disorders, other systems of classification are more important, such as the category of problem drugs found in the World Drug Reports ([15] as the most recent example). For a recent general discussion of how best to define addictive disorders comprising both substance use disorders and other behavioral addictions, see the overview of ALICE RAP [16, 17].

The overview of the burden of disease caused by addictive disorders presented in this chapter is restricted to the health burdens caused by such disorders (i.e. mortality, years of life lost to premature mortality (YLL), years of life lost to disability (YLD), and/or disability adjusted life years (DALYs) lost attributable to addictive disorders; see [18]). The most important measure of the health burden caused by addictive disorders is the DALYs lost [19], which is the sum of YLL and YLD (i.e. a summary measure of health) [19]. All estimates of the health burden caused by addictive disorders were obtained from the most recent iteration of the Global Burden of Disease and Injury (GBD) study (for the last relevant publication on the topic, see [20] and http://vizhub.healthdata.org/gbd-compare/). Although other estimates of the burden of addictive disorders exist, estimates from the GBD study are presented in this chapter, as they are comparable estimates across substances; however, the GBD study estimates do have limitations. Substance use disorders as defined by the GBD 2010 included only dependence as defined by the DSM-IV [21] or ICD-10 [14], and not abuse (DSM-IV: [19]) or harmful use (ICD-10: [14]). Thus, it is implicitly assumed that the disability weight [22] for people with "abuse" or "harmful use" is the same as for similar people without those disorders. Lastly, the GBD study does not provide explicit estimates for tobacco use disorders, but is restricted to smoking as a risk factor.

Alcohol Use Disorders

Alcohol has been used by societies for thousands of years [23]. Furthermore, the industrialization of alcohol production and the globalization of alcohol marketing and promotion led to an increase in alcohol consumption worldwide in the 20th century [24]. Alcohol consumption is causally associated with both positive (at low levels of alcohol consumption for people who do not engage in heavy episodic drinking) and negative medical consequences [25], and is the fifth leading risk factor for the global burden of disease [26]. Alcohol use disorders

(AUDs) in general, and alcohol dependence (AD) specifically, are some of the most severe health effects caused by the prolonged harmful use of alcohol [7]. Furthermore, with a prevalence of approximately 4%, AUDs are some of the most common mental disorders worldwide [20]. Due to the detrimental effects of the chronic heavy use of alcohol, people with an AUD have a life expectancy that is more than 10 years lower than people without an AUD [27, 28]. Additionally, AUDs are often linked to the majority of the alcohol-attributable burden of disease and death [29, 30] since the risk relationship between the average volume of alcohol consumed and most disease and injury endpoints is exponential [25]. However, despite the prevalence of AUDs and the burden they cause, AD was only first suggested in 1976 by Edwards and Gross [31].

The following section on AUDs provides an overview of the diagnostic criteria for AUDs, the epidemiology of alcohol use and AUDs (data for this section were obtained from the Global Status Report on Alcohol and Health [24]), and the burden of disease attributable to alcohol use and AUDs (data for this section were obtained from the GBD 2010 study [20]).

Epidemiology of Alcohol Use and Alcohol Use Disorders

The consumption of alcohol is a common behavior in most high-income countries; the average prevalence of lifetime abstainers in high-income countries is below 20% [24]. However, in low- and middle-income countries, lifetime abstinence from consumption of alcohol is more common [24]. Additionally, in countries with a high proportion of Muslims (i.e. 80% and more), lifetime abstention rates are often as high as 80%, even among people with high socioeconomic status [24].

Similar to the prevalence of alcohol consumption, the prevalence of AUDs varies considerably between countries due to religious, economic, and other differences [24]. In 2010, an estimated 95 million people worldwide met the criteria for AD [20]. The lowest prevalence of AUDs (past 12 months) at 0.3% among adults was observed in Eastern Mediterranean countries (e.g. Afghanistan, Egypt, Lebanon, Pakistan, and Somalia), whereas the Americas (including South and Central America) and Europe showed the highest prevalence at 6.0% and 7.5%, respectively [24]. Figure 1.1 outlines the prevalence of AUDs by World Health Organization (WHO) region.

In all WHO regions, the prevalence of AUDs among men was more than double that of the prevalence of AUDs among women. Among men, the highest past year prevalence of AUDs was in the European region (12.6%), followed by the Americas (9.0%). For women, the highest prevalence of AUDs was in the Americas (3.2%), followed by the European region (2.9%). For both men and women, the lowest prevalence of AUDs was observed in the Eastern Mediterranean region (0.2%).

For AD in particular, the global past year prevalence was 2.3% in 2010. As with the prevalence of AUDs, the highest prevalence rates of AD were observed

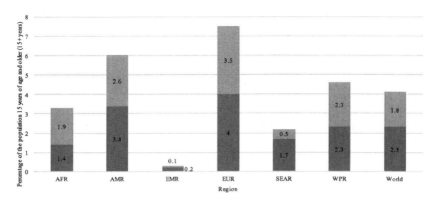

Figure 1.1 Prevalence of alcohol use disorders (AUDs) by WHO region and the world, 2010 [24]

in the European region (4%) and the Americas (3.4%). Furthermore, AD has become an increasingly important public health issue, with an observed increase in the prevalence of AD globally from 1990 to 2010 [20].

The Health Burden Caused by the Consumption of Alcohol

Over 230 three-digit ICD-10 code diseases (communicable as well as non-communicable) and injuries are causally linked to alcohol consumption [32, 33] (see Table 1.1 for an overview). Furthermore, for more than 30 of these conditions, alcohol consumption is a necessary cause (and the burdens caused by these diseases and injuries are wholly attributable to alcohol consumption), such as alcoholic cirrhosis of the liver, poisoning by alcohol, alcoholic polyneuropathy, and AUDs.

The incidence and mortality of all outcomes causally associated with alcohol use are generally determined by the volume of pure alcohol consumed and the pattern in which alcohol is consumed (in some rare cases, the harms caused by alcohol are also dependent on the quality of the alcoholic beverage) [25]. Furthermore, although persons of low socioeconomic status are more likely to be lifetime abstainers [34], these individuals have been shown to have a twofold to 12-fold elevated risk of dying from an alcohol-attributable cause of death [35].

As high levels of alcohol use or heavy episodic drinking characterize AUDs, people with an AUD are more likely to experience diseases and injuries causally related to alcohol consumption when compared to people without an AUD. A recent study from Denmark, Finland and Sweden observed that people with an AUD have a 24- to 28-year shorter life expectancy than the general population

Table 1.1 Conditions causally associated with alcohol use and corresponding ICD-10 codes

Cause of mortality or morbidity	ICD-10 code
Infectious diseases	
Tuberculosis	A15–A19
HIV/AIDS	B20–B24
Cancer	
Lip, oral cavity and pharyngeal cancers	C00–C14
Oesophageal cancer	C15
Liver cancer	C22
Laryngeal cancer	C32
Breast cancer	C50
Colon cancer	C18
Rectal cancer	C20
Endocrine, nutritional, and metabolic diseases	
Diabetes mellitus	E10–E14
Alcohol-induced pseudo-Cushing's syndrome	E24.4*
Neuropsychiatric diseases	
Alcohol use disorders	F10
Degeneration of nervous system attributed to alcohol	G31.2*
Epilepsy	G40–G41
Alcoholic polyneuropathy	G62.1*
Alcoholic myopathy	G72.1*
Cardiovascular diseases	
Hypertensive disease	I10–I15
Ischemic heart disease	I20–I25
Alcoholic cardiomyopathy	I42.6
Cardiac arrhythmias	I47–I49
Ischemic stroke, haemorrhagic, and other non-ischemic stroke	I60–I66
Digestive diseases	
Alcoholic gastritis	K29.2
Cirrhosis of the liver	K70*, K74
Acute and chronic pancreatitis	K85, K85.2*, K86.0*, K86.1
Respiratory infections	
Lower respiratory infections	J10–J18, J20–J22

continued . . .

Table 1.1 Continued

Cause of mortality or morbidity	ICD-10 code
Conditions arising during pregnancy or the prenatal period	
Maternal care for (suspected) damage to fetus from alcohol	O35.4*
Fetus and newborn affected by maternal use of alcohol	P04.3*
Low birth weight	P05–P07
Fetal alcohol syndrome (dysmorphic)	Q86.0
External causes	
Toxic effect of alcohol	T51
Unintentional injuries (transport injuries, poisonings, falls, fires, drowning, other)	V01–X59, Y15*, Y40–Y86, Y88, Y89, Y90*, X45*
Intentional injuries (self-inflicted injuries, homicide)	X60–Y09, Y87

Note: Conditions that are 100% attributable to alcohol use are indicated with an asterisk (*) [32]

[27], which coincides with the high standardized mortality rates among people with AUDs [36–38].

Burden of Disease Attributable to Alcohol Consumption

In 2010, alcohol consumption caused 2.7 million deaths globally (1.8 million deaths among men and 0.9 million deaths among women), accounting for 5.2% of all deaths in 2010 (6.3% of all deaths among men and 3.8% of all deaths among women) [20, 26]. The burden of disease attributable to alcohol consumption totaled 98 million DALYs lost in 2010 (75 million DALYs lost among men and 23 million DALYs lost among women), accounting for 3.9% of all DALYs lost (5.5% of all DALYs lost among men and 2.0% of all DALYs lost among women). Furthermore, alcohol consumption is the fifth most important risk factor for the burden of disease globally, and was the top risk factor for the burden of disease among people 15 to 49 years of age [39]. This observation can be partially explained by the fact that the diseases that are causally related to alcohol consumption harm people who are younger in age as well as those who are older in age [39].

There is also considerable regional variance, with alcohol use accounting for approximately 13% of the total burden of disease in Eastern Europe, but for less than 1% in the Central Sub-Saharan, North Africa and Middle East regions. Figure 1.2 outlines the percentage of the total burden of disease attributable to alcohol consumption in 2010.

Although the burden of disease attributable to alcohol consumption is large, this burden has decreased since 1990, with the burden of disease due to alcohol consumption decreasing from 1,637 DALYs lost per 100,000 people in 1990 to 1,444 DALYs lost per 100,000 people in 2010.

Epidemiology and Public Health Burden   9

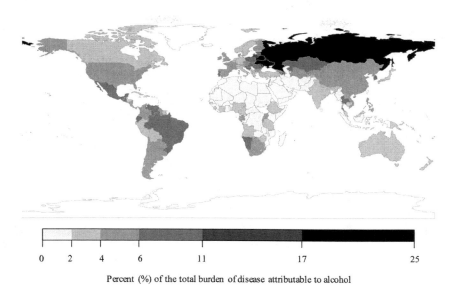

Percent (%) of the total burden of disease attributable to alcohol

Figure 1.2 Percentage of the total burden of disease (measured in disability adjusted life years lost) attributable to alcohol consumption in 2010 [84]

Burden of Disease Attributable to Alcohol Use Disorders

In 2010, AUDs accounted for 111,000 deaths and 18 million DALYs lost. For women, AUDs accounted for about 100 in 100,000 DALYs lost in 2010, while the rate for men in 2010 was much higher, with 400 in 100,000 DALYs lost. The burden of disease attributable to AUDs has decreased since 1990 from 275 deaths per 100,000 people to 259 deaths per 100,000 people in 2010.

Among mental and substance use disorders, AUDs are responsible for 44% of the YLL within this category [20]. The magnitude of the burden of disease caused by AUDs is dependent on age. AUD-attributable YLDs are highest for the age group of 20 to 50 years; death rates increase steadily from the age of 20 and peak around the age of 55, with relatively high rates for older age groups. In absolute terms, the majority of AUD-attributable deaths occur between the ages of 40 and 60 years. Figure 1.3 outlines the number of deaths per 100,000 people attributable to alcohol consumption in 2010.

With respect to regional differences, DALYs lost due to AUDs were highest in the Eastern Europe region, accounting for approximately 1,000 of every 100,000 observed DALYs lost, and were lowest for the Western Sub-Saharan Africa, North Africa and the Middle East regions, accounting for less than 70 in every 100,000 observed DALYs lost. In the North America, Western and Central Europe regions, DALYs lost ranged from between 350 and 400 per 100,000 observed DALYS lost. Globally, the absolute burden of disease attributable to AUDs has increased over the past 20 years. Due to a decreasing

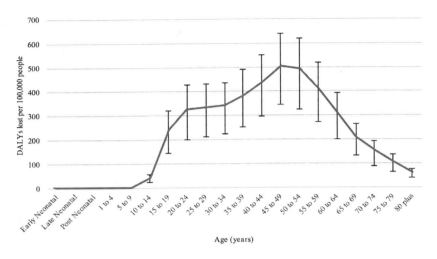

Figure 1.3 Deaths per 100,000 by age group attributable to alcohol use disorders (AUDs) globally in 2010 [84]

burden from infectious diseases and demographic shifts in the population, the relative importance of AUDs and their related burdens are increasing worldwide, particularly for developing countries [20]. Figure 1.4 outlines the DALYs lost per 100,000 people attributable to alcohol consumption in 2010.

The presented burdens of AUDs are based on deaths where AUDs have been explicitly mentioned as the cause. Thus, these data may be biased, as AUDs are not usually mentioned on death certificates, but are mainly indirect causes of death due to the impact of the heavy use of alcohol. Thus, the presented burden of AUDs excludes causal sequences, when heavy drinking by people with AUDs causes disease (e.g. liver cirrhosis [40]) or injury in some cases leading to death. Furthermore, as previously mentioned, as the risk relationship between alcohol consumption and disease/injury outcomes is exponential [25, 30, 41, 42], AUDs account for much of the burden of disease described above with regard to alcohol use. For example, an analysis of the burden of disease attributable to alcohol consumption in the EU found that the majority of this burden was due to AUDs [29].

Alcohol Consumption and Alcohol Use Disorders as a Risk Factor for Health Outcomes Not Measured in the Global Burden of Disease and Injury Study

The burden of disease attributable to alcohol consumption does not always include harms caused by the drinking of others, such as resulting from traffic accidents [43, 44]. Indeed, these harms are hypothesized to create a large burden; an Australian study observed that 70% of respondents were negatively affected

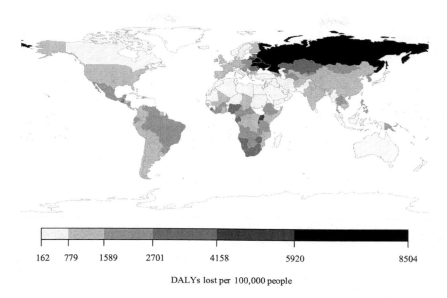

Figure 1.4 Age-standardized disability adjusted life years (DALYs) lost attributable to alcohol consumption globally in 2010 per 100,000 people [84]

by the drinking of strangers, and 30% of respondents reported negative effects from the alcohol use of a person close to them [44].

Conclusions

Both the consumption of alcohol and AUDs are prevalent globally. However, the consumption of alcohol and the prevalence of AUDs are greater in high-income countries when compared to both low- and middle-income countries. As alcohol consumption is related to over 230 three-digit ICD-10 codes, alcohol and AUDs cause a large burden of disease globally. In 2010, 2.7 million deaths and 97 million DALYs lost were attributable to alcohol consumption, and alcohol was the fifth leading risk factor for the global burden of disease. AUDs in particular were responsible for 111,000 deaths and 18 million DALYs lost. Thus, as the burden caused by alcohol consumption is large, interventions are required to further reduce alcohol consumption, the prevalence of AUDs, and their resulting burdens.

Tobacco-Related Disorders

An increase in smoking rates in the 20th century in high-income countries [45–48], followed by similar increases in mid- and lower-income countries [49], has led to an epidemic of diseases caused by tobacco use and tobacco dependence [50, 51], not only for the tobacco user [47], but also for people exposed to tobacco smoke [48]. Although the harms caused by tobacco smoke were suggested in 1898 by Rottmann, the health harms and dependence caused by tobacco smoking and other forms of tobacco use have only been recognized since the 1940s and 1950s with the emergence of case-control and cohort studies [52, 53] and from the strengthening of animal model research on the effects of tobacco smoke [52]. The understanding of the harms caused by tobacco use were furthered again in the 1960s with the outlining of criteria for causality by Hill [54], and by the 1964 surgeon general's report on the relationship between cigarette smoking and cancer, which included a summary of the empirical association between smoking and cancer as produced through a meta-analysis [55]. Furthermore, the dependence-producing properties of tobacco products have only been known widely since the 1980s [56].

Tobacco use, including cigarette smoking and other forms such as chewing tobacco, produce dependence caused by the nicotine contained in tobacco products [57]; the dependence-producing properties of tobacco products are recognized by the WHO [58] and the American Psychiatric Association [7, 59]. This production of dependence through the use of the tobacco plant is responsible for adverse effects on health such as cardio-toxicity [60] and decreased immune system functioning [61]. However, most health-related consequences caused by tobacco use are attributable to the 2,500 toxins in the tobacco plant [62] and to the 5,300 chemical substances present in tobacco smoke [63–65]. In particular, these substances lead to increases in the risk of infectious and parasitic diseases, respiratory infections, conditions arising during the perinatal period, malignant neoplasms, neuropsychiatric conditions, cardiovascular diseases, digestive diseases, and respiratory diseases [66]. The increased risk of these diseases and conditions accumulates with use and depends on the age of the person when they started using tobacco, the route of administration, the average number of cigarettes smoked per day, the characteristics of the cigarette (such as tar and nicotine content), and smoking behaviors such as inhalation characteristics [67].

The following section outlines the epidemiology of tobacco use and tobacco use disorders, as well as the epidemiology of the burdens that result from tobacco use and tobacco use disorders.

Definition of Tobacco Use Disorders

The continued problematic use of tobacco over time (i.e. daily use of either cigarettes or smokeless tobacco) can lead to clinical impairment and/or distress in an individual, which is clinically recognized as a tobacco use disorder [7]. Tobacco use disorders are commonly measured using the criteria set out in the various versions of the DSM-5 [7] (the DSM-IV measures nicotine dependence), or using Fagerström's criteria for nicotine dependence (a subtype of tobacco use disorders) [68]; however, other instruments are also used to measure tobacco use disorders.

Epidemiology of Tobacco Use and Tobacco Use Disorders

There is a critical public health need to monitor trends in the use of tobacco in terms of both prevalence and total volume of consumption, as well as in the prevalence of tobacco use disorders [69]. However, historical data on the prevalence of smoking in developing countries are limited [46, 70], with only approximately one-third of all countries monitoring tobacco use by conducting nationally representative youth and adult surveys at least once every five years [71]. Additionally, efforts to track cigarette consumption per capita have not been systematic over time, and the data on tobacco consumption differ substantially by source [72–74].

Two recent improvements in data collection and synthesis have enhanced the monitoring of tobacco use and tobacco use disorders. First, the Tobacco Atlas has facilitated the use of tobacco data by assembling these data in one location [75]. Second, investments in multi-country survey programs have expanded the data on tobacco use and tobacco use disorders [71].

Prevalence of Tobacco Use

Globally, tobacco consumption is large and widespread, with smoking being prevalent in low-, middle- and high-income countries [69]. Figure 1.5 outlines the age-adjusted prevalence of daily smoking per 100,000 people.

Due to increases in public health prevention measures, such as increases in tobacco taxation, enforcement of bans on tobacco advertising, and protection

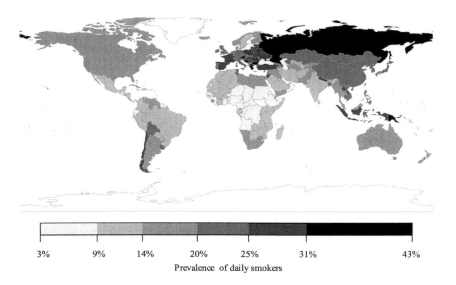

Figure 1.5 Age-standardized prevalence of daily tobacco use in 2012 by country [69]

of people from tobacco smoke [76, 77] (see [76] for the WHO best buys), the prevalence of daily smoking decreased from 1980 to 2012; the estimated age-standardized prevalence of daily tobacco smoking for men declined from 41.2% to 31.1%, an average annual rate of decline of 0.9%, and for women declined from 10.6% to 6.2%, or 1.7% per year [69]. The largest annualized rates of change worldwide between 1980 and 2012 were achieved among people 15 to 19 years of age (−1.8% in daily smoking rates among men and −2.8% in daily smoking rates among women) [69].

In high-income countries, the prevalence of daily smoking in men peaks at 45 to 54 years of age, after which it decreases. Among women in high-income countries, the prevalence of daily smoking peaks at 20 to 29 years of age, and then decreases. In comparison to high-income countries, in developing countries daily tobacco use in men peaks at 25 to 40 years of age, after which it decreases, and in women daily tobacco use peaks at 75 years of age and older [69].

Prevalence of Tobacco Use Disorders

As with tobacco use, tobacco use disorders are hypothesized to be prevalent globally [78]. In the United States, the past year prevalence of tobacco use disorders (as measured through tobacco dependence) (DSM-IV) was 12.8% in adults 18 years of age and older, with these rates being similar among women (11.5%) and among men (14.1%) [79]. As previously mentioned, since dependence is a subtype tobacco use disorder, the prevalence of tobacco use disorders is higher than that of tobacco dependence.

Burden of Tobacco Use and Tobacco Use Disorders

Tobacco use is causally related to various diseases in the body through both primary exposure and secondary exposure [47]. Specifically, primary exposure to tobacco is causally related to the development of malignant neoplasms (specifically cancer of the larynx, oropharynx, oesophagus, trachea, bronchus and lung, stomach, pancreas, kidney and ureter, colon, cervix and bladder, as well as acute myeloid leukemia), cardiovascular diseases (stroke, aortic aneurysm, coronary heart disease, and atherosclerotic peripheral vascular disease), respiratory diseases (chronic obstructive pulmonary disease (COPD), pneumonia, asthma, and other respiratory effects), blindness, cataracts, periodontitis, hip fractures, and reproductive effects in women (including reduced fertility) [47, 80].

Additionally, secondary exposure to tobacco has been found to be causally related to health complications for the fetus (including tissue damage particularly to the lung and brain, and preterm delivery, which in turn leads to death and disability among newborns) [80]. Table 1.2 outlines the diseases and injuries that are causally related to the smoking of tobacco products.

Tobacco use causes a large burden of disease globally [81, 82]. Among tobacco users, approximately one-half of deaths are attributable to tobacco use (i.e. the number of deaths that would not have occurred if no one used tobacco products [83]).

Table 1.2 Diseases that are causally related to tobacco use

Cause of mortality or morbidity	ICD-10 code
Infectious diseases	
Tuberculosis	A15–A19
Neoplasms	
Lip, oral cavity and pharyngeal cancers	C00–C14
Oesophageal cancer	C15
Laryngeal cancer	C32
Stomach cancer	C16
Pancreas cancer	C25
Trachea, bronchus and lung cancers	C33–C34
Cervical cancer	C53
Urinary tract cancer	C64–C68
Renal cell carcinoma	C64
Bladder cancer	C67
Acute myeloid leukemia	C92
Neuropsychiatric conditions	
Mental and behavioral disorders due to use of psychoactive substances (tobacco use disorders)	F17
Diseases of the eye and adnexa	
Visual impairment, including blindness	H54
Cataracts	H25–H26
Cardiovascular diseases	
Ischemic heart disease	I20–I25
Heart failure	I50–I52, I23, I25.0, I97.0, I97.1, I98.1
Cardiac arrhythmias	I47–I49
Cerebrovascular disease	I60–I69
Pulmonary circulatory disease	I26–I28
Atherosclerosis	I70–I79
Respiratory diseases	
Pneumonia and influenza	J10–J18
Chronic obstructive pulmonary disease	J40–J44
Asthma	J45
Digestive diseases	
Diabetes	E08–E13
Ulcers	K25–K28
Periodontitis	K5.2–K5.4

continued...

16 Shield et al.

Table 1.2 Continued

Cause of mortality or morbidity	ICD-10 code
Conditions arising during the perinatal period (maternal use)	
Low birth weight and short gestation; neonatal conditions	P02.0–P02.2, P04.8, P05–P07, P96.1
Fetus and newborn affected by maternal use of drugs and tobacco	P04.2, P04.4
Sudden infant death syndrome	R95
Unintentional injuries	
Hip fracture	S72.0
Toxic effect of tobacco and nicotine	T65.2
Fires	X00–X09

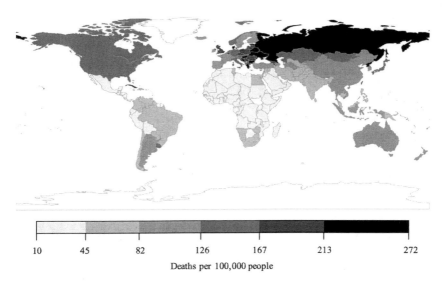

Figure 1.6 Age-standardized deaths attributable to tobacco smoking globally in 2010 per 100,000 people [84]

Burden of Tobacco Use

In 2010, tobacco use caused approximately 6.3 million deaths globally, representing 11.9% of all deaths, with these deaths caused by tobacco use leading to 137.8 million YLL (6.3% of all YLL). This difference in the percentage of all deaths caused by tobacco use and the percentage of all YLLs caused by tobacco use is due to the age at which tobacco-related deaths occur. Specifically, the majority (72.6%) of tobacco-attributable deaths occur after 55 years of age. Figure

1.6 outlines the number of deaths attributable to smoking in 2012 by country. Furthermore, the burden of deaths caused by tobacco use was 2.5 times higher among men, causing 4.5 million deaths among men compared to 1.8 million deaths among women.

As with the number of deaths, the total tobacco-attributable burden of disease was substantial, with 156.8 million DALYs lost representing 6.3% of all DALYs lost [26]. Furthermore, as with the burden of mortality caused by tobacco use, the burden of disease caused by tobacco use affects mainly people who are older in age, with the majority (73.5%) of tobacco-attributable DALYs occurring after 45 years of age. Additionally, the majority of the burden of disease caused by tobacco use is due to premature mortality rather than disability: globally, in 2010, 87.9% of all DALYs lost caused by tobacco use were due to premature mortality, while 12.1% of all DALYs lost caused by tobacco use were due to disability. Figure 1.7 outlines the number of DALYs lost attributable to tobacco smoking in 2010.

In accordance with the prevalence of daily smoking in the general population, the greatest population-adjusted burden of deaths and DALYs lost per 100,000 people occurred in the Eastern Europe, Central Europe, Western Europe, North America and Asian Pacific regions; however, as with the prevalence of daily smoking, there is a large variation within geographic regions. Furthermore, the burden of disease attributable to tobacco smoking in 2010 was similar in high-income and low- to middle-income countries. Specifically, in high-income countries, tobacco smoking caused 91.5 deaths and 2,259 DALYs lost per 100,000 people, and in developing countries, tobacco smoking caused 98.3 deaths and 2415 DALYs lost per 100,000 people.

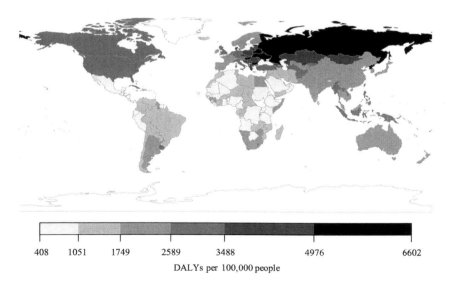

Figure 1.7 Age-standardized disability adjusted life years (DALYs) lost attributable to tobacco smoking globally in 2010 per 100,000 people [84]

The estimated age-standardized deaths attributable to tobacco use have decreased from 1990, when the number of tobacco-attributable deaths was 2,863 per 100,000 people [84]. In 2010, the number of tobacco-attributable deaths was 2,276 deaths per 100,000 people [84]. Furthermore, the burden attributable to tobacco smoking decreased from 3,379 DALYs lost per 100,000 people in 1990 to 2,385 DALYS lost per 100,000 people in 2010. This decrease in the burden of tobacco smoking over time can be attributed to two main sources. First, as previously mentioned, due to increased public health measures such as increases in tobacco taxation [85], there has been a decrease in the prevalence of daily cigarette consumption in high-income and low- to middle-income countries [69]. Second, there has been a decrease in the burden of some of the diseases associated with tobacco use, such as neoplasms, due to improvements in prevention, screening, and treatment [86, 87].

Burden of Tobacco Use Disorders

The GBD 2010 study does not estimate the prevalence of tobacco use disorders, or the number of deaths or DALYs lost attributable to tobacco use disorders, as the disability caused by these disorders is considered to be negligible [26]. Smokers with tobacco use disorders have reported a poorer quality of life than have subjects without a tobacco use disorder, even after adjustment for sociodemographic characteristics [88, 89]; however, the impact of tobacco use disorders on quality of life is likely low, and thus the main burden of tobacco use disorders is likely indirect and due to the other health effects caused by tobacco smoking among those who have a tobacco use disorder.

Conclusions

Similar to the prevalence of tobacco use, the prevalence of tobacco use disorders is hypothesized to be high; however, data on the prevalence of tobacco use disorders are sparse and the prevalence of tobacco use disorders in most countries is unknown. Although the prevalence of tobacco smoking and the resulting attributable burden has declined globally in high-income and low- to middle-income countries, tobacco smoking and the resulting attributable burden remains large, and interventions are required to further reduce both the prevalence of smoking and its resulting burden.

Illicit Drug Use Disorders

The United Nations Office on Drugs and Crime estimates that there are 243 million illicit drug users worldwide, with the vast majority of these individuals abusing opioids, cannabis or stimulants (cocaine and amphetamines) [15]. A primary concern of illicit drug use is the subsequent transition to illicit drug dependence, a state characterized by maladaptive patterns of illicit drug use leading to clinically significant impairments, as manifested by specified symptoms [21].

Illicit drug use is an important public health problem due to its prevalence, the prevalence of illicit drug disorders, and the observation that illicit drug use results in significant individual-level harms [90], and considerable costs to society (due to impacts on healthcare, criminal justice and lost productivity [91–94]) [90]. To address these issues, a variety of public health and justice policies have been established in a number of countries; some of these policies have proven to be effective (such as approaches to harm reduction [95]), while other policies have led to increased harms (such as increased law enforcement [96, 97]). Indeed, the global harms caused by illicit drug use have increased (although not significantly) from 1990 to 2010 [26, 90].

Based largely on findings from the GBD 2010 study [98–100], the following section outlines the epidemiology of illicit drug use and illicit drug use disorders, as well as the burden of disease attributable to them. Specifically, the following discussion focuses on the health-related burden of disease, rather than on the social- or economic-related burden of disease, as comprehensive global data on these latter burdens are generally lacking, with some regional exceptions [91–94].

Epidemiology of Illicit Drug Dependence

The global prevalence of opioid, cannabis, and stimulant (cocaine and amphetamine) dependence is outlined in Figure 1.8. These data highlight that opioid and amphetamine dependence are the two most prevalent forms of illicit drug dependence worldwide, followed by cannabis and cocaine dependence [98].

In 2010, there were 15.5 million people with opioid dependence, 13.1 million people with cannabis dependence, 6.9 million people with cocaine dependence, and 17.2 million people with amphetamine dependence. The current global prevalence of opioid dependence represents an increase of 5.1 million cases from 1990 [100]. Australasia, Western Europe and North America, High-Income are the regions most impacted by opioid dependence, as they display prevalence rates considerably higher than the global average [100]. The current situation in Australasia and Western Europe is not surprising as these regions have a history of opioid dependence dating back to 1990 [100]. The North America, High-Income region, on the other hand, has witnessed a dramatic increase in the prevalence of opioid dependence since 1990, when the prevalence was slightly above the global average [100]. This may be due, in part, to a substantial increase in the consumption of prescription opioids in this region over the last two decades [101–103]. Regions with a considerably lower prevalence of opioid dependence than the global average include Sub-Saharan Africa East, Sub-Saharan Africa West, and Asia Southeast [100].

Although the global prevalence of cannabis dependence has not changed since 1990, population growth over time has resulted in an additional 2 million cases [99]. The North America, High-Income region has historically, as well as currently, one of the highest prevalence rates of cannabis dependence globally (0.60%); the prevalence in this region is second only to Australasia (0.68%) [99]. In contrast, the Sub-Saharan Africa West region has the lowest prevalence of cannabis dependence [99]. Broadly speaking, the prevalence of cannabis dependence is generally higher in high-income regions compared to low- and middle-income regions and to the global average [99].

Comparisons across time suggest no marked differences in the global prevalence of cocaine or amphetamine dependence since 1990, but there are some regional exceptions [104]. For example, the prevalence rate of amphetamine dependence has not changed in the North America, High-Income region since 1990, but the prevalence rate of cocaine dependence has risen in this region from 0.43% to 0.53% [104]. Regions that have among the highest prevalence rates of cocaine dependence include North America, High-Income and Latin America Tropical and Caribbean, while the lowest prevalence rates are observed in regions across Asia [104]. Regions that have among the highest prevalence rates of amphetamine dependence include Asia Southeast, Australasia, and Latin America Tropical, while the lowest prevalence rates are observed in the Latin America Andean, Eastern Europe, and Asia East regions [104].

Further comparisons by demographics reveal that the prevalence of illicit drug dependence is higher among males than among females, irrespective of the illicit drug type (Figure 1.8). For example, male to female ratios for the global prevalence of opioid and cannabis dependence currently stand at 2.5 and 1.8, respectively [99, 100]. Furthermore, the prevalence of illicit drug dependence peaks among young adults, namely 25 to 29 years of age for opioid dependence [100], 20 to 24 years of age for cannabis dependence [99], 25 to 34 years of age for cocaine dependence, and 20 to 35 years of age for amphetamine dependence [104].

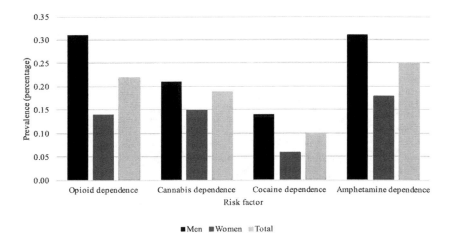

Figure 1.8 Prevalence of opioid, cannabis, cocaine, and amphetamine dependence by sex in 2010 [98–100, 104]

Burdens of Illicit Drug Use and Illicit Drug Dependence

The GBD 2010 study [84] modeled the effects of illicit drugs and illicit drug dependence (a disease category completely attributable to illicit drug use) on schizophrenia (attributable to cannabis use), hepatitis B and C (attributable to injection drug use), HIV (attributable to injection drug use), and suicide (attributable to opioid, cocaine, and amphetamine dependence) [98]. Furthermore, as an elevated risk of mortality due to cannabis dependence is not apparent, the corresponding burden of disease computations is limited to disability [105].

Burden of Illicit Drug Use

In 2010, 158,000 deaths (109,000 deaths among men and 48,000 deaths among women) and 24 million DALYs lost (16 million DALYs lost among men and 8 million DALYs lost among women) were attributable to illicit drug use. This represents 0.3% of all deaths in 2010 and 1.0% of all DALYs lost in 2010. Of the burden of disease caused by illicit drug use, 7 million DALYs lost were caused by YLL, while 17 million DALYs lost were caused by YLD. Therefore, in 2010, drug use had a much greater impact on morbidity than on mortality. Furthermore, illicit drug use in 2010 was the fifteenth leading risk factor for the total burden of disease.

The burden of illicit drug use has increased from 1990, when it caused 1.4 deaths per 100,000 people and 292 DALYs lost per 100,000 people; in 2010, illicit drug use caused 2.3 deaths and 343 DALYs lost per 100,000 people. This increase in the burden of disease per 100,000 people caused by illicit drug use is mainly due to an increase in the prevalence of illicit drug use disorders [98].

Burden of Illicit Drug Dependence

The attributable mortality from illicit drug dependence in 2010 was 77,000 deaths, 4 million YLLs, 16 million YLDs, and 20 million DALYs lost (Table 1.3), comprising 0.2% of all deaths and 0.8% all DALYs lost [98]. In addition, the risk attributable to opioid and stimulant dependence was a substantial contributor to disease burden (Table 1.4). As with the burden of disease caused by illicit drug use, the majority of the burden of disease attributable to illicit drug dependence was in the form of disability [98]. Furthermore, the greatest proportion of the burden of disease attributable to illicit drug dependence was due to opioid dependence (46%), followed by other drug dependence (25%), amphetamine dependence (13%), cannabis dependence (10%), and cocaine dependence (6%) [98].

Demographic comparisons of the burden of disease attributable to illicit drug dependence mirror the trends apparent for its prevalence [98–100, 104]. First, regardless of the illicit drug, DALYs lost per 100,000 people was higher among males compared to females [98–100, 104]. Second, as with the prevalence of illicit drug dependence, the burden of disease attributable to illicit drug

22 Shield et al.

Table 1.3 Burden of disease attributable to opioids, cannabis, stimulants (cocaine and amphetamine), and other drug dependence in 2010 [98–100, 104]

Illicit drug type	YLDs (millions)	YLLs (millions)	DALYs (millions)	DALYs per 100,00 people
Opioids	7.2	2.0	9.2	133.0
Cannabis	2.1	–	2.1	29.9
Stimulants				
Cocaine	1.1	0.0	1.1	16.1
Amphetamines	2.6	0.0	2.6	37.6
Other drugs	3.5	1.6	5.1	73.5

Table 1.4 Additional burden of disease attributable to opioid and stimulant (cocaine and amphetamine) dependence as risk factors for suicide in 2010 [98–100, 104]

Illicit drug type	Suicide YLDs (thousands)	Suicide YLLs (thousands)	Suicide DALYs (thousands)
Opioid	7	664	671
Stimulants			
Cocaine	3	320	324
Amphetamines	10	844	854

dependence peaked among young adults [98–100, 104]. Figure 1.9 outlines the burden of illicit drugs per 100,000 people by age.

As with the prevalence of illicit drug use and dependence, the burden of illicit drug dependence varied by country (see Figure 1.10). The North America, High-Income region had the largest burden of disease attributable to opioid dependence, with 292.1 DALYs lost per 100,000 people [100]. Regions with similarly large burdens include Eastern Europe, Australasia, and Sub-Saharan Africa South [100]. Regions at the other end of the spectrum include Sub-Saharan Africa West, Sub-Saharan Africa Central, and Asia East [100]. As with the burden of disease attributable to opioid dependence, the North America, High-Income region had among the highest number of DALYs lost per 100,000 people attributable to cannabis dependence (81.5 DALYs lost per 100,000 people) [99]. Other regions with similarly high DALYs lost attributable to cannabis dependence include Australasia, Latin America South, and Western Europe, whereas the lowest number of DALYs lost attributable to cannabis dependence are found in the Sub-Saharan Africa West, Latin America Central, and Latin America Andean regions [99]. The North America, High-Income region had the highest number of DALYs lost per 100,000 people attributable to cocaine dependence in 2010 [104]. Other regions with similarly high numbers of DALYs lost due to

Epidemiology and Public Health Burden 23

cannabis dependence include Latin America Tropical and the Caribbean; the numbers of DALYs lost in these regions are more than three times the global average [104]. The smallest burden of cocaine disorders was observed in the Asia East, Asia Southeast, and Sub-Saharan Africa East regions [104]. For amphetamine dependence, the regions with the highest number of DALYs

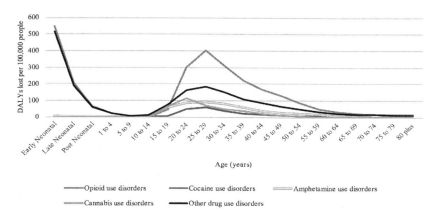

Figure 1.9 Burden of disease attributable to opioids, cannabis, and stimulants (cocaine and amphetamine) by age in 2010 [98–100, 104]

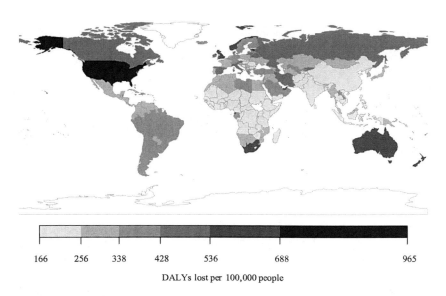

Figure 1.10 Age-standardized disability adjusted life years (DALYs) lost attributable to drug dependence globally in 2010 per 100,000 people [84]

lost per 100,000 people include Asia Southeast, Australasia, and Latin America Tropical, whereas the regions with the lowest number of DALYs lost due to amphetamine dependence include Latin America Andean, Eastern Europe, and Asia East [104].

There was also a variation in the proportion of the burden of illicit drug dependence caused by mortality and by morbidity. For most regions, the burden of disease attributable to opioid dependence is mainly comprised of YLDs [100]. In the regions of Eastern Europe, North America, High-Income and Sub-Saharan Africa South, the burden of disease attributable to opioid dependence is primarily comprised of YLLs [100]. For example, YLLs constitute 55% of the DALYs lost attributable to opioid dependence in the North America, High-Income region [100].

As was the case with the burden of illicit drug use, the burden of illicit drug dependence has increased from 0.5 deaths and 250 DALYs lost per 100,000 people in 1990 to 1.1 deaths and 288 DALYs lost per 100,000 people in 2010. Again, similar to the increase in the burden of disease attributable to illicit drug use, the increase in the burden of illicit drug dependence per 100,000 people was mainly driven by an increase in the prevalence of illicit drug disorders [100]. The largest increase was observed for opioid dependence, the burden of which in 1990 was responsible for 102 DALYs lost per 100,000 people and in 2010 was responsible for 132 DALYs lost per 100,000 people [100]. The contribution of cannabis, cocaine, and amphetamine dependence to the total burden of disease has not increased; however, due to an increase in the population size, the absolute burden of these illicit drug disorders has increased [99].

Illicit Drug Dependence as a Risk Factor for Other Health Outcomes

The GBD 2010 study excluded drug abuse and harmful use diagnoses, citing low disability weights, validity concerns, and the lack of available data [98]. Therefore, the burden due to illicit drug use and illicit drug use disorders presented in this chapter is underestimated. Furthermore, as was the case with the burden of disease caused by AUDs and tobacco dependence or tobacco use disorders, illicit drug dependence is causally related to health outcomes other than dependence and harmful use [106].

Conclusions

Globally, illicit drug use disorders are relatively prevalent, with amphetamine dependence being the most prevalent illicit drug use disorder, followed by opioid, cannabis, and cocaine dependence [98]. The burden of disease attributable to illicit drug dependence totals 20 million DALYs lost [98] (0.8% of all DALYs lost), with suicide attributable to illicit drug dependence contributing another 2 million DALYs lost [98, 107]. The largest contributor to the burden of disease attributable to illicit drug dependence was caused by opioid dependence [98].

Discussion

Given the prevalence of substance use disorders, and the burdens caused by these disorders, a clear understanding of the role of the risk factors leading to these disorders, and the effective and affordable interventions that can prevent them, should guide the development of health policies and treatment programs [108]. In particular, the magnitude of the burdens of disease caused by the use of alcohol, tobacco, and illicit drugs is large, and these substances represent some of the major risk factors for the global burden of disease [109]. The public health impact of addictive substances has been recognized by numerous organizations [110], and therefore addressing the use and abuse of these addictive substances has been designated as a global health priority, resulting in the Tobacco Framework Convention [111] and the Global Strategy to Reduce the Harmful Use of Alcohol [112]. In addition, the WHO has designated both tobacco use and alcohol use as two of the four key modifiable risk factors that contribute to the global burden of non-communicable diseases, and has proposed actions to reduce the burdens they cause [108, 113]. However, the impact of substance use disorders extends beyond non-communicable diseases, and the disease burden caused by substance use disorders is becoming increasingly recognized. Of great importance will be a Special Session of the United Nations General Assembly, in April 2016, to discuss the global drug problem and to facilitate policy reforms (UNGASS 2016). It is hoped that this session will result in more effective efforts to reduce the burden of substance use disorders, as current attempts appear to be insufficient.

Note

1. The prevalence of AUDs is the sum of the prevalence of harmful use and alcohol dependence, in line with the ICD-10 criteria.

References

1. Hill EM, Newlin DB. Evolutionary approaches to addiction. *Addiction*. 2002;97(4): 375–379.
2. Anselme P, Robinson MJ. What motivates gambling behavior? Insight into dopamine's role. *Frontiers in Behavioural Neuroscience*. 2013;7:182.
3. Oetting ER, Beauvais F. Peer cluster theory: drugs and the adolescent. *Journal of Counseling & Development*. 1986;65(1):17–22.
4. Swadi H. Individual risk factors for adolescent substance use. *Drug Alcohol Depend*. 1999;55(3):209–224.
5. Nutt DJ, King LA, Phillips LD. For the Independent Scientific Committee on Drugs. Drug harms in the UK: a multicriteria decision analysis. *Lancet*. 2010;376 (9752):1558–1565.
6. Lachenmeier DW, Rehm J. Comparative risk assessment of alcohol, tobacco, cannabis and other illicit drugs using the margin of exposure approach. *Sci Rep*. 2015;5:8126.
7. American Psychiatric Association. *Diagnostic and statistical manual of mental disorders*. 5th ed. Philadelphia (PA): American Psychiatric Association; 2013.

8. American Psychiatric Association. *Diagnostic and statistical manual of mental disorders.* 3rd ed. Washington (DC): American Psychiatric Association; 1980.
9. Petry NM. Should the scope of addictive behaviors be broadened to include pathological gambling? *Addiction.* 2006;101(Suppl 1):152–160.
10. Reuter J, Raedler T, Rose M, Hand I, Gläscher J, Büchel C. Pathological gambling is linked to reduced activation of the mesolimbic reward system. *Nat Neurosci.* 2005;8(2):147–148.
11. Slutske WS, Eisen S, True WR, Lyons MJ, Goldberg J, Tsuang M. Common genetic vulnerability for pathological gambling and alcohol dependence in men. *Arch Gen Psychiatry.* 2000;57(7): 666–673.
12. Potenza MN, Kosten TR, Rounsaville BJ. Pathological gambling. *JAMA.* 2001;286(2):141–144.
13. Hasin DS, O'Brien CP, Auriacombe M, Borges G, Bucholz K, Budney A, et al. DSM-5 criteria for substance use disorders: recommendations and rationale. *Am J Psychiatry.* 2013;170:834–851.
14. World Health Organization. *International classification of diseases and related health problems.* 10th rev. Geneva: World Health Organization; 2007.
15. United Nations Office on Drugs and Crime. *World Drug Report 2014.* New York: United Nations; 2014.
16. Rehm J, Anderson P, Gual A, Kraus L, Marmet S, Room R, et al. The tangible common denominator of substance use disorders: a reply to commentaries to Rehm et al. (2013). *Alcohol Alcohol.* 2014;49(1):118–122.
17. Rehm J, Marmet S, Anderson P, Gual A, Kraus L, Nutt DJ, et al. Defining substance use disorders: do we really need more than heavy use? *Alcohol Alcohol.* 2013;48(6):633–640.
18. Lopez AD, Mathers CD, Ezzati M, Jamison DT, Murray CJ. *Global burden of disease and risk factors.* New York & Washington (DC): World Bank & Oxford University Press; 2006.
19. Murray CJ, Acharya AK. Understanding DALYs. *J Health Econ.* 1997;16(6): 703–730.
20. Whiteford HA, Degenhardt L, Rehm J, Baxter AJ, Ferrari AJ, Erskine HE, et al. Global burden of disease attributable to mental and substance use disorders: findings from the Global Burden of Disease Study 2010. *Lancet.* 2013;382(9904): 1575–1586.
21. American Psychiatric Association. *Diagnostic and statistical manual of mental disorders.* 4th ed., text revision. Washington (DC): American Psychiatric Association; 2000.
22. Rehm J, Frick U. Valuation of health states in the U.S. study to establish disability weights: lessons from the literature. *Int J Methods Psychiatr Res.* 2010;19(1):18–33.
23. McGovern P. *Uncorking the past: the quest for wine, beer, and other alcoholic beverages.* Berkley (CA): The Regents of the University of California; 2009.
24. World Health Organization. *Global status report on alcohol and health.* Geneva: World Health Organization; 2014.
25. Rehm J, Baliunas D, Borges GL, Graham K, Irving HM, Kehoe T, et al. The relation between different dimensions of alcohol consumption and burden of disease: an overview. *Addiction.* 2010;105(5):817–843.
26. Lim SS, Vos T, Flaxman AD, Danaei G, Shibuya K, Adair-Rohani H, et al. A comparative risk assessment of burden of disease and injury attributable to 67 risk factors and risk factor clusters in 21 regions, 1990–2010: a systematic analysis for the Global Burden of Disease Study 2010. *Lancet.* 2012;380:2224–2260.

27. Westman J, Wahlbeck K, Laursen TM, Gissler M, Nordentoft M, Hallgren J, et al. Mortality and life expectancy of people with alcohol use disorder in Denmark, Finland and Sweden. *Acta Psychiat Scand*. 2015;131(4):297–306.
28. Schuckit MA. Alcohol-use disorders. *Lancet*. 2009;373(9662):492–501.
29. Rehm J, Shield KD, Rehm MX, Gmel G, Frick U. Modelling the impact of alcohol dependence on mortality burden and the effect of available treatment interventions in the European Union. *Eur Neuropsychopharmacol*. 2013;23(2):89–97.
30. Rehm J, Roerecke M. Reduction of drinking in problem drinkers and all-cause mortality. *Alcohol Alcohol*. 2013;48(4):509–513.
31. Edwards G, Gross MM. Alcohol dependence: provisional description of a clinical syndrome. *BMJ*. 1976;1(6017):1058–1061.
32. Rehm J. The risks associated with alcohol use and alcoholism. *Alcohol Research and Health*. 2011;34(2):135–143.
33. Rehm J, Mathers C, Popova S, Thavorncharoensap M, Teerawattananon Y, Patra J. Global burden of disease and injury and economic cost attributable to alcohol use and alcohol use disorders. *Lancet*. 2009;373(9682): 2223–2233.
34. Degenhardt L, Chiu WT, Sampson N, Kessler RC, Anthony JC, Angermeyer M, et al. Toward a global view of alcohol, tobacco, cannabis, and cocaine use: findings from the WHO World Mental Health Surveys. *PLoS medicine*. 2008;5(7):1053–1067.
35. Probst C, Roerecke M, Behrendt S, Rehm J. Gender differences in socioeconomic inequality of alcohol-attributable mortality: a systematic review and meta-analysis. *Drug Alcohol Rev*. 2014.
36. Harris EC, Barraclough B. Excess mortality of mental disorder. *Br J Psychiatry*. 1998;173:11–53.
37. Roerecke M, Rehm J. Alcohol use disorders and mortality: a systematic review and meta-analysis. *Addiction*. 2013;108(9):1562–1578.
38. Roerecke M, Rehm J. Cause-specific mortality risk in alcohol use disorder treatment patients: a systematic review and meta-analysis. *Int J Epidemiol*. 2014;43(3):906–919.
39. Shield KD, Rehm J. Global risk factor rankings: the importance of age-based health loss inequities caused by alcohol and other risk factors. *BMC Research Notes*. 2015;8(1):231.
40. Rehm J, Samokhvalov AV, Shield KD. Global burden of alcoholic liver diseases. *Journal of Hepatology*. 2013;59(1):160–168.
41. Rehm J, Zatonski W, Taylor B, Anderson P. Epidemiology and alcohol policy in Europe. *Addiction*. 2011;106(Suppl 1):11–19.
42. Shield KD, Parry C, Rehm J. Chronic diseases and conditions related to alcohol use. *Alcohol Res*. 2013;35(2):155–171.
43. Navarro HJ, Doran CM, Shakeshaft AP. Measuring costs of alcohol harm to others: a review of the literature. *Drug Alcohol Depend*. 2010, 114(2–3): 87–99.
44. Laslett AM, Room R, Ferris J, Wilkinson C, Livingston M, Mugavin J. Surveying the range and magnitude of alcohol's harm to others in Australia. *Addiction*. 2011;106(9):1603–1611.
45. Peto R, Lopez A, Boreham J, Thun M, Heath JC. Mortality from tobacco in developed countries: indirect estimation from national vital statistics. *Lancet*. 1992;339:1268–1278.
46. Lopez AD, Collishaw NE, Piha T. A descriptive model of the cigarette epidemic in developed countries. *Tobacco Control*. 1994;3(3):242.

47. US Department of Health and Human Services. *The health consequences of smoking: a report of the surgeon general.* Atlanta (GA): US Department of Health and Human Services—Center for Chronic Disease Prevention and Health Promotion—Office of Smoking and Health; 2004.
48. US Department of Health and Human Services. *The health consequences of involuntary exposure to tobacco smoke: a report of the surgeon general.* Atlanta (GA): US Department of Health and Human Services; 2006.
49. Giovino GA, Mirza SA, Samet JM, Gupta PC, Jarvis MJ, Bhala N, et al. Tobacco use in 3 billion individuals from 16 countries: an analysis of nationally representative cross-sectional household surveys. *Lancet.* 2012;380(9842):668–679.
50. Gaziano TA, Bitton A, Anand S, Abrahams-Gessel S, Murphy A. Growing epidemic of coronary heart disease in low-and middle-income countries. *Curr Probl Cardiol.* 2010;35(2):72–115.
51. Mathers CD, Loncar D. Projections of global mortality and burden of disease from 2002 to 2030. *PLoS medicine.* 2006;3(11):e442.
52. Proctor RN. The history of the discovery of the cigarette–lung cancer link: evidentiary traditions, corporate denial, global toll. *Tobacco Control.* 2012;21(2): 87–91.
53. Müller FH. Tabakmissbrauch und Lungencarcinom. *Zeitschrift für Krebsforschung.* 1939;49(57):e85.
54. Hill A. The environment and disease: association or causation? *Proc R Soc Med.* 1965;58:295–300.
55. US Department of Health—Education and Welfare. *Smoking and health: report of the advisory committee to the surgeon general of the public health service.* Washington (DC): US Department of Health—Education and Welfare; 1964.
56. US Department of Health and Human Services. *The health consequences of smoking: nicotine addiction. A report of the surgeon general.* Atlanta (GA): US Department of Health and Human Services; 1988.
57. Benowitz NL. Nicotine addiction. *N Engl J Med.* 2010;362(24):2295.
58. World Health Organization. *International statistical classification of diseases and related health problems, tenth revision (ICD-10).* 2nd ed. Geneva: World Health Organization; 2004.
59. American Psychiatric Association. *Diagnostic and statistical manual of mental disorders.* Washington (DC): American Psychiatric Association; 1994.
60. Benowitz NL, Gourlay SG. Cardiovascular toxicity of nicotine: implications for nicotine replacement therapy. *J Am Coll Cardiol.* 1997;29(7):1422–1431.
61. McAllister-Sistilli CG, Caggiula AR, Knopf S, Rose CA, Miller AL, Donny EC. The effects of nicotine on the immune system. *Psychoneuroendocrinology.* 1998;23(2):175–187.
62. Hecht SS, Hoffmann D. Tobacco-specific nitrosamines: an important group of carcinogens in tobacco and tobacco smoke. *Carcinogenesis.* 1988;9(6):875–884.
63. Talhout R, Schulz T, Florek E, Van Benthem J, Wester P, Opperhuizen A. Hazardous compounds in tobacco smoke. *International Journal of Environmental Research and Public Health.* 2011;8(2):613–628.
64. Rodgman A, Perfetti TA. Alphabetical component index. In: Rodgman A, Perfetti TA, editors. *The chemical components of tobacco and tobacco smoke.* Boca Raton (FL): CRC Press; 2009:1483–1784.
65. Smith CJ, Hansch C. The relative toxicity of compounds in mainstream cigarette smoke condensate. *Food Chem Toxicol.* 2000;38(7):637–646.

66. Anderson P, Rehm J, Room R. *Impact of addictive substances and behaviours on individual and societal well-being.* Oxford: Oxford University Press; 2015.
67. Ezzati M, Lopez A, Rodgers A, Murray CJL. *Comparative quantification of health risks: global and regional burden of disease attributable to selected major risk factors.* Geneva: World Health Organization; 2004.
68. Fagerström KO, Heatherton TF, Kozlowski LT. Nicotine addiction and its assessment. *Ear Nose & Throat.* 1990;69(11): 763–765.
69. Ng M, Freeman MK, Fleming TD, Robinson M, Dwyer-Lindgren L, Thomson B, et al. Smoking prevalence and cigarette consumption in 187 countries, 1980–2012. *JAMA.* 2014;311(2):183–192.
70. World Health Organization. *Tobacco or health: a global status report.* Geneva: World Health Organization; 1997.
71. World Health Organization. *WHO report on the global tobacco epidemic, 2013.* Geneva: World Health Organization; 2013.
72. US Department of Agriculture. *Tobacco Yearbook USDA Dataset.* Washington (DC): US Department of Agriculture; 2015.
73. Food and Agriculture Organization of the United Nations. *Projections of tobacco production, consumption and trade to the year 2010.* Rome: Food and Agriculture Organization of the United Nations; 2015.
74. Euromonitor International. *Tobacco industry market research.* London: Euromonitor International; 2015.
75. World Lung Foundation, American Cancer Society. *The Tobacco Atlas.* 4th ed. New York: World Lung Foundation; 2015.
76. World Health Organization. *Global status report on noncommunicable diseases 2010: description of the global burden of NCDs, their risk factors and determinants.* Geneva: World Health Organization; 2011.
77. King BA, Dube SR, Tynan MA. Current tobacco use among adults in the United States: findings from the National Adult Tobacco Survey. *Am J Public Health.* 2012;102(11):e93–e100.
78. Fagerström K. The epidemiology of smoking. *Drugs.* 2002;62(2):1–9.
79. Grant BF, Hasin DS, Chou SP, Stinson FS, Dawson DA. Nicotine dependence and psychiatric disorders in the United States: results from the national epidemiologic survey on alcohol and related conditions. *Arch Gen Psychiatry.* 2004;61(11):1107–1115.
80. U.S. Department of Health and Human Services. *A report of the surgeon general: highlights. Overview of findings regarding reproductive health.* Atlanta (GA): US Department of Health and Human Services—Centers for Disease Control and Prevention—National Center for Chronic Disease Prevention and Health Promotion—Office on Smoking and Health; 2010.
81. Lim SS, Vos T, Flaxman AD, Danaei G, Shibuya K, Adair-Rohani H, et al. A comparative risk assessment of burden of disease and injury attributable to 67 risk factors and risk factor clusters in 21 regions, 1990–2010: a systematic analysis for the Global Burden of Disease Study 2010. *Lancet.* 2012;380(9859):2224–2260.
82. Ezzati M, Lopez AD. Estimates of global mortality attributable to smoking in 2000. *Lancet.* 2003;362(9387):847–852.
83. Northridge ME. Public health methods: attributable risk as a link between causality and public health action. *Am J Public Health.* 1995;85(9):1202–1204.
84. Institute for Health Metrics and Evaluation. *GBD compare*; 2015. Available from: http://vizhub.healthdata.org/gbd-compare.

85. Frieden TR, Bloomberg MR. How to prevent 100 million deaths from tobacco. *Lancet.* 2007;369(9574):1758–1761.
86. International Agency for Research on Cancer. *World cancer report.* Geneva: International Agency for Research on Cancer; 2003.
87. Berry DA, Cronin KA, Plevritis SK, Fryback DG, Clarke L, Zelen M, et al. Effect of screening and adjuvant therapy on mortality from breast cancer. *N Engl J Med.* 2005;353(17):1784–1792.
88. Schmitz N, Kruse J, Kugler J. Disabilities, quality of life, and mental disorders associated with smoking and nicotine dependence. *Am J Psychiatry.* 2003;160(9): 1670–1676.
89. Sprangers MA, de Regt EB, Andries F, van Agt HM, Bijl RV, de Boer JB, et al. Which chronic conditions are associated with better or poorer quality of life? *J Clin Epidemiol.* 2000;53(9):895–907.
90. Degenhardt L, Hall W. Extent of illicit drug use and dependence, and their contribution to the global burden of disease. *Lancet.* 2012;379(9810): 55–70.
91. Collins DJ, Lapsley HM. *The costs of tobacco, alcohol and illicit drug abuse to Australian society in 2004/05: summary version.* Canberra: Department of Health and Ageing; 2008.
92. Rehm J, Gnam W, Popova S, Baliunas D, Brochu S, Fischer B, et al. The costs of alcohol, illegal drugs, and tobacco in Canada, 2002. *J Stud Alcohol Drugs.* 2007;68(6):886–895.
93. Fernández M. The socioeconomic impact of drug-related crimes in Chile. *International Journal of Drug Policy.* 2012;23(6):465–472.
94. Office of National Drug Control Policy. *The economic costs of drug abuse in the United States, 1992–2002.* Washington (DC): Executive Office of the President; 2004.
95. Marlatt GA. Harm reduction: come as you are. *Addict Behav.* 1996;21(6):779–788.
96. Chin G. Race, the war on drugs, and the collateral consequences of criminal conviction. *Journal of Gender, Race & Justice.* 2002;6:253.
97. Room R, Reuter P. How well do international drug conventions protect public health? *Lancet.* 2012;379(9810):84–91.
98. Degenhardt L, Whiteford HA, Ferrari AJ, Baxter AJ, Charlson FJ, Hall WD, et al. Global burden of disease attributable to illicit drug use and dependence: findings from the Global Burden of Disease Study 2010. *Lancet.* 2013;382(9904):1564–1574.
99. Degenhardt L, Ferrari AJ, Calabria B, Hall WD, Norman RE, McGrath J, et al. The global epidemiology and contribution of cannabis use and dependence to the global burden of disease: results from the GBD 2010 study. *PloS one.* 2013;8(10):e76635.
100. Degenhardt L, Charlson F, Mathers B, Hall WD, Flaxman AD, Johns N, et al. The global epidemiology and burden of opioid dependence: results from the global burden of disease 2010 study. *Addiction.* 2014;109:1320–1333.
101. Imtiaz S, Shield KD, Fischer B, Rehm J. Harms of prescription opioid use in the United States. *Subst Abuse Treat Prev Policy.* 2014;9(1):43.
102. Fischer B, Nakamura N, Urbanoski K, Rush B, Rehm J. Correlations between population levels of prescription opioid use and prescription-opioid-related substance use treatment admissions in the USA and Canada since 2001. *Public Health.* 2012;126(9):749–751.
103. Fischer B, Jones W, Urbanoski K, Skinner R, Rehm J. Correlations between prescription opioid analgesic dispensing levels and related mortality and morbidity in Ontario, Canada, 2005–2011. *Drug Alcohol Rev.* 2014;33:19–26.

104. Degenhardt L, Baxter AJ, Lee YY, Hall W, Sara GE, Johns N, et al. The global epidemiology and burden of psychostimulant dependence: findings from the Global Burden of Disease Study 2010. *Drug Alcohol Depend.* 2014;137:36–47.
105. Calabria B, Degenhardt L, Hall W, Lynskey M. Does cannabis use increase the risk of death? Systematic review of epidemiological evidence on adverse effects of cannabis use. *Drug Alcohol Rev.* 2010;29(3):318–330.
106. Degenhardt L, Whiteford H, Hall WD. The Global Burden of Disease projects: what have we learned about illicit drug use and dependence and their contribution to the global burden of disease? *Drug Alcohol Rev.* 2014;33:4–12.
107. Ferrari AJ, Norman RE, Freedman G, Baxter AJ, Pirkis JE, Harris MG, et al. The burden attributable to mental and substance use disorders as risk factors for suicide: findings from the Global Burden of Disease Study 2010. *PloS one.* 2014;9(4):e91936.
108. Babor TF, Caulkins JP, Edwards G, Fischer B, Foxcroft DR, Humphreys K, et al. *Drug policy and the public good.* Oxford: Oxford University Press; 2010.
109. Murray CJ, Lopez A. Global mortality, disability, and the contribution of risk factors: global burden of disease study. *Lancet.* 1997;349:1436–1442.
110. World Health Organization. *The global burden of disease: 2004 update.* Geneva: World Health Organization; 2008.
111. World Health Organization. *2010 global progress report on the implementation of the WHO Framework Convention on Tobacco Control.* Geneva: World Health Organization; 2010.
112. World Health Organization. *Global strategy to reduce the harmful use of alcohol.* Geneva: World Health Organization; 2010.
113. World Health Organization. *Prevention and control of NCDs: priorities for investment.* Geneva: World Health Organization; 2011.

Chapter 2

The Etiology of Addiction
A Contemporary Biopsychosocial Approach

James MacKillop and Lara A. Ray

> *A successful addiction model must synthesize pharmacological, experiential, cultural, situational, and personality components in a fluid and seamless description of addictive motivation. It must account for why a drug is more addictive in one society than another, addictive for one individual and not another, and addictive for the same individual at one time and not another. The model must make sense out of the essentially similar behavior that takes place with all compulsive involvements. In addition, the model must adequately describe the cycle of increasing yet dysfunctional reliance on an involvement until the involvement overwhelms other reinforcements available to the individual.*
>
> [1]

Introduction

The goal of the current chapter is to review contemporary perspectives on the etiology, or the causes, of addictive disorders. As illustrated by the epigraph above, this is no small task because of the complexity of these conditions and because the study of addiction is the focus of multiple disciplines using highly divergent perspectives. Furthermore, these different perspectives have not generated a single accepted account for why a person develops an addiction, but a number of empirically-grounded theoretical approaches that broadly fall into three domains—biological determinants, psychological determinants, and social determinants. These are collectively referred to as the biopsychosocial model of addiction, and the chapter will successively address these three domains, starting with neurobiological and genetic models, subsequently reviewing psychological theories, and then surveying social and societal influences. Finally, the chapter concludes with reflections on the progress and future priorities in understanding the causes of addiction.

Given the wide scope of this chapter, the emphasis will be on breadth over depth, and on theory over individual empirical studies. A fully comprehensive account of the etiology of addiction in each of these areas is beyond the scope of the chapter and incompatible with the clinical orientation of this volume. This raises the question of what the appropriate role of theory should be in the treatment of addiction. Scientific theories represent the abstracted relations among a wide array of empirical observations and, optimally, theory and treatment represent two sides of the same coin, the former describing the development of the condition and the latter seeking to reverse-engineer the acquired dysfunction. Thus, a premise of the chapter is that a foundation in the causal models of addiction provides a scientifically-minded clinician with a framework for approaching treatment. Theories don't provide a simple answer to why a given patient developed their presenting problem, but go deeper than symptoms to articulate the important processes and mechanisms that are putatively operative. Moreover, as the theories discussed below are grounded in empirical observation, theoretically-informed treatment is one key aspect of evidence-based treatment.

Biological Models of Addiction

Neurobiological Models of Addiction

Major progress has been made in understanding the effects of addictive drugs in the brain, leading to a number of influential neurobiological models. One of the earliest theories that shaped neurobiological perspectives was the *psychostimulant theory of addiction* [2], which identified a neurobiological common denominator across drugs of addictive potential via increases in dopamine release in the medial forebrain bundle, a neuronal tract within the mesolimbic dopamine pathway. Dopaminergic activation in this region was putatively responsible for subjective reward and for motivating behavior for survival and reproduction [3, 4]. Thus, mesocortical dopaminergic activity was theorized to be the common basis for the pleasure associated with drug effects and addiction potential across diverse pharmacological compounds. In terms of etiology, the principal mechanism was the sheer magnitude of dopaminergic stimulation produced compared to natural reinforcers. In contrast, subsequent theories specifically focused both on how drugs affected the brain acutely and how repeated administration gave rise to long-standing or potentially permanent brain changes, termed neuroadaptations, that cemented high levels of drug motivation.

Among more recent models, one of the most influential is the *incentive sensitization theory* [5, 6]. Again, incentive sensitization suggests that activation of mesolimbic dopamine substrates is critical to the development of the motivational and appetitive properties; however, incentive sensitization shifted the focus away from drug reward and parsed the role of dopamine more finely. Specifically, rather than mediating either the hedonic impact of the reward (i.e., its pleasure, how much it is liked) or rewarding learning, dopamine was hypothesized to subserve the incentive salience of the reward (i.e., its motivational value, how much it is wanted). Over time, via neuroadaptive changes that result from acute overstimulation of dopamine neurotransmission, sensitization of the incentive salience attribution is hypothesized to take place via associative (Pavlovian) conditioning, creating a chronic state of wanting (also called craving). Furthermore, the processes of wanting and liking are hypothesized to be dissociable, meaning that an individual sensitizes to the motivational salience of the drug without necessarily increasing how much the person likes the drug. The liking process in turn is thought to be subserved by endogenous opioids in the ventral tegmental area. In terms of behavioral consequences, incentive sensitization is hypothesized to give rise to attentional bias toward drug stimuli and high levels of craving [7].

An alternative formulation, the *cellular learning model of addiction*, makes the case that addiction should be more broadly considered a disorder of learning and memory [8, 9]. From this perspective, sensitization of dopamine neurotransmission is one part of the neurobiology of addiction, but the subsequent downstream learning processes are even more important. Specifically, this account proposes that potent psychoactive drug effects contribute to synaptic plasticity that leads to long-term increases in the salience of drug rewards and, by comparison, decreases in the salience of alternative rewards [8, 9]. This is hypothesized to take place by way of drug-induced remodeling of neuronal dendrites, axons, and synapses, either via up- or down-regulation of gene expression or expression-based effects that lead to morphological synaptic changes. Supporting this thesis, addictive drugs have been robustly found to induce alterations in gene expression associated with synaptic plasticity, including inducing ΔFosB, a relatively long-lasting transcription factor that increases sensitivity to the rewarding and locomotor stimulant effects of addictive drugs [10, 11]. Thus, the highly potent psychoactive effects of addictive drugs are theorized to become deeply instantiated in the brain via potent effects on circuitry for learning new events and remembering important ones from the past.

Other neurobiological theories contrast with the preceding models that emphasize the drug acquiring very high rewarding salience. One dominant line of inquiry has pursued addiction as a series of transitions from voluntary use to habitual use to, ultimately, compulsive use of alcohol and other drugs [12, 13]. The neurobiological substrates responsible for these changes are theorized to be a transition from processing in the ventral striatum, which is responsible for subjectively rewarding drug effects subserving goal directed behavior, to the dorsal striatum, which is responsible for motor and habit learning. This neuroadaptive change is theorized to be a transition from deliberative action-outcome instrumental learning to reflexive stimulus-response learning, such that drug-seeking ultimately becomes increasingly automatic and outside of voluntary control. A substantial body of preclinical research supports this shift [14]. The *ventral-to-dorsal striatum account* is not necessarily incompatible with incentive sensitization, but it certainly emphasizes automaticity in behavior over increasing subjective drug motivation.

The *allostatic model of addiction* [15–17] shares a parallel with the ventral-to-dorsal striatum model to the extent that it emphasizes stages in addiction characterizing the initial heavy use of alcohol and drugs for its rewarding properties followed by chronic and uncontrolled use that is no longer driven by reward-seeking. Specifically, addiction is theorized to progress through three stages: (1) binge use/intoxication; (2) withdrawal/negative affect; and (3) preoccupation/anticipation (craving). These stages map on to progressive neuroadaptive changes in the striatum, extended amygdala, hippocampus, and orbitofrontal cortex. Furthermore, the development of addiction is characterized as an aberrant homeostatic, or allostatic, process that involves changes in reward and stress circuits following persistent exposure to addictive drugs. This model is one of the few that explicitly integrates the neurobiology of the acute rewarding effects of drugs with mechanisms related to negative reinforcement associated with withdrawal and stress (e.g., corticotrophin-releasing factor, neuropeptide Y). One of the primary advantages of this model is that it integrates a wide array of findings on molecular, cellular, and neuronal changes that are associated with the pathophysiology of addiction. However, evidence from this model is drawn primarily from studies of alcohol, as opposed to other drugs of abuse.

Finally, although most of the preceding models have emphasized neuroadaptive changes in subcortical circuitry, it is worth noting that there are also contemporary neurobiological models that focus on deficits and acquired changes in prefrontal cortex functioning. In particular, neuroimaging studies and preclinical models have revealed dysregulation in subunits of the prefrontal cortex responsible for inhibitory control and reactivity to stimuli signaling drug availability [18–20]. Thus, addiction can be understood as resulting from both pathological adaptations within motivational systems and higher-level prefrontal systems.

Genetic Influences on Addiction

A limitation to most of the preceding models is that they typically describe addiction as a general process, not in relation to individual risk. In reality, addiction develops in only a minority of individuals who experiment with addictive drugs [21] and understanding which individuals are most vulnerable has important implications for both prevention and treatment. In biological models of addiction, the question of individual vulnerability largely pertains to genetic influences and genetic variation conferring etiological risk is well established. For example, there is an extensive literature using twin and adoption designs to ascertain the aggregate heritability of addictive disorders, generally suggesting 40–60% heritability [22, 23]. More recently, substantial heritability has also been identified using genomic complex trait analysis, a novel technique that generates estimates using variation in common single nucleotide polymorphisms (SNPs) across the genome [24, 25].

These studies make it clear that genetic variation is an important influence on the development of addiction, but the mechanisms by which this influence is conferred have been elusive. Candidate gene studies have generated mixed findings and atheoretical genome-wide association studies have generally not identified significant loci. However, two notable exceptions are robust evidence that variation in a locus responsible for alcohol pharmacokinetics is a protective factor against alcohol use disorder, and that variation putatively related to nicotine pharmacodynamics is a risk factor for nicotine dependence. In the first case, the *ALHD2* gene is responsible for aldehyde dehydrogenase activity, a key enzyme for breaking down acetaldehyde resulting from alcohol metabolism, and the

A allele of an SNP (rs671) within *ALDH2* results in substantially lower enzymatic activity. As a result, if A allele carriers drink alcohol, they experience an acetaldehyde buildup and a number of unpleasant symptoms, including flushing, nausea, headache, and tachycardia. The A allele is relatively common in Asian populations and effectively makes carriers "allergic" to alcohol, exerting a powerful protective effect against alcohol use disorder [26]. In the second case, a number of large-scale studies have convincingly implicated variants on chromosome 15 with nicotine dependence. This region contains the α5-α3-β4 nicotinic receptor gene cluster, and nicotinic cholinergic receptors are key sites of action for nicotine. In particular, a locus in the α5 nicotinic receptor subunit gene (*CHRNA5*), rs16969968, has been associated with significantly increased risk for developing nicotine dependence and smoking-related diseases, such as lung cancer and chronic obstructive pulmonary disease [27].

These findings represent two success stories in understanding addiction genetics, illustrating the ways that genetic variation may influence the pharmacokinetics and pharmacodynamics of drug effects to influence addiction risk. However, it is also clear that major gaps in knowledge remain and that progress in addiction genetics has been slower than anticipated, even after the development of sophisticated genome-wide techniques. In general, there is little evidence for one major "addiction gene" or a small number of highly influential loci. Instead, the current perspective is that it is likely that hundreds or thousands of variants contribute small magnitude effects to affect risk.

Difficulty in identifying genetic influences on addiction may also be a function of the heterogeneity of the clinical phenotype, given the many permutation symptoms that may be present. To address this, there is increasing interest in identifying narrower, more discrete behavioral phenotypes that are putatively more closely related to specific neurobiological processes and genetic variation in particular [28, 29]. These characteristics are also called intermediate phenotypes or endophenotypes, and are predicted both to increase power to detect specific genes underlying the risk for a given disorder and to inform mechanisms of risk or protection.

Psychological Models of Addiction

A Reinforcement-Based Approach

One of the earliest psychological theories of addictive behavior that is still actively pursued to this day is an operant learning approach. With foundations in early learning theory [30, 31], this approach theorizes that substance use is fundamentally a form of instrumental learning, meaning the behavior is primarily determined by its consequences and, more specifically, the reinforcing properties of the drug [32–34]. This comprises both positive reinforcement (i.e., effects provided by the drug that strengthen motivation), such as stimulation, social enhancement, orosensory, or gustatory properties; and negative reinforcement (i.e., states removed by the drug that strengthen motivation), such as the alleviation of anxiety, depression, other psychiatric symptoms, or withdrawal symptoms. Importantly, these different forms of positive and negative reinforcement are not mutually exclusive, operating concurrently, and in the context of punishing drug consequences and the presence (or absence) of alternative reinforcers. In broad strokes, this approach proposes that a drug's positively and negatively reinforcing properties, its punishing properties, the opportunity for alternative reinforcers, and the timing of the aforementioned jointly determine the reinforcing value of the drug, the final common pathway to use. These processes are theorized to be the proximal mechanisms by which other known risk factors (e.g., genetic and environmental vulnerabilities) contribute to substance use, and individual differences in each domain are responsible for differences in vulnerability across individuals.

Considerable evidence supports this approach, starting with data from early residential studies revealing that drug consumption could be studied experimentally and fundamentally conformed behavioral principles [35, 36]. Subsequently, human laboratory studies convincingly demonstrated that drug consumption conformed to key predictions from operant theory in terms of sensitivity to increases in response cost and the presence of alternative reinforcers [37–39].

More recently, a reinforcement-based model of addiction has been extended using behavioral economics, which integrates psychological and economic principles to understand decision-making and consumption behavior. This is a natural extension, following from recognition that operant behavior in complex environments with multiple options and different costs and benefits is essentially a behavioral microeconomy and that decision-making is a critical final common pathway to consumption behavior. Integrating economic concepts into addiction research also provides powerful tools for quantifying reinforcing value. One form of behavioral economic decision-making that has been extensively examined in relation to addiction is preference for smaller immediate rewards compared to larger delayed rewards. This is considered a behavioral economic index of impulsivity and is discussed below with other measures of impulsivity. In addition, purchase tasks that assess estimated drug consumption at escalating levels of price have been used to efficiently measure the reinforcing value of drugs, which is significantly associated with substance misuse and has been found to predict treatment response. An alternative measure characterizes substance-related reinforcement compared to non-drug alternative reinforcement, a measure of disproportionate reliance on drug-related reinforcement, and has also been linked to level of drug involvement [40–44]. Finally, a reinforcement-based approach has given rise to treatments that either seek to develop mutually exclusive alternative reinforcers to compete with drug use or directly reinforce elements of treatment, which are among some of the best supported treatments [45, 46].

Variability in Acute Drug Effects

A related perspective emphasizes on the importance of variation in the drug's subjective effects as a determinant of use and misuse. This has most extensively been investigated in relation to alcohol, but clearly has relevance to other drugs also. Early theories of alcohol effects predicted that individuals primarily drink alcohol because of its ability to reduce tension, the so-called tension reduction hypothesis. However, the evidence that a direct, consistent effect of alcohol is to alleviate tension is weak [47, 48]. Subsequently, it has become clear that alcohol's direct effects are best understood as having both stimulant and sedative properties, with the former predominating during the ascending limb of the blood–alcohol curve and the latter predominating during the descending limb [49, 50]. In addition, attenuated response to alcohol has been identified as a risk factor for lifelong alcohol misuse [51, 52], and a recent meta-analysis revealed consistent evidence that the risk factor of having a positive family history of alcohol use disorder is conferred by attenuated alcohol effects [53]. However, it is notable that other studies have prospectively linked augmented stimulant effects to greater alcohol problems while greater levels of sedative effects are protective against the development of an alcohol use disorder [54, 55], thus suggesting that important aspects of this relationship remain insufficiently understood.

Cognitive Processes

The preceding theories reflect proximal properties of substances, but cognitive models emphasize the intervening role of mental or information processing mechanisms. One dominant cognitive model emphasizes the importance of expectancies in determining addictive behavior. Expectancies refer to cognitive templates that reflect the memorial residues from previous experiences and exist to anticipate experiences and facilitate behavior. Expectancies reflect bidirectional relationships in which experiences stamp imprints into the brain's memory systems, and these imprints preemptively generate responses, effectively creating self-fulfilling behavioral prophecies. Expectancies are believed to be partially responsible for placebo effects, to medications in general [56] and to addictive drugs [57]. Furthermore, expectancy inventories on expectancies reveal the multifarious beliefs that individuals hold about drug effects [58]. For example, a wide variety of alcohol expectancies have been characterized, including global positive effects, sexual enhancement, social facilitation, assertiveness, relaxation/ tension reduction, and interpersonal power [58], and expectancies have been significantly associated with substance use cross-sectionally and longitudinally [59–61]. Importantly, expectancies do not necessarily reflect direct pharmacological actions of alcohol so much as the individual's aggregated construal of alcohol's effects, resulting from the complex intersection of pharmacology, accurate and inaccurate attributions in ambiguous social and interpersonal contexts, and the background context sociocultural messages, norms, and advertising. For example, as noted above, alcohol may not have direct anxiolytic effects, but a person may attribute tension reduction properties to drinking beer because it is consumed as part of an after-work routine or because the brand markets it in that capacity.

Related cognitive determinants are motives for substance use, the pattern of reasons that a person reports for why he or she uses the drug. Like expectancies, motives are typically assessed using self-report assessments and validated measures have revealed distinct patterns of motives. For example, most drugs are used for social, enhancement, and coping motives [62–65]. However, differences are also present across drugs. For example, pain management is important for opioid users [64, 66]; sensory expansion is a distinct motivational domain for marijuana [65]; and social conformity represents a subfactor for young adult drinkers [67]. Facets of motivation have been robustly associated with levels of substance use and clinical severity, with coping motives exhibiting particularly robust associations [64, 67]. A larger array of motives have been identified for smoking, 13 in total (see Chapter 5). Of these, tolerance, craving, loss of control, and automaticity have been identified as the primary dependence motives, and are most robustly associated with nicotine dependence [68].

Within a cognitive framework, expectancies and motives can be thought of as explicit reflective cognitive processes, or declarative "top-down" processes in which the individual reports introspectively available cognitions about the drug. An important complement to those mechanisms are implicit automatic cognitive processes, or unconscious "bottom-up" processes that reflect the salience and weighting of drugs within a person's cognitive network. Implicit cognition can be measured in a variety of different ways, but the common theme is using behavioral tasks that embed drug-related information and use behavioral performance, often interference, to reveal how salient drug information is within the person's cognitive network. Level of cognitive bias on these measures has been significantly associated with level of substance misuse [69] and has also been found to be predictive of treatment response [70, 71]. Indeed, implicit cognition has given rise to novel adjunctive retraining treatments to degrade these acquired associations [72, 73]. Implicit and explicit measures of cognition are weakly associated, with some shared variance but both independently predicting substance involvement [74].

Personality Factors

The notion of an "addictive personality" has also elicited considerable interest as a psychological determinant of addiction, but has also been controversial [75], and there is weak evidence for any singular pattern of personality characteristics that is commonly present in addiction [76]. On the other hand, there is evidence that some normative personality traits are consistently associated with addictive behavior, including positive links with neuroticism and negative links with conscientiousness and agreeableness [77–80]. However, the most robust link between characterological traits and addiction is present for associations with measures of impulsivity, broadly defined as capacity for self-control of arising impulses. Importantly, impulsivity is measured in a variety of different ways and it is increasingly understood to be a multidimensional psychological trait. Self-reported impulsive personality traits on questionnaires reveal a number of different facets. For example, the UPPS-P impulsive behavior scale comprises five subscales, including positive and negative urgency (i.e., proneness to act out during positive and negative mood states), premeditation (lack of) (i.e., level of deliberation or forethought), perseverance (lack of) (i.e., level of persistence or follow-through), and sensation seeking (i.e., preference for stimulating, exciting, or novel experiences). Of these, all of the traits have been linked to substance use, but positive and negative urgency are particularly related to clinical severity [81]. A second multidimensional measure of self-reported impulsive personality traits is the Barratt Impulsiveness Scale, which has also been robustly linked to addictive disorders and other externalizing behavior [82]. Beyond self-report, behavioral tasks can be used to measure orientation to immediate versus delayed reward (also referred to as delay discounting or delay of gratification), and capacity to inhibit prepotent motor responses (also referred to as response inhibition). In both cases, higher levels of impulsive responding have been linked to addictive disorders [83, 84]. However, it is notable that although the associations within the three domains of personality traits, delay discounting, and response inhibition are generally moderate to large, correlations across domains are generally small to negligible [85–87], suggesting they are distinct from one another.

Developmental Psychopathology

The last important psychological perspective is that of developmental psychopathology, an approach that seeks to understand psychiatric conditions as maladaptive deviations from normative human development. This perspective broadens the etiological lens to recognize influences prior to active drug use, such as prenatal influences and adverse childhood events [88, 89], and across the lifespan. In particular, a critical developmental window in the development of addiction is from adolescence to young adulthood, approximately 13–25. This is a broad window, but within it the vast majority of individuals will initiate their first exposures to addictive drugs and sizable proportions will progress to regular use and clinically significant misuse. For example, alcohol consumption peaks during emerging adulthood and is the most significant source of morbidity and mortality for this cohort [90, 91]. Furthermore, in the later phase of that time window, many individuals will naturally reduce consumption or stop using altogether, referred to as "maturing out" of drug use. In this way, it is not dissimilar to other forms of experimentation and role exploration that are present in adolescence, behaviors that are believed to be evolutionarily adaptive for developing autonomy, social status, and mate selection [92]. However, drug use during adolescence and young adulthood can also interfere with important developmental goals, such as educational attainment, career development, long-term relationships, and having a family [93–95], setting the stage for potentially lifelong problems. Notably, successful maturing out of substance use has been found to be a function of role transitions in terms of work, marriage, and parenthood [96–98]. Thus, there appear to be developmentally limited and lifetime persistent forms of substance use and substance use disorder [99], subtypes that are not unlike other externalizing behavior [100].[1] Taken together, converging data suggest that this developmental window is similar to an ethological "critical period," setting the stage for healthy and unhealthy substance use across the lifespan [101–103]. Furthermore, the preceding psychological mechanisms can also be understood within a developmental framework, with changes in expectancies, motives, and facets of impulsivity also predicting healthy and unhealthy changes in substance use during adolescence and young adulthood [104–108].

A final note pertaining to developmental psychopathology is that the perspective has been substantially enhanced by a deeper understanding of neurocognitive development. For example, the development of prefrontal cortex is gradual and protracted across adolescence and into young adulthood [109, 110]. Unfortunately, as a result, the developing brain appears to be more susceptible to neurotoxic effects of substance use [111, 112]. Furthermore, at least in preclinical models, adolescents appear to be more sensitive to reinforcing drug effects and less sensitive to the punishing effects [113]. Thus, adolescence and young adulthood represent a developmental window characterized by a surge in substance use during a period of neurocognitive vulnerability, with potential ramifications across the life span.

Social Models of Addiction

Social Networks

The importance of social factors in addiction is readily apparent from the observation that substance use is very commonly a social activity and the proverb that "birds of a feather flock together." Furthermore, there is a large empirical literature supporting this perspective. For example, social enhancement features prominently in measures of expectancies and motives [58, 62–65] and estimated substance use among close social affiliates is highly correlated with personal use [114, 115]. The importance of social influences can also be seen in clinical research. For example, in large randomized controlled trials, changes in the alcohol-related composition of the important individuals in a person's life have been found to predict treatment response, irrespective of experimental condition [116, 117]. Positive changes in social networks have been found to be mechanisms of the positive effects of Alcoholics Anonymous [118]. Furthermore, an intervention specifically developed to create a more positive social network has been shown to significantly increase behavioral and attitudinal support for not drinking and to significantly decrease drinking itself [119, 120].

The critical influence of a person's social ecology has been even more clearly revealed via social network analysis (SNA), a family of methodologies for quantitatively characterizing the structure of relationships among people [121–123]. There are broadly two SNA approaches, *egocentric* and *sociocentric*. Egocentric SNA refers to a person's self-reported social network (i.e., the network from the perspective of that individual, referred to as the "ego"). Sociocentric SNA refers to the objective social network (i.e., each person rates their relationship with each other person, such that the network is a latent property of cross-ratings). The advantage of egocentric SNA is that it provides the ego's perspective on the important people in their lives, whereas the advantage of sociocentric SNA is that it characterizes an objective network of individuals. A number of studies have examined social network dynamics relating to addictive behavior and have generated a number of important insights. For example, in early adolescents, individuals who are central to their social networks are more likely to use alcohol [124] and have been found to have more influence on their friends' alcohol use [125]. In addition, there is evidence for what are referred to as *selection dynamics* (e.g., drinkers seeking out other drinkers) and *influence dynamics* (i.e., the presence of drinkers in a network inducing more drinking), and these dynamics vary across adolescence [126–130]. Similarly, in adults, drinkers have been found to cluster together and social network characteristics predict changes in drinking over time [131–133], with parallel findings for other addictive disorders [115, 124, 129, 134].

Collectively, a social network perspective proposes that individuals self-select into networks of social relationships that are populated with people exhibiting similar levels of substance use (or lack thereof). For individuals with addiction, these networks are theorized to have a self-perpetuating influence on their members over time, including impeding behavior change in treatment. Thus, for some individuals, treatment may not just require abstaining or reducing alcohol, tobacco, cocaine, or heroin, but giving up important interpersonal relationships too. Here again, there is a maladaptive cycle in which social network influences recursively maintain the addictive behavior.

Classes of Social Influence and Mechanisms

It is important to recognize that not all members in social networks are of equal importance and the level of influence varies across the life span. In the critical period of adolescence and young adulthood, parental influences and peer influences are particularly powerful. A number of different parental influences have been identified. Arguably, the most important influence is parental substance use [135, 136], which can model the behavior, communicate perceived approval, and increase availability. In addition, parenting style is an important factor. Authoritative parenting is protective against substance use [137, 138], but the reverse is true for harsh parenting and parental hostility [139–141]. As parent–child connectedness and parental support are also negatively related to substance use [137, 138], it appears that both structure and warmth are important protective influences. Peer influences on substance use can be divided into three broad domains: overt offers, reflecting direct requests to use; modeling, reflecting passive social influence by familiar or unfamiliar peers; and social norms, reflecting the overestimation of typical behavior within a cohort [142]. All three domains are influential to varying extents [143–146]. In addition, in the case of social norms, social media campaigns have been undertaken to modify widespread overestimates, albeit with mixed evidence of efficacy [147].

Although parental and peer influences are most relevant to adolescents and young adults, dyadic influences, or significant others, are a potent social influence throughout adulthood. This is particularly an issue because individuals who use substances are more likely to be in a relationship together [148, 149], referred to as assortative mating, leading to dual-addiction couples. Like parental substance use, substance use among significant others provides a form of modeling, communicates approval, and provides access to substances [150]. However, addiction in couples is also associated with additional adverse patterns and consequences, such as intimate partner violence and poor parenting [150]. Thus, addiction among both members of a dyad represents a particularly deep embedding of the condition within a social network.

Sociocultural Influences

Finally, social influences on addiction include higher-order factors within society and culture, such as religion, economic conditions, and public policy. Religion is highly influential in overall population levels of substance use [151, 152] and, in terms of public policy, levels of taxation have major impacts on tobacco and alcohol consumption [153, 154]. Related to taxation, there is robust evidence that minimum pricing for alcohol reduces consumption [155, 156] and reduces negative consequences from drinking [157]. Other regulatory public policy influences include legal age of consumption, private versus state monopoly markets, law enforcement, density of outlets, and the availability of drink specials/"happy hours" [158]. Of course, economic and policy influences largely only pertain to legal addictive drugs or gambling because illicit drugs are unregulated. However, access to evidence-based prevention and treatments, and costs of care, are also important sociocultural factors that affect treatment for all forms of addiction [159–161]. In each of the preceding cases, these represent ways that a geographic area can have a favorable or unfavorable sociocultural climate toward the development and treatment of addiction.

Conclusions

If the goal of scientific theory is "to carve nature at its joints," then by extension, in clinical science, the goal of treatment is to intervene upon the dysfunction that is present in each of the resulting parts. A contemporary biopsychosocial approach carves addiction into three major sections and then further subdivides in a number of different ways. What emerges across these multifarious accounts is that there is no simple or singular answer to the question of why people develop addiction. Contemporary neurobiological theories of addiction offer incisive insights into addiction, emphasizing that psychoactive drugs use evolutionarily novel levels of stimulation to subvert, or even hijack, ancient brain systems that are responsible for adaptive motivation, learning, and executive control.

Psychologically, elevations in the reinforcing value of drug effects, maladaptive explicit and implicit cognitive processing, and deficits in self-regulatory capacities all contribute to persistent drug use, influences that are superimposed upon a developmental backdrop. Finally, social factors play a critical role, from family members and friends to extended social networks and a person's broader sociocultural context. A common theme in these accounts is the presence of recursive etiological processes, or feedforward processes that, once initiated and sufficiently engaged, are theorized to become self-sustaining and exacerbating. In other words, across theoretical accounts, there is convergence that addiction is a disorder of "vicious cycles," or patterns of maladaptive overconsumption that over time become increasingly difficult to change.

The array of perspectives reveals both strengths and weaknesses in the science of addiction. The contemporary approach provides a rich multidimensional perspective, spanning levels of analysis and addressing the complexity of the condition. However, rather than reflecting true synthesis across levels of analysis, a biopsychosocial approach still predominantly reflects discrete perspectives within each of these three domains. Furthermore, theoretical perspectives typically do not extend across disciplinary boundaries. Biological, psychological, and social approaches tend to be siloed away from each other, especially as methodological and disciplinary differences get larger. For example, there are no links between preclinical animal models, human developmental psychopathology, and tax policy. In this way, the field is akin to the parable about "the blind men and the elephant"—researchers in many different areas of the field are correctly identifying important aspects of a large complex problem, but no holistic theoretical viewpoint provides an overall framework.

Importantly, however, a merging of perspectives is increasingly taking place. Neuroimaging is increasingly permitting insights from preclinical models to be investigated directly in human participants affected by addiction. Genetic variables are being woven into psychological and social frameworks, and reciprocally behavioral and social measures are serving as novel phenotypes for genetic dissection or as moderators of genetic influences. Novel medications are targeting promising neural pathways from preclinical research and providing innovative mechanisms of action. These will be the advances that permit more comprehensive accounts of addiction to be developed, ones that more satisfactorily rise to the challenge of the epigraph at the chapter's start. Furthermore, even in its current incarnation, the contemporary biopsychosocial approach nonetheless provides a wealth of etiological processes and mechanisms for clinicians to consider in treating patients, making it an indispensable perspective in evidence-based treatment of addiction.

Note

1. Beyond a binary distinction, it is worth noting that a wide variety of theoretically and empirically derived addiction subtypes or trajectory profiles have been identified, but that a comprehensive review of these denominations is beyond the scope of the chapter.

References

1. Peele S, Alexander BK (1998) Theories of addiction. In: Peele S, editor. *The meaning of addiction: an unconventional view*. San Francisco (CA): Jossey-Bass.
2. Wise RA, Bozarth MA. A psychomotor stimulant theory of addiction. *Psychol Rev*. 1987;94:469–492.
3. Nesse RM, Berridge KC. Psychoactive drug use in evolutionary perspective. *Science*. 1997;278:63–66.
4. Kelley AE, Berridge KC. The neuroscience of natural rewards: relevance to addictive drugs. *J Neurosci*. 2002;22:3306–3311. doi:20026361.
5. Robinson TE, Berridge KC. The neural basis of drug craving: an incentive-sensitization theory of addiction. *Brain Res Brain Res Rev*. 1993;18:247–291.
6. Robinson TE, Berridge KC. Incentive-sensitization and addiction. *Addiction*. 2001;96:103–114. doi:10.1080/09652140020016996.
7. Robinson TE, Berridge KC. Review. The incentive sensitization theory of addiction: some current issues. *Philos Trans R Soc Lond B Biol Sci*. 2008;363:3137–3146. doi:10.1098/rstb.2008.0093.
8. Hyman SE Addiction: a disease of learning and memory. *Am J Psychiatry*. 2005;162:1414–1422. doi:10.1176/appi.ajp.162.8.1414.
9. Hyman SE, Malenka RC, Nestler EJ. Neural mechanisms of addiction: the role of reward-related learning and memory. *Annu Rev Neurosci*. 2006;29:565–598. doi:10.1146/annurev.neuro.29.051605.113009.
10. Kelz MB, Chen J, Carlezon WA, et al. Expression of the transcription factor deltaFosB in the brain controls sensitivity to cocaine. *Nature*. 1999;401:272–276. doi:10.1038/45790.
11. Colby CR, Whisler K, Steffen C, et al. Striatal cell type-specific overexpression of DeltaFosB enhances incentive for cocaine. *J Neurosci*. 2003;23:2488–2493.
12. Robbins TW, Everitt BJ. Drug addiction: bad habits add up. *Nature*. 1999;398:567–570. doi:10.1038/19208.
13. Everitt BJ, Robbins TW. Neural systems of reinforcement for drug addiction: from actions to habits to compulsion. *Nat Neurosci*. 2005;8:1481–1489. doi:10.1038/nn1579.
14. Everitt BJ, Robbins TW. From the ventral to the dorsal striatum: devolving views of their roles in drug addiction. *Neurosci Biobehav Rev*. 2013;37:1946–1954. doi:10.1016/j.neubiorev.2013.02.010.
15. Koob GF, Le Moal M. Drug addiction, dysregulation of reward, and allostasis. *Neuropsychopharmacology*. 2001;24:97–129. doi:S0893-133X(00)00195-0 [pii] 10.1016/S0893-133X(00)00195-0.
16. Koob GF, Le Moal M. Addiction and the brain antireward system. *Annu Rev Psychol*. 2008;59:29–53. doi:10.1146/annurev.psych.59.103006.093548.
17. Koob GF, Volkow ND. Neurocircuitry of addiction. *Neuropsychopharmacology*. 2010;35:217–238. doi:npp2009110 [pii] 10.1038/npp.2009.110.
18. Kalivas PW, Volkow ND. The neural basis of addiction: a pathology of motivation and choice. *Am J Psychiatry*. 2005;162:1403–1413. doi:10.1176/appi.ajp.162.8.1403.
19. Goldstein RZ, Volkow ND. Drug addiction and its underlying neurobiological basis: neuroimaging evidence for the involvement of the frontal cortex. *Am J Psychiatry*. 2002;159:1642–1652. doi:10.1176/appi.ajp.159.10.1642.

20. McClure SM, Bickel WK. A dual-systems perspective on addiction: contributions from neuroimaging and cognitive training. *Ann N Y Acad Sci.* 2014;1327:62–78. doi: 10.1111/nyas.12561.
21. Grant BF, Dawson DA, Moss HB. Disaggregating the burden of substance dependence in the United States. *Alcohol Clin Exp Res.* 2011;35:387–388. doi:10.1111/j.1530-0277.2011.01433.x.
22. Goldman D, Oroszi G, Ducci F. The genetics of addictions: uncovering the genes. *Nat Rev Genet.* 2005;6:521–532. doi:nrg1635 [pii] 10.1038/nrg1635.
23. Agrawal A, Lynskey MT. Are there genetic influences on addiction: evidence from family, adoption and twin studies. *Addiction.* 2008;103:1069–1081. doi:10.1111/j.1360-0443.2008.02213.x.
24. Palmer RHC, McGeary JE, Heath AC, et al. Shared additive genetic influences on DSM-IV criteria for alcohol dependence in subjects of European ancestry. *Addiction.* 2015;110:1922–1931. doi:10.1111/add.13070.
25. Bidwell LC, Palmer RHC, Brick L, et al. Genome-wide single nucleotide polymorphism heritability of nicotine dependence as a multidimensional phenotype. *Psychol Med.* 2016;1–11. doi:10.1017/S0033291716000453.
26. Luczak SE, Glatt SJ, Wall TL. Meta-analyses of ALDH2 and ADH1B with alcohol dependence in Asians. *Psychol Bull.* 2006;132:607–621. doi:10.1037/0033-2909.132.4.607.
27. Bierut LJ. Convergence of genetic findings for nicotine dependence and smoking related diseases with chromosome 15q24-25. *Trends Pharmacol Sci.* 2009. doi:S0165-6147(09)00168-0 [pii] 10.1016/j.tips.2009.10.004.
28. Gottesman II, Gould TD. The endophenotype concept in psychiatry: etymology and strategic intentions. *Am J Psychiatry.* 2003;160:636–645.
29. MacKillop J, Munafò MR. *Genetic influences on addiction: an intermediate phenotype approach.* Cambridge (MA): MIT Press; 2013.
30. Thorndike EL. *Animal intelligence.* New Brunswick (NJ): Transaction Publishers; 2011.
31. Skinner BF. *The behavior of organisms: an experimental analysis.* Acton (MA): Copley Publishing Group; 1966.
32. Bigelow GE. An operant behavioral perspective on alcohol abuse and dependence. In: Heather N, Peters TJ, Stockwell T, editors. *International handbook of alcohol dependence and problems.* Chichester (UK): John Wiley & Sons; 2001:299–315.
33. Higgins ST, Heil SH, Lussier JP. Clinical implications of reinforcement as a determinant of substance use disorders. *Annu Rev Psychol.* 2004;55:431–461. doi:10.1146/annurev.psych.55.090902.142033.
34. Bickel WK, Johnson MW, Koffarnus MN, et al. The behavioral economics of substance use disorders: reinforcement pathologies and their repair. *Annu Rev Clin Psychol.* 2014;10:641–677. doi:10.1146/annurev-clinpsy-032813-153724.
35. Mello NK, Mendelson JH. Operant analysis of drinking patterns of chronic alcoholics. *Nature.* 1965;206:43–46.
36. Mendelson JH, Mello NK. Experimental analysis of drinking behavior of chronic alcoholics. *Ann N Y Acad Sci.* 1966; 133:828–845.
37. Bigelow G. An operant behavioral analysis of alcohol abuse and dependence. In: Heather N, Peters TJ, Stockwell T, editors. *International handbook of alcohol dependence and problems.* Chichester (UK): John Wiley & Sons; 2001:299–315.
38. Budney AJ, Higgins ST, Hughes JR, Bickel WK. The scientific/clinical response to the cocaine epidemic: a MEDLINE search of the literature. *Drug Alcohol Depend.* 1992;30:143–149. doi:0376-8716(92)90019-9 [pii].

39. Jones JD, Comer SD. A review of human drug self-administration procedures. *Behav Pharmacol*. 2013;24:384–395. doi:10.1097/FBP.0b013e3283641c3d.
40. Correia CJ, Simons J, Carey KB, Borsari BE. Predicting drug use: application of behavioral theories of choice. *Addict Behav*. 1998;23:705–709. doi:S0306-4603(98)00027-6 [pii].
41. Correia CJ, Carey KB, Borsari B. Measuring substance-free and substance-related reinforcement in the natural environment. *Psychol Addict Behav*. 2002;16:28–34.
42. MacKillop J, Murphy JG. A behavioral economic measure of demand for alcohol predicts brief intervention outcomes. *Drug Alcohol Depend*. 2007;89:227–233. doi: S0376-8716(07)00022-1 [pii] 10.1016/j.drugalcdep.2007.01.002.
43. Murphy JG, Correia CJ, Colby SM, Vuchinich RE. Using behavioral theories of choice to predict drinking outcomes following a brief intervention. *Exp Clin Psychopharmacol*. 2005;13:93–101. doi:2005-05782-002 [pii] 10.1037/1064-1297.13.2.93.
44. Murphy JG, MacKillop J, Skidmore JR, Pederson AA. Reliability and validity of a demand curve measure of alcohol reinforcement. *Exp Clin Psychopharmacol*. 2009;17:396–404. doi:2009-23091-004 [pii] 10.1037/a0017684.
45. Stitzer M, Petry N. Contingency management for treatment of substance abuse. *Annu Rev Clin Psychol*. 2006;2:411–434. doi:10.1146/annurev.clinpsy.2.022305.095219.
46. Meyers RJ, Smith JE, Lash DN. The community reinforcement approach. *Recent Dev Alcohol*. 2003;16:183–195.
47. Cappell H, Herman CP. Alcohol and tension reduction: a review. *Q J Stud Alcohol*. 1972;33:33–64.
48. Greeley J, Oei T. Alcohol and tension reduction. In: Leonard KE, Blane HT, editors. Psychological theories of drinking and alcoholism. 2nd ed. New York: Guilford Press; 1999:14–53.
49. Martin CS, Earleywine M, Musty RE, et al. Development and validation of the Biphasic Alcohol Effects Scale. *Alcohol Clin Exp Res*. 1993;17:140–146.
50. Ray LA, MacKillop J, Leventhal A, Hutchison KE. Catching the alcohol buzz: an examination of the latent factor structure of subjective intoxication. *Alcohol Clin Exp Res*. 2009;33:2154–2161. doi:10.1111/j.1530-0277.2009.01053.x.
51. Schuckit MA. A longitudinal study of children of alcoholics. *Recent Dev Alcohol*. 1991;9:5–19.
52. Schuckit MA. Biological, psychological and environmental predictors of the alcoholism risk: a longitudinal study. *J Stud Alcohol*. 1998;59:485–494.
53. Quinn PD, Fromme K. Subjective response to alcohol challenge: a quantitative review. *Alcohol Clin Exp Res*. 2011. doi:10.1111/j.1530-0277.2011.01521.x.
54. King AC, de Wit H, McNamara PJ, Cao D. Rewarding, stimulant, and sedative alcohol responses and relationship to future binge drinking. *Arch Gen Psychiatry*. 2011;68:389–399. doi:10.1001/archgenpsychiatry.2011.26.
55. Hendershot CS, Wardell JD, McPhee MD, Ramchandani VA. A prospective study of genetic factors, human laboratory phenotypes, and heavy drinking in late adolescence. *Addict Biol*. 2016. doi:10.1111/adb.12397.
56. Stewart-Williams S, Podd J. The placebo effect: dissolving the expectancy versus conditioning debate. *Psychol Bull*. 2004;130:324–340. doi:10.1037/0033-2909.130.2.324.
57. Metrik J, Rohsenow DJ. Understanding the role of substance expectancies in addiction. In: MacKillop J, de Wit H, editors. *The Wiley-Blackwell handbook of addiction psychopharmacology*. Chichester: John Wiley & Sons; 2013:459–488.

58. Brown SA, Christiansen BA, Goldman MS. The Alcohol Expectancy Questionnaire: an instrument for the assessment of adolescent and adult alcohol expectancies. *J Stud Alcohol.* 1987;48:483–491.
59. Darkes J, Greenbaum PE, Goldman MS. Alcohol expectancy mediation of biopsychosocial risk: complex patterns of mediation. *Exp Clin Psychopharmacol.* 2004;12:27–38. doi:10.1037/1064-1297.12.1.27 2004-10475-007 [pii].
60. Smith GT, Goldman MS, Greenbaum PE, Christiansen BA. Expectancy for social facilitation from drinking: the divergent paths of high-expectancy and low-expectancy adolescents. *J Abnorm Psychol.* 1995;104:32–40.
61. Christiansen BA, Smith GT, Roehling PV, Goldman MS. Using alcohol expectancies to predict adolescent drinking behavior after one year. *J Consult Clin Psychol.* 1989;57:93–99.
62. Cooper ML, Frone MR, Russell M, Mudar P. Drinking to regulate positive and negative emotions: a motivational model of alcohol use. *J Pers Soc Psychol.* 1995;69:990–1005.
63. Ward LC, Kersh BC, Shanks D. Psychometric assessment of motives for using cocaine in men with substance use disorders. *Psychol Rep.* 1997;80:189–190. doi:10.2466/pr0.1997.80.1.189.
64. Jones RE, Spradlin A, Robinson RJ, Tragesser SL. Development and validation of the opioid prescription medication motives questionnaire: a four-factor model of reasons for use. *Psychol Addict Behav.* 2014;28:1290–1296. doi:10.1037/a0037783.
65. Simons J, Correia CJ, Carey KB. A comparison of motives for marijuana and alcohol use among experienced users. *Addict Behav.* 2000;25:153–160.
66. Barth KS, Maria MM-S, Lawson K, et al. Pain and motives for use among non-treatment seeking individuals with prescription opioid dependence. *Am J Addict.* 2013;22:486–491. doi:10.1111/j.1521-0391.2013.12038.x.
67. Kuntsche E, Knibbe R, Gmel G, Engels R. Why do young people drink? A review of drinking motives. *Clin Psychol Rev.* 2005;25:841–861. doi:10.1016/j.cpr.2005.06.002.
68. Piasecki TM, Piper ME, Baker TB. Tobacco dependence: insights from investigations of self-reported smoking motives. *Curr Dir Psychol Sci.* 2010;19:395–401. doi:10.1177/0963721410389460.
69. Rooke SE, Hine DW, Thorsteinsson EB. Implicit cognition and substance use: a meta-analysis. *Addict Behav.* 2008;33:1314–1328. doi:10.1016/j.addbeh.2008.06.009.
70. Kahler CW, Daughters SB, Leventhal AM, et al. Implicit associations between smoking and social consequences among smokers in cessation treatment. *Behav Res Ther.* 2007;45:2066–2077. doi:10.1016/j.brat.2007.03.004.
71. Carpenter KM, Martinez D, Vadhan NP, et al. Measures of attentional bias and relational responding are associated with behavioral treatment outcome for cocaine dependence. *Am J Drug Alcohol Abuse.* 2012;38:146–154. doi:10.3109/00952990.2011.643986.
72. Wiers RW, Eberl C, Rinck M, et al. Retraining automatic action tendencies changes alcoholic patients' approach bias for alcohol and improves treatment outcome. *Psychol Sci.* 2011;22:490–497. doi:10.1177/0956797611400615.
73. Attwood AS, O'Sullivan H, Leonards U, et al. Attentional bias training and cue reactivity in cigarette smokers. *Addiction.* 2008;103:1875–1882. doi:10.1111/j.1360-0443.2008.02335.x.

74. Reich RR, Below MC, Goldman MS. Explicit and implicit measures of expectancy and related alcohol cognitions: a meta-analytic comparison. *Psychol Addict Behav.* 2010;24:13–25. doi:10.1037/a0016556.
75. Nathan PE. The addictive personality is the behavior of the addict. *J Consult Clin Psychol.* 1988;56:183–188.
76. Sher KJ, Trull TJ. Personality and disinhibitory psychopathology: alcoholism and antisocial personality disorder. *J Abnorm Psychol.* 1994;103:92–102.
77. Malouff JM, Thorsteinsson EB, Rooke SE, Schutte NS. Alcohol involvement and the five-factor model of personality: a meta-analysis. *J Drug Educ.* 2007;37:277–294.
78. Malouff JM, Thorsteinsson EB, Schutte NS. The five-factor model of personality and smoking: a meta-analysis. *J Drug Educ.* 2006;36:47–58.
79. Kotov R, Gamez W, Schmidt F, Watson D. Linking "big" personality traits to anxiety, depressive, and substance use disorders: a meta-analysis. *Psychol Bull.* 2010;136:768–821. doi:10.1037/a0020327.
80. Maclaren VV, Fugelsang JA, Harrigan KA, Dixon MJ. The personality of pathological gamblers: a meta-analysis. *Clin Psychol Rev.* 2011;31:1057–1067. doi:10.1016/j.cpr.2011.02.002.
81. Coskunpinar A, Dir AL, Cyders MA. Multidimensionality in impulsivity and alcohol use: a meta-analysis using the UPPS model of impulsivity. *Alcohol Clin Exp Res.* 2013;37:1441–1450. doi:10.1111/acer.12131.
82. Stanford MS, Mathias CW, Dougherty DM, et al. Fifty years of the Barratt Impulsiveness Scale: an update and review. *Pers Individ Dif.* 2009;47:385–395.
83. MacKillop J, Amlung M, Few L, et al. Delayed reward discounting and addictive behavior: a meta-analysis. *Psychopharmacology (Berl).* 2011;216:305–321. doi:10.1007/s00213-011-2229-0.
84. Smith JL, Mattick RP, Jamadar SD, Iredale JM. Deficits in behavioural inhibition in substance abuse and addiction: a meta-analysis. *Drug Alcohol Depend.* 2014;145:1–33. doi:10.1016/j.drugalcdep.2014.08.009.
85. Stahl C, Voss A, Schmitz F, et al. Behavioral components of impulsivity. *J Exp Psychol Gen.* 2014;143:850–886. doi:10.1037/a0033981.
86. MacKillop J, Miller JD, Fortune E, et al. Multidimensional examination of impulsivity in relation to disordered gambling. *Exp Clin Psychopharmacol.* 2014;22:176–185. doi:10.1037/a0035874.
87. Cyders MA, Coskunpinar A. Measurement of constructs using self-report and behavioral lab tasks: is there overlap in nomothetic span and construct representation for impulsivity? *Clin Psychol Rev.* 2011;31:965–982. doi:10.1016/j.cpr.2011.06.001.
88. Konijnenberg C. Methodological issues in assessing the impact of prenatal drug exposure. *Subst Abuse.* 2015;9:39–44. doi:10.4137/SART.S23544.
89. Enoch MA. The role of early life stress as a predictor for alcohol and drug dependence. *Psychopharmacology (Berl).* 2011;214:17–31. doi:10.1007/s00213-010-1916-6.
90. Hingson RW, Zha W, Weitzman ER. Magnitude of and trends in alcohol-related mortality and morbidity among U.S. college students ages 18–24, 1998–2005. *J Stud Alcohol Drugs Suppl.* 2009:12–20.
91. Schulenberg JE, Maggs JL. A developmental perspective on alcohol use and heavy drinking during adolescence and the transition to young adulthood. *J Stud Alcohol Suppl.* 2002:54–70.

92. Ellis BJ, Del Giudice M, Dishion TJ, et al. The evolutionary basis of risky adolescent behavior: implications for science, policy, and practice. *Dev Psychol.* 2012;48:598–623. doi:10.1037/a0026220.
93. Bachman JG, Wadsworth KN, O'Malley PM, et al. *The decline of substance use in young adulthood: changes in social activities, role, and beliefs.* Mahwah (NJ): Erlbaum; 2002.
94. Gotham HJ, Sher KJ, Wood PK. Alcohol involvement and developmental task completion during young adulthood. *J Stud Alcohol.* 2003;64:32–42.
95. Wood MD, Sher KJ, McGowan AK. Collegiate alcohol involvement and role attainment in early adulthood: findings from a prospective high-risk study. *J Stud Alcohol.* 2000;61:278–289.
96. Lee MR, Chassin L, MacKinnon DP. Role transitions and young adult maturing out of heavy drinking: evidence for larger effects of marriage among more severe premarriage problem drinkers. *Alcohol Clin Exp Res.* 2015. doi:10.1111/acer.12715.
97. Lee MR, Chassin L, Villalta IK. Maturing out of alcohol involvement: transitions in latent drinking statuses from late adolescence to adulthood. *Dev Psychopathol.* 2013;25:1137–1153. doi:10.1017/S0954579413000424.
98. Dawson DA, Grant BF, Stinson FS, Chou PS. Maturing out of alcohol dependence: the impact of transitional life events. *J Stud Alcohol.* 2006;67:195–203.
99. Zucker RA. The four alcoholisms: a developmental account of the etiologic process. *Nebr Symp Motiv.* 1986;34:27–83.
100. Moffitt TE. Adolescence-limited and life-course-persistent antisocial behavior: a developmental taxonomy. *Psychol Rev.* 1993;100:674–701.
101. Chartier KG, Caetano R. Trends in alcohol services utilization from 1991–1992 to 2001–2002: ethnic group differences in the U.S. population. *Alcohol Clin Exp Res.* 2011;35:1485–1497. doi:10.1111/j.1530-0277.2011.01485.x.
102. Chartier KG, Caetano R. Ethnicity and health disparities in alcohol research. *Alcohol Res Heal.* 2010;33:152–160.
103. Jackson CA, Henderson M, Frank JW, Haw SJ. An overview of prevention of multiple risk behaviour in adolescence and young adulthood. *J Public Heal.* 2012;34(Suppl 1):i31–i40. doi:10.1093/pubmed/fdr113.
104. Littlefield AK, Verges A, McCarthy DM, Sher KJ. Interactions between self-reported alcohol outcome expectancies and cognitive functioning in the prediction of alcohol use and associated problems: a further examination. *Psychol Addict Behav.* 2011;25:542–546. doi:10.1037/a0022090.
105. Littlefield AK, Sher KJ, Wood PK. Do changes in drinking motives mediate the relation between personality change and "maturing out" of problem drinking? *J Abnorm Psychol.* 2010;119:93–105. doi:10.1037/a0017512.
106. Patrick ME, Wray-Lake L, Finlay AK, Maggs JL. The long arm of expectancies: adolescent alcohol expectancies predict adult alcohol use. *Alcohol Alcohol.* 2010;45:17–24. doi:10.1093/alcalc/agp066.
107. Quinn PD, Harden KP. Differential changes in impulsivity and sensation seeking and the escalation of substance use from adolescence to early adulthood. *Dev Psychopathol.* 2013;25:223–239. doi:10.1017/S0954579412000284.
108. Littlefield AK, Sher KJ, Wood PK. Is "maturing out" of problematic alcohol involvement related to personality change? *J Abnorm Psychol.* 2009;118:360–374. doi:10.1037/a0015125.
109. Paus T. Mapping brain maturation and cognitive development during adolescence. *Trends Cogn Sci.* 2005;9:60–68. doi:10.1016/j.tics.2004.12.008.

110. Casey BJ. Beyond simple models of self-control to circuit-based accounts of adolescent behavior. *Annu Rev Psychol.* 2015;66:295–319. doi:10.1146/annurev-psych-010814-015156.
111. Jacobus J, Tapert SF. Neurotoxic effects of alcohol in adolescence. *Annu Rev Clin Psychol.* 2013;9:703–721. doi:10.1146/annurev-clinpsy-050212-185610.
112. Jacobus J, Tapert SF. Effects of cannabis on the adolescent brain. *Curr Pharm Des.* 2014;20:2186–2193.
113. Spear LP, Varlinskaya EI. Sensitivity to ethanol and other hedonic stimuli in an animal model of adolescence: implications for prevention science? *Dev Psychobiol.* 2010;52:236–243. doi:10.1002/dev.20457.
114. MacKillop J, Acker JD, Bollinger J, et al. The Brief Alcohol Social Density Assessment (BASDA): convergent, criterion-related and incremental validity. *J Stud Alcohol Drugs.* 2013;74(5):810–15.
115. Fortune EE, MacKillop J, Miller JD, et al. Social density of gambling and its association with gambling problems: an initial investigation. *J Gambl Stud.* 2012. doi:10.1007/s10899-012-9303-3.
116. Stout RL, Kelly JF, Magill M, Pagano ME. Association between social influences and drinking outcomes across three years. *J Stud Alcohol Drugs.* 2012;73:489–497.
117. Longabaugh R, Wirtz PW, Zywiak WH, O'Malley SS. Network support as a prognostic indicator of drinking outcomes: the COMBINE study. *J Stud Alcohol Drugs.* 2010;71:837–846.
118. Kelly JF, Stout RL, Magill M, Tonigan JS. The role of Alcoholics Anonymous in mobilizing adaptive social network changes: a prospective lagged mediational analysis. *Drug Alcohol Depend.* 2011;114:119–126. doi:10.1016/j.drugalcdep.2010.09.009.
119. Litt MD, Kadden RM, Kabela-Cormier E, Petry N. Changing network support for drinking: initial findings from the network support project. *J Consult Clin Psychol.* 2007;75:542–555. doi:2007-11558-004 [pii] 10.1037/0022-006X.75.4.542.
120. Litt MD, Kadden RM, Kabela-Cormier E, Petry NM. Changing network support for drinking: network support project 2-year follow-up. *J Consult Clin Psychol.* 2009;77:229–242. doi:2009-03774-004 [pii] 10.1037/a0015252.
121. Borgatti SP, Mehra A, Brass DJ, Labianca G. Network analysis in the social sciences. *Science.* 2009;323:892–895. doi:10.1126/science.1165821.
122. Rosenquist JN. Lessons from social network analyses for behavioral medicine. *Curr Opin Psychiatry.* 2011;24:139–143. doi:10.1097/YCO.0b013e3283438061.
123. Burt RS, Kilduff M, Tasselli S. Social network analysis: foundations and frontiers on advantage. *Annu Rev Psychol.* 2013;64:527–547. doi:10.1146/annurev-psych-113011-143828.
124. Ennett ST, Bauman KE, Hussong A, et al. The peer context of adolescent substance use: findings from social network analysis. *J Res Adolesc.* 2006;16:159–186. doi:10.1111/j.1532-7795.2006.00127.x.
125. Crosnoe R, Needham B. Holism, contextual variability, and the study of friendships in adolescent development. *Child Dev.* 2004;75:264–279.
126. Mundt MP. The impact of peer social networks on adolescent alcohol use initiation. *Acad Pediatr.* 2011;11:414–421. doi:10.1016/j.acap.2011.05.005.
127. Mundt MP, Mercken L, Zakletskaia L. Peer selection and influence effects on adolescent alcohol use: a stochastic actor-based model. *BMC Pediatr.* 2012;12:115. doi:10.1186/1471-2431-12-115.

128. Fujimoto K, Valente TW. Decomposing the components of friendship and friends' influence on adolescent drinking and smoking. *J Adolesc Health.* 2012;51:136–143. doi:10.1016/j.jadohealth.2011.11.013.
129. Fujimoto K, Valente TW. Social network influences on adolescent substance use: disentangling structural equivalence from cohesion. *Soc Sci Med.* 2012;74: 1952–1960. doi:10.1016/j.socscimed.2012.02.009.
130. Cruz JE, Emery RE, Turkheimer E. Peer network drinking predicts increased alcohol use from adolescence to early adulthood after controlling for genetic and shared environmental selection. *Dev Psychol.* 2012;48:1390–1402. doi:10.1037/a0027515.
131. Rosenquist JN, Murabito J, Fowler JH, Christakis NA. The spread of alcohol consumption behavior in a large social network. *Ann Intern Med.* 2010;152: 426–433. doi:10.7326/0003-4819-152-7-201004060-00007.
132. Bullers S, Cooper ML, Russell M. Social network drinking and adult alcohol involvement: a longitudinal exploration of the direction of influence. *Addict Behav.* 2001;26:181–199.
133. Lau-Barraco C, Braitman AL, Leonard KE, Padilla M. Drinking buddies and their prospective influence on alcohol outcomes: alcohol expectancies as a mediator. *Psychol Addict Behav.* 2012;26:747–758. doi:10.1037/a0028909.
134. Meisel MK, Clifton AD, MacKillop J, et al. Egocentric social network analysis of pathological gambling. *Addiction.* 2013;108:584–591. doi:10.1111/add.12014.
135. Grant BF. The impact of a family history of alcoholism on the relationship between age at onset of alcohol use and DSM-IV alcohol dependence: results from the National Longitudinal Alcohol Epidemiologic Survey. *Alcohol Health Res World.* 1998;22:144–147.
136. Den Exter Blokland EAW, Engels RCME, Hale WW, et al. Lifetime parental smoking history and cessation and early adolescent smoking behavior. *Prev Med (Baltim).* 2004;38:359–368. doi:10.1016/j.ypmed.2003.11.008.
137. Ryan SM, Jorm AF, Lubman DI. Parenting factors associated with reduced adolescent alcohol use: a systematic review of longitudinal studies. *Aust N Z J Psychiatry.* 2010;44:774–783. doi:10.1080/00048674.2010.501759.
138. Resnick MD, Bearman PS, Blum RW, et al. Protecting adolescents from harm: findings from the National Longitudinal Study on Adolescent Health. *JAMA.* 1997;278:823–832.
139. Johnson V, Pandina RJ. Effects of the family environment on adolescent substance use, delinquency, and coping styles. *Am J Drug Alcohol Abuse.* 1991;17:71–88.
140. Lamis DA, Malone PS, Lansford JE, Lochman JE. Maternal depressive symptoms as a predictor of alcohol use onset and heavy episodic drinking in youths. *J Consult Clin Psychol.* 2012;80:887–896. doi:10.1037/a0028959.
141. Bailey JA, Hill KG, Oesterle S, Hawkins JD. Parenting practices and problem behavior across three generations: monitoring, harsh discipline, and drug use in the intergenerational transmission of externalizing behavior. *Dev Psychol.* 2009;45:1214–1226. doi:10.1037/a0016129.
142. Borsari B, Carey KB. Peer influences on college drinking: a review of the research. *J Subst Abus.* 2001;13:391–424.
143. Jaccard J, Blanton H, Dodge T. Peer influences on risk behavior: an analysis of the effects of a close friend. *Dev Psychol.* 2005;41:135–147. doi:10.1037/0012-1649.41.1.135.

144. Graham JW, Marks G, Hansen WB. Social influence processes affecting adolescent substance use. *J Appl Psychol.* 1991;76:291–298.
145. Perkins HW, Meilman PW, Leichliter JS, et al. Misperceptions of the norms for the frequency of alcohol and other drug use on college campuses. *J Am Coll Health.* 1999;47:253–258. doi:10.1080/07448489909595656.
146. Wolfson S. Students' estimates of the prevalence of drug use: evidence for a false consensus effect. *Psychol Addict Behav.* 2000;14:295–298.
147. Lewis MA, Neighbors C. Social norms approaches using descriptive drinking norms education: a review of the research on personalized normative feedback. *J Am Coll Health.* 2006;54:213–218. doi:10.3200/JACH.54.4.213-218.
148. Agrawal A, Heath AC, Grant JD, et al. Assortative mating for cigarette smoking and for alcohol consumption in female Australian twins and their spouses. *Behav Genet.* 2006;36:553–566. doi:10.1007/s10519-006-9081-8.
149. Grant JD, Heath AC, Bucholz KK, et al. Spousal concordance for alcohol dependence: evidence for assortative mating or spousal interaction effects? *Alcohol Clin Exp Res.* 2007;31:717–728. doi:10.1111/j.1530-0277.2007.00356.x.
150. Leonard KE, Eiden RD. Marital and family processes in the context of alcohol use and alcohol disorders. *Annu Rev Clin Psychol.* 2007;3:285–310. doi:10.1146/annurev.clinpsy.3.022806.091424.
151. AlMarri TSK, Oei TPS. Alcohol and substance use in the Arabian Gulf region: a review. *Int J Psychol.* 2009;44:222–233. doi:10.1080/00207590801888752.
152. Roberts SCM. Macro-level gender equality and alcohol consumption: a multi-level analysis across U.S. States. *Soc Sci Med.* 2012;75:60–68. doi:10.1016/j.socscimed.2012.02.017.
153. Chaloupka FJ, Yurekli A, Fong GT. Tobacco taxes as a tobacco control strategy. *Tob Control.* 2012;21:172–180. doi:10.1136/tobaccocontrol-2011-050417.
154. Wagenaar AC, Salois MJ, Komro KA. Effects of beverage alcohol price and tax levels on drinking: a meta-analysis of 1003 estimates from 112 studies. *Addiction.* 2009;104:179–190. doi:10.1111/j.1360-0443.2008.02438.x.
155. Stockwell T, Auld MC, Zhao J, Martin G. Does minimum pricing reduce alcohol consumption? The experience of a Canadian province. *Addiction.* 2012;107:912–920. doi:10.1111/j.1360-0443.2011.03763.x.
156. Stockwell T, Zhao J, Giesbrecht N, et al. The raising of minimum alcohol prices in Saskatchewan, Canada: impacts on consumption and implications for public health. *Am J Public Health.* 2012;102:e103–e110. doi:10.2105/AJPH.2012.301094.
157. Stockwell T, Zhao J, Marzell M, et al. Relationships between minimum alcohol pricing and crime during the partial privatization of a Canadian government alcohol monopoly. *J Stud Alcohol Drugs.* 2015;76:628–634.
158. Treno AJ, Marzell M, Gruenewald PJ, Holder H. A review of alcohol and other drug control policy research. *J Stud Alcohol Drugs.* 2014;75(Suppl 1):98–107.
159. Bridging the Gap between Practice and Research: Forging Partnerships with Community-Based Drug and Alcohol Treatment—PubMed—NCBI. Available from: www.ncbi.nlm.nih.gov/pubmed/25101381.
160. Oliva EM, Maisel NC, Gordon AJ, Harris AHS. Barriers to use of pharmacotherapy for addiction disorders and how to overcome them. *Curr Psychiatry Rep.* 2011;13:374–381. doi:10.1007/s11920-011-0222-2.
161. Carroll KM. Lost in translation? Moving contingency management and cognitive behavioral therapy into clinical practice. *Ann N Y Acad Sci.* 2014;1327:94–111. doi:10.1111/nyas.12501.

Chapter 3

Evidence-Based Treatment of Addictive Disorders

An Overview

John F. Kelly, Brandon G. Bergman, and Cristi L. O'Connor

Treatment for addictive disorders encompasses a broad array of psychological, social, and pharmacological interventions that are deployed to ameliorate the suffering and functional disabilities brought about by alcohol and other drugs, as well as behavioral or "process" addictive disorders, such as gambling. These interventions can be delivered by professionals with varying degrees of training and experience, as well as non-professional volunteers (e.g., Alcoholics Anonymous [AA]). Evidence-based practice (EBP) and empirically supported treatment (EST) are terms used to describe both general practices and specific treatments, respectively, that have been tested under rigorous research conditions to help ensure that such practices and treatments result in the most optimal health outcomes for individuals suffering from addictive disorders. In this chapter, we briefly describe the rationale, origins, and definitions of EBPs and ESTs, provide examples, and discuss the related benefits and some of the challenges in implementing such interventions in an integrated fashion in real-world clinical and community settings.

Introduction

The rise of managed care insurance plans in the latter part of the 20th century in the United States was intended to curtail what many saw as inefficient utilization of healthcare resources and federal healthcare dollars. The ultimate goal of this initiative was to enhance patients' outcomes with as few resources as possible, in order to implement more cost-efficient care. This movement was paralleled by calls for the need to ground psychiatric clinical care in a base of clinical research [1]. This shift was based on the premise that clinical care is at its most efficient when the care is informed by scientific research, spawning development of the "evidence-based treatment" paradigm in psychiatry, mental health, and substance use disorder treatment.

In order to provide some context for the chapters on specific addictive disorders that follow, in this chapter we describe and review: (a) the nature and strength of evidence and its relationship to clinical research designs and the research process; (b) the origins and definitions of evidence-based approaches; (c) a description and comparison of medical and contextual models of evidence-based treatment; (d) challenges in the implementation and regulation of evidence-based treatments; (e) why a practitioner might deviate from the specific guidelines of an evidence-based treatment; (f) the Veterans Administration Quality Enhancement Research Initiative (QUERI) as an example of implementing and evaluating evidence-based treatment in practice; and (g) a proposal to enhance evidence-based treatment paradigms by highlighting *practice-based evidence and measurement-based practice*. We conclude with considerations for future directions of the evidence-based treatment paradigm, as related to substance use disorder (SUD) treatment.

Research Designs, the Research Process, and Strength of Evidence

At its core, clinical evidence is concerned with cause and effect. Specifically, we want to know how likely it is that if we implement a particular clinical intervention, it will result in, or cause, a related outcome. Whether it concerns the causal factors in the etiology of a disorder or whether an intervention is seen to "work" to ameliorate or cure the disorder, we want to know the causal connection. In the 1960s, epidemiologist Sir Austin Bradford Hill outlined several criteria that can be used to help determine whether there is a causal impact of an intervention on an outcome [2]. These are outlined in Table 3.1, and include specificity, temporal precedence, experimentation, analogy, dose-response, plausibility, coherence, and consistency. To illustrate how these criteria relate to evidence-based practice, it may be helpful to consider the following. If a new addiction treatment is assumed to be efficacious, then one would have more confidence that it is causally related to the change in the outcome if: the outcome was due only to that specific intervention (*specificity*); it was clear that the intervention was delivered before the outcome changed (*temporal precedence*); there was *experimental evidence* (i.e., sufficient number of participants had been randomly assigned to receive the new intervention compared to another condition and the new intervention found to be superior); there is a stronger effect on the outcome with an increase in dose of the treatment (biological gradient/*dose-response*); it is theoretically plausible that the intervention could cause a positive change in the outcome (*plausibility*); similar treatments have been shown to cause change in the outcome being considered, or a similar outcome (*analogy*); and the results are the same or similar across different studies by different researchers at different times (*consistency*). Bradford Hill proposed that as more of these criteria are satisfied, the confidence in a causal connection is increased.

According to the American Psychological Association (APA) Presidential Task Force on Evidence-Based Practice [3], there are several forms of evidence, defined as a body of facts or information derived from scientific investigation. Specifically, "scientific investigation" can include clinical observation, qualitative research, case studies, single-case designs, public health or ecological designs, processes or mechanisms of change research, naturalistic or effectiveness studies, randomized controlled trials, and systematic reviews and meta-analyses. Each of these types of evidence possesses strengths and weaknesses.

Table 3.1 The Bradford Hill criteria for evaluating causal and effect relations

Criterion	Explanation
1. Strength of association	A small association does not mean that there is not a causal effect, though the larger the association, the more likely that it is causal.
2. Temporality	The effect has to occur after the cause (and if there is an expected delay between the cause and expected effect, then the effect must occur after that delay).
3. Specificity	Causation is likely if there is a very specific population at a specific site and disease with no other likely explanation. The more specific an association between a factor and an effect, the bigger the probability of a causal relationship. [1]
4. Consistency	Consistent findings observed by different persons in different places with different samples strengthens the likelihood of an effect.
5. Biological gradient	Greater exposure should generally lead to greater incidence of the effect. However, in some cases, the mere presence of the factor can trigger the effect. In other cases, an inverse proportion is observed: greater exposure leads to lower incidence.
6. Plausibility	A plausible mechanism between cause and effect is helpful (but Hill noted that knowledge of the mechanism is limited by current knowledge).
7. Coherence	Coherence between epidemiological and laboratory findings increases the likelihood of an effect. However, Hill noted that "lack of such [laboratory] evidence cannot nullify the epidemiological effect on associations."
8. Experiment	Occasionally, it is possible to appeal to experimental evidence.
9. Analogy	The effect of similar factors may be considered.

Source: Bradford Hill [2]

Clinical observation, for example, is one type of evidence, and skilled clinicians naturally often generate "hypotheses" pertaining to causes, maintaining conditions, and addiction relapse risk factors that can form the basis for their interventions. Based on a hypothesis, an intervention is implemented and implicitly tested, and hopefully a positive outcome achieved. A weakness of evidence purely from clinical observation is that what appears effective, and is remembered as such, can be susceptible to perceptual and recall biases. In other words, these clinical impressions, while important in generating hypotheses, are not without human error in determining their causal link to behavior change. Without controlled experimentation, it is unclear to what extent any positive change is due exclusively to the clinician and treatment delivery versus some client or other factors that lie outside of treatment. Consequently, without systematic, objective, and valid measurement of patients' response to the intervention in comparison to a standardized placebo or other treatment, it is difficult to know where to attribute any positive effect in a causal way. This is not always possible to do, however, as is the case in very rare diseases where only relatively few clinical cases exist. Important to note, therefore, is that there is no one research design that is "right" in every case. Rather, it is critical to choose the strongest design to best answer the research question at hand regarding cause and effect [4]. Discerning the cause and amount of change in the outcome is crucial in clinical research, because without it large amounts of financial resources and effort could be spent to disseminate an intervention perceived to "work" (i.e., cause meaningful salutary changes), only to find that the widespread adoption and implementation of the intervention does not actually improve patients' outcomes enough to justify the effort, or produce discernible benefits at all.

Also important when determining the strength of the evidence for any given intervention is the strength of the comparison treatment condition against which it has been tested. If a novel behavioral intervention has been tested against other active treatments (e.g., cognitive behavioral therapy [CBT]), the relative benefit might be smaller, for example, than if the same treatment is tested against a non-active "placebo" condition (e.g., relaxation training). In pharmacological research, of course, there is always a standardized "placebo" condition intended to look and feel identical to the active medication but without the presumed active ingredients. In behavioral therapy research, however, finding a standardized "placebo" has been more challenging, but equally important. Without it, we are unable to determine which specific treatment might be the most optimal as the effect sizes will co-vary along with the strength of the comparison condition. For this reason, Finney [5] has called for the standardization of a comparison condition in behavioral SUD treatment research so that effect sizes can be compared meaningfully across different studies, as is done in pharmacological research. More specifically, Finney [5] suggests treatments might be compared, for example, to four standardized sessions of brief motivational interviewing.

Some research questions cannot be addressed with certain research designs because of the nature of the problem. For instance, if a researcher wants to investigate the effect of the presence of major depression on relapse to alcohol use for individuals suffering from an alcohol use disorder (AUD), a randomized controlled trial cannot be used because we cannot randomly assign some individuals to have depression and some not. In other words, the independent variable (major depression) is not under the researcher's control; in this case, an alternate, quasi-experimental design would be used where groups of AUD patients with and without major depression ideally would be matched on other variables that might also relate to and affect the outcome (e.g., age, gender, severity of AUD, other types of psychiatric illness, etc.). Using this matching strategy, for example, the groups would be as similar as possible, except that one group would have major depression and the other would not.

On the other hand, if a researcher wanted to investigate the effect of a medication or a specific behavioral therapy on reducing AUD relapse risk for patients with co-occurring major depression, patients *could* be assigned at random to receive the medication or placebo, or to receive behavioral therapy or its comparison, because the independent variable (treatment) is under the researcher's control. This latter type of experimental study carries the largest degree of confidence that any observed advantage for the treatment is due, in fact, to the treatment, and not to other factors [6]. Thus, in theory, the process of random assignment will, on average, even out any preexisting differences in the comparison conditions being tested, so that the only difference between the groups is the variable of interest—or the independent variable. It is important to note, however, the sample size must be large enough for this to be true, and, in general, larger samples increase the likelihood that random assignment will even out participant factors. A sample size of at least 20 individuals per condition is needed to ensure the probability remains *lower than .05* that any difference between randomly assigned groups is accounted for by a non-independent variable (which would reduce the confidence in a causal association between treatment and outcome) [7].

Tightly controlled approaches are excellent for determining causal associations, but their weakness is that the focus at this stage of the research is on determining whether this is a true benefit attributable to a particular treatment under ideal conditions (i.e., it tries to establish a causal connection). As such, these studies often exclude individuals with other types of problems such that the sample on which the study results are based may be somewhat different from individuals seen in "typical" treatment settings. For example, a trial testing the efficacy of a new medication for AUD may exclude patients with co-occurring major depressive disorder, although this co-occurrence is common in real-world clinical settings [8]. These types of studies also use clinicians that are often experienced and receive intensive training and supervision in the new treatment to ensure that the treatment is delivered exactly as intended without hindrance. These features may not apply in real-world busy clinical settings, where providers have varying degrees of experience and supervision, and where crises and emergencies can interrupt treatment flow. Thus, many have argued treatments tested under these conditions are not generalizable to the majority of clinical settings [9, 10].

As a result of the generalizability problem from results of tightly controlled clinical trials, treatments are typically developed in phases beginning with pre-clinical phases up through phase 3 clinical trials [11, 12]. Table 3.2 describes these phases for pharmacological and behavioral interventions. These vary slightly across pharmacological and psychological interventions but are generally similar, going from the more tightly controlled studies with high "internal validity" to the more "externally valid" effectiveness studies with greater real-world generalizability. The ideal scenario would be that a new treatment shown to work under tightly controlled conditions would also be seen to produce at least as large a benefit when implemented under real-world clinical conditions.

The Origins and Definitions of Evidence-Based Approaches

Establishing causal connections in pharmacology research is somewhat more straightforward than it is in psychotherapy research because, as noted above, any

Table 3.2 Phase model of treatment research for pharmacological and behavioral treatments

Stage	Phase	Pharmacological study	Behavioral study
Treatment development	Preclinical	Testing in non-human subjects and in vitro studies	–
	Phase 0	Increased information about medication properties (e.g., half-life)	Basic research about constructs to be modified by treatment (e.g., cognitive biases)
	Phase 1	Pilot tests on healthy volunteers	1a: Manual development 1b: Pilot tests on target population and manual refinement
	Phase 2	Randomized trial to test efficacy and safety relative to placebo	Randomized trial to test efficacy and safety relative to comparison group (no treatment, inactive treatment, active treatment)
Treatment implementation	Phase 3	Effectiveness tests in real-world clinical settings	Effectiveness tests in real-world clinical settings
	Phase 4	Ongoing monitoring of medication's impact on public health (e.g., adverse events)	–

Source: Friedman, Furberg, and DeMets [11] and Rounsaville, Carroll, and Onken [12]

new active treatment is always compared to a standardized placebo in a randomized controlled experimental study design, and there are few other variables to confound the causal connections under study (although a patient who is "assigned" to an active medication condition may not always take it as prescribed, and this can create a confound in the estimated efficacy of a medication). Research on psychosocial treatments are more complicated as there is not just a "technological" aspect of the treatment, which is presumed to be the carrier of the causal effect (e.g., skills training in CBT), but also the characteristics and skill of the therapist, as well as the relationship, rapport, and alliance between the therapist and the patient.

In an effort to "survive in [the] heyday of biological psychiatry," "to spotlight [psychology's] achievements in data-based psychological interventions," and to "[promote] psychological interventions to the public and third party payors," Division 12 of the APA (clinical psychology) convened a task force of psychologists with varying theoretical orientations that formally defined *empirically validated treatments* (EVTs) [13]. Their efforts to establish criteria that mirror the double-blind placebo randomized controlled trials (RCTs) used to evaluate medications so as "not to leave psychologists at a serious disadvantage" was stated explicitly. The task force set forth criteria for *well-established* EVTs and *probably efficacious* EVTs. Table 3.3 below describes evidence levels and criteria for EVTs, as well as more recent designations, including EBP. To be deemed *well established*, a treatment needed to be superior to another treatment or psychological placebo (e.g., attention or relaxation condition) in two "good" group design studies, conducted by two different investigative teams, or equivalent to an already *well established* treatment. In addition, a *well-established* treatment could receive that designation from "a large series" of single case studies with "good experimental design" demonstrating efficacy relative to another treatment. In both cases, the treatment needed to be manualized and the treatment samples clearly described. To be deemed *probably efficacious*, the treatment needed to be superior relative to a waitlist control group in two studies, or meeting some but not all the criteria for a *well-established* EVT (e.g., only one study showing its effectiveness relative to another treatment, two studies with samples that were too variable in their presenting problem, or a "small" rather than "large" series of single case studies).

Chambless and Hollon [14] further refined this work in defining *empirically supported therapies* (ESTs) with a clearer emphasis on RCTs, in order to maximize the likelihood that any observed improvements are not due to factors beyond the treatment, such as patient (e.g., motivation) or social factors (e.g., the composition of an individual's social network), or the passage of time. They defined a treatment as *efficacious* if it was superior in two RCTs with separate investigators to a no-treatment control, or *efficacious and specific* if superior to a medication or psychological placebo (e.g., psychoeducation group). It is considered *possibly efficacious* if superior in only one RCT or with one investigative team. They also specified single case designs that are acceptable (e.g., multiple baseline or A-B-A-B), and offered a guideline requiring three positive single case studies conducted by two separate investigative teams to be deemed *efficacious*. Similarly, as with the Division 12 Task Force, they recommend the treatment be for a specific problem or issue, and that the treatment is manualized. Although the paper considers other key clinical research domains, such as clinical versus statistical significance and clinical utility outlined above in greater detail (e.g., generalizability of findings to clinical practice), their EST definition views these issues as secondary.

It is important to note that "clinical significance" [16] is particularly relevant for practicing clinicians, as it moves beyond statistical value of whether there is a reliable difference unlikely to occur by chance, to whether there is a reliable difference that is meaningful in the lives of patients (e.g., does it actually reduce suffering and increase an individual's functioning in their day-to-day life?). A three-point reduction on an outcome measure may be "statistically significant" and publishable in a scientific journal, for instance, but this reduction may not feel any different to people suffering from a psychiatric illness, such as SUD. In other words, before appropriating funding to disseminate and implement an intervention based on an accumulation of statistically significant findings, it will be important to consider whether the expenditure and effort will actually benefit the patient in a meaningful way. This is why, in addition

Evidence-Based Treatment 61

Table 3.3 Summary of evidence-based treatment criteria and definitions

Term	Criteria/definition
Empirically validated treatment (EVT)[1]	
Well established	I. At least two good group design studies, conducted by different investigators, demonstrating efficacy in one or more of the following ways:
	(a) Superior to pill or psychological placebo or to another treatment.
	(b) Equivalent to an already established treatment in studies with adequate statistical power.
	OR
	II. A large series of single case design studies demonstrating efficacy. These studies must have:
	(a) Used good experimental designs.
	(b) Compared the intervention to another treatment as in I(a).
	Further criteria for both I and II:
	III. Studies must be conducted with treatment manuals.
	IV. Characteristics of the client samples must be clearly specified.
Probably efficacious	I. Two studies showing the treatment are more effective than a waiting list control group.
	OR
	II. Two studies otherwise meeting the well-established treatment criteria I, III, and IV, but both are conducted by the same investigator. Or one good study demonstrating effectiveness by these same criteria.
	OR
	III. At least two good studies demonstrating effectiveness but flawed by heterogeneity of the client samples.
	OR
	IV. A small series of single case design studies otherwise meeting the well-established treatment criteria of II, III, and IV.
Empirically supported therapy (EST)[2]	
EST	I. Comparison with a no-treatment control group, alternative treatment group, or placebo (a) in a randomized control trial, controlled single case experiment, or equivalent time-samples design; and (b) in which the EST is statistically significantly superior to no treatment, placebo, or alternative treatments, or in which the EST is equivalent to a treatment already established in efficacy, and power is sufficient to detect moderate differences.

continued ...

Table 3.3 Continued

Term	Criteria/definition
	II. These studies must have been conducted with (a) a treatment manual or its logical equivalent; (b) a population, treated for specified problems, for whom inclusion criteria have been delineated in a reliable, valid manner; (c) reliable and valid outcome assessment measures, at minimum tapping the problems targeted for change; and (d) appropriate data analysis.
Efficacious	In addition to I and II, for a designation of efficacious, the superiority of the EST must have been shown in at least two independent research settings (sample size of three or more at each site in the case of single case experiments). If there is conflicting evidence, the preponderance of the well-controlled data must support the EST's efficacy.
Possibly efficacious	In addition to I and II, for a designation of possibly efficacious, one study (sample size of three or more in the case of single case experiments) suffices in the absence of conflicting evidence.
Efficacious and specific	In addition to I and II, for a designation of efficacious and specific, the EST must have been shown to be statistically significantly superior to pill or psychological placebo or to an alternative bona fide treatment in at least two independent research settings. If there is conflicting evidence, the preponderance of the well-controlled data must support the EST's efficacy and specificity.

Evidence-based practice (EBP)[3]

Evidence-based practice in psychology	The integration of the best available research with clinical expertise in the context of patient characteristics, culture, and preferences.

Source: 1. Chambless and Hollon [14]; 2. American Psychological Association [13]; 3. Levant [15]

to statistical significance, confidence intervals and standardized effect sizes are also important to calculate and report. Also, when Miller and Manuel [17] surveyed clinicians on the degree of clinical difference that would need to be present for them to adopt a treatment, for dichotomous outcomes (e.g., total abstinence), a 10% difference between the treatment and comparison was deemed meaningful (e.g., 40% of those who received the treatment versus 30% of those who received the comparison), and for continuous outcomes (e.g., percent days abstinent), a doubling or halving was deemed meaningful (e.g., treatment group has 70% days abstinent, on average, versus 35% for the comparison group).

In selecting an EST, practitioners may choose to consult an existing list of ESTs, which may vary considerably in the criteria used. These may be found in one of several research articles (see [6], for example), or websites hosted by federally funded organizations or universities (e.g., University of Washington). In the National Registry of Evidence-Based Programs and Practices (NREPP), hosted by the United States Substance Abuse and Mental Health Services Administration (SAMHSA), an intervention need only be superior to a comparison condition of any kind in a true experiment (randomized trial) or quasi-experiment (participants are not randomized to condition). This stands, in contrast, for example, to the EST definition described above. Obviously, with only one or two studies, confidence in the results might be lower than if several studies showed the same benefits (i.e., there is deemed to be "consistency"; see [2]), especially if sample sizes are low and the degree of conferred benefit small in the one or two studies completed (i.e., uncertain clinical significance, despite statistical significance). In fact, there are more than 330 ESTs for SUD listed in the NREPP database, and it may be difficult to determine from these the most optimal intervention.

Finally, in 2005, an APA task force defined *evidence-based practice* [15], which intended to address the critiques of relying solely on evidence from RCTs in setting clinical practice guidelines (e.g., [9, 10]). Although related concepts, EBP considers ESTs as one integral type of scientific evidence to inform clinical practice with a given patient. Specifically, EBP is defined as the "integration of the best available research with clinical expertise in the context of patient characteristics, culture, and preferences." One clear addition to the definition of EBP relative to EST is the judgment and expertise of the clinician, and patient characteristics beyond the problem for which they are seeking help. Within this definition, RCTs are viewed as but one type of evidence, though, as mentioned above, carrying with them the greatest ability to establish a causal connection between the treatment and any related benefit.

Multisite trials are often employed to test interventions that have been demonstrated to be effective in studies conducted at a single site. These studies are typically hybrids of efficacy and effectiveness studies (or phase 2 and phase 3 trials; see Table 3.3 above). The National Institute on Drug Abuse Clinical Trials Network (NIDA-CTN), for example, conducts multisite randomized controlled trials using existing community programs with the interventions provided using staff already employed by those programs. A puzzling but consistent finding in multisite trials, such as those conducted by the NIDA-CTN in treating SUD, has been that differences are often observed *between sites* in the efficacy of the exact same treatments delivered by highly qualified and well-supervised clinicians, who show a high level of adherence and competence in delivering the treatment. It is important to note that these differences have not been explained by differences in patient factors (i.e., the case mix). What then accounts for these between-site differences in the delivery of the exact same behavioral treatment? What differences in practice or contexts might account for such variations? This question has led to much scrutiny of therapeutic intervention models and has raised concerns about the fit of the theoretical models specified to describe and explain how exactly SUD interventions confer benefits.

The Medical versus Contextual Model of Treatments

ESTs as outlined by the Division 12 Task Force and Chambless and Hollon [13, 14] evaluate the efficacy of different therapies based on the "medical model," also known as the "technology" model [18]. This model posits that a person with an illness is prescribed a specific treatment (e.g., a medication) that will lead to a cure or reduce the symptoms of the illness. In other words, the medication is the active causal ingredient leading to a salutary change. The intent to boost psychotherapy research so that it rivaled the kind of credibility given to pharmacological interventions for psychiatric disorders in a growing paradigm of managed care was a major aim of conforming to the well-established and highly regarded medical model. The idea transferred to psychotherapy research from this medical model was that the therapist is presumed to be a "constant," and not a "variable," and that the most crucial thing in treatment is adherence to, and competence in, delivering the "behavioral pill" exactly as intended. In other words, like a medication, the content of the psychotherapeutic intervention was responsible for patient improvement. Many have argued, however, that boiling down more complex psychosocial interventions to an analogue of medication was too narrow a view. Specifically, characterizing interventions as being delivered by "disembodied therapists" [19] and targeting psychiatric disorders ignored the curative power of the therapeutic relationship and its various components [18].

In contrast with this medical model of ESTs, the *contextual model* [20, 21] suggested that patients improve through a combination of: (a) the relationship or alliance between the therapist and themselves; (b) a belief that they will get better, also referred to as the "instillation of hope" [22] or "remoralization" [23]; and (c) through a set of specific ingredients that addresses the problem for which they present. Lambert and Barley [24] suggest that, in psychotherapeutic clinical outcomes studies, specific (i.e., "medical model" type) techniques, while important, account for about 15% of the outcome variance. These techniques are only about half as influential as *common* therapeutic factors such as the degree of therapeutic alliance between clinicians and those they try to help, as well as individual patient factors (e.g., motivation). Division 29 of the APA (psychotherapy) commissioned its own task force in 2001 to examine the nature of *empirically supported therapy relationships* (ESRs). Based on a volume of literature reviews in the area [19], the task force concluded that the therapeutic alliance, cohesion in group therapy, therapist empathy, and goal consensus and collaboration were *demonstrably effective* elements of therapeutic outcome. This is likely because the therapist plays not just a role as "technician," but also as an understanding ally, supporter, coach, and cheerleader. Clearly, however, there must be also some implicit theory as to how the presenting condition and chief complaint is to be addressed that must make sense in the context of the presenting condition—a rationale that explains the nature of the disorder and coherent steps to facilitate remission [25] (e.g., when treating addiction, there is likely to be talk of withdrawal, tolerance, causes, and maintaining conditions of the disorder, and may include psychodynamic, behavioral, or social-cognitive formulations of how people can get and stay in remission). In other words, while the context appears to be crucial in creating the right conditions for change, specific elements are offered within this context (e.g., avoiding high-risk individuals and situations).

Challenges in Implementing ESTs

As noted in our discussion of the phased approach to clinical research, there is a distinction between efficacy studies, testing interventions in the context of structured and highly monitored conditions, and effectiveness studies, testing interventions in real-world clinical settings. ESTs could be challenging to implement in real-world clinical settings for a number of reasons, including but not limited to ingrained clinical habits of practitioners, the balance between training in new strategies and the large caseloads of community practitioners, and clinicians' views that research does not address questions relevant to them [26]. Counterintuitively, many studies have shown that, despite the *efficacy* of certain interventions under tightly controlled conditions, they may be no more *effective* in real-world settings than treatment-as-usual [27, 28]. For example, Morgenstern, Blanchard, Morgan, Labouvie, and Hayaki [29] showed that, among outpatients in community treatment, implementation of a highly standardized cognitive behavioral intervention for SUD did not enhance treatment retention or abstinence compared to low-standardization CBT or treatment-as-usual (TAU), an unstandardized 12-step-oriented treatment. Importantly, this lack of additional benefit occurred even though therapists in the highly standardized CBT condition demonstrated greater technical skills and adherence to the treatment relative to the other comparison conditions. Consistent with the discussion of common factors above, nonspecific effects, including treatment attendance and therapeutic alliance, accounted for nearly 20% of outcome variance.

Similarly, in multisite trials of motivational interviewing (MI) conducted in the NIDA CTN, four separate multisite clinical trials comparing MI treatments to TAU were conducted and found to be no better than TAU, despite showing benefits in smaller single-site trials [30–33]. For example, the implementation of three-session, individually delivered MI did not result in superior patient retention or more negative urine toxicology screens relative to TAU, which included case management and encouragement to attend 12-step meetings [34]. In fact, as noted by Miller and Moyers [27], the modal treatment effect size for *all* NIDA CTN trials testing EBTs intended to show enhancements in real-world clinical care relative to TAU was zero. It is also worth noting that, as highlighted above, some treatment sites had better outcomes than others, irrespective of treatment received (e.g., MI versus TAU).

Despite the explicit theory and practice differences among these different intervention approaches (e.g., MI versus 12-step), these largely null findings suggest a robust contribution of nonspecific therapeutic factors and patient differences to treatment outcomes [27]. Put another way, there are influential therapeutic factors at work that have not yet been "specified" in these clinical models that need to be assessed and included in explanatory models if we are to understand more fully the causal connections between intervention implementation and patients' outcomes [35].

Another important challenge in the delivery of ESTs is that, for the most part, psychopharmacology and psychosocial treatments are often tested separately in clinical trials. However, many programs are increasingly offering both forms of treatment [36]. For example, among privately funded programs, between 2002 and 2007, the use of naltrexone (opioid antagonist used to address alcohol or opioid use disorder) has increased from 30% to 40%, and the use of buprenorphine/naloxone (a partial opioid agonist) has increased from 15% to 45%. Among publicly funded programs, naltrexone has remained stable at 15%, while buprenorphine has increased from 5% to 25%. Although a program's theoretical orientation may make it less likely to adopt SUD medications (e.g., 12-step oriented treatment programs appear less likely to adopt certain types of medication [36]), this practice is changing. For example, the Hazelden Betty Ford Foundation, one of the most well-known 12-step oriented treatment programs in the world that offers ESTs, including 12-step facilitation (TSF), motivational enhancement (a treatment based on MI), and CBT, has begun systematically to offer medications such as naltrexone and buprenorphine for patients with opioid use disorders, as part of its Comprehensive Opioid Response with 12 steps (COR-12). While this combination of treatments is conceived to be superior than either intervention alone, it is unknown whether the implementation of these interventions may be additive, multiplicative, or perhaps, counterintuitively, whether one may subtract from the benefits provided by the other leading to a diminishing return.

Another challenge to implementing ESTs is that, even among the most methodologically rigorous studies where pharmacological and psychosocial approaches are tested together, such as the large multisite clinical trial known as the COMBINE study [37, 38] and the Prescription Opioid Addiction Treatment Study [39], adding a specialized psychosocial treatment may not improve positive responses to an efficacious medication and standard medical management (e.g., weekly check-ins with a nonspecialist physician or nurse). Of note, medical management in these studies includes strong encouragement to remain abstinent, and to attend 12-step mutual-help groups, which can be powerful interventions themselves [40]. As such, the effect of this straightforward intervention plus medication may be potent enough that individual specialized addiction therapy provides no incremental benefit. That said, the large multisite COMBINE study also did not find that adding a medication to a specialized behavioral addiction intervention improved outcomes. Thus, as noted previously, conducting some kind of active intervention is likely to produce similar benefits. Community-based SUD treatment may be enhanced through further trials of ESTs in clinical settings that reflect the real-world multimodal (psychosocial and psychopharmacological) nature of frontline treatment.

"Acceptable Deviation" from Evidence-Based Practice

Strong therapist "adherence" to, and "competence" in, delivering a specific treatment protocol are prized qualities in evaluating the effects of a new behavioral therapy for SUD in efficacy studies. Adhering closely to a treatment manual and delivering its contents with a high degree of fidelity and competence are critical factors in helping to determine whether it is, in fact, the contents of a particular treatment that are the "active ingredients," and thus responsible for any observed benefits. Ideally, this same degree of adherence and competence would occur in real-world clinical settings. Without clinical judgment, however, blind adherence to an "empirically supported" treatment protocol may be therapeutically counterproductive and even harmful. The recommended indicated minimum therapeutic dose of methadone for an opioid-dependent patient, for instance, is at least 60 mg [41, 42]. However, if a patient has been stably in remission for the past five years and has never been above a dose of 40 mg, it would be unwise clinically to raise the patient's dose to 60 mg; doing so, in fact, could jeopardize the patient's recovery. Consequently, in keeping with the broader definition of "evidence-based practice," acceptable deviations from the empirically supported treatment regimen are justified and must involve common sense and good clinical judgment.

The Science of Implementing and Evaluating Empirically Supported Treatments in Real-World Clinical Settings: The VA Quality Enhancement Research Initiative (QUERI) example

Since the formation of NIDA and the National Institute on Alcohol Abuse and Alcoholism (NIAAA) in the 1970s in the United States, there has been a proliferation of new pharmacological and behavioral treatments designed, tested, and found efficacious. Consequently, there has been pressure to implement these new treatments in real-world clinical settings. The challenges in getting programs and clinicians to adopt and implement new empirically supported practices is not as straightforward a state of affairs as one might anticipate. This has given rise to an entirely new field of "implementation science." There are multiple challenges involved in educating program directors and clinical providers about the nature of evidence and the degree of expected benefit from implementation in order to get their buy-in, and motivate decision-makers to spend a large amount of time and money in training the workforce. The Veterans Administration (VA) with its national healthcare system has had a vested interest in the implementation of ESTs, in order to enhance quality and reduce costs, thereby maximizing clinical efficiency. The Quality Enhancement Research Initiative (QUERI) began in 1998 as a VA specific effort to implement ESTs in frontline clinical settings and to evaluate the benefits of this implementation. The six steps of the QUERI process are outlined in Table 3.4. One of the most

Table 3.4 The steps of the Quality Enhancement Research Initiative to help improve patients' outcomes by helping clinical programs adopt, implement, and sustain EBPs

QUERI steps	Example
Identify gap in EBP	• 60% of methadone clinics' average methadone dosing is lower than the recommended 60 mg • 68% of methadone clinics are not providing any recommended counseling along with provision of methadone
Develop and implement a strategy for change	• Gain leadership buy-in for the need for change • Conduct on-site in-services to educate clinics and providers about the gaps in EBP
Test strategy	• Conduct a 1-to-2 year evaluation of the implementation of best practices
Document system improvements	• Obtain feedback and provide evidence to programs and providers that the treatment system is improving as a result of the implementation
Document outcomes and Quality of Life improvements	• Provide evidence that patients are now better off as a result of the EBP implementation

Source: US Department of Veterans Affairs [43]

crucial steps in this process is the sixth and final step: providing evidence that the implementation of the new practice does, in fact, result in real-world improvements in patients' outcomes. This is the ultimate goal of developing, testing, and delivering ESTs, but cannot be assumed. Indeed, as outlined above, counterintuitively, implementation of "best practices" in the treatment of SUD may not always, and possibly only rarely, results in improvements in patients' outcomes and quality of life.

Another important aspect of evaluating evidence is understanding why an EST may or may not work and whether the presumed mechanisms through which it is purported to transfer its beneficial effects do so when observed empirically. Suchman [44], and later Finney [45], described a process analysis model whereby it is possible to evaluate where in the treatment process chain there are particular poor linkages or failures. He describes three different types of failures that can occur in evaluating the causal chain of how treatments work: implementation failures, program failures, and theory failures. During the course of CBT for SUD, for example, patients' relapse prevention (RP) coping skills are expected to increase. If, however, coping skills remain stable or decrease, this would be considered an "implementation failure," because a crucial during-treatment change (increase in coping skills) would have not been achieved, and, consequently, either a more intensive or different approach would need to be tried to enhance the acquisition of these skills. If, on the other hand, coping skills were observed to increase, but in following the intervention patients over time, they are unable to deploy such skills in the real world, then this would be viewed as a "program failure" since a crucial proximal outcome of the program (i.e., day-to-day use of relapse prevention coping skills) was not observed. Finally, if these skills are, in fact, able to be deployed following the intervention, but they are not observed to have any bearing on whether someone relapses to SUD or not, then there is presumed to be a "theory" failure in that the major theory underlying the intervention (i.e., patients relapse because they do not have the skills to prevent SUD relapse, and treatment therefore needs to teach such RP coping skills in order to prevent SUD relapse) is unsupported.

If an intervention is predicted to be superior to an already established intervention but this effect is not observed empirically, evaluating the intervention using this process analysis model at each one of these junctures will help identify where in the treatment process chain a "failure" has occurred. Even in the context of null results, such an analysis may allow for more targeted refinements of the intervention and a re-evaluation of this refined approach in its ability to enhance patient care. If an EST has no advantage relative to TAU, it may not mean that intervention is of no use; rather, it could mean that it was not implemented properly, or there were unforeseen patient barriers to deploying the new skills following the intervention. As an example of this process analysis approach, Morgenstern, Kuerbis, Amrhein, Hail, Lynch, and McKay [46] conducted a study examining the mechanisms through which a specific EST, MI, reduces alcohol use. This randomized controlled clinical trial found that MI increased the major purported mechanisms of the therapy (i.e., increased verbalized intentions and reasons for reducing alcohol use, as well as commitment to change, also known as "change talk"), producing an "implementation" success. However, the increase in "change talk" did not result in better alcohol outcomes than a non-therapist feedback-only "self-change" condition, indicating a "theory failure."

Practice-Based Evidence and Measurement-Based Practice

Adopting and implementing ESTs in real-world clinical settings clearly is not without challenges. One disappointment has been that when the EST is actually delivered in real-world clinical settings, it does not result in improved patients' outcomes [27, 29]. Another challenge is that clinicians, even when trained and supervised initially to implement a new EST, typically drift and return to prior practice or assume that what they are practicing is in fact the EST, when it may only partially resemble the EST or not resemble it at all [30]. Because some of the initial "efficacy" results may be "lost in translation" as they are implemented in real-world settings, it has been argued that evidence-based practice be augmented with "practice-based evidence" [47]. In keeping with this idea, we argue for a "measurement-based practice" paradigm whereby real-time outcome measurement (i.e., patient-reported during-treatment outcomes) is used to validate approaches and allow for immediate feedback to patients, clinicians, and programs, and enable clinical improvements and innovations to be tried and evaluated in the frontline, real-world context. In the general psychotherapy literature, for example, when therapists received quantitative feedback about patient progress, their patients had outcomes that were twice as good compared to therapists who did not receive such feedback [48]. With the use of the same kinds of validated standardized metrics used in clinical research studies, captured by brief self-report measures prior to each treatment session, this approach provides estimates of patients' response to treatment, the effectiveness of individual clinicians and the clinical program overall, and identification of vulnerable subgroups of patients for whom standardized approaches may not be working well. In these patients with poorer outcomes, clinical innovations and enhancements can be tried and evaluated in a matter of months instead of the years it takes to conduct and disseminate clinical trials. Thus, measurement-based practice is "evidence-based practice" as it is practiced in the setting that matters most—the actual treatment program or clinical practice treating those specific patients. Sophisticated electronic health records and data capture systems are being developed to be better able to do this. However, these platforms will need to be tailored to capture standardized clinical outcomes specific to particular clinical disorders such as SUD and able to provide immediate feedback to program administrators on the effectiveness of any EST implementation, so that it may inform its optimal adaptation to maximize clinical benefit in that program's own specific context and patient population.

We believe this measurement-based approach to be the future of efficient care delivery in healthcare, including the treatment of SUD, as it enables continuous quality improvement. This degree of data capture and ready data availability will also inform better clinical decision-making, facilitate greater accountability within and across SUD programs, and motivate and empower SUD programs and clinicians to deliver more effective care. Because of the use of standardized measurement that can be compared across programs, this approach can help identify "over-performing" clinicians and programs so that new innovations in practice and program structures can be detected and highlighted, and eventually disseminated to benefit more individuals suffering from SUD.

Conclusions

To maximize effectiveness and efficiency, and reduce waste in any area of healthcare, we want solid evidence in identifying the most optimal treatments. Because of the cost involved in the adoption, implementation, and maintenance of new practices, it is critical that any newly adopted intervention results in genuine benefits to those suffering. With high volume, high burden disorders such as SUD, EBP, and EST have been defined, and novel treatments and practices developed and implemented. The past two decades of research on testing the active ingredients of SUD treatments has resulted in important knowledge: that a variety of active treatments produce very similar outcomes and that relational, therapist, and client factors account for more outcome variance than differences in active treatments. Consequently, "evidence-based practice," although commonly conceived as delivery of a specific "technique," also contains a great deal of evidence for the importance of a set of common therapeutic principles or elements, such as therapist empathy, as well the importance of client factors such as recovery motivation [49] and abstinence self-efficacy [50]. Frontline, real-time, measurement-based practice is likely to open the door to the next era of data-informed clinical care. Accurate assessment using brief, clinically meaningful, psychometrically validated tools, which measure during-treatment "outcomes" in clinical settings, may elucidate important context variables that might be responsible for clinic "over-performance," as well as under-performance, and will provide immediately available, real-world data with optimal relevance. This measurement-based practice paradigm that we propose can rapidly inform clinical practice and inform new treatment innovations that can be tested and evaluated quickly. As a result, the measurement-based practice paradigm creates continual quality improvement that also can inform the field more broadly about real-world effects, and consequently may be the most pragmatic and efficient model of "evidence-based practice."

References

1. Reed GM, Eisman E. Uses and misuses of evidence: managed care, treatment guidelines, and outcomes measurement in professional practice. In: Goodheart CD, Kazdin AE, Sternberg RJ, editors. *Evidence-based psychotherapy: where practice and research meet*. Washington (DC): American Psychological Association; 2006:13–35.
2. Hill AB. The environment and disease: association or causation? *Proceedings of the Royal Society of Medicine*. 1965;58:295–300.
3. APA Presidential Task Force on Evidence-Based Practice. Evidence-based practice in psychology, *The American Psychologist*. 2006;61:271–285.
4. Campbell DT, Fiske DW. Convergent and discriminant validation by the multitrait-multimethod matrix. *Psychological Bulletin*. 1959;56:81–105.
5. Finney JW. Limitations in using existing alcohol treatment trials to develop practice guidelines. *Addiction*. 2000;95:1491–1500.
6. Miller WR, Zweben J, Johnson WR. Evidence-based treatment: why, what, where, when, and how? *Journal of Substance Abuse Treatment*. 2005;29:267–276.
7. Hser YI, Anglin MD. Cost-effectiveness of drug abuse treatment: relevant issues and alternatie longitudinal modeling approaches. *NIDA Res Monogr*. 1991;113:67–93.
8. Muller CA, Geisel O, Pelz P, Higl V, Kruger J, Stickel A, et al. High-dose baclofen for the treatment of alcohol dependence (BACLAD study): a randomized, placebo-controlled trial. *European Neuropsychopharmacology*. 2015;25:1167–1177.
9. Westen D, Novotny CM, Thompson-Brenner H. The empirical status of empirically supported psychotherapies: assumptions, findings, and reporting in controlled clinical trials. *Psychological Bulletin*. 2004;130:631–663.
10. Westen D, Novotny CM, Thompson-Brenner H. EBP ≠ EST: reply to Crits-Christoph et al. (2005) and Weisz et al. (2005). *Psychological Bulletin*. 2005;131:427–433.

11. Friedman LM, Furberg CD, DeMets DL. *Fundamentals of clinical trials*. New York: Springer-Verlag; 2010.
12. Rounsaville BJ, Carroll KM, Onken LS. A stage model of behavioral therapies research: getting started and moving on from stage I. *Clinical Psychology: Science and Practice*. 2001;8:133–142.
13. American Psychological Association. Task Force on Promotion and Dissemination of Psychological Procedures. A Report Adopted by the Division 12 Board; 1993. Washington (DC): Society of Clinical Psychology, American Psychological Association.
14. Chambless DL, Hollon SD. Defining empirically supported therapies. *Journal of Consulting and Clinical Psychology*. 1998;66:7–18.
15. Levant RF. *Report of the 2005 presidential task force on evidence-based practice*. Washington (DC): American Psychological Association; 2005.
16. Jacobson NS, Truax P. Clinical significance: a statistical approach to defining meaningful change in psychotherapy research. *Journal of Consulting and Clinical Psychology*. 1991;59:12–19.
17. Miller WR, Manuel JK. How large must a treatment effect be before it matters to practitioners? An estimation method and demonstration. *Drug and Alcohol Review*. 2008;27:524–528.
18. Morgenstern J, McKay JR. Rethinking the paradigms that inform behavioral treatment research for substance use disorders. *Addiction*. 2007;102:1377–1389.
19. Norcross JC, editor. *Psychotherapy relationships that work: therapist contributions and responsiveness to patients*. New York: Oxford University Press; 2002.
20. Wampold BE. *The great psychotherapy debate: models, methods, and findings*. Mahwah (NJ): Lawrence Erlbaum Associates; 2001.
21. Wampold BE, Imel ZE. *The great psychotherapy debate: the evidence for what makes psychotherapy work*. New York: Routledge; 2015.
22. Yalom ID, Leszcz M. *The theory and practice of group psychotherapy*. 5th ed. New York: Basic Books; 2005.
23. Howard KI, Lueger RJ, Maling MS, Martinovich Z. A phase model of psychotherapy outcome: causal mediation of change. *Journal of Consulting and Clinical Psychology*. 1993;61:678–685.
24. Lambert MJ, Barley DE. Research summary on the therapeutic relationship and psychotherapy outcome. In: Norcross JC, editor. *Psychotherapy relationships that work: therapist contributions and responsiveness to patients*. New York: Oxford University Press; 2002:17–32.
25. Frank JD, Frank JB. *Persuasion and healing: a comparative study of psychotherapy*. 3rd ed. Baltimore (MD): Johns Hopkins University Press; 1993.
26. Lamb S, Greenlick MR, McCarty D. *Bridging the gap between practice and research: forging partnerships with community-based drug and alcohol treatment*. Washington (DC): National Academy Press; 1998.
27. Miller WR, Moyers TB. The forest and the trees: relational and specific factors in addiction treatment. *Addiction*. 2015;110:401–413.
28. Wells EA, Saxon AJ, Calsyn DA, Jackson TR, Donovan DM. Study results from the Clinical Trials Network's first 10 years: where do they lead? *Journal of Substance Abuse Treatment*. 2010;38(Suppl 1):S14–S30.
29. Morgenstern J, Blanchard KA, Morgan TJ, Labouvie E, Hayaki J. Testing the effectiveness of cognitive-behavioral treatment for substance abuse in a community

setting: within treatment and posttreatment findings. *Journal of Consulting and Clinical Psychology.* 2001;69:1007–1017.
30. Carroll KM, Ball SA, Nich C, Martino S, Frankforter TL, Farentinos C, et al. Motivational interviewing to improve treatment engagement and outcome in individuals seeking treatment for substance abuse: a multisite effectiveness study. *Drug Alcohol Depend.* 2006;81:301–312.
31. Carroll KM, Libby B, Sheehan J, Hyland N. Motivational interviewing to enhance treatment initiation in substance abusers: an effectiveness study. *The American Journal on Addictions.* 2001;10:335–339.
32. Carroll KM, Martino S, Ball SA, Nich C, Frankforter T, Anez LM, et al. A multisite randomized effectiveness trial of motivational enhancement therapy for Spanish-speaking substance users. *Journal of Consulting and Clinical Psychology.* 2009;77:993–999.
33. Winhusen T, Kropp F, Babcock D, Hague D, Erickson SJ, Renz C, et al. Motivational enhancement therapy to improve treatment utilization and outcome in pregnant substance users. *Journal of Substance Abuse Treatment.* 2008; 35:161–173.
34. Ball SA, Martino S, Nich C, Frankforter TL, Van Horn D, Crits-Christoph P, et al. Site matters: multisite randomized trial of motivational enhancement therapy in community drug abuse clinics. *Journal of Consulting and Clinical Psychology.* 2007;75:556–567.
35. Pedhazur EJ. *Multiple regression in behavioral research.* New York: Holt, Rinehart, & Winston; 1982.
36. Roman PM, Abraham AJ, Knudsen HK. Using medication-assisted treatment for substance use disorders: evidence of barriers and facilitators of implementation. *Addictive Behaviors.* 2011;36:584–589.
37. Anton RF, O'Malley SS, Ciraulo DA, Cisler RA, Couper D, Donovan DM. Combined pharmacotherapies and behavioral interventions for alcohol dependence. The COMBINE study: a randomized controlled trial. *Journal of the American Medical Association.* 2006;295:2003–2017.
38. COMBINE Study Group. Testing combined pharmacotherapies and behavioral interventions in alcohol dependence: rationale and methods. *Alcohol Clin Exp Res.* 2003;27:1107–1122.
39. Weiss RD, Potter JS, Fiellin DA, Byrne M, Connery HS, Dickinson W, et al. Adjunctive counseling during brief and extended buprenorphine-naloxone treatment for prescription opioid dependence: a 2-phase randomized controlled trial. *Arch Gen Psychiatry.* 2011;68:1238–1246.
40. Kelly JF, Yeterian JD. Mutual-help groups for alcohol and other substance use disorders. In: McCrady BS, Epstein EE, editors. *Addictions: a comprehensive guidebook.* New York: Oxford University Press; 2013:500–525.
41. Ball JC, Ross A. *The effectiveness of methadone maintenance treatment.* New York: Springer-Verlag; 1991.
42. Caplehorn JR, Bell J, Kleinbaum DG, Gebski VJ. Methadone dose and heroin use during maintenance treatment. *Addiction.* 1993;88:119–124.
43. US Department of Veterans Affairs. *VA&HSE&D QUERI Implementation Guide.* 2013. Washington (DC): US Department of Veterans Affairs.
44. Suchman EA. Social patterns of illness and medical care. *Journal of Health and Human Behavior.* 1965;6:2–16.

45. Finney JW. Enhancing substance abuse treatment evaluations: examining mediators and moderators of treatment effects, *J Subst Abuse*. 1995;7:135–150.
46. Morgenstern J, Kuerbis A, Amrhein P, Hail L, Lynch K, McKay JR. Motivational interviewing: a pilot test of active ingredients and mechanisms of change. *Psychol Addict Behav*. 2012;26:859–869.
47. Kelly JF. Accounting for practice-based evidence in evidence-based practice. *The Brown University Digest of Addiction Theory and Application*. 2008;68.
48. Lambert MJ, Whipple JL, Smart DW, Vermeersch DA, Nielsen SL, Hawkins EJ. The effects of providing therapists with feedback on patient progress during psychotherapy: are outcomes enhanced? *Psychotherapy Research*. 2001;11:49–68.
49. Kelly JF, Greene MC. Beyond motivation: initial validation of the commitment to sobriety scale. *Journal of Substance Abuse Treatment*. 2014;46:257–263.
50. Hoeppner BB, Kelly JF, Urbanoski KA, Slaymaker V. Comparative utility of a single-item versus multiple-item measure of self-efficacy in predicting relapse among young adults. *Journal of Substance Abuse Treatment*. 2011;41:305–312.

Part II

Integrated Treatment for Specific Addictive Disorders

Chapter 4
Alcohol Use Disorder

George A. Kenna and Lorenzo Leggio

Introduction

Prevalence of Alcohol Use Disorder

Alcohol use disorder (AUD) is a risk factor for more than 60 diseases and types of injuries, and result in approximately 2.5 million deaths per year worldwide [1]. Public health problems caused by harmful use of alcohol represent a substantial health, social, and economic burden [2]. While not always considered a medical problem, AUD is a chronic, relapsing condition with a multifactorial etiology that includes genetic, neurobiological, and environmental components [3]. The Diagnostic and Statistical Manual of Mental Disorders (DSM)-5 [4] integrates the two previous DSM-IV disorders (alcohol abuse and alcohol dependence, AD) [5] into a single disorder called "alcohol use disorder (AUD)" with mild (2–3 criteria), moderate (4–5 criteria), and severe (≥6 criteria) sub-classifications. For a lifetime diagnosis for DSM-5 AUD, at least two or more of the 11 diagnostic criteria within any 12-month period must be met [4].

Recent epidemiological data suggest 12-month (the immediate prior 12 months) and lifetime prevalences of DSM-5 AUD to be 13.9% and 29.1%, respectively, with prevalence highest for men (17.6% and 36.0%), white (14.0% and 32.6%), and Native American (19.2% and 43.4%), with the most severe AUD highest among those with the lowest income (1.8% and 1.5%, respectively) [6]. Therefore, interventions that reduce AUDs may have important public health implications, including both biological and behavioral treatments. Moreover, as AUD is a complex behavioral disorder, the evidence suggests that different stages of the disease may require different prevention and treatment strategies [7].

Alcoholism treatment can be effective in reducing alcohol consumption and reducing the economic, social, and medical consequences of alcohol use [8]. There are many treatment modalities available, including formal treatment delivered by professionals all the way to self-help (e.g., 12-step). There are about one million persons in the United States (US) at any given time receiving formal addiction treatment, and most of those are receiving treatment for either alcoholism alone or a co-addiction with other drugs. However, because almost 18 million people abuse or are dependent on alcohol, there is a significant treatment gap, and many persons who could benefit from treatment are not receiving it.

Evidence-Based Psychological Interventions

The most commonly employed evidence-based psychological/psychosocial interventions for the treatment of AUD include some form of cognitive behavioral therapy (CBT), motivational enhancement therapy (MET), and/or 12-step facilitation (TSF). Cognitive behavioral therapy is focused on handling thoughts about alcohol, dealing with urges, refusing drinks, and avoiding situations that might lead to relapse. The emphasis is on increasing the patient's ability to cope with situations that commonly precipitate relapse. Motivational enhancement therapy, based on principles of motivational psychology, is focused on producing internally motivated change, helps patients identify internal motivational strategies, and provides structured feedback about alcohol-related problems. Twelve-step facilitation is based on the principles of Alcoholics Anonymous (AA) and introduces the first three steps of AA to promote active participation in AA.

Project MATCH was designed to match the most effective psychosocial treatments to individual patient characteristics. Some examples of the matching characteristics included motivational readiness to change, psychiatric severity, and social support for drinking. The sample included 952 outpatients and 774 recent inpatients [9]. Patients were randomly assigned to receive either CBT, MET, or TSF for 12 weeks, with the primary outcome variables percent days abstinent (PDA) and drinks per drinking day (DDD). Results revealed that, overall, all three treatment groups did equally well. At the end of the 12-week treatment phase, a higher percentage of CBT and TSF patients were abstinent relative to patients who received MET. Furthermore, a lower percentage of patients in the CBT and TSF groups experienced alcohol-related negative consequences relative to patients in the MET group. Differences between treatment conditions were significant for the outpatient group, through one year post-treatment only [10]. Project MATCH [10] suggested that MET, CBT, and facilitating the patient's entry and retention in AA appeared to be equally effective at maintaining abstinence.

Counseling

A systematic review of 23 randomized trials (with duration ≥6 months) evaluating behavioral counseling for adolescents and adults with an AUD (using DSM-IV criteria) concluded that behavioral counseling may reduce alcohol consumption in patients with AUD. Behavioral counseling interventions included brief advice, feedback, MI, and CBT strategies such as self-completed action plans, written health education or self-help materials, drinking diaries, and problem-solving exercises. Control interventions included usual care, educational materials, and advice from a nurse. Compared to control interventions at 12 months, behavioral counseling was associated with reduced alcohol consumption in adults and young adults/college students; however, there was insufficient evidence to draw conclusions about the effect of behavioral counseling on accidents, injuries, or alcohol-related liver problems in adults [11].

Brief Interventions

Modest evidence suggests that brief interventions (BIs) may reduce mortality in heavy drinkers, that brief primary care physician (PCP) intervention can decrease alcohol use, problem drinking, and hospitalization in problem drinkers, and that BIs in primary care settings may reduce alcohol consumption in hazardous drinkers, including patients not specifically seeking alcohol-related treatment. The US Preventive Services Task Force (USPSTF) recommends screening adults aged 18 years and older for alcohol misuse and providing persons engaging in risky or hazardous drinking with brief behavioral counseling to reduce alcohol misuse [12]. Brief interventions may include MI of varying length and number, CBT, self-completed action plans, written health education or self-help materials, requests to keep drinking diaries, written personalized feedback, follow-up telephone counseling, and exercises to complete at home.

A review of four trials with 1,540 heavy drinkers reported sufficient evidence to suggest that BIs may reduce mortality in heavy drinkers. The BIs, however, varied in duration, frequency, and manner of delivery, and the follow-up time frames varied from 1 to 10 years. The pooled relative risk of death for those receiving BI was 0.47 [13]. Another systematic review compared in-person versus computer-delivered personalized feedback interventions for alcohol misuse in 2,441 adolescents and young adults, and reported that personalized feedback delivered in person or by computer has a similar efficacy for decreasing short-term alcohol use and alcohol-related problems in adolescents and young adults. In comparing in-person to computer-delivered personalized feedback interventions, no significant differences in any alcohol use variables or alcohol-related problems were found at short-term follow-up; however, in-person personalized feedback interventions were associated with significantly reduced drinks per week and alcohol quantity at >4 months [14].

Good evidence suggests that a brief PCP intervention can decrease alcohol use, problem drinking, and hospitalization in problem drinkers. In a randomized trial, 774 men and women problem drinkers were randomized to receive either a workbook-based intervention during two 15-minute physician visits one month apart (and contract to reduce alcohol intake) versus a booklet on general health. The intervention consisted of two physician visits and two nurse follow-up phone calls covering review of normative drinking, patient-specific alcohol effects, worksheet on drinking cues, drinking diary cards, and drinking agreement in prescription format. In comparing workbook-based intervention versus control at 12 months, women decreased alcohol consumption by 47% versus 16% ($p < 0.001$, number needed to treat 4), and men decreased their alcohol consumption by 37% versus 23% ($p < 0.001$, NNT 8). While there were no differences in days of hospitalization in women, the total days of hospitalization in men was 178 versus 314 ($p < 0.01$), respectively. The intervention significantly reduced seven-day alcohol use, number of binge drinking episodes, frequency of excessive drinking, and a trend toward fewer emergency department visits [15]. At four-year follow-up, there were no significant differences between treatment and control groups in overall drinking rates, in rates of heavy drinking in men, or in binge drinking rates in women. There were significant differences seen, however, between treatment and control groups in female heavy drinkers and male binge drinkers [16]. Randomized trials support the role of primary care-delivered interventions to reduce at-risk drinking [17, 18].

Brief interventions in primary care settings may also reduce alcohol consumption in hazardous drinkers, including patients not specifically seeking alcohol-related treatment. For example, in a systematic review, 29 randomized trials were compared based on BIs for reducing alcohol consumption versus control treatment delivered in general practice or emergency departments with participants not seeking alcohol treatment. Brief intervention reduced alcohol consumption compared to control after ≥1 year follow-up [19]. Also, in a systematic review of BIs or MIs with 5,639 outpatients actively attending primary care and not seeking alcohol treatment, BI was associated with a reduction in alcohol use at six or 12 months by about three drinks per week; Project TrEAT accounted for about 40% of this analysis [20].

Furthermore, in a systematic review of 56 randomized trials, BIs (compared to no intervention) significantly reduced drinking at 3–12 months, there was modest benefit after 12 months (not statistically significant), and results at >3–6 months follow-up were significant only if trials with heavy drinkers were excluded [21].

Longer-Term Interventions

Cognitive behavioral therapy (CBT) appears associated with increased abstinence, but focus and duration of sessions may influence its effectiveness. Based on a randomized trial with low adherence, 284 patients with depression and hazardous alcohol consumption were offered a single CBT session then randomized to nine alcohol-related sessions versus nine depression-related sessions versus nine integrated depression and alcohol-related sessions versus no further treatment. Multiple sessions were significantly associated with a greater reduction in average drinks and drinking days and a greater reduction in depressive symptoms. Integrated treatment was associated with greater overall reduction in drinking days and level of depression, with greater improvements observed in men with alcohol-related sessions versus depression-related sessions (greater reduction in number of daily drinks, mean change 4.62 versus 0.34) and single-focused sessions versus integrated sessions. Greater improvements were observed in women with depression-related versus alcohol-related sessions (greater reduction in number of daily drinks, mean change 4.22 versus 0.24) and integrated sessions versus single-focused sessions [22].

Alcohol interventions have also been tested outside the US. For example, 742 patients in the United Kingdom with alcohol problems were randomized to social behavior and network therapy (cognitive and behavioral strategies to help patients build social networks supportive of change, eight sessions lasting 50 minutes over 8–12 weeks) versus MET (three sessions lasting 50 minutes over 8–12 weeks). Strong evidence suggests that social behavior and network therapy are as effective as MET for reducing alcohol-related problems at one-year follow-up [23].

More complex approaches have also been examined. In a trial of 210, participants with AD were randomized to one of three groups: (1) case management (i.e., active control, attendance at AA was neither encouraged nor discouraged); (2) network support (i.e., 12 one-hour sessions to help patient change social network to one more supportive of abstinence and less supportive of drinking, attendance at AA was encouraged); or (3) network support plus contingency management (i.e., network support plus prize drawing if verified completion of assigned tasks). Results suggest that network support might increase abstinence rates. Comparing case management versus network support versus network support plus contingency management, the proportion of days abstinent at 15 months, respectively, was about 60% versus 75% versus 70%, and proportion of patients abstinent for prior 90 days at 15 months was about 22% versus 40% versus 28%. Network support, however, did not affect social support for drinking, but appeared to increase behavioral and attitudinal support for abstinence [24]; however, network support alone was associated with a mean 80% days abstinent compared to just over 60% in the other groups at two years post-treatment [25].

In a trial of men scoring ≥8 on the Alcohol Use Disorders Identification Test, 112 patients were randomized to stepped care intervention versus five minutes of minimal intervention that was delivered by a nurse and followed for six months. Stepped care appeared no more effective than minimal intervention for reducing alcohol consumption [26]. Further evidence also suggests that stepped care may not reduce alcohol consumption compared to minimal intervention [27].

Computer-Based Interventions

A systematic review of 24 randomized trials compared non-guided computer-based interventions versus minimally active interventions (assessment-only, usual care, generic non-tailored information or education material) or brief intervention for reducing alcohol consumption in adults. Modest evidence suggests that non-guided computer-based interventions may reduce alcohol consumption in adults compared to minimally active interventions. Compared to minimally active interventions, non-guided computer-based interventions were associated with reduced alcohol consumption and binge drinking in students and reduced alcohol consumption in non-students [28]. Also, in a trial of 80 non-dependent problem drinkers randomized to a Web-based protocol to promote moderate drinking versus control, the Web-based protocol was associated with a significant increase in days abstinent at 12 months, suggesting that a Web-based protocol might increase abstinence in non-dependent problem drinkers [29].

Evidence-Based Pharmacological Interventions

Currently, most alcoholism treatment is psychosocially oriented and conducted outside medical settings by non-medical personnel, such as counselors. Several psychosocial treatments have been shown to be effective in achieving and maintaining abstinence and/or reducing heavy drinking. However, psychosocial treatments alone are often not effective for everyone, and pharmacologic interventions are considered primarily as adjunct therapy for patients receiving psychosocial interventions [30]. While we are aware of many other medications researched or sometimes used off-label for alcoholism, due to space limitations this chapter can only briefly cover the medications originally approved for the indication of AD treatment by the Food and Drug Administration (FDA), and encourage readers to seek out other more comprehensive resources on this topic (e.g., [31]).

FDA-Approved Medications

Disulfiram

More than a half-century ago, the FDA approved the use of disulfiram for the management of AD in selected, highly motivated patients in conjunction with supportive and psychotherapeutic treatment. Disulfiram is an aldehyde dehydrogenase inhibitor that acts as an alcohol deterrent by producing unpleasant symptoms even with small amounts of alcohol. Disulfiram reinforces an individual's desire to stop drinking by providing a psychological disincentive associated with the increase in acetaldehyde, resulting in hypotension, flushing, nausea, and vomiting when patients consume alcohol [31]. By contrast to the pharmacological effects of the other approved pharmacotherapies, the psychological effect of disulfiram makes it a difficult drug to test in a double-blind placebo-controlled drug trial. As a result, disulfiram has demonstrated mixed results as a treatment for AD [32].

The initial dose of disulfiram is 500 mg orally once daily for one to two weeks, and the dose may be reduced if adverse effects (e.g., hepatitis, hepatic failure, skin eruptions, drowsiness, fatigue, erectile dysfunction, headache, metallic or garlic-like aftertaste, psychotic reactions) occur. Treatment may be required for months or years. In prescribing disulfiram, caution should be used in patients who are elderly or who have hepatic or renal impairment. It is also contraindicated in patients with severe myocardial disease, coronary occlusion, or psychosis. In addition to alcohol, concomitant use with isoniazid, metronidazole, and possibly phenytoin should be avoided. In clinical practice, to avoid a reaction, often patients who are of a mindset will discontinue taking disulfiram for a few days in anticipation of relapsing to alcohol use [31].

In a pivotal study, with partial blinding and low compliance rates, in addition to counseling from alcohol rehabilitation specialists, 605 male alcoholic patients received either 250 mg disulfiram, 1 mg disulfiram, or placebo for one year. The 1 mg disulfiram was considered a disulfiram control group because it is an amount of disulfiram that is not enough to cause aversive symptoms. Riboflavin added to all pills was used as a tracer to assess adherence. To determine if the threat of becoming ill is sufficient to maintain adherence, patients who were given disulfiram were not told which dosage they were receiving [33]. Disulfiram was found to possibly reduce days of drinking but did not improve total abstinence at one year. In this study, all patients knew if they received disulfiram or placebo, but were blinded to dosages of disulfiram to test the role of the patient's fear of a disulfiram-ethanol reaction; however, low compliance rates, as verified by urine tests, suggested limited clinical usefulness [33].

In summary, the evidence that disulfiram may reduce alcohol consumption in patients with AD is modest. Based on a systematic review of 22 low-to-moderate quality randomized trials comparing disulfiram versus any control in 2,414 patients with AD, disulfiram was associated with decreased alcohol consumption in the analysis of all trials. However, results suggest possibly greater benefit with supervised medication intake compared to unsupervised medication intake. Comparators in these studies included placebo, no disulfiram, naltrexone, and acamprosate [34].

Naltrexone

One of alcohol's many actions includes the release of β-endorphins from neurons. A higher concentration of β-endorphin results in an inhibition of gamma-aminobutyric acid (GABA) neurons that facilitate the disinhibition of dopamine neurons located in the ventral tegmental area, which in turn project to the nucleus accumbens (NAc). In addition to direct stimulation of the NAc to release dopamine, this mediated action also results in the release of dopamine at the NAc. This increased dopamine activity is related to the positively reinforcing effects of alcohol and is thought to be associated with the development of AD [31]. Naltrexone is an opiate antagonist that, in theory, blocks this mesolimbic activation by alcohol.

The FDA-approved naltrexone for adjunctive use with a medically supervised behavior modification program in the treatment of AD after successful trials reported that naltrexone significantly reduced alcohol craving and consumption in AD patients taking naltrexone [35, 36], though not all trials have been positive [37]. Naltrexone is available orally and for intramuscular use. Naltrexone is contraindicated if patients are taking opiate agonists, experiencing opiate withdrawal, acute hepatitis, or hepatic failure. The typical maintenance dose is 50 mg orally once daily in the absence of opiates (smaller doses may be used initially following opiate cessation) or naltrexone 380 mg intramuscularly every four weeks as an alternative, more treatment-compliant route. A naltrexone challenge test is recommended in patients who may be physically dependent on opiates. Adverse effects include hepatotoxicity, insomnia, anxiety, nervousness, nausea, vomiting, headache, or fatigue.

Based on systematic reviews, naltrexone is an effective medication to treat AD, albeit the evidence for the effectiveness of naltrexone is modest, as data suggest that naltrexone may reduce heavy drinking and relapse rate in AD patients. First, in a Cochrane review of 50 randomized trials of opioid antagonists in 7,793 patients with AD, 47 trials evaluated naltrexone [38]. For naltrexone compared to placebo, there was a reduced risk of heavy drinking in analysis of 28 trials with 4,433 patients (NNT 7-17). There was also a reduced risk of any drinking in an analysis of 27 trials with 4,693 patients. Naltrexone also decreased the number of drinking days in an analysis of 26 trials with 3,882 patients, and decreased heavy drinking days in analysis of 15 trials with 1,715 patients; however, side effects were significantly more common with naltrexone, and included abdominal pain, decreased appetite, nausea, vomiting, daytime sleepiness, drowsiness, fatigue, insomnia, lethargy, somnolence, weakness, blurred vision, decreased libido, depression, dizziness, and nightmares. At 3–12 months after treatment was discontinued, naltrexone reduced risk of heavy drinking in analysis of five trials with 1,061 patients (NNT 6-130). Injectable naltrexone appears to be effective, based on the analysis of four trials, but not all outcomes were statistically significant. In three trials, naltrexone was compared to acamprosate, with no significant differences in efficacy. In a meta-analysis of side effects, naltrexone was associated with more nausea and somnolence, and acamprosate was associated with more diarrhea. No significant difference in efficacy was found in single trials comparing naltrexone to any other drug [38]. A second systematic review of 122 randomized trials and one cohort study evaluated the efficacy of pharmacotherapy for AUD in 22,803 adult outpatients. All of these trials had a treatment duration of 12–52 weeks; most of the trials enrolled patients following detoxification or required a sobriety period ≥3 days, and also included psychosocial co-interventions. In 44 trials that compared naltrexone versus placebo, naltrexone 50 mg/day oral was associated with a significantly reduced risk of return to heavy drinking and reduced the risk of return to any drinking. However, naltrexone (any formulation) was associated with a significantly increased risk of study withdrawal for adverse events [39].

Acamprosate

Acamprosate calcium helps maintain abstinence to alcohol through a mechanism that may involve an interaction with glutamate and GABA neurotransmitter systems centrally. Acamprosate, a glutamatergic antagonist and possibly GABA agonist, is thought to work by normalizing the glutamatergic excitation that occurs in alcohol withdrawal, though the mechanism of action is not clearly understood. It possesses a dose-dependent reduction of alcohol intake specific for the type of alcohol and the mechanisms of dependence, without exhibiting anticonvulsant, antidepressant, or anxiolytic properties [40]. The dose of acamprosate is 666 mg (two tablets) orally three times daily with meals. It may be started as soon as possible after achieving abstinence. If creatinine clearance is 30–50 mL/minute, the dose should be adjusted to use 333 mg three times daily. Acamprosate is contraindicated if the creatinine clearance is <30 mL/minute. It can be used in combination with naltrexone or disulfiram, as it has a different mechanism of action. Acamprosate has a low potential for significant drug interactions, but diarrhea and asthenia are common adverse effects, and suicide and suicidality have been occasionally reported [40].

Most of the large clinical trials testing acamprosate in AD were conducted in Europe, where they resulted in strong effect sizes in improving drinking outcomes (i.e., acamprosate effectively maintained complete abstinence in detoxified AD patients). In particular, three European multicenter randomized double-blind placebo-controlled studies showed that acamprosate, in addition to psychosocial treatment, promoted alcohol abstinence [41–43] and was an effective treatment for alcoholism [44]. Together, while acamprosate may reduce the risk of return to any drinking, it does not appear to reduce the risk of return to heavy drinking in adult outpatients with AUD. A systematic review compared acamprosate versus placebo, reporting that no significant difference in return to heavy drinking was found in an analysis of 16 trials with 4,847 patients, though acamprosate was associated with a reduced risk of return to any drinking ($p < 0.001$) and fewer drinking days [39].

Alternately, however, based on a systematic review of 24 randomized trials evaluating acamprosate in 6,894 AD patients after completing detoxification, evidence suggests that acamprosate may reduce the risk of any drinking after completion of detoxification and fewer drinking days. In this analysis, patients were mostly men (median age 42 years), and study drugs were acamprosate in 2,563 patients, placebo in 2,929 patients, and naltrexone in 402 patients. In analyses of acamprosate compared to placebo, acamprosate reduced the risk of any drinking (number needed to harm [NNH] 9) and increased the PDA, however, it also increased the risk of diarrhea (NNH 9). While there was a lower risk of dropouts overall, there was a higher risk of dropouts due to adverse events [45].

Comparing Naltrexone and Acamprosate

There appears strong evidence that acamprosate and naltrexone similarly reduce the risk for drinking after detoxification in AD patients, but evidence for the combination of the two drugs is inconsistent. Three trials with 800 patients compared acamprosate versus naltrexone (the COMBINE study provided 76.5% of the patients for this comparison [46]) and found no significant differences in return to any drinking, PDA, or return to heavy drinking. Acamprosate was associated with higher risk of diarrhea ($p < 0.0001$) and naltrexone was associated with a higher risk of nausea ($p = 0.003$), fatigue ($p = 0.03$), and somnolence ($p = 0.013$). Two trials compared the combination of acamprosate plus naltrexone versus placebo (the COMBINE study provided 88.5% of the patients for this comparison [46]) and reported no significant differences in return to any drinking (and also heavy drinking) or PDA; however, adverse effects were significantly more common with combination therapy, including diarrhea, decreased appetite, nausea, and vomiting. Two trials compared the combination of acamprosate plus naltrexone versus acamprosate alone. The COMBINE trial [46] provided 88.5% of the patients for this comparison and found no significant differences in return to any drinking or PDA [38]. Four trials compared acamprosate versus naltrexone and reported no significant differences in return to any drinking, return to heavy drinking, or number of drinking days [39].

In a European trial of 160 patients with alcoholism following detoxification randomized to naltrexone versus acamprosate versus combination versus placebo for 12 weeks, naltrexone and acamprosate each reduced relapse rates, and the combination was more effective than acamprosate alone. The overall relapse rate was 42.5%, with relapse rates of 22.5% with combination therapy, 30% with naltrexone, 42.5% with acamprosate, and 75% with placebo. The combination had significantly lower relapse rates compared to placebo (p = 0.008) or acamprosate alone (p = 0.04), but comparison with naltrexone was not statistically significant [47]. A second large European trial (PREDICT) that followed the design of the COMBINE trial reported that neither acamprosate nor naltrexone supplied any additional benefit compared with placebo, which is at variance with a positive naltrexone effect being reported in the COMBINE study [48].

Strategies and Considerations for Integrating Psychological and Pharmacological Therapies

All FDA-approved medications for the treatment of AD are indicated for use with a psychosocial intervention. Thus, researchers have examined if certain combinations of pharmacotherapy and psychosocial interventions show greater efficacy than other combinations. Pharmacotherapy for AUD should always be delivered in a psychosocial context that may affect the outcome of treatment. In the past couple of decades, there has been an increased interest in the use of new treatments, including pharmacotherapies in conjunction with psychosocial therapies, which treatment providers and patients hope can improve outcomes. The underlying physiological cause of AUD is treatable using pharmacotherapies, and conceivably addresses some of the biological aspects of alcoholism, as research suggests that approximately half of the risk for developing AD is genetic [49]. The rigorous study of different psychotherapeutic treatments for AUD has shown several distinct approaches to be effective. Treating a complex behavioral disorder such as AUD with both pharmacotherapy and psychosocial therapy may give individuals the best options for recovery. The multiplicity of brain systems affected by alcohol gives the clinician an advantage in having many targets for medications to alleviate the effects of alcohol. Many psychosocial interventions for AUD, including AA, can be integrated successfully with pharmacotherapy. Psychosocial interventions, ranging from brief MM to more intensive manualized psychotherapies, have all been shown to produce positive outcomes in certain studies, depending on the specific medication and the study context. Particularly successful examples include the use of behavioral marital therapy plus a disulfiram contract for patients taking that medication [50], or the combination of naltrexone or acamprosate with CBT or psychosocial support. Ongoing research examining the optimal combinations of medications with different psychosocial treatments for AD may further inform the field.

Medication Adherence

Medication adherence focuses on encouraging patients to take their medications as prescribed, as well as whether they continue to take their prescribed medication. As with other chronic conditions, rates of non-adherence in the pharmacologic treatment of substance use disorders (SUDs) is high [51]. Adherence rates are a major issue with all oral medications for the treatment of AUDs. The previously discussed randomized, controlled VA Cooperative Study that examined the efficacy of disulfiram in 605 patients with AD is an example of how poor adherence affects outcomes [33]. Only 20% of the patients were adherent as monitored by detection of riboflavin in at least five urine samples over one year. Abstinence rates were significantly higher in men who were adherent to treatment relative to non-adherent patients. However, among the adherent patients, abstinence rates were not significantly greater in the disulfiram-treated patients relative to the placebo control groups. Although disulfiram showed poor efficacy in this controlled clinical trial, many clinicians use disulfiram in practice because it is effective in patients who actually adhere to the medication best facilitated by a family member or friend.

For naltrexone, a double-blind placebo-controlled study examined rates of relapse in 196 AD patients by treatment adherence and medication group. In addition to receiving counseling from a healthcare provider, patients were randomly assigned to receive either 50 mg/day of oral naltrexone or placebo pills for 12 weeks. Adherence was defined as attending 80% of the counseling sessions and patient self-reports of taking naltrexone as prescribed. Results showed that there was no difference between placebo and naltrexone in rates of relapse for patients who were non-adherent. However, in patients who were adherent, participants taking naltrexone showed a significantly lower rate of relapse relative to patients taking placebo ($p < .001$). This is consistent with a recent systematic review of naltrexone clinical trials that suggested that modest effect sizes for naltrexone may be attributable, at least in part, to variability in naltrexone adherence rates [52].

Patients taking acamprosate were randomly assigned to receive compliance therapy plus usual care, or usual care only, for four months. Compliance therapy consisted of a combination of different therapeutic techniques in which concerns about and benefits of the medication were addressed and strategies for relapse prevention were reviewed in four to six one-hour sessions. Participants in the compliance therapy group had better adherence rates ($p < .05$) and took significantly longer to experience an extended relapse ($p < .05$). The lack of a statistically significant difference between patients receiving compliance therapy plus usual care and patients receiving usual care alone in the number of days to first drink and the number of days to relapse was most likely due to a small sample size [53].

There are several reasons for patient non-adherence. Adherence rates decrease with increasing complexity of the dosing regimen. Patients are more likely to miss doses with medication regimens that are frequent relative to infrequent dosing, and with dosing that is difficult to incorporate into daily living (e.g., medication that must be taken so many hours before or after eating). Additionally, medication-related adverse effects (real or anticipated) might also deter patients from adhering to a dosing regimen, and there is evidence that even patient anticipation of adverse events contributes to poor adherence rates [54, 55]. Another factor that is associated with poor adherence is having a co-occurring psychiatric or medical disorder. Patients with depression are less likely to adhere to medication regimens for chronic conditions [56]. Patients with an SUD in addition to another psychiatric or medical disorder are also more likely to miss doses [50]. An additional common reason for patient non-adherence is the denial of the existence or severity of the illness. Patients are more prone to non-adherence if they do not believe that they have an illness or if they are convinced that the illness is not harmful [51].

There are important manual-based interventions available for clinicians that target patient adherence. Medical management (MM) is an intervention that is administered by a healthcare professional. During the initial session, the healthcare professional reviews the diagnosis, the negative consequences of drinking, recommends abstinence, provides information about medications, and develops a medication adherence plan. MM encourages attendance at AA meetings or other community support groups. Follow-up MM sessions review drinking, overall functioning, medication adherence, and adverse effects. Problems with medication adherence are addressed. This intervention was successfully implemented in the COMBINE study, a large, randomized controlled clinical trial of the efficacy of combining medications and behavioral interventions for the treatment of AD [46].

BRENDA (Biopsychosocial, Report, Empathy, Needs, Direct advice, and Assessment) is a manual-based supportive counseling technique that provides support for abstinence and targets medication adherence [57]. It was developed for use in non-specialty settings by physicians or nurse practitioners, or by psychiatrists in private practice. BRENDA includes a combination of MM and MET, a technique discussed earlier aimed at increasing intrinsic motivation for making a behavioral change [9]. If the patient is resistant to treatment recommendations, then a re-evaluation of biopsychosocial barriers to adherence and treatment goals might be necessary.

Naltrexone in an extended-release injectable suspension has shown promising results in improving patient adherence to medication regimens treating AUDs. In a large, randomized, double-blind, placebo-controlled, multicenter trial, patients with AD were randomly assigned to one of three treatment groups for six months: 380 mg extended-release naltrexone (XR-NTX), 190 mg

XR-NTX, or placebo injections each month. All patients received 12 sessions of BRENDA supportive counseling. Results demonstrated that 74% of patients received at least four of the six monthly injections, and 64% of patients received all six injections. Compared with placebo, 380 mg of long-acting naltrexone resulted in a 25% decrease in the event rate of heavy drinking days and 190 mg of naltrexone resulted in a 17% decrease. Pretreatment abstinence and sex each demonstrated a significant interaction with the medication group on treatment outcome, as men and those with pretreatment abstinence both exhibited greater treatment effects. These results suggest that using a long-acting depot medication for the treatment of AD may be an effective method for improving patient adherence [58].

One study examined the contribution of medication adherence and AA meeting attendance to maintaining abstinence. In this study, 122 inpatients with AD were randomly assigned to receive medication or placebo and strongly encouraged to attend AA meetings. Medication adherence was defined as taking medication as prescribed for a minimum of 15 days per month, for the first four out of six months of the follow-up period. Findings demonstrated that medication adherence and AA meeting attendance have a reciprocal association, in that greater medication adherence leads to better AA meeting attendance, and vice versa. Furthermore, both medication adherence and AA meeting attendance independently contributed to greater rates of abstinence at 18 months post-treatment. This finding argues against the belief held by some clinicians that taking medications and attending AA meetings are not complementary [59].

An early study examined whether patients taking oral naltrexone would show greater improvements in treatment outcomes with coping skills versus supportive therapy. A group of 97 recently abstinent patients were randomly assigned to 12 weeks of either naltrexone or placebo plus either coping skills therapy or supportive therapy. Comparing continuous abstinence rates over 12 weeks of treatment, a significantly greater percentage of participants receiving naltrexone plus supportive therapy never relapsed relative to the other treatment groups. They also reported that the percentage of patients remaining abstinent who received naltrexone and coping skills therapy may be higher than patients who did not receive naltrexone; however, no statistical comparison was made. The greater emphasis on abstinence in the supportive therapy treatment, in combination with naltrexone, may have contributed to the greater rates of continuous abstinence relative to the other treatment groups. However, among non-abstinent patients, the percentage who did not relapse was highest for those who received naltrexone and coping skills therapy [35]. Additionally, in a study of 197 patients taking naltrexone 50 mg daily who were randomized to CBT versus primary care management, results suggest that CBT and primary care management have similar abstinence rates at 10 weeks in patients taking naltrexone. However, heavy drinking ≤2 days during the previous 28 days was 86.5% with CBT versus 84.1% with primary care management (not significant [60]).

Important Comorbidities and Other Pertinent Considerations

Co-occurring psychiatric disorders are common in patients with an AUD diagnosis, and complicate the course and the treatment of the disorder, but they frequently don't receive specialized treatment that addresses both conditions. Although pharmacological and psychosocial treatments for AUDs and psychiatric disorders can be integrated to help these patients, relatively few clinical studies have tested these types of treatments. Teasing apart overlapping underlying psychiatric disorders and AUD is difficult for many reasons beyond the scope of this chapter; however, as mental health and substance abuse facilities expand their services for patients with dual disorders, further research is needed to guide the treatment of this patient population [51].

Numerous aspects of comorbidity suggest that medications might be particularly important for this group of individuals with AUDs, because many already are used to taking medications for their psychiatric disorder and dosing can be integrated into a medication schedule for the comorbid condition. Some AUD individuals with comorbid diagnoses, however, face greater difficulties in accessing and using traditional alcoholism treatment and self-help groups in which many members do not have comorbid disorders. Moreover, the cognitive symptoms common in comorbid mental disorders may destabilize a patient's motivation and ability to perform assignments often integrated into psychosocial treatments, particularly in the early stage of recovery. Patients with thought disorders or slowed thinking secondary to depression may have difficulty concentrating and learning or completing assignments in treatment that are based on CBT [61]. When using medications to treat AUD patients with comorbid disorders, it is also important to define whether these types of medications affect psychosis, exacerbate affective or anxiety symptoms, or symptoms of PTSD. A study of naltrexone found that it did not worsen the symptoms associated with schizophrenia [62], although case reports have suggested that naltrexone may precipitate panic attacks [63].

Developments in effective psychotherapy for AUD, along with the recognition that pharmacotherapy alone may not adequately address all the treatment requirements of comorbid patients, has led to some progress of specialized psychotherapy for this population. The use of effective psychosocial treatments is particularly important among these patients for several reasons: (1) there are some cases where pharmacotherapy may not be recommended; (2) psychosocial treatments may be effective in treating functional deficits in patients with chronic psychiatric disorders, such as schizophrenia; (3) pharmacologic treatment enhanced with psychosocial approaches is important for patients with poor medication compliance; and (4) effective psychosocial treatments are important for patients for whom early abstinence may be associated with a worsening of psychiatric symptoms, such as patients with PTSD who may experience anxiety with the cessation of alcohol use [51].

All medications that are currently FDA-approved for the treatment of AD are indicated for use with a psychosocial intervention, as historically pharmacologic therapy has been found to be most effective when given with some form of specialized counseling (e.g., MM, CBT). Recent data with several medications (e.g., naltrexone, acamprosate) discussed in this section suggest that the primary care model of management, in which the patient meets regularly with a primary care provider to discuss progress toward nondrinking goals and medication issues, with an emphasis on adherence, might be equally effective as specialized counseling (e.g., CBI), but perhaps not as long-lasting, especially if the medication is stopped.

Future Directions in the Integrative Treatment of Alcohol Use Disorder

One of the major problems with the current pharmacotherapies for AUD is that they are only moderately effective and the efficacy of some of the potential new medications are limited to certain alcoholic subtypes. In a review by Kranzler and Edenberg [64], the authors suggest that the convergence of research in AUD treatment and genetics of AUD is leading to the possibility of matching patients with certain treatments. For example, naltrexone is a modestly effective treatment for AUD, although ineffective for certain individuals. Recent studies have sought to more fully understand the role certain opioid receptor genes play. Patients with one or two Asp40 alleles taking naltrexone were significantly less likely than patients with Asn40 homozygotes taking naltrexone to relapse to heavy drinking [65]. The COMBINE study also found a positive moderating effect on the Asp40 allele in reducing the percentage of heavy drinking days [66]. With regard to dopaminergic genes, a number of studies have focused on the variation of the *DRD4*, which encodes the D4 dopamine receptor [67]. The L allele of *DRD4* has been associated with craving or drinking alcohol in some studies [68–70], but other studies found no association [71, 72].

A recent analysis of pharmacogenetic studies of AUD treatment concluded, however, that the extant data are inconclusive [49]. Studies that use greater methodological rigor and better statistical controls, such as corrections for multiple testing, may help to resolve these inconsistent findings. These procedures could also lead to the discovery of more robust and clinically meaningful moderator effects. As the field evolves through methodological standardization and the use of larger study samples, pharmacogenetic research has the potential to inform clinical care by enhancing therapeutic effects and personalizing treatments. These efforts may also provide insights into the mechanisms by which medications reduce heavy drinking or promote abstinence in patients with an AUD [49]. Current research also suggests that genetic knowledge of various neurotransmitter systems show that the presence or absence of specific alleles may at some point improve the efficacy of drugs to reduce craving or prolonging abstinence. Subtypes of AD have been shown to differ to some degree, as a function of allelic variation. Advances in the neurobiology of addiction have led to the identification of some genes and provide the basis for understanding specific risk loci. However, regardless of the explosion of genetic knowledge in AUDs, there are presently few clinical applications. Nonetheless, it is envisioned that future clinical practice will eventually use the extant genetic knowledge and technology. In addition to the increasing genetic knowledge, it is hoped that future clinical practice will also be able to use other potential predictors of treatment response, such as possible neuroimaging biomarkers and/or challenge tests. Also import is recognizing the various classification schemes of subtypes of alcoholics that may also impact outcomes [73].

Because of the large population affected, making access to treatment must be a priority for healthcare. Additionally, recognizing the other barriers to use and lack of treatment options, new research on a wider variety of efficacious psychological and pharmacological treatments, and how they can be best matched, is necessary. On the one hand, these researchers and corporations recognize the large untapped market failed by current therapies. On the other, pharmaceutical companies must also be cognizant of how they approach marketing such new drug discoveries. In particular, pharmaceutical companies use sophisticated marketing tools containing emotional appeals, but minimally educate consumers about their diseases. In particular, vulnerable populations, such as those with AUDs and other mentally ill patients, may be unduly influenced by advertising due to their compromised cognitive state. There must be hope for real abstinence and transition to a more healthy and productive lifestyle. Potentially future efforts promoting effective treatments may help to produce an effective paradigm shift toward treatment without misappropriating expectations of successful recovery in this compromised population.

Alcoholism affects a substantial proportion of the US population at some point in their lives. In addition to current drug treatments for alcoholism that appear to be underutilized, psychotherapies are fundamentally important to drive successful pharmacotherapy. Pharmacotherapies guided by pharmacogenomics and facilitated by psychotherapy will someday intervene at specific points in neurological pathways to facilitate alcohol treatment. However, while significant advances are being made toward finding more efficacious approaches to treat the disorder, acceptance of treatment by those affected, as well as treatment providers, may in the end be the keys to realizing the potential these drugs may ultimately have. It is unlikely there will ever be one treatment that "cures" AUD; therefore, we need to continue our efforts in identifying treatments that can be the best fit for a specific patient. Moreover, we need to continue investigating the role the psychosocial environment plays in combination with pharmacotherapy. Pharmacotherapy for AUD should always be considered an adjunct therapy to psychosocial interventions, and this combination approach should best address the high relapse rates of AUD. Making medications and psychosocial treatments affordable and available to all that need them however must become the ultimate goal for treatment access.

Table 4.1 Summary table

KEY RESEARCH FINDINGS
1. Alcohol use disorders are generally a worldwide problem with significant social, public health, and economic implications.
2. A paradigm shift in thinking about addiction as a brain disease has changed the focus of treatment of alcoholism to the same as that of any other lifelong pharmacological treatment.
3. Treatment of alcoholism is complex and challenging, and determining effective psychosocial treatments is essential to attenuate the detrimental effects of excessive alcohol consumption.
4. New and exciting data are driving a better understanding of how the currently approved medications combined with behavioral therapy can better serve our patient populations.
5. Recognizing that there are several alcoholic subtypes is important to facilitate the most effective pharmacological and behavioral treatment outcomes.
RECOMMENDATIONS FOR EVIDENCE-BASED PRACTICE
1. Treatment providers should actively assess AUDs and help set reduced drinking goals.
2. Patients with significant current or past withdrawal syndrome may require detoxification before starting outpatient medication management.
3. Providers should discuss and offer medications for AUD and should recognize the heterogeneity of AUDs that requires a menu of medication options discussed with the patient.
4. Medications do not work alone, and instead are shown to be more effective when accompanied by lifestyle changes that support reduced drinking goals and psychosocial therapy to facilitate medication adherence.
5. Providers who start a patient on pharmacotherapy should schedule a one-month follow-up to assess side effects, adherence, and efficacy. Effective treatment should be continued for at least six to 12 months. If a treatment fails, the provider should consider trying an alternative pharmacotherapy or refer the patient to specialty care for closer follow-up.
6. Every effort must be made to provide universal affordable access to treatment.
7. Recognize that there is no one best approach for "curing" AUD, and that several treatments combining pharmacotherapy with psychotherapy may need to be tried to obtain the best desired result for any particular patient.
RECOMMENDATIONS FOR FUTURE RESEARCH
1. Identification of novel medications for treating remains an important priority.
2. Understanding individual differences that interact with medications to influence outcome is highly important.
3. Understanding the mechanisms of behavior change that underlie successful and unsuccessful treatment is highly warranted.

References

1. World Health Organization. *World Health Organization global status report on alcohol.* Geneva: World Health Organization; 2011.
2. Rehm J, Anderson P, Barry J, et al. Prevalence of and potential influencing factors for alcohol dependence in Europe. *Eur Addict Res.* 2015;21:6–18. doi:10.1159/000365284.
3. O'Connor PG. Alcohol abuse and dependence. In: Goldman L, Ausiello D, editors. *Cecil Med.* 23rd ed. Philadelphia (PA): Saunders Elsevier. 2007:167–173.
4. American Psychiatric Association. *Diagnostic and statistical manual of mental disorders.* 2013. doi:10.1176/appi.books.9780890425596.744053.
5. American Psychiatric Association. *Diagnostic and statistical manual of mental disorders.* 4th ed. 1994. Washington (DC): American Psychiatric Association.
6. Grant BF, Goldstein RB, Saha TD, et al. Epidemiology of DSM-5 alcohol use disorder: results from the National Epidemiologic Survey on Alcohol and Related Conditions III. *JAMA Psychiatry.* 2015;72:757–766. doi:10.1001/jamapsychiatry.2015.0584.
7. Petrakis IL. A rational approach to the pharmacotherapy of alcohol dependence. *J Clin Psychopharmacol.* 2006;26:S3–S12. doi:10.1097/01.jcp.0000248602.68607.81.
8. Miller WR, Walters ST, Bennett ME. How effective is alcoholism treatment in the United States? *J Stud Alcohol.* 2001;62:211–220.
9. Allen JP, Mattson ME, Miller WR, et al. Matching alcoholism treatments to client heterogeneity: Project MATCH posttreatment drinking outcomes. *J Stud Alcohol.* 1997;58:7–29.
10. Project MATCH Research Group. Matching alcoholism treatments to client heterogeneity: treatment main effects and matching effects on drinking during treatment. *J Stud Alcohol.* 1998;59:631–639.
11. Jonas DE, Garbutt JC, Amick HR, et al. Behavioral counseling after screening for alcohol misuse in primary care: a systematic review and meta-analysis for the U.S. Preventive Services Task Force. *Ann Intern Med.* 2012;157:645–654. doi:10.7326/0003-4819-157-9-201211060-00544.
12. Moyer VA. Screening and behavioral counseling interventions in primary care to reduce alcohol misuse: U.S. Preventive Services Task Force recommendation statement. *Ann Intern Med.* 2013;159:210–218. doi:10.7326/0003-4819-159-3-201308060-00652.
13. Cuijpers P, Riper H, Lemmers L. The effects on mortality of brief interventions for problem drinking: a meta-analysis. *Addiction.* 2004;99:839–845. doi:10.1111/j.1360-0443.2004.00778.x.
14. Cadigan JM, Haeny AM, Martens MP, et al. Personalized drinking feedback: a meta-analysis of in-person versus computer-delivered interventions. *J Consult Clin Psychol.* 2015;83:430–437. doi:10.1037/a0038394.
15. Fleming MF, Barry KL, Manwell LB, et al. Brief physician advice for problem alcohol drinkers: a randomized controlled trial in community-based primary care practices. *JAMA.* 1997;277:1039–1045. doi:10.1001/jama.1997.03540370029032.
16. Fleming MF, Mundt MP, French MT, et al. Brief physician advice for problem drinkers: long-term efficacy and benefit-cost analysis. *Alcohol Clin Exp Res.* 2002;26:36–43. doi:10.1111/j.1530-0277.2002.tb02429.x.
17. Fleming MF, Manwell LB, Barry KL, et al. Brief physician advice for alcohol problems in older adults: a randomized community-based trial. *J Fam Pract.* 1999;48:378–384.

18. Moore AA, Blow FC, Hoffing M, et al. Primary care-based intervention to reduce at-risk drinking in older adults: a randomized controlled trial. *Addiction.* 2011; 106:111–120. doi:10.1111/j.1360-0443.2010.03229.x.
19. Kaner EFS, Beyer F, Dickinson HO, et al. Effectiveness of brief alcohol interventions in primary care populations. *Cochrane Database Syst Rev.* 2007; CD004148. doi:10.1002/14651858.CD004148.pub3.
20. Bertholet N, Daeppen JB, Wietlisbach V, et al. Reduction of alcohol consumption by brief alcohol intervention in primary care: systematic review and meta-analysis. *Arch Intern Med.* 2005;165:986–995. doi:10.1001/archinte.165.9.986.
21. Moyer A, Finney JW, Swearingen CE, Vergun P. Brief interventions for alcohol problems: a meta-analytic review of controlled investigations in treatment-seeking and non-treatment-seeking populations. *Addiction.* 2002;97:279–292. doi:10.1046/j.1360-0443.2002.00018.x.
22. Baker AL, Kavanagh DJ, Kay-Lambkin FJ, et al. Randomized controlled trial of cognitive-behavioural therapy for coexisting depression and alcohol problems: short-term outcome. *Addiction.* 2010;105:87–99. doi:10.1111/j.1360-0443.2009.02757.x.
23. UKATT Research Team. Effectiveness of treatment for alcohol problems: findings of the randomised UK alcohol treatment trial (UKATT). *BMJ.* 2005;331:541. doi:10.1136/bmj.331.7516.541.
24. Litt MD, Kadden RM, Kabela-Cormier E, Petry N. Changing network support for drinking: initial findings from the network support project. *J Consult Clin Psychol.* 2007;75:542–555. doi:10.1037/0022-006X.75.4.542.
25. Litt MD, Kadden RM, Kabela-Cormier E, Petry NM. Changing network support for drinking: network support project 2-year follow-up. *J Consult Clin Psychol.* 2009;77:229–242. doi:10.1037/a0015252.
26. Drummond C, Coulton S, James D, et al. Effectiveness and cost-effectiveness of a stepped care intervention for alcohol use disorders in primary care: pilot study. *Br J Psychiatry.* 2009;195:448–456. doi:10.1192/bjp.bp.108.056697.
27. Watson J, Crosby H, Dale V, et al. AESOPS: a randomised controlled trial of the clinical effectiveness and cost-effectiveness of opportunistic screening and stepped care interventions for older hazardous alcohol users in primary care. *Heal Technol Assess.* 2013;17:1–158. doi:10.3310/hta17250.
28. Khadjesari Z, Murray E, Hewitt C, et al. Can stand-alone computer-based interventions reduce alcohol consumption? A systematic review. *Addiction.* 2011;106:267–282. doi:10.1111/j.1360-0443.2010.03214.x.
29. Hester RK, Delaney HD, Campbell W. ModerateDrinking.Com and moderation management: outcomes of a randomized clinical trial with non-dependent problem drinkers. *J Consult Clin Psychol.* 2011;79:215–224. doi:10.1037/a0022487.
30. Garbutt JC. The state of pharmacotherapy for the treatment of alcohol dependence. *J Subst Abuse Treat.* 2009;36:S15–S23;quiz S24–S25. doi:10.1016/j.jsat.2008.08.008.
31. Edwards S, Kenna GA, Swift RM, Leggio L. Current and promising pharmacotherapies, and novel research target areas in the treatment of alcohol dependence: a review. *Curr Pharm Des.* 2011;17:1323–1332. doi:10.2174/138161211796150765.
32. Garbutt JC, West SL, Carey TS, et al. Pharmacological treatment of alcohol dependence: a review of the evidence. *JAMA.* 1999;281:1318–1325. doi:10.1001/jama.281.14.1318.

33. Fuller RK, Branchey L, Brightwell DR, et al. Disulfiram treatment of alcoholism: a Veterans Administration cooperative study. *JAMA*. 1986;256:1449–1455. doi:10.1001/jama.1986.03380110055026.
34. Skinner MD, Lahmek P, Pham H, Aubin HJ. Disulfiram efficacy in the treatment of alcohol dependence: a meta-analysis. *PLoS One*. 2014;9:e87366. doi:10.1371/journal.pone.0087366.
35. O'Malley SS, Jaffe AJ, Chang G, et al. Naltrexone and coping skills therapy for alcohol dependence: a controlled study. *Arch Gen Psychiatry*. 1992;49:881–887. doi:10.1001/archpsyc.1992.01820110045007.
36. Volpicelli JR, Alterman AI, Hayashida M, O'Brien CP. Naltrexone in the treatment of alcohol dependence. *Arch Gen Psychiatry*. 1992;49:876–880.
37. Krystal JH, Cramer JA, Krol WF, et al. Naltrexone in the treatment of alcohol dependence. *N Engl J Med*. 2001;345:1734–1739. doi:doi:10.1056/NEJMoa011127.
38. Rösner S, Hackl-Herrwerth A, Leucht S, et al. Acamprosate for alcohol dependence. *Cochrane Database Syst Rev*. 2010;CD004332. doi:10.1002/14651858.CD004332.pub2.
39. Jonas DE, Amick HR, Feltner C, et al. Pharmacotherapy for adults with alcohol use disorders in outpatient settings: a systematic review and meta-analysis. *JAMA*. 2014;311:1889–1900. doi:10.1001/jama.2014.3628.
40. Plosker GL. Acamprosate: a review of its use in alcohol dependence. *Drugs*. 2015;75:1255–1268. doi:10.1007/s40265-015-0423-9.
41. Paille FM, Guelfi JD, Perkins AC, et al. Double-blind randomized multicentre trial of acamprosate in maintaining abstinence from alcohol. *Alcohol Alcohol*. 1995;30:239–247.
42. Pelc I, Verbanck P, Le Bon O, et al. Efficacy and safety of acamprosate in the treatment of detoxified alcohol-dependent patients: a 90-day placebo-controlled dose-finding study. *Br J Psychiatry*. 1997;171:73–77. doi:10.1192/bjp.171.1.73.
43. Sass H, Soyka M, Mann K, Zieglgänsberger W. Relapse prevention by acamprosate: results from a placebo-controlled study on alcohol dependence. *Arch Gen Psychiatry*. 1996;53:673–680. doi:ISSN: 0003-990X.
44. Mann K, Lehert P, Morgan MY. The efficacy of acamprosate in the maintenance of abstinence in alcohol-dependent individuals: results of a meta-analysis. *Alcohol Clin Exp Res*. 2004;28:51–63. doi:10.1097/01.ALC.0000108656.81563.05.
45. Rösner S, Hackl-Herrwerth A, Leucht S, et al. Opioid antagonists for alcohol dependence. *Cochrane Database Syst Rev*. 2010;CD001867. doi:10.1002/14651858.CD001867.pub2.
46. Anton RF, O'Malley SS, Ciraulo DA, et al. Combined pharmacotherapies and behavioral interventions for alcohol dependence. The COMBINE study: a randomized controlled trial. *JAMA*. 2006;295:2003–2017. doi:10.1016/S0084-3970(08)70391-8.
47. Kiefer F, Jahn H, Tarnaske T, et al. Comparing and combining naltrexone and acamprosate in relapse prevention of alcoholism: a double-blind, placebo-controlled study. *Arch Gen Psychiatry*. 2003;60:92–99. doi:10.1001/archpsyc.60.1.92.
48. Mann K, Lemenager T, Hoffmann S, et al. Results of a double-blind, placebo-controlled pharmacotherapy trial in alcoholism conducted in Germany and comparison with the US COMBINE study. *Addict Biol*. 2013;18:937–946. doi:10.1111/adb.12012.

49. Jones JD, Comer SD, Kranzler HR. The pharmacogenetics of alcohol use disorder. *Alcohol Clin Exp Res*. 2015;39:391–402. doi:10.1111/acer.12643.
50. Lacro JP, Dunn LB, Dolder CR, et al. Prevalence of and risk factors for medication nonadherence in patients with schizophrenia: a comprehensive review of recent literature. *J Clin Psychiatry*. 2002;63:892–909. doi:http://dx.doi.org/10.4088/JCP.v63n1007.
51. Weiss RD. Adherence to pharmacotherapy in patients with alcohol and opioid dependence. *Addiction*. 2004;99:1382–1392. doi:10.1111/j.1360-0443.2004.00884.x.
52. Swift R, Oslin DW, Alexander M, Forman R. Adherence monitoring in naltrexone pharmacotherapy trials: a systematic review. *J Stud Alcohol Drugs*. 2011;72:1012–1018.
53. Reid SC, Teesson M, Sannibale C, et al. The efficacy of compliance therapy in pharmacotherapy for alcohol dependence: a randomized controlled trial. *J Stud Alcohol*. 2005;66:833–841.
54. Ammassari A, Trotta MP, Murri R. Correlates and predictors of adherence to highly active antiretroviral therapy: overview of published literature. *J Acquir Immune Defic Syndr*. 2002;31(Suppl 3):S123–S127. doi:10.1097/00126334-200212153-00007.
55. Claxton AJ, Cramer J, Pierce C. A systematic review of the associations between dose regimens and medication compliance. *Clin Ther*. 2001;23:1296–1310. doi:10.1016/S0149-2918(01)80109-0.
56. DiMatteo MR, Lepper HS, Croghan TW. Depression is a risk factor for noncompliance with medical treatment. *Arch Intern Med*. 2000;160:2101. doi:10.1001/archinte.160.14.2101.
57. Pettinati HM, Volpicelli JR, Pierce JD, O'Brien CP. Improving naltrexone response: an intervention for medical practitioners to enhance medication compliance in alcohol dependent patients. *J Addict Dis*. 2000;19:71–83. doi:10.1300/J069v19n01_06.
58. Garbutt JC, Kranzler HR, O'Malley SS, et al. Efficacy and tolerability of long-acting injectable naltrexone for alcohol dependence: a randomized controlled trial. *JAMA*. 1995. doi:10.1001/jama.293.13.1617.
59. Pisani VD, Fawcett J, Clark D, McGuire M. Relative contributions of medication adherence and AA meeting attendance to abstinent outcome for chronic alcoholics. *J Stud Alcohol*. 1993;54:115–119.
60. O'Malley SS, Rounsaville BJ, Farren C, et al. Initial and maintenance naltrexone treatment for alcohol dependence using primary care vs specialty care: a nested sequence of 3 randomized trials. *Arch Intern Med*. 2003;163:1695–1704. doi:10.1001/archinte.163.14.1695.
61. Petrakis IL, Gonzalez G, Rosenheck R, Krystal JH. Comorbidity of alcoholism and psychiatric disorders: an overview. *Alcohol Res Heal*. 2002;26:81–89.
62. Sernyak MJ, Glazer WM, Heninger GR, et al. Naltrexone augmentation of neuroleptics in schizophrenia. *J Clin Psychopharmacol*. 1998;18:248–251.
63. Luby ED, Marrazzi MA. A panic attack precipitated by opiate blockade: a case study. *J Clin Psychopharmacol*. 1987;7:361–362.
64. Kranzler HR, Edenberg HJ. Pharmacogenetics of alcohol and alcohol dependence treatment. *Curr Pharm Des*. 2010;16:2141–2148. doi:BSP/CPD/E-Pub/000113 [pii].

65. Oslin DW, Berrettini W, Kranzler HR, et al. A functional polymorphism of the mu-opioid receptor gene is associated with naltrexone response in alcohol-dependent patients. *Neuropsychopharmacology*. 2003;28:1546–1552. doi:10.1038/sj.npp.1300219\r1300219 [pii].

66. Anton RF, Oroszi G, O'Malley S, et al. An evaluation of mu-opioid receptor (OPRM1) as a predictor of naltrexone response in the treatment of alcohol dependence. *Arch Gen Psychiatry*. 2008;65:135–144. doi:10.1001/archpsyc.65.2.135.

67. Ray LA, Bryan A, MacKillop J, et al. The dopamine D4 Receptor (DRD4) gene exon III polymorphism, problematic alcohol use and novelty seeking: direct and mediated genetic effects. *Addict Biol*. 2009;14:238–244. doi:10.1111/j.1369-1600.2008.00120.x.

68. Hutchison KE, Wooden A, Swift RM, et al. Olanzapine reduces craving for alcohol: a DRD4 VNTR polymorphism by pharmacotherapy interaction. *Neuropsychopharmacology*. 2003;28:1882–1888. doi:10.1038/sj.npp.1300264.

69. Hutchison KE, Ray L, Sandman E, et al. The effect of olanzapine on craving and alcohol consumption. *Neuropsychopharmacology*. 2006;31:1310–1317. doi:10.1038/sj.npp.1300917.

70. MacKillop J, Menges DP, McGeary JE, Lisman SA. Effects of craving and DRD4 VNTR genotype on the relative value of alcohol: an initial human laboratory study. *Behav Brain Funct*. 2007;3:11. doi:10.1186/1744-9081-3-11.

71. McGeary JE, Monti PM, Rohsenow DJ, et al. Genetic moderators of naltrexone's effects on alcohol cue reactivity. *Alcohol Clin Exp Res*. 2006;30:1288–1296. doi:10.1111/j.1530-0277.2006.00156.x.

72. van den Wildenberg E, Janssen RGJ, Hutchison KE, et al. Polymorphisms of the dopamine D4 receptor gene (DRD4 VNTR) and cannabinoid CB1 receptor gene (CNR1) are not strongly related to cue-reactivity after alcohol exposure. *Addict Biol*. 2007;12:210–220. doi:10.1111/j.1369-1600.2007.00064.x.

73. Leggio L, Kenna GA, Fenton M, et al. Typologies of alcohol dependence: from Jellinek to genetics and beyond. *Neuropsychol Rev*. 2009;19:115–129. doi:10.1007/s11065-008-9080-z.

Chapter 5

Tobacco Use Disorder

James MacKillop, Joshua C. Gray, Max M. Owens, Jennifer Laude, and Sean David

Acknowledgments: This work was supported in part by the Peter Boris Chair in Addictions Research

Introduction

Smoking remains a major public health problem worldwide. Although the prevalence varies considerably by nation, approximately one in five adults smoke globally [1]. Among smokers, approximately half meet criteria for tobacco use disorder [2, 3], the formal psychiatric diagnosis of addiction to nicotine, making it among the most prevalent of all psychiatric disorders. In addition to being widespread, smoking continues to be a major cause of preventable morbidity and mortality around the world, estimated to contribute to almost 10% of deaths globally [1]. The three principal causes of smoking-related illness and death are cardiovascular disease, cancer, and respiratory disease, but smoking also causes or contributes to an array of other medical problems [4]. As an example of the effects on mortality, a 50-year observational study found the life expectancy of smokers was approximately 10 years shorter than nonsmokers, and smokers were twice as likely to die during middle age [5]. Compounding the public health burden, smoking results in massive economic costs to society. In the United States alone, the estimated annual economic burden of smoking is $300 billion in lost productivity and healthcare costs [4, 6]. Thus, the tobacco industry largely operates based on privatized profits from cigarette sales and socialized costs to consumers and society as a whole.

Among smokers, approximately 70% report wanting to quit permanently [7], and there are compelling reasons to do so. In time, a former smoker's risk of cardiovascular disease and other conditions return to the level of nonsmokers. For example, quitting smoking by age 30 has been found to be associated with mortality rates that were indistinguishable from nonsmokers [5]. The unfortunate reality, however, is that only a minority of quit attempts are successful. Among smokers who are trying to quit unassisted, the cessation rate is approximately 1 in 20 [7]. The rate of success goes up dramatically when individuals receive evidence-based treatments, both psychological and pharmacological, and this chapter will review those practices. Following the general outline of the volume, the first section focuses on psychological treatments, the second section focuses on pharmacological treatments, and the third section focuses on strategies and considerations for integrating the two domains. Following the discussion of specific treatment elements, the fourth section focuses on pertinent treatment considerations, including common psychiatric comorbidities and weight gain following treatment. Finally, we consider the overall state of smoking cessation research and identify future directions to improve outcomes.

In terms of the broader context, treating tobacco use disorder takes a variety of different forms, but can be broadly divided into three domains: (1) systemic strategies that reduce risk for all individuals (e.g., rational tax policy, barriers to access for minors, prevention, public health media messaging); (2) widespread screening and brief intervention at first points of clinical contact (e.g., primary care, emergency department); and (3) formal interventions for treatment-seeking individuals via specialist care. Although there is extensive evidence that systems-level factors, such as tobacco taxation, substantially influence smoking behavior [8, 9], the primary focus of this chapter will be the second two domains, namely clinician-delivered treatments.

Evidence-Based Psychological Interventions

For the purposes of the chapter, psychological treatments are broadly defined as interpersonal interactions between a clinician and a patient that seek to improve the patient's well-being. In the treatment of tobacco use disorder, these interventions fall into two categories: (1) brief interventions, typically referred to as minimal contact interventions; and (2) formal multi-session treatment regimens, delivered either individually or in a group.

Minimal Contact Interventions

Minimal contact interventions (MCIs) are intended for a wide variety of health-care professionals, including psychologists, psychiatrists, primary care physicians, nurses, dentists, and social workers. The format is simple, comprising universal screening of an individual's tobacco use status and, for smokers identified, conducting an immediate further brief evaluation and providing recommendations. The typical protocol for MCIs is commonly referred to as the Five As: (1) ASK (i.e., ask the patient if he or she is a tobacco user) (2) ADVISE (i.e., if so, make a clear clinical recommendation for the individual to attempt cessation); (3) ASSESS (i.e., evaluate the willingness to make a cessation attempt and set a quit date); (4) ASSIST (i.e., provide direct assistance for individuals who are willing to make a cessation attempt); and (5) ARRANGE (i.e., arrange for a follow-up to review progress) [9].

Minimal contact interventions range in duration from 3 to 20 minutes, with most of the variability being in how much assistance is given. At the short end, assistance may simply be providing a list of community resources (e.g., treatment programs, quit/helplines). At the long end, assistance can include a deeper discussion of strategies for cessation that would be most helpful for the individual (e.g., developing a quit plan, discussing strategies for implementation) and may engage psychotherapeutic techniques such as motivational interviewing, described below. Despite their brevity, MCIs have consistently been found to increase overall quit rates significantly [9, 10], albeit by modest amounts in absolute terms. From a public health standpoint, universally implementing MCIs creates a healthcare environment in which clinicians do not overlook or ignore smoking, and smokers consistently receive meaningful recommendations and useful resources. For individuals who are motivated to stop smoking, MCIs may be the catalyst for a quit attempt or pursuit of more intensive treatment. Given the low cost and widespread applicability, clinicians in virtually all healthcare environments where smokers may be present are recommended to conduct MCIs, unless otherwise contraindicated or inapplicable.

Formal Treatment Programs

Formal treatment comes in many forms, but can be broadly defined as being provided by a smoking cessation specialist and having more than one treatment interaction. A further designation among formal treatments is whether or not it is "intensive treatment," defined as four or more sessions that each last more than 10 minutes each [9]. Generally speaking, there is robust evidence from systematic reviews that face-to-face individual treatment significantly improves the probability of successful smoking cessation [10], both delivered individually or in a group. The magnitude of this effect is a substantial increase in the probability of long-term (6–12 month) success. To put this in context, the effect of providing formal treatment is approximately three times the magnitude of MCIs and equivalent to several efficacious pharmacotherapies (single form nicotine replacement, bupoprion, cytisine), discussed below.

In terms of the content that comprises formal individual or group treatments, arguably the most well-supported psychological approach to tobacco use disorder is motivational interviewing (MI) [11, 12], a client-centered, directive psychological technique to help patients resolve ambivalence and change their behavior. In-session, the clinician implementing MI focuses on empathetically exploring the causes for ambivalence and selectively reinforces the patient's personal motives for cessation, seeking to maximize language reflecting motivation for and commitment to change. The theoretical foundations for this approach draw on the Rogerian tradition, in which empathy creates a powerful interpersonal context for a patient to explore change, and social psychological principles, namely avoiding the reactance response that is often elicited by instructing patients what to do and the powerful influence of listening to oneself argue on behalf of change [13]. Put simply, in the context of a constructive therapeutic relationship, MI seeks to use the patient's own priorities and language to catalyze behavioral change.

In terms of general processes, MI uses four tactics for achieving these goals [14]. The first is to express empathy for the patient, creating a nonjudgmental interpersonal relationship that will encourage forthright discussion. The second is to develop discrepancy with the patient by discussing negative consequences of the target behavior. The third is to roll with any resistance that arises, rather than pushing back if a patient expresses doubts or retreats from making a change.

The fourth is to support self-efficacy, which refers to cultivating a sense of self-confidence and personal drive in the quitting process. With regard to the key areas that MI should address for smoking cessation, a useful heuristic is the Five Rs (1) RELEVANCE (i.e., the personally relevant reasons that smoking cessation is important to the patient); (2) RISKS (i.e., personally relevant health risks to the patient); (3) REWARDS (i.e., the patient's perceived benefits of terminating smoking, such as health benefits, money saved, self-esteem); (4) ROADBLOCKS (i.e., the patient's perceived barriers to success, including the people, places, and consequences such as withdrawal or weight gain); and (5) REPETITION (i.e., completion of a motivational interview repeatedly for patients who are unwilling to attempt cessation or experience a failed quit attempt) [9].

Other treatment strategies that have been identified include the incorporation of supportive counseling, cognitive behavioral approaches, and contingency management. Supportive counseling largely overlaps with empathic aspects of MI, communicating concern for the patient and willingness to help, encouraging the individual during the quit attempt, emphasizing the patient's successes and the evidence supporting smoking cessation treatments [9]. Cognitive behavioral strategies and contingency management (CM) both come from a learning theory approach (see Chapter 3), focusing on skills training and directly reinforcing abstinence, respectively. Also referred to as relapse prevention, a cognitive behavioral approach typically comprises a functional analysis of the patient's antecedents and consequences of smoking to understand the topography of smoking behavior and associated motivational mechanisms. The functional analysis is used to identify the common antecedents of smoking, referred to as "high-risk situations" or "triggers," followed by skills training to navigate these situations during the quit attempt. High-risk situations are idiographically identified, but commonly include specific people, places, times of day/routines, affective states (including negative mood, positive mood, withdrawal symptoms), and drinking or other drug use. In other words, the functional analysis is the who, what, when, and why of the patient's smoking. Treatment then focuses on first learning to identify high-risk situations, preparing to minimize risk in advance of the quit date, and then troubleshooting the identified and newly arising high-risk situations that emerge after the quit attempt has been initiated. For example, patients may be recommended to use behavioral strategies such as avoiding the high-risk situation altogether, altering it in some way to reduce risk, or using a substitute as a sensorimotor replacement instead of a cigarette. Other strategies focus on cognitive risk factors, such as trivializing smoking a cigarette ("How bad can just one be?") or, alternatively, being excessively demoralized by a lapse ("Now I've slipped there's no way I'll be able to quit, I may as well have another"), referred to as the abstinence violation effect. Of note, these strategies were found to be effective in a meta-analysis of active ingredients in psychological treatment in the 2008 clinical practice guidelines [9], but subsequent systematic reviews and meta-analyses have generated mixed findings [15, 16]. This suggests that the efficacy of cognitive behavioral strategies may systematically vary based on the components included or based on the patient population addressed.

Contingency management uses financial incentives to directly reinforce tobacco abstinence, typically verified using expired carbon monoxide. Procedurally, patients in CM protocols receive regular testing for abstinence or smoking reduction and receive immediate feedback in the form of gift cards, vouchers, or opportunities for small prizes [17]. In addition, alternative strategies exist in which individuals may deposit their own resources that are only refunded based on success [18], a form of precommitment. Of note, CM is not intended to be a curative treatment so much as a way to create immediate short-term positively or negatively reinforcing consequences for smoking. In doing so, the hope is to help the patient be maximally successful early in treatment to facilitate long-term behavior change. The approach is less a face-to-face psychological intervention than a behavioral regimen that can be added to additional treatment components. Nonetheless, an extensive evidence base supports the efficacy of contingency management in smoking cessation treatment [19, 20], and, where feasible, CM should be considered as a potential element in multicomponent treatment programs.

Evidence-Based Pharmacological Interventions

Nicotine Replacement Therapy

Nicotine replacement therapy (NRT) provides low doses of nicotine to reduce withdrawal symptoms associated with smoking cessation, weaning the individual away from physiological dependence on nicotine. Many forms of NRT are available, including transdermal patches, gum, lozenges, nasal spray, and inhalers. While transdermal patches are long-acting and designed to be worn continuously throughout the day, the other forms of NRT are short-acting and are administered as needed (*pro re nata; prn*) [10]. Transdermal patches and *prn* NRT are putatively complementary approaches because the slow nicotine release of the transdermal patch can address chronic withdrawal symptoms and the quick release of nicotine from *prn* NRT can address acute "breakthrough" cravings. Indeed, while robust evidence supports the efficacy of individual forms of NRT, combination NRT shows even greater efficacy. For example, a meta-analysis of 117 studies with over 50,000 participants found that any form of NRT increases the likelihood of quitting smoking successfully by 50–70%, and the use of combination NRT approach was even more effective [21]. Furthermore, in some instances, combination NRT has been found to be comparable in efficacy to the leading prescription medication for smoking cessation, varenicline [22].

Nicotine replacement therapy is generally safe, with no serious side effects commonly reported. The most common side effect of NRT, occurring in about half of users, is irritation at the site of administration (e.g., skin for patch, nasal passage for inhaler) [21]. This can be effectively managed through use of hydrocortisone cream and rotating patch sites [9]. Less common side effects include nausea, gastrointestinal complaints, and insomnia [23], the latter being manageable by patients discontinuing NRT prior to bedtime or using a 16-hour patch designed to be taken off before bedtime [9]. Although a minority of subjects have reported increased rates of heart palpitations or chest pain [21, 23], there is no evidence of increased cardiovascular risk, regardless of whether users have preexisting cardiovascular conditions [24, 25]. Furthermore, long-term use of gum and inhaler NRT (i.e., ranging from one to five years) has been demonstrated to be safe, NRT has minimal abuse liability, and its discontinuation is rarely associated with physical or psychological symptoms of withdrawal [26, 27].

An important NRT consideration is determining the optimal dosage and treatment course. In general, an eight-week course is recommended, and patients who smoke more than 10 cigarettes daily are recommended to begin with a 21 mg patch, and those who smoke fewer than 10 are recommended to begin with 14 mg. However, a logical consideration is that highly dependent smokers may benefit from an increased dosage and duration of NRT. A clinical rule of thumb is to approximate the number of milligrams of transdermal nicotine to the typical number of cigarettes per day (e.g., one 20-cigarette pack/day = 21 mg, two packs/day = 42 mg). However, in a pooled analysis of eight studies, a higher-dose nicotine patch, either 42 mg/24-hour or 25 mg/16-hour, was only slightly more effective than the standard-dose patch [21]. Nonetheless, level of nicotine consumption and severity of nicotine withdrawal are "two sides of the same coin," meaning that the dose of nicotine replacement should attempt to scale to the individual's consumption. In terms of extended duration, using NRT beyond an eight-week course appears to have minimal impact on long-term rates of abstinence [28–30]. However, one study found extended use of the patch and long-term counseling led to a significant reduction in cigarettes smoked per day [29], supporting NRT as a possible harm reduction strategy in those who are unable to achieve abstinence. Somewhat counterintuitively, it has also been found that initiation of NRT while still smoking is both safe and may increase the likelihood of long-term abstinence [29, 31–33].

In sum, NRT has robust efficacy and a highly tolerable side effect profile, making it a pharmacological treatment of first resort. Combining transdermal patches to manage overall withdrawal and short-acting formulations for acute cravings reflects the best practice regimen. Even in patients who are not completely abstinent, NRT use may be encouraged to reduce smoking.

Varenicline

Varenicline (Chantix®/Champix®) is a partial nicotinic receptor agonist, stimulating $\alpha_4\beta_2$ and $\alpha_3\beta_4$ receptors, to provide relief from withdrawal while simultaneously inhibiting the rewarding effects of smoking [34–36], and is the most commonly prescribed pharmacological agent for facilitating smoking cessation [37]. Recommended dosing for varenicline is 1 mg twice a day for 12 weeks, with a titration period during the first week (.5 mg days 1–3, .5 mg twice daily days 4–7), and the quit date set on the second week [22]. Numerous studies support the efficacy of varenicline [38], which generates 12-month abstinence rates of ~35%. This rate is typically superior to other pharmacotherapies. Recent meta-analyses found varenicline to be more effective than individual forms of NRT or bupropion, with one finding it superior to combination NRT (e.g., patch and gum) as well [22, 39]. In addition, it is possible that varenicline may be used synergistically with other therapies. A meta-analysis of three randomized controlled trials found that combination therapy of varenicline and the nicotine patch was more effective than varenicline and placebo, and effects persisted to a six-month follow-up [40]. Finally, a recent review of the four studies comparing varenicline monotherapy to combination varenicline and bupropion concluded that initial evidence suggests the combination is superior [41]. In sum, varenicline is arguably the most efficacious medication currently available and there is potential for synergistic gains from combining it with other pharmacotherapies, although further investigation of combination approaches is needed.

Although there is robust evidence of efficacy, varenicline does have a notable side effect profile. Possible side effects fall into three domains: (1) adverse psychological effects, such as mood disturbance, sleep problems, and suicidality; (2) adverse cardiovascular events; and (3) gastrointestinal symptoms. In the first case, varenicline has carried an FDA "black box" warning since 2009, which advises prescribers and users to monitor any behavioral or mood changes or suicidal thoughts that occur [42]. This was a result of reports of adverse psychiatric events from the general public during post-marketing surveillance (following the approval and widespread availability of the drug). Disproportionate levels of psychiatric side effects were not present in the controlled trials that supported the initial approval. Subsequently, a recent meta-analysis of 39 randomized controlled trials concluded there was no evidence of any increased suicidality (ideation or successful or unsuccessful attempts), depression, irritability, aggression, or death [43]. In fact, the meta-analysis even identified a reduced risk for anxiety among participants receiving varenicline. However, it was notable that varenicline was reliably associated with increased risk of sleep disorders, abnormal dreams, and fatigue. With regard to cardiovascular side effects, two meta-analyses of major adverse cardiovascular events (MACE; i.e., cardiovascular-related death, non-fatal myocardial infarction, non-fatal stroke) found a non-significant trend toward an increased risk among individuals taking varenicline. However, the overall incidence was very low (<1% in both groups and <.2% difference in rate of incidence across groups), leading to the conclusion that the risk of MACE is "small, and statistically and clinically insignificant" [44, 45]. Finally, with regard to gastrointestinal side effects, a meta-analysis of 12 randomized placebo-controlled studies found that use of varenicline significantly increased the likelihood of experiencing nausea, constipation, and flatulence [46]. These effects are primarily related to discomfort rather than long-term or serious physical harm. Thus, there is limited controlled evidence implicating varenicline with psychiatric symptoms suicidality and MACE, but common side effects are sleep/dream disturbance and gastrointestinal symptoms.

Bupropion

Bupropion hydrochloride (Zyban®) is a nonselective inhibitor of dopamine and norepinephrine transporters and an antagonist of nicotinic acetylcholine receptors [47]. It was originally used to treat depression [48] but is also efficacious in treating tobacco use disorder [49]. Given its pharmacodynamics, the mechanisms of efficacy are thought to be blocking the rewarding effects of nicotine and reducing withdrawal symptoms following cessation, particularly craving and negative affect [50–52]. Recommended dosing is 150 mg twice per day for 7–12 weeks with a titration period during the first three days (150 mg once per day for days 1–3), and a quit date set on the eighth day [10, 53]. The efficacy of bupropion is well supported by numerous studies. A recent meta-analysis of 36 trials concluded that bupropion led to a quit rate of 17% compared to 9% in response to placebo [53]. Despite evidence of increased efficacy compared to placebo, bupropion is similarly effective to individual forms of NRT, but less effective than varenicline and combination NRT [49].

Bupropion's most common side effects are insomnia (~30–40%) and dry mouth (~10–13%) [54, 55]. Despite the FDA warning that bupropion might be associated with serious neuropsychiatric symptoms and even suicide [56], more recent large-scale studies have not supported this risk [49, 57]. Nonetheless, additional clinician monitoring is probably warranted, compared to NRT, for example. Finally, bupropion is toxic at high doses, and at standard prescription doses it is associated with a seizure rate of approximately 1:1,000 pts [53, 58]. Bupropion has not been tested for increased risk in individuals with a history of seizures (for obvious reasons), for whom it should be assumed to be contraindicated.

Cytisine

Cytisine (Tabex®) is a partial agonist of the nicotinic acetylcholine receptor with a special affinity for the $\alpha_4\beta_2$ receptor subtype [59], and is thought to reduce craving and withdrawal symptoms that occur after tobacco cessation [60]. While its mechanism of action is similar to varenicline, it has a much shorter half-life (5 hours versus 24 hours) and is more rapidly eliminated from the body [61]. The recommended dosing is one 1.5 mg tablet every two hours for the first three days of use, every two and a half hours for days 4–12, every three hours for days 13–16, every four hours for days 17–20, and every six hours for days 21–25 [62]. Individuals are recommended to quit smoking entirely on the fifth day of use, and smoking beyond this is discouraged.

In terms of efficacy, a recent meta-analysis of seven controlled clinical trials found cytisine to be more effective than placebo (RR = 1.59), with an even higher rate of success in the two controlled trials that biochemically verified abstinence (RR = 3.29) [63]. Additionally, a recent clinical trial found it to be more effective than NRT for smoking cessation [64]. Though cytisine has not been tested against varenicline or bupropion in a clinical trial, cytisine's efficacy compared to placebo is similar to that of varenicline and bupropion, and greater when only the most well-controlled trials are considered [22, 63, 65]. Additionally, cytisine's production is estimated to cost between 5 and 50% as much as other cessation medications [66]. Given its equal or greater efficacy, its shorter course of treatment, and lower cost of production, a report commissioned by the British National Institute for Health Research estimated that cytisine was both more efficacious and more cost-effective than varenicline based on existing evidence [65].

Cytisine appears to be highly tolerable. The largest meta-analysis conducted for clinical trials of cytisine found an equal number of serious adverse events in those receiving cytisine and placebo [63]. Non-serious gastrointestinal problems are the most common side effect of cytisine (12% in those taking cytisine compared to 7% placebo) [63]. Naturalistic studies of cytisine have found up to 15% reported terminating use of cytisine due to non-serious gastrointestinal discomfort [67]. It has been reported that this effect is most common during the first few days of use and declines as treatment progresses [59]. However, clinicians should exercise caution when using cytisine for patients already experiencing gastrointestinal disorder. There have been no other side effects that have been consistently linked to cytisine beyond those typically experienced by smokers attempting to quit [63, 67].

Though it has been prescribed as a smoking cessation medication in Eastern Europe since 1964, it is, unfortunately, not formally approved beyond that region, albeit available for purchase online. Certainly, more research on cytisine under real-world conditions and in specific patient populations is needed to fully confirm its efficacy and safety [65, 68], but given its relative efficacy, low cost, safety, and mild side effects compared to other smoking cessation medications, the case for using cytisine is strong in jurisdictions where it is available.

Second-Line and Experimental Medications

A number of second-line medications are available for smoking cessation, including clonidine and nortryptiline. Clonidine is an antihypertensive drug and nortryptiline is a tricyclic antidepressant, and both have exhibited efficacy in treating tobacco use disorder [9]. However, both have comparatively significant side effect profiles, making them more appropriate for full consideration if a patient does not succeed with the preceding first-line medications.

A number of novel experimental therapeutics are also being investigated as smoking cessation pharmacotherapies. These include topiramate, an anticonvulsant; d-cycloserine, a nooptropic; and atomoxetine, a non-stimulant medication for attention deficit hyperactivity disorder [69]. Of these, atomoxetine is particularly promising given its preclinical effects on discounting of future rewards [70–72], a form of impulsivity reflecting ability to delay gratification. Steep discounting of future rewards has been robustly shown to predict smoking cessation response [73–75]. These compounds are promising, but it is premature to conclude that any of these agents warrant widespread "off-label" use in smoking cessation at this point. In contrast, although there has been substantial interest in naltrexone, an opioid receptor antagonist, a recent meta-analysis revealed no beneficial effects across eight trials [76].

Probably the most controversial novel candidate therapeutic is electronic cigarettes (e-cigarettes), which could either serve as novel NRT delivery devices or novel forms of risk. The prototypical e-cigarette delivers aerosol by heating fluid containing nicotine (although non-nicotine solutions are available) that users draw into their mouth and lungs, mimicking the action of conventional smoking. The release of nicotine via heat rather than the burning of tobacco substantially reduces the inhalation of carcinogens [77–79]. However, there has been concern as to whether components in e-cigarettes cause adverse health effects. The propellants used in these devices (e.g. propylene glycol) decompose into carcinogens such as formaldehyde when aerosolized, which impair respiratory function [79], and could increase the risk of cancer and lung disease [80–82]. Toxic metals in e-cigarettes have been reported at concentrations higher than those in combustible cigarettes [83] and toxicities specific to e-cigarettes have also been identified [84].

In addition to health concerns over the use of e-cigarettes, there is mixed evidence demonstrating their effectiveness as smoking cessation aids [149]. Two placebo-controlled clinical trials have found that e-cigarettes are efficacious for smoking cessation, however, many more are underway and will clarify the relative efficacy. Furthermore, one study found e-cigarettes to be equally as effective smoking cessation aids as NRT [85]. Furthermore, e-cigarettes have been deemed to be less risky, cause fewer negative physical feelings, provide more satisfaction, and are better at reducing craving, negative affect, and stress than NRT [86]. On the other hand, it may also be the case e-cigarettes re-normalize smoking behavior [87]. Population-based studies indicate e-cigarettes significantly lower the odds of achieving sustained abstinence from smoking [78, 88, 89, 150] and some adolescents progress from e-cigarettes to combustible cigarettes [90]. It is possible that e-cigarettes could place smokers at risk of escalating to regular, frequent use of combustible tobacco [90, 91]. However, e-cigarettes may also be useful for harm reduction purposes in regular smokers of combustible cigarettes. Clinical studies have confirmed e-cigarettes deliver less nicotine per puff than combustible cigarettes [77], but experienced users can intake levels of nicotine similar to those produced by combustible cigarettes [78, 92]. Further, the dilutions of nicotine used in these devices are not required by law to meet standards for labeling or nicotine content, and as such, concentrations vary [77]. Collectively, the state of the clinical science on e-cigarettes is still in its infancy, and they are controversial products in the nicotine consumption and cessation marketplace. Although e-cigarettes may be ultimately useful for smoking cessation or harm reduction, clinicians should be cautious about making specific recommendations at this point.

Strategies and Considerations for Integrating Psychological and Pharmacological Interventions

The preceding sections identified the efficacious individual strategies for treating tobacco use disorder, but given how challenging smoking cessation is for many patients, a best practice approach includes combining psychological and pharmacological strategies. Indeed, it may be the case that combinations of psychological approaches and multiple pharmacotherapies are optimal [41, 93], as is already established for dual-form NRT. However, at this point, there are no established guidelines for integrating psychological and pharmacological approaches in specific synergistic ways. Rather, the general recommendation is to include both domains, and whether differentially beneficial interactions are present remains an empirical question.

Nonetheless, in terms of practically integrating treatment approaches, a thorough assessment of the patient in a variety of domains can provide a useful framework for integrating treatment. Table 5.1 presents a number of instruments that can be used to idiographically assess the patient and optimally implement psychological and pharmacological approaches. The majority are psychometrically validated and available without cost in the public domain. Included are measures of level of tobacco use disorder, motivation to change, motives for smoking, and smoking-related high-risk situations. These can be complemented by assessments of smoking-relevant traits (e.g., forms of impulsivity, anhedonia, or hostility), other substance use, symptoms of commonly comorbid psychiatric disorders, and cognitive functioning for a holistic sense of the patient. The guiding principle is an emphasis on matching as many active treatment ingredients as possible to the presenting symptoms and vulnerabilities of the patient.

Another way to think about assessment is as a framework for thinking about the functional role of each treatment component. What are the most pertinent motivational maintaining factors? How will a psychological or pharmacological component address each factor? Furthermore, in addition to a comprehensive intake evaluation, an important strategy for optimal success is continued evaluation of the pertinent domains as treatment unfolds. Are cravings and other withdrawal symptoms dissipating over time? Is self-efficacy increasing over time? Are fluctuations in commitment to the quit attempt observable? These are the kinds of questions that ongoing assessment can provide to an empirically-minded clinician.

Important Comorbidities and Other Pertinent Considerations

Most of the preceding approaches have been developed in trials focusing on smokers who only have tobacco use disorder. However, tobacco use disorder is commonly comorbid with other psychiatric conditions [94, 95], and smokers with comorbid disorders exhibit higher levels of tobacco consumption, greater

Table 5.1 Assessment instruments for a multidimensional pretreatment smoking profile

Assessment	Domain(s)
Fagerstrom Test for Nicotine Dependence [139]	Severity of nicotine dependence (tobacco use disorder)
Readiness Rulers [140]	Single-item measures of cessation attempt readiness, confidence, and importance
Wisconsin Inventory of Smoking Dependence Motives (Full/Brief) [141, 142]	Twelve domains of motives for smoking: four primary dependence subscales—craving, automaticity, tolerance, loss of control; eight secondary dependence subscales—affiliative attachment, behavioral choice, cognitive enhancement, cue exposure, negative reinforcement, positive reinforcement, taste, social goads
Smoking Self-Efficacy Questionnaire [143]	Confidence for resisting smoking in response to internal and external temptations
Questionnaire of Smoking Urges (Full/Brief) [144, 145]	Cravings to smoke for pleasure/reward (positive reinforcement) and to alleviate aversive states (negative reinforcement)
Obsessive Compulsive Smoking Scale [146]	Cravings; two subscales—preoccupation with smoking and compulsive drive
Smoking-related Weight Concerns Scale [124]	Relevance of post-cessation weight gain; two subscales—weight concerns and weight efficacy after quitting
Commitment to Quitting Smoking Scale [147]	Dedication to smoking cessation success
Smoking History Questionnaire	Smoking developmental milestones (e.g., age of first cigarette, first daily cigarette), historical trends (e.g., maximum ever, longest duration of quitting), and previous cessation strategies
Expired Carbon Monoxide [148]	Recent smoking behavior and heaviness of smoking topography; relatively transient (state-like)
Salivary Cotinine [148]	Recent smoking behavior and heaviness of smoke consumption; relatively stable (trait-like)

Note: Some redundancy is present, and these assessments are anticipated to be part of a larger battery with measures of concurrent substance use, commonly comorbid psychiatric conditions, cognitive functioning, and potentially other measures.

addiction severity, and even less success in quitting [46, 94, 96, 97]. These individuals represent a generally higher severity cohort, at even greater risk of smoking-related disease, and, by one estimate, the life expectancy of smokers with comorbid psychiatric disorders is 25 years less than the general population [98].

The treatment of tobacco use disorder among individuals with other psychiatric conditions can present a number of challenges. For instance, individuals with comorbid disorders appear to experience exaggerated nicotine withdrawal symptoms [99–101] and the symptoms of nicotine withdrawal can mimic symptoms of patients' primary psychiatric illness [102, 103]. As such, clinicians should help patients recognize withdrawal and should aggressively treat it [104]. Longer-term treatments (>12 weeks) may be needed for prolonged abstinence in these populations [9, 105], and it is critical clinicians be persistent in their efforts, as often more than one quit attempt is needed for sustained abstinence [103]. In terms of general treatment considerations, smoking cessation clinicians should ensure individuals receive mental health treatment for their disorders, as this increases the likelihood they achieve long-term abstinence from smoking [106]. Finally, physicians will also need to consider drug interactions when applying pharmacotherapies in those with psychiatric illness. Current smokers may need different doses of psychotropic medications to attain therapeutic levels and the dose may need to be tapered upon smoking cessation [107].

In terms of specific comorbidities, among the highest is the overlap between tobacco use disorder and schizophrenia/schizoaffective disorder [108, 109]. Smoking-related illness is a substantial cause of mortality among individuals with schizophrenia [110, 111]. Nonetheless, individuals with these comorbidities are able to maintain abstinence or greatly reduce smoking using pharmacotherapies. Indeed, clinical trials have found that varenicline and bupropion effective and safe in terms of symptom exacerbation [112]. Surprisingly, NRT monotherapy has not been systematically examined in this cohort, but has been found to be efficacious in combination with bupropion [112].

A second highly common comorbidity is between tobacco use disorder and other substance use disorders (SUDs) [3], although rates differ as a function of the type of substance used [113]. Unsuccessful quit attempts may be due in part to treatment providers' misperception that smoking cessation adversely affects SUD treatment [114]. On the contrary, quitting smoking predicts favorable substance use outcomes [115]. Indeed, the National Institutes of Health stress the benefits of quitting smoking for people with SUDs [28, 106]. Despite this, SUD treatment facilities have tended to deprioritize tobacco use treatment [114, 116, 117]. This is problematic given that people with SUDs are more likely to die from tobacco-related complications than other drug-related causes [118, 119]. In a recent systematic review of smoking cessation treatment among individuals with SUDs, NRT, cognitive behavioral strategies, contingency management, and combinations of the preceding all showed evidence of increasing abstinence, although from a modestly sized evidence base [120]. Given the substantial comorbidity, treatment of tobacco use disorder should be an available component of all substance use disorder treatment programs.

These are by no means the only significantly elevated forms of comorbidity. Rates of anxiety disorders, affective disorders, and ADHD are also significantly elevated among smokers [2, 121, 122]. In general, the results suggest smoking cessation interventions targeting the general population have not worked as effectively for persons with comorbid conditions, and developing higher-intensity combinations of existing strategies and novel interventions will be essential for improving success rates. This is particularly important because the general population trends toward declines in smoking have not been realized among individuals with psychiatric disorders [106], meaning that the overall smoker population is becoming more psychiatrically complicated over time.

Independent of concurrent psychiatric conditions, another important clinical consideration is weight gain. It is well documented that people who stop smoking gain weight, with a recent meta-analysis suggesting an average of 4–5 kg (~10 lbs) after one year of abstinence [123]. Smoking for weight control is a motive for tobacco use [124], and fear of weight gain could deter individuals from initiating or persisting in smoking cessation [125], despite the benefits of smoking cessation robustly exceeding the health risks owing to weight gain [123, 126–128]. Importantly, however, there are ambiguities in this relationship. Concerns about weight gain may be specific to female smokers [129], and some large studies have not found weight gain to be a risk factor for relapse [130]. Among individuals for whom it is a concern, there are a number of strategies to address it. The combination of smoking cessation and weight management treatment has been shown to positively affect both outcomes in the short-term, albeit with no long-term synergistic effects [131]. In addition, a Cochrane review determined NRT, bupropion, and varenicline marginally reduced weight gain following smoking cessation [123]. Two further considerations are that it is important to note that not all patients gain weight [123], and it appears that weight may recalibrate compared to nonsmokers after long-term cessation [132, 133]. Collectively, the reality of post-cessation weight gain for many patients suggests that clinicians should at least inform patients of a range of cessation-induced weight gain, but would also be wise to evaluate the extent to which smoking is used for weight management, the patient's perspectives on weight gain, and the need for combined smoking cessation and weight management treatment.

Conclusions and Future Directions

The contemporary state of treatment for tobacco use disorder juxtaposes sobering realities with substantial reasons for optimism. On the one hand, the morbidity, mortality, and economic burden of smoking remains immense, and controlled intervention research suggests that even with the most efficacious treatments, long-term success for any single quit attempt is the exception, not the rule. On the other hand, there are an array of efficacious strategies that have been developed, both psychological and pharmacological, and the use of these strategies increases a person's chance for success substantially, increasing rates of success up to fourfold by some estimates [10]. To be sure, there are no silver bullets among the treatments reviewed, but the evidence-informed clinician has a diverse toolkit available to maximize the probability of success. In terms of integration, rather than specific combinations of approaches, the evidence suggests "more is better," defining more as intensive behavioral treatment (≥ 4 sessions) and using both behavioral and pharmacological treatment, at least combining multiple forms of NRT and possibly combining other pharmacotherapies. In addition, thorough idiographic assessment of the patient's presentation is recommended to reveal the specific domains that need to be addressed.

Fundamentally, however, there is substantial progress that remains to be made. There is clearly a need for novel additional psychological strategies and medications. There has been discussion of tailoring treatment to the individual patient for some time [134], but relatively little empirical work on specific strategies or algorithms to do so. Stepped care, or escalating treatment based on initial response, has promise [135], but has only begun to be explored. Personalized medicine by leveraging psychological (e.g., motivational or self-regulatory profiles) and biological markers (e.g., metabolic indices or genetic markers) has great promise [136–138], but is in its infancy. Relatedly, whether more truly is better or whether there are optimal combinations of active ingredients remains an open empirical question. Finally, with regard to populations with comorbid conditions, there is a need to move beyond establishing the viability of the standard practices to developing maximally efficacious high-intensity regimens. Ultimately, progress will need to be made on each of these fronts to substantially improve smoking cessation success for individual patients and at the population level.

References

1. Gowing LR, Ali RL, Allsop S, et al. Global statistics on addictive behaviours: 2014 status report. *Addiction.* 2015;110:904–919. doi:10.1111/add.12899.
2. Breslau N. Psychiatric comorbidity of smoking and nicotine dependence. *Behav Genet.* 1995;25:95–101.
3. Grant BF, Hasin DS, Chou SP, et al. Nicotine dependence and psychiatric disorders in the United States: results from the national epidemiologic survey on alcohol and related conditions. *Arch Gen Psychiatry.* 2004;61:1107–1115. doi:61/11/1107 [pii] 10.1001/archpsyc.61.11.1107.
4. Author is Department of Health and Human Services (DHHS). *The health consequences of smoking—50 years of progress: a report of the surgeon general.* Atlanta (GA): DHHS; 2014.
5. Doll R, Peto R, Boreham J, Sutherland I. Mortality in relation to smoking: 50 years' observations on male British doctors. *BMJ.* 2004;328:1519. doi:10.1136/bmj.38142.554479.AE.
6. Xu X, Bishop EE, Kennedy SM, et al. Annual healthcare spending attributable to cigarette smoking: an update. *Am J Prev Med.* 2015;48:326–333. doi:10.1016/j.amepre.2014.10.012.
7. Center for Disease Control. Quitting smoking among adults—United States, 2001–2010. *Morb Mortal Wkly Rep.* 2011;60:1513–1519.

Table 5.2 Summary table

KEY RESEARCH FINDINGS
1. Smoking and the psychiatric condition of tobacco use disorder remain highly prevalent.
2. Smoking is among the largest preventable causes of morbidity and mortality worldwide.
3. Although population-level declines are present in the developed world, these trends are attenuated among individuals of low socioeconomic status.
4. Tobacco use disorder is commonly comorbid with other psychiatric disorders; smokers are significantly more likely to meet criteria for a number of conditions and, among patient groups with other conditions, the prevalence of smoking is significantly higher.
5. Common comorbidities include other substance use disorders, schizophrenia/schizoaffective disorder, and major depressive disorder.

RECOMMENDATIONS FOR EVIDENCE-BASED PRACTICE
1. All clinicians who interact with ambulatory smokers should provide minimal contact interventions (i.e., the Five As).
2. Face-to-face psychological treatment has been found to be efficacious, both individually and in groups; more than four sessions is associated with better outcomes.
3. Efficacious ingredients in psychological treatment include motivational interviewing and cognitive behavioral strategies.
4. Contingency management has shown short-term efficacy.
5. All patients should be treated with first-line pharmacotherapies (i.e., nicotine replacement therapy [NRT], varenicline, bupropion).
6. NRT is efficacious and well tolerated; combination NRT generates superior outcomes to single-modality NRT.
7. Varenicline is associated with the highest efficacy, but has a more significant side effect profile; however, concerns about neuropsychiatric and cardiovascular side effects have not been supported in controlled studies.
8. Bupropion and cytisine are also efficacious medications, although the latter is not widely available.
9. The risks and benefits of e-cigarettes are not well understood and use in clinical practice would be premature.
10. Combined psychological and pharmacological treatment optimizes outcomes.

RECOMMENDATIONS FOR FUTURE RESEARCH
1. Novel psychological and pharmacological treatments are needed to improve treatment response.
2. Empirical investigation of tailoring and integration strategies is warranted.
3. Personalization using psychological or biological profiles has promise for optimizing outcome.

8. Chaloupka FJ, Straif K, Leon ME. Effectiveness of tax and price policies in tobacco control. *Tob Control.* 2010. doi:tc.2010.039982 [pii] 10.1136/tc.2010.039982.
9. Fiore MC, Jaen CR, Baker TB, et al. *Treating tobacco use and dependence: 2008 update.* Clinical Practice Guideline. Rockville (MD): US Department lf Healthy and Human Services. Publich Health Service; May 2008.
10. West R, Raw M, McNeill A, et al. Healthcare interventions to promote and assist tobacco cessation: a review of efficacy, effectiveness and affordability for use in national guideline development. *Addiction.* 2015;110:1388–1403. doi:10.1111/add.12998.
11. Heckman CJ, Egleston BL, Hofmann MT. Systematic review and meta-analysis. *Efficacy.* 2011;19:410–416. doi:10.1136/tc.2009.033175.
12. Lindson-Hawley N, Thompson TP, Begh R. Motivational interviewing for smoking cessation. *Cochrane Database Syst Rev.* 2015;3:CD006936. doi:10.1002/14651858.CD006936.pub3.
13. Miller WR, Rose GS. Toward a theory of motivational interviewing. *Am Psychol.* 2009;64:527–537. doi:10.1037/a0016830.
14. Miller WR, Rollnick S. *Motivational interviewing: helping people change.* 3rd ed. New York: Guilford Press; 2012.
15. Song F, Huttunen-Lenz M, Holland R. Effectiveness of complex psycho-educational interventions for smoking relapse prevention: an exploratory meta-analysis. *J Public Health (Oxf).* 2010;32:350–359. doi:10.1093/pubmed/fdp109.
16. Hajek P, Stead LF, West R, et al. Relapse prevention interventions for smoking cessation. *Cochrane Database Syst Rev.* 2013;8:CD003999. doi:10.1002/14651858.CD003999.pub4.
17. Ledgerwood DM, Arfken CL, Petry NM, Alessi SM. Prize contingency management for smoking cessation: a randomized trial. *Drug Alcohol Depend.* 2014;140:208–212. doi:10.1016/j.drugalcdep.2014.03.032.
18. Halpern SD, French B, Small DS, et al. Randomized trial of four financial-incentive programs for smoking cessation. *N Engl J Med.* 2015;372:2108–2117. doi:10.1056/NEJMoa1414293.
19. Ledgerwood DM. Contingency management for smoking cessation: where do we go from here? *Curr Drug Abuse Rev.* 2008;1:340–349.
20. Cahill K, Hartmann-Boyce J, Perera R. Incentives for smoking cessation. *Cochrane Database Syst Rev.* 2015;5:CD004307. doi:10.1002/14651858.CD004307.pub5.
21. Stead LF, Perera R, Bullen C, et al. Nicotine replacement therapy for smoking cessation. *Cochrane Database Syst Rev.* 2012. doi:10.1002/14651858.CD000146.pub3.
22. Cahill K, Stevens S, Perera R, Lancaster T. Pharmacological interventions for smoking cessation: an overview and network meta-analysis. *Cochrane Database Syst Rev.* 2013;5:CD009329. doi:10.1002/14651858.CD009329.pub2.
23. Mills EJ, Wu P, Lockhart I, et al. Adverse events associated with nicotine replacement therapy (NRT) for smoking cessation: a systematic review and meta-analysis of one hundred and twenty studies involving 177,390 individuals. *Tob Induc Dis.* 2010;8:1–15.
24. Mills EJ, Thorlund K, Eapen S, et al. Cardiovascular events associated with smoking cessation pharmacotherapies: a network meta-analysis. *Circulation.* 2014;129:28–41. doi:10.1161/CIRCULATIONAHA.113.003961.
25. Sharma A, Thakar S, Lavie CJ, et al. Cardiovascular adverse events associated with smoking-cessation pharmacotherapies. *Curr Cardiol Rep.* 2015;17:554. doi:10.1007/s11886-014-0554-8.

26. Croghan IT, Hurt RD, Dakhil SR, et al. Randomized comparison of a nicotine inhaler and bupropion for smoking cessation and relapse prevention. *Mayo Clin Proc.* 2007;82:186–195. doi:10.4065/82.2.186.
27. Murray RP, Bailey WC, Daniels K, et al. Gum used safety of nicotine polacrilex by 3,094 participants in the lung health study. *Chest.* 1996;109:438–445.
28. Hall SM, Humfleet GL, Muñoz RF, et al. Extended treatment of older cigarette smokers. *Addiction.* 2009;104:1043–1052. doi:10.1111/j.1360-0443.2009.02548.x.
29. Joseph AM, Fu SS, Lindgren B, et al. Chronic disease management for tobacco dependence. *Arch Intern Med.* 2011;171:1894–1900.
30. Schnoll RA, Goelz PM, Veluz-Wilkins A, et al. Long-term nicotine replacement therapy: a randomized clinical trial. *JAMA Intern Med.* 2015;175:504–511. doi:10.1001/jamainternmed.2014.8313.
31. Rose JE, Herskovic JE, Behm FM, Westman EC. Precessation treatment with nicotine patch significantly increases abstinence rates relative to conventional treatment. *Nicotine Tob Res.* 2009;11:1067–1075. doi:10.1093/ntr/ntp103.
32. Rose JE, Behm FM, Westman EC, Kukovich P. Precessation treatment with nicotine skin patch facilitates smoking cessation. *Nicotine Tob Res.* 2006;8:89–101. doi:10.1080/14622200500431866.
33. Etter J, Huguelet P, Perneger T, Cornuz J. Nicotine gum treatment before smoking cessation: a randomized trial. *Arch Intern Med.* 2009;169:1025–1034. doi:10.1001/archinternmed.2009.12.
34. Mihalak KB, Carroll FI, Luetje CW. Varenicline is a partial agonist at alpha4beta2 and a full agonist at alpha7 neuronal nicotinic receptors. *Mol Pharmacol.* 2006;70:801–805. doi:10.1124/mol.106.025130.
35. Coe JW, Brooks PR, Vetelino MG, et al. Varenicline: an alpha4beta2 nicotinic receptor partial agonist for smoking cessation. *J Med Chem.* 2005;48:3474–3477. doi:10.1021/jm050069n.
36. Arias HR, Feuerbach D, Targowska-Duda K, et al. Pharmacological and molecular studies on the interaction of varenicline with different nicotinic acetylcholine receptor subtypes: potential mechanism underlying partial agonism at human α4β2 and α3β4 subtypes. *Biochim Biophys Acta.* 2015;1848:731–741. doi:10.1016/j.bbamem.2014.11.003.
37. Kasza KA, Cummings KM, Carpenter MJ, et al. Use of stop-smoking medications in the United States before and after the introduction of varenicline. *Addiction.* 2015;110:346–355. doi:10.1111/add.12778.
38. Agboola SA, Coleman T, McNeill A, Leonardi-Bee J. Abstinence and relapse among smokers who use varenicline in a quit attempt: a pooled analysis of randomized controlled trials. *Addiction.* 2015;110:1182–1193. doi:10.1111/add.12941.
39. Mills EJ, Wu P, Lockhart I, et al. Comparisons of high-dose and combination nicotine replacement therapy, varenicline, and bupropion for smoking cessation: a systematic review and multiple treatment meta-analysis. *Ann Med.* 2012;44:588–597.
40. Chang PH, Chiang CH, Ho WC, et al. Combination therapy of varenicline with nicotine replacement therapy is better than varenicline alone: a systematic review and meta-analysis of randomized controlled trials. *BMC Public Health.* 2015;15:689. doi:10.1186/s12889-015-2055-0.
41. Vogeler T, McClain C, Evoy KE. Combination bupropion SR and varenicline for smoking cessation: a systematic review. *Am J Drug Alcohol Abuse.* 2016;42(2):129–139. doi:10.3109/00952990.2015.1117480.

42. United States Food and Drug Administration. *Information for healthcare professionals: varenicline (marketed as Chantix) and bupropion (marketed as Zyban, Wellbutrin, and generics)*. Washington (DC): United States Food and Drug Administration; 2009.
43. Thomas KH, Martin RM, Knipe DW, et al. Risk of neuropsychiatric adverse events associated with varenicline: systematic review and meta-analysis. *BMJ*. 2015;350:h1109. doi:10.1136/bmj.h1109.
44. Prochaska JJ, Hilton JF. Risk of cardiovascular serious adverse events associated with varenicline use for tobacco cessation: systematic review and meta-analysis. *BMJ*. 2012;344:e2856. doi:10.1136/bmj.e2856.
45. Ware JH, Vetrovec GW, Miller AB, et al. Cardiovascular safety of varenicline: patient-level meta-analysis of randomized, blinded, placebo-controlled trials. *Am J Ther*. 2013;20:235–246.
46. Leung LK, Patafio FM, Rosser WW. Gastrointestinal adverse effects of varenicline at maintenance dose: a meta-analysis. *BMC Clin Pharmacol*. 2011;11:15. doi:10.1186/1472-6904-11-15.
47. Dwoskin LP, Rauhut AS, King-Pospisil KA, Bardo MT. Review of the pharmacology and clinical profile of bupropion, an antidepressant and tobacco use cessation agent. *CNS Drug Rev*. 2006;12:178–207. doi:10.1111/j.1527-3458.2006.00178.x.
48. Thase ME, Haight BR, Richard N, et al. Remission rates following antidepressant therapy with bupropion or selective serotonin reuptake inhibitors: a meta-analysis of original data from 7 randomized controlled trials. *J Clin Psychiatry*. 2005;66:974–981.
49. Cahill K, Stevens S, Lancaster T. Pharmacological treatments for smoking cessation. *JAMA*. 2014;311:193–194. doi:10.1001/jama.2013.283787.
50. West R, Baker CL, Cappelleri JC, Bushmakin AG. Effect of varenicline and bupropion SR on craving, nicotine withdrawal symptoms, and rewarding effects of smoking during a quit attempt. *Psychopharmacology (Berl)*. 2008;197:371–377. doi:10.1007/s00213-007-1041-3.
51. Cryan JF, Bruijnzeel AW, Skjei KL, Markou A. Bupropion enhances brain reward function and reverses the affective and somatic aspects of nicotine withdrawal in the rat. *Psychopharmacology (Berl)*. 2003;168:347–358. doi:10.1007/s00213-003-1445-7.
52. Lerman C, Roth D, Kaufmann V, et al. Mediating mechanisms for the impact of bupropion in smoking cessation treatment. *Drug Alcohol Depend*. 2002;67:219–223. doi:10.1016/S0376-8716(02)00067-4.
53. Hughes JR, Stead LF, Hartmann-Boyce J, Cahill K, Lancaster T. Antidepressants for smoking cessation. *Cochrane Database Syst Rev*. 2014;8(1):CD000031. doi:10.1002/14651858.CD000031.pub4.
54. Jorenby DE, Leischow SJ, Nides MA, et al. A controlled trial of sustained-release bupropion, a nicotine patch, or both for smoking cessation. *N Engl J Med*. 1999;340:685–691.
55. Hurt RD, Sachs DP, Glover ED, et al. A comparison of sustained-release bupropion and placebo for smoking cessation. *N Engl J Med*. 1997;337:1195–1202.
56. FDA. *Public health advisory: FDA requires new boxed warnings for smoking cessation drugs Chantix and Zyban*. Washington (DC): Food and Drug Administration; 2009.
57. European Agency for the Evaluation of Medicines for Human Use. *Opinion following an article 36 referral: bupropion hydrochloride*. London: European Agency for the Evaluation of Medicines for Human Use; 2002.

58. Dunner DL, Zisook S, Billow AA, et al. A prospective safety surveillance study for bupropion sustained-release in the treatment of depression. *J Clin Psychiatry*. 1998;59:366–373.
59. Tutka P, Zatoński W. Cytisine for the treatment of nicotine addiction: from a molecule to therapeutic efficacy. *Pharmacol Reports*. 2006;58:777–798.
60. Coe JW, Brooks PR, Vetelino MG, et al. Varenicline: an α4β2 nicotinic receptor partial agonist for smoking cessation. *J Med Chem*. 2005;48:3474–3477. doi:10.1021/jm050069n.
61. Jeong SH, Newcombe D, Sheridan J, Tingle M. Pharmacokinetics of cytisine, an α4β2 nicotinic receptor partial agonist, in healthy smokers following a single dose. *Drug Test Anal*. 2015;7:475–482. doi:10.1002/dta.1707.
62. Sopharma Pharmaceuticals. Tabex; 2016.
63. Hajek P, McRobbie H, Myers K. Efficacy of cytisine in helping smokers quit: systematic review and meta-analysis. *Thorax*. 2013;68:1037–1042. doi:10.1136/thoraxjnl-2012-203035.
64. Walker N, Howe C, Glover M, et al. Cytisine versus nicotine for smoking cessation. *N Engl J Med*. 2014;371:2353–2362. doi:10.1056/NEJMoa1407764.
65. Leaviss J, Sullivan W, Ren S, et al. What is the clinical effectiveness and cost-effectiveness of cytisine compared with varenicline for smoking cessation? A systematic review and economic evaluation. *Health Technol Assess (Rockv)*. 2014;18:1–119. doi:10.3310/hta18330.
66. Prochaska JJ, Benowitz NL. Smoking cessation and the cardiovascular patient. *Curr Opin Cardiol*. 2015;30:506–511. doi:10.1097/HCO.0000000000000204.
67. Zatonski W, Cedzynska M, Tutka P, West R. An uncontrolled trial of cytisine (Tabex) for smoking cessation. *Tob Control*. 2006;15:481–484. doi:10.1136/tc.2006.016097.
68. Carson KV, Brinn MP, Robertson TA, et al. Current and emerging pharmacotherapeutic options for smoking cessation. *Subst Abus Res Treat*. 2013;7:85–105. doi:10.4137/SART.S8108.
69. Elrashidi MY, Ebbert JO. Emerging drugs for the treatment of tobacco dependence: 2014 update. *Expert Opin Emerg Drugs*. 2014;19:243–260. doi:10.1517/14728214.2014.899580.
70. Robinson ESJ, Eagle DM, Mar AC, et al. Similar effects of the selective noradrenaline reuptake inhibitor atomoxetine on three distinct forms of impulsivity in the rat. *Neuropsychopharmacology*. 2008;33:1028–1037. doi:10.1038/sj.npp.1301487.
71. Sun H, Cocker PJ, Zeeb FD, Winstanley CA. Chronic atomoxetine treatment during adolescence decreases impulsive choice, but not impulsive action, in adult rats and alters markers of synaptic plasticity in the orbitofrontal cortex. *Psychopharmacology (Berl)*. 2012;219:285–301. doi:10.1007/s00213-011-2419-9.
72. Turner M, Wilding E, Cassidy E, Dommett EJ. Effects of atomoxetine on locomotor activity and impulsivity in the spontaneously hypertensive rat. *Behav Brain Res*. 2013;243:28–37. doi:10.1016/j.bbr.2012.12.025.
73. MacKillop J, Kahler CW. Delayed reward discounting predicts treatment response for heavy drinkers receiving smoking cessation treatment. *Drug Alcohol Depend*. 2009;104:197–203. doi:S0376-8716(09)00174-4 [pii] 10.1016/j.drugalcdep.2009.04.020.
74. Krishnan-Sarin S, Reynolds B, Duhig AM, et al. Behavioral impulsivity predicts treatment outcome in a smoking cessation program for adolescent smokers. *Drug Alcohol Depend*. 2007;88:79–82. doi:10.1016/j.drugalcdep.2006.09.006.

75. Sheffer C, MacKillop J, McGeary J, et al. Delay discounting, locus of control, and cognitive impulsiveness independently predict tobacco dependence treatment outcomes in a highly dependent, lower socioeconomic group of smokers. *Am J Addict.* 2012;21:221–232. doi:10.1111/j.1521-0391.2012.00224.x.
76. David SP, Chu IM, Lancaster T, et al. Systematic review and meta-analysis of opioid antagonists for smoking cessation. *BMJ Open.* 2014;4:e004393. doi:10.1136/bmjopen-2013-004393.
77. Goniewicz ML, Kuma T, Gawron M, et al. Nicotine levels in electronic cigarettes. *Nicotine Tob Res.* 2013;15:158–166. doi:10.1093/ntr/nts103.
78. Grana R, Benowitz N, Glantz SA. E-cigarettes: a scientific review. *Circulation.* 2014;129:1972–1986. doi:10.1161/CIRCULATIONAHA.114.007667.
79. Rahman MA, Hann N, Wilson A, Worrall-Carter L. Electronic cigarettes: patterns of use, health effects, use in smoking cessation and regulatory issues. *Tob Induc Dis.* 2014;12:21.
80. Wu Q, Jiang D, Minor M, Chu HW. Electronic cigarette liquid increases inflammation and virus infection in primary human airway epithelial cells. *PLoS One.* 2014. doi:10.1371/journal.pone.0108342.
81. Jensen RP, Wentai LB, Pankow JF, et al. Hidden formaldehyde in e-cigarette aerosols. *N Engl J Med.* 2015;3724:392–394. doi:10.1056/NEJMc1413069.
82. Rowell TR, Tarran R. Will chronic e-cigarette use cause lung disease? *Am J Physiol Lung Cell Mol Physiol.* 2015. doi: 10.1152/ajplung.00272.2015.
83. Williams M, Villarreal A, Bozhilov K, et al. Metal and silicate particles including nanoparticles are present in electronic cigarette cartomizer fluid and aerosol. *PLoS One.* 2013. doi:10.1371/journal.pone.0057987.
84. Crotty Alexander LE, Vyas A, Schraufnagel DE, Malhotra A. Electronic cigarettes: the new face of nicotine delivery and addiction. *J Thorac Dis.* 2015;7:E248–E251. doi:10.3978/j.issn.2072-1439.2015.07.37.
85. Bullen C, Howe C, Laugesen M, et al. Electronic cigarettes for smoking cessation: a randomised controlled trial. *Lancet.* 2013;382:1629–1637. doi:10.1016/S0140-6736(13)61842-5.
86. Harrell PT, Marquinez NS, Correa JB, et al. Expectancies for cigarettes, e-cigarettes, and nicotine replacement therapies among e-cigarette users (aka vapers). *Nicotine Tob Res.* 2015;17:193–200. doi:10.1093/ntr/ntu149.
87. Fairchild AL, Bayer R, Colgrove J. The renormalization of smoking? E-cigarettes and the tobacco "endgame". *N Engl J Med.* 2014;370:293–295.
88. Adkison SE, O'Connor RJ, Bansal-Travers M, et al. Electronic nicotine delivery systems: International Tobacco Control Four-Country Survey. *Am J Prev Med.* 2013;44:207–215. doi:10.1016/j.amepre.2012.10.018.
89. Vickerman KA, Carpenter KM, Altman T, et al. Use of electronic cigarettes among state tobacco cessation quitline callers. *Nicotine Tob Res.* 2013;15:1787–1791. doi:10.1093/ntr/ntt061.
90. Leventhal AM, Strong DR, Kirkpatrick MG, et al. Association of electronic cigarette use with initiation of combustible tobacco product smoking in early adolescence. *JAMA.* 2015;314:700. doi:10.1001/jama.2015.8950.
91. Lee S, Grana RA, Glantz SA. Electronic cigarette use among Korean adolescents: a cross-sectional study of market penetration, dual use, and relationship to quit attempts and former smoking. *J Adolesc Heal.* 2014;54:684–690. doi:10.1016/j.jadohealth.2013.11.003.

92. Farsalinos KE, Spyrou A, Stefopoulos C, et al. Nicotine absorption from electronic cigarette use: comparison between experienced consumers (vapers) and naïve users (smokers). *Sci Rep.* 2015;5:11269. doi:10.1038/srep11269.
93. Loh WY, Piper ME, Schlam TR, et al. Should all smokers use combination smoking cessation pharmacotherapy? Using novel analytic methods to detect differential treatment effects over 8 weeks of pharmacotherapy. *Nicotine Tob Res.* 2012;14:131–141. doi:10.1093/ntr/ntr147.
94. Grant BF, Hasin DS, Chou SP, et al. Nicotine dependence and psychiatric disorders in the United States: results from the national epidemiologic survey on alcohol and related conditions. *Arch Gen Psychiatry.* 2004;61:1107–1115. doi:10.1001/archpsyc.61.11.1107.
95. Lasser K, Boyd JW, Woolhandler S, et al. Smoking and mental illness. *JAMA.* 2000;284:2606. doi:10.1001/jama.284.20.2606.
96. McClave AK, McKnight-Eily LR, Davis SP, Dube SR. Smoking characteristics of adults with selected lifetime mental illnesses: results from the 2007 national health interview survey. *Am J Public Health.* 2010;100:2464–2472. doi:10.2105/AJPH.2009.188136.
97. (CDC) C for DC and P. Vital signs: current cigarette smoking among adults aged ≥18 years with mental illness—United States, 2009–2011. *MMWR Morb Mortal Wkly Rep.* 2013;62:81–87.
98. Kessler RC, Chiu WT, Demler O, Walters EE. Prevalence, severity, and comorbidity of 12-month DSM-IV disorders in the National Comorbidity Survey Replication. *Arch Gen Psychiatry.* 2005;62:617–627. doi:10.1001/archpsyc.62.6.617.
99. Borrelli B, Niaura R, Keuthen NJ, et al. Development of major depressive disorder during smoking-cessation treatment. *J Clin Psychiatry.* 1996;57:534–538.
100. Kinnunen T, Doherty K, Militello F, Garvey A. Depression and smoking cessation: characteristics of depressed smokers and effects of nicotine replacement. *J Consult Clin Psychol.* 1996;64:791–798. doi:10.1037/0022-006X.64.4.791.
101. Niaura R, Britt DM, Borrelli B, et al. History and symptoms of depression among smokers during a self-initiated quit attempt. *Nicotine Tob Res.* 1999;1:251–257. doi:10.1080/14622299050011371.
102. Rigotti NA. Strategies to help a smoker who is struggling to quit. *JAMA.* 2012;308:1573–1580. doi:10.1001/jama.2012.13043.
103. Cerimele JM, Halperin AC, Saxon AJ. Tobacco use treatment in primary care patients with psychiatric illness. *J Am Board Fam Med.* 2014;27:399–410. doi:10.3122/jabfm.2014.03.130252.
104. Smith PH, Homish GG, Giovino GA, Kozlowski LT. Cigarette smoking and mental illness: a study of nicotine withdrawal. *Am J Public Health.* 2014. doi:10.2105/AJPH.2013.301502.
105. Evins AE, Cather C, Pratt SA, et al. Maintenance treatment with varenicline for smoking cessation in patients with schizophrenia and bipolar disorder: a randomized clinical trial. *JAMA.* 2014;311:145–154. doi:10.1001/jama.2013.285113.
106. Cook BL, Wayne GF, Kafali EN, et al. Trends in smoking among adults with mental illness and association between mental health treatment and smoking cessation. *JAMA.* 2014;311:172–182. doi:10.1001/jama.2013.284985.
107. Kroon LA. Drug interactions with smoking. *Am J Heal Pharm.* 2007;64:1917–1921. doi:10.2146/ajhp060414.

108. Lasser K, Boyd JW, Woolhandler S, et al. Smoking and mental illness: a population-based prevalence study. *JAMA*. 2000;284:2606–2610. doi:joc00268 [pii].
109. De Leon J, Diaz FJ. A meta-analysis of worldwide studies demonstrates an association between schizophrenia and tobacco smoking behaviors. *Schizophr Res*. 2005;76:135–157. doi:S0920-9964(05)00075-7 [pii] 10.1016/j.schres.2005.02.010.
110. Brown S, Inskip H, Barraclough B. Causes of the excess mortality of schizophrenia. *Br J Psychiatry*. 2000;177:212–217.
111. Bushe CJ, Taylor M, Haukka J. Mortality in schizophrenia: a measurable clinical endpoint. *J Psychopharmacol*. 2010;24:17–25. doi:10.1177/1359786810382468.
112. Evins AE, Cather C. Effective cessation strategies for smokers with schizophrenia. *Int Rev Neurobiol*. 2015;124:133–147. doi:10.1016/bs.irn.2015.08.001.
113. Guydish J, Passalacqua E, Pagano A, et al. An international systematic review of smoking prevalence in addiction treatment. *Addiction*. 2015. doi:10.1111/add.13099.
114. Guydish J, Passalacqua E, Tajima B, Manser ST. Staff smoking and other barriers to nicotine dependence intervention in addiction treatment settings: a review. *J Psychoactive Drugs*. 2007;39:423–433. doi:10.1080/02791072.2007.10399881.
115. Tsoh JY, Chi FW, Mertens JR, Weisner CM. Stopping smoking during first year of substance use treatment predicted 9-year alcohol and drug treatment outcomes. *Drug Alcohol Depend*. 2011;114:110–118. doi:10.1016/j.drugalcdep.2010.09.008.
116. Currie SR, Nesbitt K, Wood C, Lawson A. Survey of smoking cessation services in Canadian addiction programs. *J Subst Abuse Treat*. 2003;24:59–65. doi:10.1016/S0740-5472(02)00344-6.
117. Prochaska JJ, Fletcher L, Hall SE, Hall SM. Return to smoking following a smoke-free psychiatric hospitalization. *Am J Addict*. 2006;15:15–22. doi:10.1080/10550490500419011.
118. Hser YI, McCarthy WJ, Anglin MD. Tobacco use as a distal predictor of mortality among long-term narcotics addicts. *Prev Med (Baltim)*. 1994;23:61–69. doi:10.1006/pmed.1994.1009.
119. Hurt RD, Offord KP, Croghan IT, et al. Mortality following inpatient addictions treatment: role of tobacco use in a community-based cohort. *JAMA*. 1996;275:1097–1103. doi:10.1001/jama.275.14.1097.
120. Thurgood SL, McNeill A, Clark-Carter D, Brose LS. A systematic review of smoking cessation interventions for adults in substance abuse treatment or recovery. *Nicotine Tob Res*. 2016;18:993–1001. doi:10.1093/ntr/ntv127.
121. Goodwin RD, Zvolensky MJ, Keyes KM, Hasin DS. Mental disorders and cigarette use among adults in the United States. *Am J Addict*. 2012;21:416–423. doi:10.1111/j.1521-0391.2012.00263.x.
122. Capusan AJ, Bendtsen P, Marteinsdottir I, Larsson H. Comorbidity of adult ADHD and its subtypes with substance use disorder in a large population-based epidemiological study. *J Atten Disord*. 2016. doi:10.1177/1087054715626511.
123. Aubin HJ, Farley A, Lycett D, et al. Weight gain in smokers after quitting cigarettes: meta-analysis. *BMJ*. 2012;345:e4439.
124. Borrelli B, Mermelstein R. The role of weight concern and self-efficacy in smoking cessation and weight gain among smokers in a clinic-based cessation program. *Addict Behav*. 1998;23:609–622.
125. Clark MM, Hurt RD, Croghan IT, et al. The prevalence of weight concerns in a smoking abstinence clinical trial. *Addict Behav*. 2006;31:1144–1152. doi:10.1016/j.addbeh.2005.08.011.

126. Koster A, Leitzmann MF, Schatzkin A, et al. The combined relations of adiposity and smoking on mortality. *Am J Clin Nutr.* 2008;88:1206–1212. doi:10.3945/ajcn.2008.26298.
127. Rom O, Reznick AZ, Keidar Z, et al. Smoking cessation-related weight gain-beneficial effects on muscle mass, strength and bone health. *Addiction.* 2015;110:326–335. doi:10.1111/add.12761.
128. Chinn S, Jarvis D, Melotti R, et al. Smoking cessation, lung function, and weight gain: a follow-up study. *Lancet.* 2005;365:1629–1635. doi:10.1016/S0140-6736(05)66511-7.
129. Jeffery RW, Hennrikus DJ, Lando HA, et al. Reconciling conflicting findings regarding postcessation weight concerns and success in smoking cessation. *Health Psychol.* 2000;19:242–246.
130. Zhou X, Nonnemaker J, Sherrill B, et al. Attempts to quit smoking and relapse: factors associated with success or failure from the ATTEMPT cohort study. *Addict Behav.* 2009;34:365–373. doi:10.1016/j.addbeh.2008.11.013.
131. Spring B, Howe D, Berendsen M, et al. Behavioral intervention to promote smoking cessation and prevent weight gain: a systematic review and meta-analysis. *Addiction.* 2009;104:1472–1486. doi:10.1111/j.1360-0443.2009.02610.x.
132. Mizoue T, Ueda R, Tokui N, et al. Body mass decrease after initial gain following smoking cessation. *Int J Epidemiol.* 1998;27:984–988.
133. Munafò MR, Tilling K, Ben-Shlomo Y. Smoking status and body mass index: a longitudinal study. *Nicotine Tob Res.* 2009;11:765–771. doi:10.1093/ntr/ntp062.
134. Niaura R, Abrams DB. Smoking cessation: progress, priorities, and prospectus. *J Consult Clin Psychol.* 2002;70:494–509.
135. Effectiveness of a stepped primary care smoking cessation intervention: cluster randomized clinical trial (ISTAPS study)—PubMed—NCBI. Available from: www.ncbi.nlm.nih.gov/pubmed/21561497.
136. King DP, Paciga S, Pickering E, et al. Smoking cessation pharmacogenetics: analysis of varenicline and bupropion in placebo-controlled clinical trials. *Neuropsychopharmacology.* 2012;37:641–650. doi:10.1038/npp.2011.232.
137. Chen LS, Bloom AJ, Baker TB, et al. Pharmacotherapy effects on smoking cessation vary with nicotine metabolism gene (CYP2A6). *Addiction.* 2014;109:128–137. doi:10.1111/add.12353.
138. Shiffman S, West R, Gilbert D. Recommendation for the assessment of tobacco craving and withdrawal in smoking cessation trials. *Nicotine Tob Res.* 2004;6:599–614. doi:10.1080/14622200410001734067.
139. Heatherton TF, Kozlowski LT, Frecker RC, Fagerstom KO. The Fagerstrom Test for Nicotine Dependence: a revision of the Fagerstrom Tolerance Questionnaire. *Addiction.* 1991;86:1119–1127. doi:10.1111/j.1360-0443.1991.tb01879.x.
140. Zimmerman GL, Olsen CG, Bosworth MF. A "stages of change" approach to helping patients change behavior. *Am Fam Physician.* 2000;61:1409–1416.
141. Piper ME, Piasecki TM, Federman EB, et al. A multiple motives approach to tobacco dependence: the Wisconsin Inventory of Smoking Dependence Motives (WISDM-68). *J Consult Clin Psychol.* 2004;72:139–154. doi:10.1037/0022-006X.72.2.139 2004-12113-001 [pii].
142. Smith SS, Piper ME, Bolt DM, et al. Development of the brief Wisconsin Inventory of Smoking Dependence Motives. *Nicotine Tob Res.* 2010;12:489–499. doi:10.1093/ntr/ntq032.

143. Etter JF, Bergman MM, Humair JP, Perneger TV. Development and validation of a scale measuring self-efficacy of current and former smokers. *Addiction.* 2000;95:901–913.
144. Tiffany ST, Drobes DJ. The development and initial validation of a questionnaire on smoking urges. *Br J Addict.* 1991;86:1467–1476.
145. Cox LS, Tiffany ST, Christen AG. Evaluation of the brief questionnaire of smoking urges (QSU-brief) in laboratory and clinical settings. *Nicotine Tob Res.* 2001;3:7–16. doi:10.1080/14622200020032051.
146. Hitsman B, Shen BJ, Cohen RA, et al. Measuring smoking-related preoccupation and compulsive drive: evaluation of the obsessive compulsive smoking scale. *Psychopharmacology (Berl).* 2010;211:377–387. doi:10.1007/s00213-010-1910-z.
147. Kahler CW, Lachance HR, Strong DR, et al. The commitment to quitting smoking scale: initial validation in a smoking cessation trial for heavy social drinkers. *Addict Behav.* 2007;32:2420–2424. doi:10.1016/j.addbeh.2007.04.002.
148. Biochemical verification of tobacco use and cessation. *Nicotine Tob Res.* 2002; 4:149–159. doi:10.1080/14622200210123581.
149. Hartmann-Boyce, J., McRobbie, H., Bullen, C., Begh, R., Stead, L. F., & Hajek, P. Electronic cigarettes for smoking cessation. *Cochrane Database Syst Rev.* 2016 Sep 14;9:CD010216.
150. Kalkhoran, S., & Glantz, S. A. E-cigarettes and smoking cessation in real-world and clinical settings: a systematic review and meta-analysis. *The Lancet Respiratory Medicine.* 2016;4(2):116–128.

Chapter 6

Opioid Use Disorder

Monica Bawor, Brittany Dennis, James MacKillop, and Zainab Samaan

Introduction

Opioid use disorder (OUD) is a chronic relapsing disease and a major source of morbidity and mortality worldwide [1]. OUD is characterized by DSM-5 as a problematic pattern of opioid consumption causing significant impairment in social and physical functioning within a one-year period [2]. OUD has replaced previously used diagnoses of opioid abuse and dependence, although these terms are widely used in the literature that predates DSM-5. Globally, OUD affects approximately 15 million individuals [3]. The rates of opioid abuse and diverson continue to rise, and recent estimates suggest 25 million individuals initated using illicit opioids over the nine-year period between 2002 and 2011 [4]. Parallel to increasing opioid use, opioid-related mortality rates have increased steadily, such that the World Health Organization (WHO) estimates 69,000 people die from opioid overdose each year [3]. Patients with OUD are also at high risk of HIV [5], hepatitis [5], and cardiac disease, such as infective endocarditis [6, 7]. Finally, individuals with OUD are subject to numerous psychiatric comorbidities and psychosocial challenges [8].

Several treatment modalities are available to treat OUD, including both psychosocial and pharmacological interventions. However, the establishment of effective interventions for the management of OUD is challenging due to the major lack of consensus over defining and measuring outcomes. A recent review of 60 randomized controlled trials assessing pharmacological therapies for OUD revealed overwhelming variability in the definition and measurement of the outcomes used to establish treatment effectives [9]. The majority of trials used diverse definitions, measurements, and time frames when assessing broader outcome domains. For instance, outcomes were defined as abstinence from opioid use, measured by either urine drug screen or self-report for periods varying from days to months; reduction in illicit opioid use by various percentages or cutoff values; or risk outcomes such as injecting behavior, among many other methods. Physical symptoms and psychosocial outcomes, as well as psychiatric health outcomes, were also defined and measured with large variability [9]. Such vast variability in the methods for defining and measuring treatment response highlights the difficulty in establishing evidence-based OUD treatment. These challenges notwithstanding, however, this chapter reviews the current treatment options for treating OUD that have the strongest basis in empirical evidence. In addition, strategies for integrating pharmacological and psychosocial treatments and special considerations within this population are discussed.

Evidence-Based Psychosocial Interventions

There is growing evidence supporting the therapeutic benefits for psychosocial interventions in the treatment of psychiatric and substance use disorders [10, 11]. Psychosocial interventions make use of specific psychological, behavioral, and social strategies to achieve a particular treatment goal, and can be implemented in inpatient, outpatient, or residential treatment settings. Evidence for the efficacy of psychosocial interventions as a stand-alone treatment strategy for the treatment of opioid use disorders is limited and largely based on observational studies [12], and therefore it is unclear whether they provide adequate therapeutic benefit when administered alone. Psychosocial interventions are most often evaluated in combination with a concurrent pharmacological treatment, typically opioid substitution therapy.

Cognitive Behavioral Therapy

Cognitive behavioral therapy (CBT) has been widely adapted for use in the treatment of substance use disorders [13, 14]. CBT for substance use disorders employs the use of social learning theory and principles of operant conditioning to help patients understand the psychological basis of their substance use and the consequences of their behavior through directed self-monitoring [15]. Patients learn to recognize situations in which they are most susceptible to engage in drug use, while making use of cognitive and behavioral strategies to actively deal with these circumstances [16, 17]. CBT can include a broad range of interventions, applicable in both individual and group formats, and administered using either standardized or idiographic approaches [15].

There are several variants of CBT, which can provide a range of options to choose from, and the flexibility to tailor an intervention to a specific individual and treatment goal [15]. This does, however, produce a fairly heterogeneous body of literature, which can pose a limitation in making evidence-based comparisons in systematic reviews of the effectiveness of CBT in OUD.

CBT is effective in reducing depressive symptoms compared to a discussion-type group intervention in the context of OUD [18] and in decreasing opioid use, as well as the risk of injecting behavior compared to methadone treatment alone [19, 20], among individuals receiving methadone maintenance treatment (MMT) for OUD. High-intensity CBT, including 30- to 40-minute sessions of relapse prevention, cognitive restructuring, and coping skills training for 26 weeks, was also shown to improve treatment completion among patients with OUD and chronic cocaine use treated with methadone [21]; however, there are conflicting findings with respect to treatment retention that suggest there is no additional benefit of CBT [20]. A meta-analysis of CBT for substance use disorders found evidence of significant positive acute, short-term, and long-term effects, but only a small number of opioid-focused studies were included [22]. Based on data from RCTs, CBT as an added therapy is effective in reducing illicit opioid use, comorbid depressive symptoms, and drug-related risk behavior in patients with OUD. When considering other treatment outcomes, the benefits of CBT in combination with pharmacological treatment are no greater than that of methadone or buprenorphine alone in abstinence, treatment retention, withdrawal symptoms, craving, other substance use, and sexual risk behavior [19, 21, 23, 24].

An alternative form of CBT is relapse prevention (RP) [25], and a meta-analysis comprised of 26 randomized and observational studies evaluating the effectiveness of RP revealed a moderate effect ($r = 0.014$, 95% confidence interval [CI] = 0.10 to 0.17, $k = 26$) in reducing substance use among patients with alcohol and polysubstance use disorders, but a more pronounced effect for improvement in overall psychosocial adjustment ($r = 0.48$, 95% CI = 0.42 to 0.53, $k = 10$) compared to primarily discussion-type and no-treatment controls [26]. The specific effect of RP in OUD was not examined. Like other forms of CBT, there is general but not specific support for RP in treating OUD.

Dialectical behavior therapy (DBT) is a well-established comprehensive cognitive behavioral program used particularly for borderline personality disorder [27]. It differs from standard CBT or RP for substance use disorders in that it is not specifically focused on substance use, but it shares cognitive behavioral foundations and an emphasis on skills training. The fundamental principle of DBT is to enhance quality of life, brought upon by the synthesis of two opposing goals: change and acceptance [28]. A specific version of DBT was developed for substance use disorders, incorporating concepts to encourage abstinence and reduce adverse events [29]. DBT can be provided in an inpatient or outpatient setting via individual therapy, group skills training, or telephone consultation [30].

The evidence for DBT in the treatment of substance use disorders is based on two RCTs, which showed a benefit for DBT in reducing opioid use, and improving global and social adjustment compared to baseline, as well as to other treatment conditions (treatment as usual or comprehensive validation therapy plus 12-step facilitation) [30, 31]. DBT, however, did not demonstrate any effect on treatment retention in OUD in either of these studies.

Although there have been positive changes associated with DBT with respect to reducing opioid use and improving social functioning, this has only been examined among two RCTs; therefore, more research is needed to substantiate these findings.

Overall, there is merit for administering CBT-based strategies in OUD patients with comorbid psychiatric disorders, especially for depression or anxiety [18]. However, the mixed results of the available studies, in addition to their small samples and methodological limitations, including the different outcome measures used, suggest that additional research may help to identify the limitations of CBT-based interventions and provide a consensus on measuring patient-important outcomes for more effective implementation in OUD.

Reinforcement-Based Treatment

Contingency management (CM) is a behavioral approach that borrows concepts from operant learning theory in order to promote abstinence from substances. This strategy employs positive reinforcement to encourage patients to meet their treatment goals. Patients are given the opportunity to receive payment, prizes, or take-home pharmacological maintenance doses if they comply with specified treatment criteria (e.g., drug-free urine screens, regular attendance at the clinic, abstinence from drugs over a given time period, etc.) [16]. Usually, a mutually agreed-upon behavioral contract is developed to ensure that both the patient and his or her treating clinician are aware of their obligations and potential consequences [32].

CM has been examined extensively in the treatment of OUD across various treatment conditions and utilizing different intervention models. Considering two separate meta-analyses, an overall reduction in opioid use was shown among patients in CM interventions compared to either MMT alone or a control condition [33, 34]. However, there appeared to be no additional effect of CM in decreasing opioid use among patients receiving buprenorphine maintenance treatment [24, 35]. There is also documented support from both meta-analyses and RCTs for the effectiveness of CM for increased short-term abstinence from opioids [36–39]. With respect to treatment retention, data from a 2011 Cochrane review by Amato and colleagues [16] indicated that CM, when added to pharmacotherapy, did not have any greater effect than pharmacotherapy alone in treatment retention. Several studies have also demonstrated the benefits of CM in reducing cocaine use among OUD patients receiving MMT [40–45]. Furthermore, CM has been implemented in detoxification settings (methadone and naltrexone), where it demonstrated efficacy in reducing opioid use and relapse, and improving treatment retention [46–49]. Data from RCTs and meta-analyses suggests that CM is an effective treatment intervention for OUD when used either in combination with methadone specifically or in detoxification settings.

Another variant of reinforcement-based treatment is the community reinforcement approach (CRA), which encourages patients to examine significant reinforcers in the major aspects of their lives and identify alternative positive and negative reinforcers and contingencies that will compete with their drug use [16]. Initially developed for the treatment of alcohol use disorder [50], it has been adapted for use in other substance use disorders. A systematic review of CRA and OUD [51] found two RCTs that evaluated treatment outcomes after CRA intervention [52, 53]. Among patients treated with methadone for OUD, CRA was found to increase opioid-negative urine screens compared to MMT alone, but showed no effect on treatment retention or injection drug use

[53]. In a buprenorphine detoxification setting, patients receiving CRA intervention with incentives demonstrated better treatment completion and greater likelihood of achieving eight consecutive weeks of abstinence from opioids compared to standard buprenorphine tapering [52]. Further observational comparison studies demonstrated efficacy in reducing the number of arrests when receiving maintenance treatment with naltrexone combined with intensive CRA versus methadone maintenance among heroin-dependent patients [54].

Although CRA is less commonly used compared to CM, the available literature supports its use as an adjunct to pharmacotherapy in the treatment of OUD for reducing opioid use and increasing treatment completion.

Motivational Interventions

Motivational enhancement therapy (MET) is a standardized intervention utilized in the treatment of substance use disorders, whereby patients are encouraged to strengthen their intrinsic motivation to facilitate change in drug-related thoughts and behavior [32]. It typically involves four structured sessions and is performed in an individual, patient-centered format [32]. Motivational interviewing (MI) is the precursor of MET, often consisting of a single brief treatment session, and is generally used in combination with other substance use treatment interventions (i.e., CBT, CM, pharmacological treatment) [55] for various substance use disorders. Manuals for administering motivational interventions for alcohol use disorders have been developed by the Project MATCH group in association with the National Institute on Alcohol Abuse and Alcoholism (NIAAA) [56]; however, they have yet to be specifically adapted for use in OUD.

A large Cochrane systematic review included 59 studies evaluating MI and MET interventions among 13,342 patients with alcohol and drug use disorders. Overall, they found a strong effect of motivational interviewing in reducing substance use post-intervention, although subgroup analyses based on specific substance of use were not performed [57]. Evidence from randomized trials showed that when MI was administered in combination with either CBT or MMT, patients reported less anxiety, fewer physical and emotional limitations and opioid-related problems, and had better compliance with the treatment regimen [58, 59]; however, studies found conflicting results regarding rates of relapse (either less frequent relapse in MI group [59], or no difference in relapse rates between groups [58]). Therefore, there is generally evidence supporting the use of MET or MI in OUD specifically when considering abstinence from opioids, relapse, or treatment retention, albeit not unequivocal.

Family/Couples Therapy

Both family therapy and behavioral couples therapy (BCT) are often used as a counseling approach to better cope with substance use disorders [60]. The basis of these therapeutic strategies relies on the assumption that the quality of relationships with a family member or significant other influences one's own substance use behavior, such that an individual is more likely to abuse drugs if their important relationships are causing them significant distress [60]. It also takes into consideration the effects that one's substance use problems has on family members and significant others [61]. This form of therapy incorporates psychoeducation, reinforcement contingencies for relationship contact, and participating in mutually pleasurable activities that discourage opportunities for engaging in drug use [61].

A meta-analysis of 15 RCTs has shown considerable support for higher treatment retention with family therapy compared to non-family therapy modalities, and is considered a cost-effective adjunct to MMT [62]. Data from a randomized trial also demonstrates positive changes in drug use, treatment attendance, and family management for individuals receiving a pharmacological treatment plus family skills training or behavioral family counseling [63, 64]. A systematic review and meta-analysis including 12 RCTs demonstrated a clear advantage of BCT compared to individual-based treatments in terms of drug use frequency and relationship satisfaction across both alcohol and substance use disorders [65]. There is also supporting evidence for a reduction in positive opioid and cocaine urine screens, as well as family and social problems for patients receiving intensive BCT in addition to MMT [66]. Given these findings, it is likely that including BCT or an alternative family-focused intervention into the treatment regimen for OUD will produce positive treatment and psychosocial outcomes.

Evidence-Based Pharmacological Interventions

OUD is commonly treated using pharmacological treatments, known formally as opioid substitution therapies (OSTs) or opioid replacement therapies (ORTs). Opioids exert a physical dependence, and as such immediate cessation can cause extreme physical craving and withdrawal [67]. The debilitating symptoms of physical withdrawal are a large barrier for patients trying to achieve abstinence from opioids [68]. Eliminating such symptoms using OST/ORT affords patients the opportunity to avoid intense physical discomfort, receive supervision during a period of serious vulnerability, as well as think clearly about reducing or stopping opioid use altogether without being driven to the debilitating effects of withdrawal [69]. The substitution therapies work to replace short-acting opioids such as heroin or oxycodone with longer-acting and less euphoric opioids, with the aim of reducing symptoms of craving and withdrawal [69]. These pharmacological interventions include opioid agonist agents, while opioid antagonists are often reserved for relapse prevention among patients with OUD [70]. These therapies are administered under the supervision of a physician, often accompanied by routine urine drug screening, as well as weekly medical assessment [71]. Patients are usually supervised over the course of a year, whereby the addiction specialist will help the patient to set personal goals and regain control of his or her life, while slowing tapering off the OST/ORT [69].

Methadone Maintenance Treatment

Methadone is a synthetic diphenylheptane opioid agonist [72]. For the management of OUD, methadone is administered once per day orally (although sublingual, intramuscular, and IV are options). Split dosing can be used for patients with comorbid chronic pain to reduce the hyperalgesic effects of methadone [72]. Patients are often initiated on a dose between 20 and 30 mg/day [72]. Treating physicians may increase the dose after an initial three-day trial of the starting dose; this increase will go up by 5–10 mg/day [72]. Dose increases continue until patients are stabilized for a 24-hour period and symptoms of withdrawal are eliminated [72]. Upon reaching an optimal dose, as determined through strict assessment of patient withdrawal and physical craving symptoms, patients are monitored until tapering is deemed appropriate by clinicians and the patients' overall health and social circumstances. Additional components of the MMT regime include weekly urine drug screening to assess for substance use and monitor methadone intake.

Efficacy

To date, methadone is the oldest and most common and efficaciously used OST [73, 74]. Methadone is effective in reducing opioid use, craving, and risk behaviors such as needle-sharing, which are known to increase the risk of HIV and hepatitis transmission [75]. When compared to non-pharmacological therapies, methadone is effective for reducing treatment attrition and illicit opioid use; however, no differences were found when evaluating criminal behavior or mortality compared to no treatment or other treatments [76]. Higher doses of methadone (60–100 mg/day) are shown to have the greatest benefit for improving retention and reducing illicit opioid use [77]. However, there is still uncertainty of methadone's long-term treatment efficacy in patients with OUD, with rates varying from 20 to 70% [78, 79]. This stems largely from the lack of an established outcome for determining effectiveness, as well as the inconsistent definitions and measurements used for effectiveness outcomes in the literature.

Contraindications and Adverse Effects of MMT

For patients with known hypersensitivity to any component of the methadone formulation, substantial respiratory depression, acute or severe bronchial asthma, and/or known paralytic ileus, MMT should be avoided [72]. Special attention should be paid to treatment initiation and dose increases; patients are at highest risk for life-threatening respiratory depression during this time [72]. Due to the effects of methadone on cardiac conductivity, patients with cardiac abnormalities should be closely monitored during MMT. Methadone is known to cause prolongation of the QT interval as well as serious cardiac effects, including arrhythmia and torsades de pointes [80]. Pregnant women deemed eligible for

MMT based on opioid use disorder criteria should be treated with MMT, as this is less dangerous than opioid withdrawal during pregnancy [72]. The neonate should be monitored for signs of respiratory depression and opioid withdrawal symptoms, which may develop in the first 24–72 hours of life and up to 2 weeks of age [72]. Opioid withdrawal and detoxification are not recommended during pregnancy, and the dose of methadone may be increased or given in divided doses in the third trimester due to increased metabolism of methadone [72].

Treatment Recommendations

There is considerable high-quality evidence (randomized controlled trials as well as Cochrane reviews of randomized controlled trials) to suggest methadone is the most effective therapy for managing patients with OUD [76, 77]. Trial evidence demonstrates methadone is most effective at doses >60 mg/day [77]. The evidence informing MMT is of higher quality and abundance in comparison to other maintenance treatments for OUD, largely because it is the oldest approved therapy for opioid dependence, and thus the standard of care. Confidence in the estimates generated from these trials is graded moderate to high [76, 77].

Combination Buprenorphine/Naloxone

Combination buprenorphine/naloxone (trade name: Suboxone®) is a relatively new intervention comprising a 4:1 combination of buprenorphine and naloxone administered sublingually. Combination buprenorphine/naloxone employs partial opioid agonistic effects because naloxone is not adequately absorbed sublingually [81]. Combination buprenorphine/naloxone's target effects are less potent than full opioid agonists such as methadone, promoting less physical dependence in comparison to various other full opioid agonists [82]. It is recommended to initiate patients on a buprenorphine/naloxone dose of 2 mg/0.5 mg per day, increasing by increments of 2 mg/0.5 mg per day until symptoms of withdrawal are suppressed [83]. It is suggested 16 mg of buprenorphine is an optimal maintenance dose [84]. While buprenorphine is available in singular form, the combination tablet with naloxone is demonstrated to enhance medication effectiveness [85–87]. Naloxone is included in the combination therapy to prevent misuse of opioids while patients are maintained on therapy; if patients were to inject the buprenorphine/naloxone tablet or misuse illicit opioids during their treatment course, naloxone will precipitate withdrawal symptoms [85–87].

Efficacy

Evidence from a systematic review of randomized trials evaluating buprenorphine/naloxone against placebo found it to be efficacious for retaining patients on therapy (any dose above 2 mg/day) and, at a dose >16 mg/day, suppressing illicit opioid use [84]. When compared against methadone, the findings are less clear. In fixed-dose, low-dose, and flexible-dose trials, buprenorphine retains fewer patients and is equally effective in reducing opioid use as MMT [84]. These findings are likely impacted by the clinically low doses selected for the trials.

Contraindications and Adverse Effects of Combination Buprenorphine/Naloxone

These medication should not be used in patients with preexisting sensitivity or allergy to agents included in the buprenorphine/naloxone formula. Buprenorphine/naloxone combination has similar potential for adverse effects as MMT; these include respiratory depression, central nervous system depression (especially for patients on benzodiazepines or other opioids), and jaundice for patients with hepatitis [83]. Buprenorphine does have the potential to impair mental abilities required for performing dangerous tasks; however, this impairment is likely to occur during dosing, not maintenance phases [83]. Buprenorphine/naloxone can interact with cytochrome-P450 3A4 inhibitors and inducers, antiretroviral, and benzodiazepine medications [83].

Treatment Recommendations

Buprenorphine maintenance therapy is an efficacious therapy for deterring opioid abuse at doses >16 mg/day [84]. While demonstrated to be equally effective for reducing illicit opioid consumption, evidence generated from randomized trials suggests buprenorphine has higher rates of attrition. At the present time, we cannot make firm conclusions to suggest that buprenorphine is superior to MMT. Our conclusions are based on the high-quality evidence (all randomized trials) summarized in the latest systematic review from the Cochrane Collaboration [84]. Confidence in the estimates generated from these trials is graded moderate to high [84].

Naltrexone

Naltrexone works as a competitive opioid receptor antagonist, acting on the opioid receptors of the brain to inhibit the effects of opioids [88]. Naltrexone is used as an alternative therapy for OUD in countries such as Russia where other opioid substitution therapies are prohibited [89]. While this treatment is available in oral tablets, the lack of patient adherence to the oral form has given rise to long-acting injectable and implant versions [88]. An important feature of naltrexone is that the medication does not induce a tolerance over time [90], which is reported with MMT [69]. Before starting naltrexone, patients should be confirmed off opioids for seven days [91].

Efficacy

Naltrexone will not alleviate the symptoms of opioid withdrawal; it blocks the effect of opioids, thus preventing further misuse [88]. Findings from a recent systematic review from the Cochrane Collaboration suggest naltrexone has limited effectiveness [92]. Naltrexone is demonstrated to be effective for reducing criminal behavior in patients with OUD [92]; however, its effectiveness for improving retention and reducing illicit opioid use is substantially weaker when compared to maintenance therapies such as combination buprenorphine/naloxone, as well as benzodiazepines [92]. Naltrexone is not suggested for use as a maintenance therapy; its effectiveness is greatest for relapse prevention when supplemented with other therapies [70].

Contraindications and Adverse Effects of Naltrexone

Naltrexone has important contraindications and adverse effects that require consideration. Naltrexone eliminates tolerance to opioids, which inadvertently increases the patient's risk of overdose during a lapse or relapse [91]. Among all the pharmacological therapies approved for OUD treatment, naltrexone has the highest risk for mortality [91], three to seven times that of methadone [93]. Naltrexone should also be used with caution among patients with renal impairment (excreted through urine), and those with hepatic impairment [91].

Treatment Recommendations

Naltrexone should be used in the absence of other effective maintenance therapies such as methadone and buprenorphine. Naltrexone may be used as a method to prevent relapse in this population, but should not be used strictly to manage OUD if methadone and buprenorphine are available. Confidence in the estimates generated from these trials was not graded in the most recent Cochrane review; however, the trials were found to suffer from high risk of bias for blinding and incomplete outcome data assessment domains [92].

Other Maintenance Therapies

Heroin Assisted Therapy (HAT)

Emerging research focuses on the treatment of marginalized populations with OUD that have failed previous pharmacotherapies. Specific attention is paid to the use of heroin for these subpopulations. Heroin assisted therapy (HAT) administers injectable diacetylmorphine, the active component of heroin, for patients with severe OUD who were using heroin. HAT is demonstrated effective for decreasing illicit opioid use and criminal behavior, as well as improving treatment retention and psychosocial functioning [94, 95]. Prescription heroin is also provided alongside methadone in some of the trials [95].

HAT is indicated for patients with severe heroin addiction who have failed other maintenance therapies; trials evaluating the effectiveness of HAT are tested solely in this subpopulation of severely addicted patients [95]. HAT should not be used in patients without a chronic heroin dependence.

Levo-α-acetylmethadol (LAAM)

Previously, a formulation of levo-α-acetylmethadol (LAAM) was approved for the management of OUD in Canada and the United States. LAAM has been demonstrated superior to methadone for reducing illicit opioid use; however, this formulation had higher attrition rates than MMT [96]. LAAM was removed from market when demonstrated to increase risk for QT prolongation and cardiac arrhythmia in patients with OUD [97], and is not recommended.

Strategies for Integrating Psychological and Pharmacological Treatments

Appropriate disease management should consider the combination of pharmacological and psychosocial interventions. Indeed, it has been shown that adjunct psychosocial therapies can improve OST effectiveness [98]. Adjunct therapies include the preceding interventions that have been found to be effective, as well as mutual support networks, such as Narcotics Anonymous. However, despite their proven effectiveness in combination with pharmacological treatments [98], psychosocial interventions are not adequately amalgamated into routine care [99]. Integration of such therapies requires careful consideration of the patient population, resources available, and federal/state/provincial guideline recommendations, as well as the accepted treatment paradigms in different countries or states. To start, management of patients will require a centralized access to provide both types of therapies for OUD patients, or partnerships with effective communication between such facilitates is required.

Pharmacological maintenance therapies are typically delivered at designated addiction treatment clinics. While in theory these clinics may provide onsite services such as psychosocial interventions or case management, this type of integrated care is neither mandatory nor common. Integrating a partnership between addiction psychologists, psychiatrists, nurses, case managers, and mutual support organizations requires: (1) a common acceptance of the multifaceted OUD; (2) an acceptance for individualized interventions; (3) open communication with patients and clinical teams; and (4) an interdisciplinary/interprofessional perspective. An open communication between these diverse clinicians is the first step in building the partnership for holistic care for patients with OUD. Using an integrated care approach decreases burden on the individual clinicians by distributing responsibility of care. This has been demonstrated to improve long-term outcomes for patients across multiple specialties, including emergency medicine [100] and primary care [101]. Although fully integrated treatment has not been empirically evaluated in terms of enhancing OUD treatment response and systematic evaluation is needed, the evidence from other integrated care models suggests this is a promising model for OUD also.

Important Comorbidities and Pertinent Considerations

The presence of psychiatric and physical comorbidities is high among patients with OUD, and may substantially influence the effects of both psychosocial and pharmacological treatment.

Chronic Pain

Opioids are commonly used for the management of pain, and not surprisingly patients with chronic pain incur a substantial risk for OUD [102]. Incident cases of OUD among patients prescribed opioids for pain is estimated to be 27% [102]. On the other hand, chronic non-cancer pain (CNCP) is highly prevalent among patients with OUD; specifically, 37–55.3% of patients receiving opioid substitution therapy report comorbid pain [103–105]. The risks associated with CNCP are especially high among OUD patients treated with opioid substitution therapy; CNCP is a strong predictor for relapse within the OST setting [106, 107]. Studies identifying predictors for adverse outcomes among patients treated with methadone found patients reporting pain to have higher incidence of opioid abuse and psychiatric symptoms [106, 107]. Patients who continue to abuse opioids while on OST have an increased risk for cardiovascular abnormalities [108, 109], overdose [110, 111], and death [110], emphasizing the importance of distinguishing the risk factors for continued opioid abuse while on OST. Thus, patients with pain should be monitored closely, which could be accomplished through more frequent clinic visits, twice weekly urine screens, or targeting adjunct therapies to manage pain, such as alternative analgesics, counseling, or case management, for this high risk population. Split dosing of methadone is suggested as a possible management strategy for patients with comorbid pain [69].

Infectious Disease

The high rates of intravenous (IV) drug use among patients with OUD are paralleled by high rates of HIV, hepatitis, and other infectious disease. Such high rates of infection are concerning since it may moderate the impact of pharmacological treatment (e.g., MMT) among patients with OUD. Among OUD patients with HIV and hepatitis, patients treated with methadone are demonstrated to have increased adherence to anti-retroviral therapy, as well as improved likelihood of virological suppression and CD4 cell count response [112]. Such findings suggest patients with comorbid infectious disease fare better when managed with a maintenance therapy. While it is important to address how methadone affects a patient's ability to adhere to infectious disease treatment, it should be noted that current research fails to address the impact of comorbid HIV and/or hepatitis C infections on a patient's propensity for OUD relapse.

Psychiatric Comorbidities

Patients with OUD have very high rates of comorbid psychiatric disorders [113, 114]. The prevalence of mood, anxiety, or personality disorders is estimated to be as high as 73%, 61%, and 65%, respectively [115–117]. It has been demonstrated that the presence of such disorders also adversely effects the outcomes of patients with OUD [118–120], including poor drug treatment outcomes such as continued illicit substance use [117, 119]. For example, one study found patients with major depression consume larger quantities of illicit substances compared to patients without depression [118]. This is concerning since the efficacy of the preceding psychosocial and pharmacological interventions is not established in patients with comorbid disorders. In fact, landmark trials assessing OSTs commonly exclude patients with psychiatric history, comorbid non-opioid drug or alcohol use disorders, abnormal liver function (thus excluding a significant proportion of IV drug use with possible comorbid hepatitis), and concomitant psychiatric medication use [121–126]. Application of such criteria could render treatment effects in trials that are not generalizable to the true patient population.

Polysubstance Use

Patients with OUD often experience problems with other substances of abuse, including alcohol, benzodiazepines, cocaine, and cannabis. Among patients with OUD receiving OST, rates of current polysubstance use are reported to vary between 20 and 66% [127–129]. Persistent polysubstance use interferes with treatment outcomes, leads to drug–drug interactions, and can have detrimental effects on overall psychosocial functioning and quality of life. For instance, cocaine use among patients with OUD on methadone has been linked with significantly lower treatment retention, as well as lower rates of negative urine screens for opioids [130]. Problematic use of benzodiazepines while receiving MMT is associated with higher rates of positive opioid and cocaine urine screens, as well as more frequent overdose and opioid-related mortality [128, 131]. While alcohol use among OUD patients in MMT can lead to similar adverse outcomes, it also increases the likelihood of hospitalizations and emergency department visits related to overdoses [132]. Although cannabis has not been found to directly interfere with methadone treatment outcomes [133], it may increase the risk of psychotic or affective disorders among this vulnerable population [134].

Treatment for OUD with methadone has been associated with improved rates of abstinence from both alcohol and cocaine, especially with higher methadone dose [127, 130, 135]. Several studies have also demonstrated the benefits of contingency management strategies and behavioral couples therapy in reducing cocaine use among OUD patients [40–45, 66]. It is recommended that multiple treatment models, ideally consisting of both pharmacological and psychosocial therapies, be applied simultaneously in order to most effectively treat concurrent polysubstance use among individuals with OUD.

Sex and Gender Differences

Women experience a greater burden of disease from opioid dependence with respect to medical problems, health outcomes, and social impairment [136–138]. They are at greater risk for HIV infection, chronic pain, and affective disorders, including depression and anxiety [139–141]. Other common barriers include childcare obligations, lack of income or unemployment, substance abuse by partners or other family members, history of sexual abuse or trauma, lack of access to resources, and social stigma attributed to addiction [142].

There is conflicting evidence as to whether women are likely to remain in treatment longer than men when enrolled in an MMT program [137, 143–145]; however, overall they do not show measurable differences in continued opioid use during treatment compared to men [146, 147]. Women maintained on buprenorphine showed significantly fewer positive opioid urine screens compared to men, and also compared to women receiving methadone [146]. Women tend to utilize available social services such as individual counseling or group therapy more often than men [138, 148], suggesting that they would fare well in psychosocial interventions for treating OUD.

Opioids also interact with sex hormones and play an important role in reproductive function across menstrual cycles, pregnancy, and menopause [149, 150]. As a result, women have a greater chance of experiencing problems with irregularities in menstruation and infertility [151].

Similarly, men experience sex hormone imbalances associated with opioid use. Testosterone levels are suppressed in men using opioids, whether used for the management of pain conditions or for the treatment of OUD with opioid maintenance therapies [152]. In the context of MMT, testosterone suppression is dependent on methadone dose [152]. Deficiency in testosterone can lead to sexual problems, including hypogonadism, erectile dysfunction, and decreased sex drive, as well as changes in weight and muscle mass, hair loss, and a reduction in bone density [153]. It can also cause mood disturbances, difficulty concentrating, and increased fatigue [154], which collectively may negatively impact quality of life and make treatment of OUD all the more challenging. Treatment providers are encouraged to take these effects into consideration when deciding on an appropriate maintenance treatment program, and ensure that the lowest possible effective dose is being prescribed. Studies also recommend testosterone replacement therapy (TRT) for men with testosterone levels falling below the lower reference limit of 300 ng/dL, provided that no known contraindications are present (such as prostate cancer or male breast cancer). Testosterone levels should be monitored regularly throughout TRT, as well as during long-term opioid use.

Future Directions

OUD is a highly complex disorder with physical, psychological, and social dimensions. Therefore, no single intervention alone is able to successfully deal with the numerous problems that patients face on a regular basis. Furthermore, societal stigmatization, sex, gender, and accessibility to health services can all influence treatment initiation and success in this population. Integrating both psychosocial and pharmacological interventions is the ideal approach as it caters to multiple aspects of the disorder, yet there is much work that remains to be done in this area.

First, as we have highlighted in this chapter, much more research is required to demonstrate the effectiveness of certain interventions where treatments effects are unclear. It is important to understand which treatments are effective for specific subgroups and marginalized individuals with OUD in order to maximize treatment success.

Second, there needs to be a direct discourse that involves patients when implementing treatment. Using qualitative methods, studies should aim to understand the outcomes that are most important to patients, as these may differ from that of the treatment provider. Identifying patient-specific needs is also likely to improve their overall treatment adherence and recovery.

Finally, the cost-effectiveness of the integrated treatment model should be systematically evaluated. The data generally suggest that the combined use of pharmacological and psychosocial strategies leads to improved outcomes, both within treatment and in overall social functioning. This is likely to reduce public health costs driven by opioid-related hospitalizations, unemployment, and crime, but this is nonetheless an empirical question. Each of these priorities will need to be pursued to ultimately contain and reduce the escalating prevalence of OUD.

References

1. National Consensus Development Panel on Effective Medical Treatment of Opiate Addiction. Effective medical treatment of opiate addiction. *JAMA*. 1998;280: 1936–1943.
2. American Psychiatric Association. Diagnostic and statistical manual of mental disorders. 5th ed. *Am J Psychiatry*. 2013. doi:10.1176/appi.books.9780890425596. 744053.
3. WHO. Management of substance abuse. *World Heal Organ*. 2014;1. doi:11/01/16.
4. SAMHSA (2012) *Results from the 2011 National Survey on Drug Use and Health: summary of national findings*. NSDUH Ser. H-44, HHS Publ. no. 12-4713. Rockville (MD): Substance Abuse and Mental Health Services Administration.
5. Zhang L, Zhang D, Chen W, et al. High prevalence of HIV, HCV and tuberculosis and associated risk behaviours among new entrants of methadone maintenance treatment clinics in Guangdong Province, China. *PLoS One*. 2013. doi:10.1371/journal.pone.0076931.
6. Chong E, Poh KK, Shen L, et al. Infective endocarditis secondary to intravenous Subutex abuse. *Singapore Med J*. 2009;50:34–42.

Table 6.1 Summary table

KEY RESEARCH FINDINGS
1. CBT in combination with methadone is effective for reducing illicit opioid use, comorbid depressive symptoms, and drug-related risk behavior, but shows no added benefit for abstinence from opioids, treatment retention, withdrawal symptoms, other substance use, sexual risk behavior, or methadone-related adverse events.
2. CM has demonstrated efficacy in reducing opioid use and promoting abstinence from opioids.
3. Methadone, especially in higher doses (60–100 mg/day), has been shown to have greatest benefit for improving retention and reducing illicit opioid use.
4. HAT has been associated with a decrease in illicit opioid use and criminal behavior, as well as improvements in treatment retention and psychosocial functioning in patients who failed other OSTs.
5. Chronic non-cancer pain is highly prevalent among patients with OUD, and has been identified as a strong predictor for relapse and presence of psychiatric symptoms within the OST setting.
6. Psychiatric comorbidity and polysubstance use have been associated with negative treatment outcomes, including shorter treatment retention, higher opioid relapse rates, more frequent overdose and opioid-related mortality, and increases in hospitalizations and emergency department visits related to overdoses.
7. Women experience a greater burden of OUD with respect to medical problems, health outcomes, and social impairment, and they often face significant barriers to accessing or receiving treatment.
8. Testosterone levels in men are suppressed in response to opioids, whether used for the management of pain conditions or for the treatment of OUD with opioid maintenance therapies. In the context of MMT, testosterone suppression is dependent on methadone dose.

RECOMMENDATIONS FOR EVIDENCE-BASED PRACTICE
1. CBT, when used as an adjunct to methadone maintenance treatment, is beneficial for improving depression and anxiety symptoms, and reducing illicit opioid use and opioid-related risk behavior among patients with OUD.
2. When combined with pharmacological therapy, CM is a practical approach to promote reduction in opioid and other drug use, as well as to improve abstinence from opioids.
3. Including BCT or an alternative family-focused intervention into the treatment regimen for opioid use disorder is likely to produce positive treatment and psychosocial outcomes.
4. Methadone and buprenorphine/naloxone have proved efficacious for retaining patients on therapy and suppressing illicit opioid use, and are therefore recommended for use as maintenance therapies to treat OUD.

Table 6.1 Continued

RECOMMENDATIONS FOR EVIDENCE-BASED PRACTICE ... *continued*
5. Integration of pharmacological and psychosocial therapies is recommended, with additional consideration for the patient population, available resources, guideline recommendations, and accepted treatment paradigms across regions.
6. Patients with pain should be monitored closely (i.e., through more frequent clinic visits, twice weekly urine screens, or targeting adjunct therapies such as alternative analgesics, counseling, or case management at this population) and implementation of a split dosing is suggested.
7. It is recommended that multiple treatment models, ideally consisting of both pharmacological and psychosocial therapies, be applied simultaneously in order to most effectively treat concurrent psychiatric comorbidity and polysubstance use among individuals with OUD.
8. For men whose testosterone levels are significantly suppressed, administration of the lowest possible effective methadone dose and consideration of testosterone replacement therapy in the absence of contraindications is encouraged, in addition to regular monitoring of testosterone levels.
9. Although MMT has demonstrated safety and efficacy in the treatment of pregnant women with OUD, emerging research suggests that buprenorphine may be a safer alternative, as it has not demonstrated any increased risk to either mother or fetus. It is also recommended that an increase in methadone dosage or administration of a split-dose strategy be considered, especially in the third trimester.
RECOMMENDATIONS FOR FUTURE RESEARCH
1. Additional research is needed in order to establish the specific efficacy of psychosocial interventions, including specific variations of CBT and MET.
2. The efficacy and cost-effectiveness of integrated pharmacological and psychosocial treatment models requires evaluation, based on data suggesting their combined use will lead to improved treatment outcomes.
3. Using qualitative methods, studies should aim to understand the outcomes that are most important to patients as these may differ from that of the treatment provider. Identifying patient-specific needs is likely to improve their overall treatment and recovery. Understanding gender/sex differences in etiology and recovery is a priority.
4. It is important to understand which treatments are effective for specific subgroups and marginalized individuals (i.e., women, individuals with psychiatric comorbidity, polysubstance use, chronic pain, HIV) with OUD using appropriate randomized study designs.
5. Translation of research into practice through widespread dissemination and inclusion in best practice guidelines is necessary, and it is encouraged that such research is used as a platform to inform changes to policy surrounding treatment of individuals with OUD.
6. Stronger evidence that is based on well-designed trials and high-quality observational studies is needed in order to have confidence in the results and develop stronger conclusions.

7. Ho RC, Ho EC, Tan CH, Mak A. Pulmonary hypertension in first episode infective endocarditis among intravenous buprenorphine users: case report. *Am J Drug Alcohol Abus.* 2009;35:199–202. doi:10.1080/00952990902939719.
8. Zapata JT, Katims DS, Yin Z. A two-year study of patterns and predictors of substance use among Mexican American youth. *Adolescence.* 1998;33:391–403.
9. Dennis B, Roshanov P, Bonner A, et al. Comparative effectiveness of opioid substitution and antagonist therapies for patients with opioid addiction: a systematic review and network meta-analysis (under review).
10. Dutra L, Stathopoulou G, Basden SL, et al. A meta-analytic review of psychosocial interventions for substance use disorders. *Am J Psychiatry.* 2008;165:179–187. doi:10.1176/appi.ajp.2007.06111851.
11. Drake RE, O'Neal EL, Wallach MA. A systematic review of psychosocial research on psychosocial interventions for people with co-occurring severe mental and substance use disorders. *J Subst Abuse Treat.* 2008;34:123–138. doi:10.1016/j.jsat.2007.01.011.
12. Mayet S, Farrell M, Ferri M, et al. Psychosocial treatment for opiate abuse and dependence. *Cochrane Database Syst Rev.* 2005:CD004330. doi:10.1002/14651858.CD004330.pub2.
13. Kadden R, Carroll KM, Donovan D, Cooney N, Monti P, Abrams D, et al. *Cognitive-behavioral coping skills therapy manual: a clinical research guide for therapists treating individuals with alcohol abuse and dependence.* NIAAA Project MATCH Monograph Series Vol. 3. DHHS Pub. No. (ADM)92-1895. Rockville (MD): National Institute on Alcohol Abuse and Alcoholism; 1992.
14. Carroll K. A cognitive-behavioral approach: treating cocaine addiction. Rockville (MD): National Institutes on Drug Abuse (NIDA), US Department of Health and Human Services; 1998.
15. McHugh RK, Hearon BA, Otto MW. Cognitive behavioral therapy for substance use disorders. *Psychiatr Clin North Am.* 2010;33:511–525. doi:10.1016/j.psc.2010.04.012.
16. Amato L, Minozzi S, Davoli M, Vecchi S. Psychosocial combined with agonist maintenance treatments versus agonist maintenance treatments alone for treatment of opioid dependence. *Cochrane Database Syst Rev.* 2011;10:CD004147. doi:10.1002/14651858.CD004147.
17. Carroll KM, Onken LS. Behavioral therapies for drug abuse. *Am J Psychiatry.* 2005;162:1452–1460. doi:10.1176/appi.ajp.162.8.1452.
18. Abrahms JL. A cognitive-behavioral versus nondirective group treatment program for opioid-addicted persons: an adjunct to methadone maintenance. *Int J Addict.* 1979;14:503–511. doi:10.3109/10826087909054598.
19. O'Neill K, Baker A, Cooke M, et al. Evaluation of a cognitive-behavioural intervention for pregnant injecting drug users at risk of HIV infection. *Addiction.* 1996;91:1115–1126. doi:10.1046/j.1360-0443.1996.91811154.x.
20. Pan S, Jiang H, Du J, et al. Efficacy of cognitive behavioral therapy on opiate use and retention in methadone maintenance treatment in China: a randomised trial. *PLoS One.* 2015. doi:10.1371/journal.pone.0127598.
21. Rosenblum A, Magura S, Palij M, et al. Enhanced treatment outcomes for cocaine-using methadone patients. *Drug Alcohol Depend.* 1999;54:207–218. doi:10.1016/S0376-8716(98)00166-5.
22. Magill M, Ray LA. Cognitive-behavioral treatment with adult alcohol and illicit drug users: a meta-analysis of randomized controlled trials. *J Stud Alcohol Drugs.* 2009;70:516–527.

23. Fiellin DA, Barry DT, Sullivan LE, et al. A randomized trial of cognitive behavioral therapy in primary care-based buprenorphine. *Am J Med.* 2013;126:74.e11–17. doi:10.1016/j.amjmed.2012.07.005.
24. Ling W, Hillhouse M, Ang A, et al. Comparison of behavioral treatment conditions in buprenorphine maintenance. *Addiction.* 2013;108:1788–1798. doi:10.1111/add.12266.
25. Marlatt GA, Donovan DM. *Relapse prevention: maintenance strategies in the treatment of addictive behaviors.* New York: Guilford Press; 2005.
26. Irvin JE, Bowers CA, Dunn ME, Wang MC. Efficacy of relapse prevention: a meta-analytic review. *J Consult Clin Psychol.* 1999;67:563–570. doi:10.1037/0022-006X.67.4.563.
27. Lee NK, Cameron J, Jenner L. A systematic review of interventions for co-occurring substance use and borderline personality disorders. *Drug Alcohol Rev.* 2015;34:663–672. doi:10.1111/dar.12267.
28. Linehan MM. Dialectical behavioral therapy: a cognitive behavioral approach to parasuicide. *J Pers Disord.* 1987;1:328–333. doi:10.1521/pedi.1987.1.4.328.
29. Dimeff LA, Linehan MM. Dialectical behavior therapy for substance abusers. *Addict Sci Clin Pract.* 2008;4:39–47.
30. Linehan MM, Dimeff LA, Reynolds SK, et al. Dialectical behavior therapy versus comprehensive validation therapy plus 12-step for the treatment of opioid dependent women meeting criteria for borderline personality disorder. *Drug Alcohol Depend.* 2002;67:13–26. doi:10.1016/S0376-8716(02)00011-X.
31. Linehan MM, Schmidt H, Dimeff LA, et al. Dialectical behavior therapy for patients with borderline personality disorder and drug-dependence. *Am J Addict.* 1999;8:279–292. doi:10.1080/105504999305686.
32. Haug N, Sorensen J, Gruber V, Song Y. Relapse prevention for opioid dependence. In: Marlatt GA, Donovan DM. *Relapse prevention: maintenance strategies in the treatment of addictive behaviors.* 2nd ed. New York: Guilford Press; 2005:151–178.
33. Prendergast M, Podus D, Finney J, et al. Contingency management for treatment of substance use disorders: a meta-analysis. *Addiction.* 2006;101:1546–1560. doi:10.1111/j.1360-0443.2006.01581.x.
34. Griffith JD, Rowan-Szal GA, Roark RR, Simpson DD. Contingency management in outpatient methadone treatment: a meta-analysis. *Drug Alcohol Depend.* 2000;58:55–66. doi:10.1016/S0376-8716(99)00068-X.
35. Downey KK, Helmus TC, Schuster CR. Treatment of heroin-dependent polydrug abusers with contingency management and buprenorphine maintenance. *Exp Clin Psychopharmacol.* 2000. doi:10.1037//1064-1297.8.2.176.
36. Benishek LA, Dugosh KL, Kirby KC, et al. Prize-based contingency management for the treatment of substance abusers: a meta-analysis. *Addiction.* 2014;109:1426–1436. doi:10.1111/add.12589.
37. Olmstead TA, Petry NM. The cost-effectiveness of prize-based and voucher-based contingency management in a population of cocaine- or opioid-dependent outpatients. *Drug Alcohol Depend.* 2009;102:108–115. doi:10.1016/j.drugalcdep.2009.02.005.
38. Petry NM, Martin B. Low-cost contingency management for treating cocaine- and opioid-abusing methadone patients. *J Consult Clin Psychol.* 2002;70:398–405. doi:10.1037/0022-006X.70.2.398.
39. Chopra MP, Landes RD, Gatchalian KM, et al. Buprenorphine medication versus voucher contingencies in promoting abstinence from opioids and cocaine. *Exp Clin Psychopharmacol.* 2009;17:226–236. doi:10.1037/a0016597.

40. Silverman K, Higgins ST, Brooner RK, et al. Sustained cocaine abstinence in methadone maintenance patients through voucher-based reinforcement therapy. *Arch Gen Psychiatry*. 1996;53:409–415. doi:10.1001/archpsyc.1996.01830050045007.
41. Silverman K, Wong CJ, Umbricht-Schneiter A, et al. Broad beneficial effects of cocaine abstinence reinforcement among methadone patients. *J Consult Clin Psychol*. 1998;66:811–824. doi:10.1037/0022-006X.66.5.811.
42. Silverman K, Robles E, Mudric T, et al. A randomized trial of long-term reinforcement of cocaine abstinence in methadone-maintained patients who inject drugs. *J Consult Clin Psychol*. 2004;72:839–854. doi:10.1037/0022-006X.72.5.839.
43. Petry NM, Martin B, Simcic F. Prize reinforcement contingency management for cocaine dependence: integration with group therapy in a methadone clinic. *J Consult Clin Psychol*. 2005;73:354–359. doi:10.1037/0022-006X.73.2.354.
44. Higgins ST, Wong CJ, Badger GJ, et al. Contingent reinforcement increases cocaine abstinence during outpatient treatment and 1 year of follow-up. *J Consult Clin Psychol*. 2000;68:64–72. doi:10.1037/0022-006X.68.1.64.
45. Peirce JM, Petry NM, Stitzer ML, et al. Effects of lower-cost incentives on stimulant abstinence in methadone maintenance treatment: a National Drug Abuse Treatment Clinical Trials Network study. *Arch Gen Psychiatry*. 2006;63:201–208. doi:63/2/201 [pii]\r10.1001/archpsyc.63.2.201.
46. Carroll KM, Ball SA, Nich C, et al. Targeting behavioral therapies to enhance naltrexone treatment of opioid dependence: efficacy of contingency management and significant other involvement. *Arch Gen Psychiatry*. 2001;58:755–761. doi:10.1001/archpsyc.58.8.755.
47. Higgins ST, Stitzer ML, Bigelow GE, Liebson IA. Contingent methadone delivery: effects on illicit-opiate use. *Drug Alcohol Depend*. 1986;17:311–322. doi:10.1016/0376-8716(86)90080-3.
48. Robles E, Stitzer ML, Strain EC, et al. Voucher-based reinforcement of opiate abstinence during methadone detoxification. *Drug Alcohol Depend*. 2002;65:179–189. doi:10.1016/S0376-8716(01)00160-0.
49. Katz EC, Chutuape MA, Jones H, et al. Abstinence incentive effects in a short-term outpatient detoxification program. *Exp Clin Psychopharmacol*. 2004;12:262–268. doi:10.1037/1064-1297.12.4.262.
50. Azrin NH. Improvements in the community-reinforcement approach to alcoholism. *Behav Res Ther*. 1976;14:339–348. doi:10.1016/0005-7967(76)90021-8.
51. Roozen HG, Boulogne JJ, Van Tulder MW, et al. A systematic review of the effectiveness of the community reinforcement approach in alcohol, cocaine and opioid addiction. *Drug Alcohol Depend*. 2004;74:1–13. doi:10.1016/j.drugalcdep.2003.12.006.
52. Bickel WK, Amass L, Higgins ST, et al. Effects of adding behavioral treatment to opioid detoxification with buprenorphine. *J Consult Clin Psychol*. 1997;65:803–810. doi:10.1037/0022-006X.65.5.803.
53. Abbott PJ, Weller SB, Delaney HD, Moore BA. Community reinforcement approach in the treatment of opiate addicts. *Am J Drug Alcohol Abus*. 1998;24:17–30.
54. Roozen HG, Kerkhof AJFM, Van Den Brink W. Experiences with an outpatient relapse program (community reinforcement approach) combined with naltrexone in the treatment of opioid-dependence: effect on addictive behaviors and the predictive value of psychiatric comorbidity. *Eur Addict Res*. 2003;9:53–58. doi:10.1159/000068808.

55. Foxcroft DR, Coombes L, Wood S, et al. Motivational interviewing for alcohol misuse in young adults. *Cochrane Database Syst Rev.* 2014;8:CD007025. doi:10.1002/14651858.CD007025.pub2.
56. Miller WR. *Motivational enhancement therapy manual: a clinical research guide for therapists treating individuals with alcohol abuse and dependence.* DIANE Publishing; 1995.
57. Smedslund G, Berg RC, Hammerstrøm KT, et al. Motivational interviewing for substance abuse. *Cochrane Database Syst Rev.* 2011:CD008063. doi:10.1002/14651858.CD008063.pub2.
58. Zhong N, Yuan Y, Chen H, et al. Effects of a randomized comprehensive psychosocial intervention based on cognitive behavioral therapy theory and motivational interviewing techniques for community rehabilitation of patients with opioid use disorders in Shanghai, China. *J Addict Med.* 2016;9:322–330. doi:10.1097/ADM.0000000000000139.
59. Saunders B, Wilkinson C, Phillips M. The impact of a brief motivational intervention with opiate users attending a methadone programme. *Addiction.* 1995;90:415–424. doi:10.1111/j.1360-0443.1995.tb03788.x.
60. Epstein EE, McCrady BS. Behavioral couples treatment of alcohol and drug use disorders: current status and innovations. *Clin Psychol Rev.* 1998;18:689–711.
61. O'Farrell TJ, Fals-Stewart W. Behavioral couples therapy for alcoholism and drug abuse. *J Subst Abuse Treat.* 2000;18:51–54. doi:10.1016/S0740-5472(99)00026-4.
62. Stanton MD, Shadish WR. Outcome, attrition, and family-couples treatment for drug abuse: a meta-analysis and review of the controlled, comparative studies. *Psychol Bull.* 1997;122:170–191.
63. Catalano RF, Gainey RR, Fleming CB, et al. An experimental intervention with families of substance abusers: one-year follow-up of the focus on families project. *Addiction.* 1999;94:241–254.
64. Fals-Stewart W, O'Farrell T. Behavioral family counseling and naltrexone for male opioid-dependent patients. *J Consult Clin Psychol.* 2003;71:432–442. doi:10.1037/0022-006X.71.3.432.
65. Powers MB, Vedel E, Emmelkamp PMG. Behavioral couples therapy (BCT) for alcohol and drug use disorders: a meta-analysis. *Clin Psychol Rev.* 2008;28:952–962. doi:10.1016/j.cpr.2008.02.002.
66. Fals-Stewart W, O'Farrell TJ, Birchler GR. Behavioral couples therapy for male methadone maintenance patients: effects on drug-using behavior and relationship adjustment. *Behav Ther.* 2001;32:391–411. doi:http://dx.doi.org/10.1016/S0005-7894%2801%2980010-1.
67. Praveen KT, Law F, O'Shea J, Melichar J. Opioid dependence. *BMJ Clin. Evid.* 2011.
68. Mars SG, Bourgois P, Karandinos G, et al. "Every 'never' I ever said came true": transitions from opioid pills to heroin injecting. *Int J Drug Policy.* 2014;25:257–266. doi:10.1016/j.drugpo.2013.10.004.
69. Methadone Maintenance Treatment. *Program standards and clinical guidelines.* Toronto: Methadone Maintenance Treatment; 2011.
70. World Health Organization. *Guidelines for the psychosocially assisted pharmacological treatment of opioid dependence.* Geneva: World Health Organization; 2009.
71. National Guideline Clearinghouse. *VA/DoD clinical practice guideline for management of substance use disorders (SUD).* Rockville, MD: National Guideline Clearinghouse; 2014.

72. Dolophine® (methadone hydrochloride) tablets prescribing information; 2012.
73. WHO. The world health report 2002: reducing risks, promoting healthy life. *Educ Health*. 2002;16:230. doi:10.1080/1357628031000116808.
74. Ezzati M, Lopez AD, Rodgers A, et al. Selected major risk factors and global and regional burden of disease. *Lancet*. 2002;360:1347–1360. doi:10.1016/S0140-6736(02)11403-6.
75. Metzger DS, Woody GE, McLellan AT, et al. Human immunodeficiency virus seroconversion among intravenous drug users in- and out-of-treatment: an 18-month prospective follow-up. *JAIDS*. 1993;6:1049–1056.
76. Mattick RP, Breen C, Kimber J, Davoli M. Methadone maintenance therapy versus no opioid replacement therapy for opioid dependence. *Cochrane Database Syst Rev*. 2009:CD002209. doi:10.1002/14651858.CD002209.pub2.
77. Faggiano F, Vigna-Taglianti F, Versino E, Lemma P. Methadone maintenance at different dosages for opioid dependence. *Cochrane Database Syst Rev*. 2003: CD002208. doi:10.1002/14651858.CD002208.
78. Bell J, Burrell T, Indig D, Gilmour S. Cycling in and out of treatment: participation in methadone treatment in NSW, 1990–2002. *Drug Alcohol Depend*. 2006;81: 55–61. doi:10.1016/j.drugalcdep.2005.05.010.
79. Termorshuizen F, Krol A, Prins M, et al. Prediction of relapse to frequent heroin use and the role of methadone prescription: an analysis of the Amsterdam Cohort Study among drug users. *Drug Alcohol Depend*. 2005;79:231–240. doi:10.1016/j.drugalcdep.2005.01.013.
80. Pearson EC, Woosley RL. QT prolongation and torsades de pointes among methadone users: reports to the FDA spontaneous reporting system. *Pharmacoepidemiol Drug Saf*. 2005;14:747–753. doi:10.1002/pds.1112.
81. Mendelson J, Jones RT, Welm S, et al. Buprenorphine and naloxone combinations: the effects of three dose ratios in morphine-stabilized, opiate-dependent volunteers. *Psychopharmacology (Berl)*. 1999;141:37–46. doi:10.1007/s002130050804.
82. Orman JS, Keating GM. Buprenorphine/naloxone: a review of its use in the treatment of opioid dependence. *Drugs*. 2009;69:577–607. doi:10.2165/00003495-200969050-00006.
83. Buprenorphine and naloxone—buprenorphine hydrochloride and naloxone hydrochloride dihydrate tablet; 2014.
84. Mattick RP, Breen C, Kimber J, et al. Buprenorphine maintenance versus placebo or methadone maintenance for opioid dependence (review). *Cochrane Database Syst Rev*. 2014;2:CD002207. doi:10.1002/14651858.CD002207.pub4.Copyright.
85. Mauger S, Fraser R, Gill K. Utilizing buprenorphine-naloxone to treat illicit and prescription-opioid dependence. *Neuropsychiatr Dis Treat*. 2014;10:587–598. doi:10.2147/NDT.S39692.
86. Chapleo CB, Walter DS. The buprenorphine-naloxone combination product. *Res Clin Forums*. 1997;19:55–58.
87. Robinson SE. Buprenorphine-containing treatments: place in the management of opioid addiction. *CNS Drugs*. 2006;20:697–712. doi:10.2165/00023210-200620090-00001.
88. Sullivan MA, Bisaga A, Mariani JJ, et al. Naltrexone treatment for opioid dependence: does its effectiveness depend on testing the blockade? *Drug Alcohol Depend*. 2013;133:80–85. doi:10.1016/j.drugalcdep.2013.05.030.
89. Davey M. Australia's success in methadone treatment could guide Russia, UN says. *Guard*. 2014. Available from: www.theguardian.com/society/2014/jul/22/australia-best-placed-to-convince-russia-on-methadone-says-un-envoy.

90. Krupitsky E, Zvartau E, Woody G. Use of naltrexone to treat opioid addiction in a country in which methadone and buprenorphine are not available. *Curr Psychiatry Rep.* 2010;12:448–453. doi:10.1007/s11920-010-0135-5.
91. Naltrexone hydrochloride—naltrexone hydrochloride tablet, film coated; 2013.
92. Minozzi S, Amato L, Vecchi S, et al. Oral naltrexone maintenance treatment for opioid dependence. *Cochrane Database Syst Rev.* 2011;CD001333. doi:10.1002/14651858.CD001333.pub4.
93. Gibson AE, Degenhardt LJ. Mortality related to pharmacotherapies for opioid dependence: a comparative analysis of coronial records. *Drug Alcohol Rev.* 2007; 26:405–410. doi:779503844 [pii].
94. Oviedo-Joekes E, Brissette S, Marsh DC, et al. Diacetylmorphine versus methadone for the treatment of opioid addiction. *N Engl J Med.* 2009;361:777–786. doi:10.1056/NEJMoa0810635.
95. Ferri M, Davoli M, Ca P. Heroin maintenance for chronic heroin-dependent individuals (review). *Cochrane Database Syst Rev.* 2012. doi:10.1002/14651858.CD003410.pub4.
96. Clark N, Lintzeris N, Gijsbers A, et al. LAAM maintenance vs methadone maintenance for heroin dependence. *Cochrane Database Syst Rev.* 2002;CD002210. doi:10.1002/14651858.CD002210.
97. Soyka M, Kranzler HR, van den Brink W, et al. The World Federation of Societies of Biological Psychiatry (WFSBP) guidelines for the biological treatment of substance use and related disorders. Part 2: opioid dependence. *World J Biol Psychiatry.* 2011;12:160–187. doi:10.3109/15622975.2011.561872.
98. Wang L, Wei X, Wang X, et al. Long-term effects of methadone maintenance treatment with different psychosocial intervention models. *PLoS One.* 2014. doi:10.1371/journal.pone.0087931.
99. IOM (Institute of Medicine). *Psychosocial interventions for mental and substance use disorders: a framework for establishing evidence-based standards.* Washington (DC): The National Academies Press; 2015.
100. Dinh MM, Green TC, Bein KJ, et al. Emergency department clinical redesign, team-based care and improvements in hospital performance: a time series analysis. *Emerg Med Australas.* 2015;27:317–322. doi:10.1111/1742-6723.12424.
101. Iddins BW, Frank JS, Kannar P, et al. Evaluation of team-based care in an urban free clinic setting. *Nurs Adm Q.* 2015;39:254–262. doi:10.1097/NAQ.0000000000000103.
102. Pohl M, Smith L. Chronic pain and addiction: challenging co-occurring disorders. *J Psychoactive Drugs.* 2012;44:119–124. doi:10.1080/02791072.2012.684621.
103. Rosenblum A, Joseph H, Fong C, et al. Prevalence and characteristics of chronic pain among chemically dependent patients in methadone maintenance and residential treatment facilities. *JAMA.* 2003;289:2370–2378. doi:10.1001/jama.289.18.2370.
104. Peles E, Schreiber S, Gordon J, Adelson M. Significantly higher methadone dose for methadone maintenance treatment (MMT) patients with chronic pain. *Pain.* 2005;113:340–346. doi:10.1016/j.pain.2004.11.011.
105. Dhingra L, Masson C, Perlman DC, et al. Epidemiology of pain among outpatients in methadone maintenance treatment programs. *Drug Alcohol Depend.* 2013;128: 161–165. doi:10.1016/j.drugalcdep.2012.08.003.
106. Jamison RN, Kauffman J, Katz NP. Characteristics of methadone maintenance patients with chronic pain. *J Pain Symptom Manage.* 2000;19:53–62. doi:10.1016/S0885-3924(99)00144-X.

107. Dennis BB, Samaan MC, Bawor M, et al. Evaluation of clinical and inflammatory profile in opioid addiction patients with comorbid pain: results from a multicenter investigation. *Neuropsychiatr Dis Treat.* 2014;10:2239–2247. doi:10.2147/NDT.S72785.
108. Peles E, Bodner G, Kreek MJ, et al. Corrected-QT intervals as related to methadone dose and serum level in methadone maintenance treatment (MMT) patients: a cross-sectional study. *Addiction.* 2007;102:289–300. doi:10.1111/j.1360-0443.2006.01668.x.
109. Krantz MJ, Kutinsky IB, Robertson AD, Mehler PS. Dose-related effects of methadone on QT prolongation in a series of patients with torsade de pointes. *Pharmacotherapy.* 2003;23:802–805.
110. Cao X, Wu Z, Li L, et al. Mortality among methadone maintenance clients in China: a six-year cohort study. *PLoS One.* 2013. doi:10.1371/journal.pone.0082476.
111. Bohnert ASB, Ilgen MA, Trafton JA, et al. Trends and regional variation in opioid overdose mortality among Veterans Health Administration patients, fiscal year 2001 to 2009. *Clin J Pain.* 2014;30:605–612. doi:10.1097/AJP.0000000000000011.
112. Pettes T, Wood E, Guillemi S, et al. Methadone use among HIV-positive injection drug users in a Canadian setting. *J Subst Abuse Treat.* 2010;39:174–179. doi:10.1016/j.jsat.2010.05.001.
113. Wu LT, Woody GE, Yang C, Blazer DG. How do prescription opioid users differ from users of heroin or other drugs in psychopathology: results from the National Epidemiologic Survey on Alcohol and Related Conditions. *J Addict Med.* 2011;5:28–35.
114. Pilowsky DJ, Wu LT, Burchett B, et al. Co-occurring amphetamine use and associated medical and psychiatric comorbidity among opioid-dependent adults: results from the Clinical Trials Network. *Subst Abuse Rehabil.* 2011;2:133–144. doi:10.2147/SAR.S20895.
115. Conway KP, Compton W, Stinson FS, Grant BF. Lifetime comorbidity of DSM-IV mood and anxiety disorders and specific drug use disorders: results from the National Epidemiologic Survey on Alcohol and Related Conditions. *J Clin Psychiatry.* 2006;67:247–257.
116. Darke S, Kaye S, Finlay-Jones R. Antisocial personality disorder, psychopathy and injecting heroin use. *Drug Alcohol Depend.* 1998;52:63–69. doi:10.1016/S0376-8716(98)00058-1.
117. Ngo HTT, Tait RJ, Hulse GK. Hospital psychiatric comorbidity and its role in heroin dependence treatment outcomes using naltrexone implant or methadone maintenance. *J Psychopharmacol.* 2011;25:774–782. doi:10.1177/0269881110364266.
118. Compton WM, Cottler LB, Jacobs JL, et al. The role of psychiatric disorders in predicting drug dependence treatment outcomes. *Am J Psychiatry.* 2003;160:890–895. doi:10.1176/appi.ajp.160.5.890.
119. Rounsaville BJ, Weissman MM, Crits-Christoph K, et al. Diagnosis and symptoms of depression in opiate addicts: course and relationship to treatment outcome. *Arch Gen Psychiatry.* 1982;39:151–156. doi:10.1001/archpsyc.1982.04290020021004.
120. Rounsaville BJ, Kosten TR, Weissman MM, Kleber HD. Prognostic significance of psychopathology in treated opiate addicts: a 2.5-year follow-up study. *Arch Gen Psychiatry.* 1986;43:739–745. doi:10.1001/archpsyc.1986.01800080025004.

121. Fudala PJ, Bridge TP, Herbert S, et al. Office-based treatment of opiate addiction with a sublingual-tablet formulation of buprenorphine and naloxone. *N Engl J Med*. 2003;349:949–958. doi:10.1056/NEJMoa022164.
122. Sees KL, Delucchi KL, Masson C, et al. Methadone maintenance vs 180-day psychosocially enriched detoxification for treatment of opioid dependence: a randomized controlled trial. *JAMA*. 2000. doi:10.1097/00132586-200104000-00058.
123. Woody GE, Poole SA, Subramaniam G, et al. Extended vs short-term buprenorphine-naloxone for treatment of opioid-addicted youth: a randomized trial. *JAMA*. 2008;300:2003–2011. doi:10.1001/jama.2008.574.
124. Strain EC, Bigelow GE, Liebson IA, Stitzer ML. Moderate- vs high-dose methadone in the treatment of opioid dependence: a randomized trial. *JAMA*. 1999;281:1000–1005. doi:joc81302 [pii].
125. Woody GE, McLellan AT, Luborsky L, O'Brien CP. Twelve-month follow-up of psychotherapy for opiate dependence. *Am J Psychiatry*. 1987;144:590–596.
126. Johnson RE, Jaffe JH, Fudala PJ. A controlled trial of buprenorphine treatment for opioid dependence. *JAMA*. 1992;267:2750–2755. doi:10.1001/jama.1992.03480200058024.
127. Maremmani I, Pani PP, Mellini A, et al. Alcohol and cocaine use and abuse among opioid addicts engaged in a methadone maintenance treatment program. *J Addict Dis*. 2007;26:61–70. doi:10.1300/J069v26n01_08.
128. Brands B, Blake J, Marsh DC, et al. The impact of benzodiazepine use on methadone maintenance treatment outcomes. *J Addict Dis*. 2008;27:37–48. doi:10.1080/10550880802122620.
129. Maremmani I, Stefania C, Pacini M, et al. Differential substance abuse patterns distribute according to gender in heroin addicts. *J Psychoactive Drugs*. 2010;42:89–95. doi:10.1080/02791072.2010.10399789.
130. DeMaria PA, Sterling R, Weinstein SP. The effect of stimulant and sedative use on treatment outcome of patients admitted to methadone maintenance treatment. *Am J Addict*. 2000;9:145–153.
131. Leece P, Cavacuiti C, Macdonald EM, et al. Predictors of opioid-related death during methadone therapy. *J Subst Abuse Treat*. 2015;57:30–35. doi:10.1016/j.jsat.2015.04.008.
132. Ryder N, Cullen W, Barry J, et al. Prevalence of problem alcohol use among patients attending primary care for methadone treatment. *BMC Fam Pract*. 2009;10:42. doi:10.1186/1471-2296-10-42.
133. Epstein DH, Preston KL. Does cannabis use predict poor outcome for heroin-dependent patients on maintenance treatment? Past findings and more evidence against. *Addiction*. 2003;98:269–279. doi:10.1046/j.1360-0443.2003.00310.x.
134. Moore THM, Zammit S, Lingford-Hughes A, et al. Cannabis use and risk of psychotic or affective mental health outcomes: a systematic review. *Lancet*. 2007;370:319–328. doi:10.1016/S0140-6736(07)61162-3.
135. Peles E, Kreek MJ, Kellogg S, Adelson M. High methadone dose significantly reduces cocaine use in methadone maintenance treatment (MMT) patients. *J Addict Dis*. 2006;25:43–50. doi:10.1300/J069v25n01_07.
136. Anglin MD, Hser YI, Booth MW. Sex differences in addict careers. 3. Addiction. *Am J Drug Alcohol Abuse*. 1987;13:253–280.
137. Peles E, Adelson M. Gender differences and pregnant women in a methadone maintenance treatment (MMT) clinic. *J Addict Dis*. 2006;25:39–45. doi:10.1300/J069v25n02_06.

138. Schiff M, Levit S, Moreno RC. Retention and illicit drug use among methadone patients in Israel: a gender comparison. *Addict Behav.* 2007;32:2108–2119. doi:10.1016/j.addbeh.2007.01.010.
139. Camacho LM, Bartholomew NG, Joe GW, et al. Gender, cocaine and during-treatment HIV risk reduction among injection opioid users in methadone maintenance. *Drug Alcohol Depend.* 1996;41:1–7. doi:10.1016/0376-8716(96)01235-5.
140. Hurley RW, Adams MCB. Sex, gender, and pain: an overview of a complex field. *Anesth Analg.* 2008;107:309–317. doi:10.1213/01.ane.0b013e31816ba437.
141. Sordo L, Chahua M, Bravo MJ, et al. Depression among regular heroin users: the influence of gender. *Addict Behav.* 2012;37:148–152. doi:10.1016/j.addbeh.2011.09.009.
142. Brady KT. *Women and addiction: a comprehensive handbook.* New York: Guilford Press; 2009.
143. Deck D, Carlson MJ. Retention in publicly funded methadone maintenance treatment in two Western states. *J Behav Heal Serv Res.* 2005;32:43–60.
144. Hser YI, Anglin MD, Liu Y. A survival analysis of gender and ethnic differences in responsiveness to methadone maintenance treatment. *Int J Addict.* 1990;25:1295–1315. doi: 10.3109/10826089009068465.
145. Chatham LR, Hiller ML, Rowan-Szal GA, et al. Gender differences at admission and follow-up in a sample of methadone maintenance clients. *Subst Use Misuse.* 1999;34:1137–1165. doi:http://dx.doi.org/10.3109/10826089909039401.
146. Jones HE, Fitzgerald H, Johnson RE. Males and females differ in response to opioid agonist medications. *Am J Addict.* 2005;14:223–233. doi:10.1080/10550490590949569.
147. Schottenfeld RS, Pakes JR, Kosten TR. Prognostic factors in buprenorphine-versus methadone-maintained patients. *J Nerv Ment Dis.* 1998;186:35–43. doi:10.1097/00005053-199801000-00006.
148. Barry D, Beitel M, Breuer T, et al. Group-based strategies for stress reduction in methadone maintenance treatment: what do patients want? *J Addict.* 2011;5:181–187. doi:10.1097/ADM.0b013e3181ee77cl.
149. Zubieta JK, Smith YR, Bueller JA, et al. Mu-opioid receptor-mediated antinociceptive responses differ in men and women. *J Neurosci.* 2002;22:5100–5107. doi:22/12/5100 [pii].
150. Sinchak K, Micevych PE. Progesterone blockade of estrogen activation of mu-opioid receptors regulates reproductive behavior. *J Neurosci.* 2001;21:5723–5729. doi:21/15/5723 [pii].
151. Nelson-Zlupko L, Kauffman E, Dore MM. Gender differences in drug addiction and treatment: implications for social work intervention with substance-abusing women. *Soc Work.* 1995;40:45–54. doi:10.1093/sw/40.1.45.
152. Bawor M, Bami H, Dennis BB, et al. Testosterone suppression in opioid users: a systematic review and meta-analysis. *Drug Alcohol Depend.* 2015;149:1–9. doi:10.1016/j.drugalcdep.2015.01.038.
153. Smith HS, Elliott JA. Opioid-induced androgen deficiency (OPIAD). *Pain Physician.* 2012;15:ES145–156.
154. Börjesson G, Mårtensson A, Holmer HI, Westerling D. F633 low testosterone levels in men with long-term opioid treatment. *Eur J Pain Suppl.* 2011;5:178.

Chapter 7

Cannabis Use Disorder

Jane Metrik and Divya Ramesh

Introduction

Cannabis is the most commonly used psychoactive substance in the world, with 43.7% of the United States population over 12 years of age reporting using it at least once in their life and 12.6% using in the past year [1]. Among young adults aged 18–25, approximately one-third report using it in the past year, with 19.1% using in the past month [1]. Of current (past month) users, 41.1% report using marijuana daily or almost daily [1].

Approximately 2.9% of the US adult population (18+ years) [2] and approximately 10% of individuals who have used cannabis on at least one occasion [3, 4] meet criteria for cannabis dependence, as defined by the fourth edition of the American Psychiatric Association's (APA) *Diagnostic and Statistical Manual of Mental Disorders* (DSM) [5, 6]. With the recent change from DSM-IV to DSM-5 diagnostic criteria for substance use disorders [7], cannabis use disorder (CUD) is now defined as a problematic pattern of cannabis use leading to clinically relevant impairment or distress occurring within a 12-month period as manifested by cannabinoid tolerance and withdrawal; increasing amounts of cannabis use over time; inability to control consumption; craving; and recurrent cannabis use having negative implications on social, professional, and educational life [8]. As with other DSM-5 substance use disorders, diagnosis of CUD is based on a unidimensional symptom count with the level of severity ranging from mild (2–3 symptoms), moderate (4–5), to severe (6–11). The transition to DSM-5 only modestly affected prevalence rates of CUD, relative to DSM-IV cannabis abuse/dependence diagnoses [9, 10].

CUD is significantly more common among men than women and most prevalent in the 18–29-year-old group relative to older ages [2, 11]. CUD is most likely to develop within the first five years of onset of use, which tends to occur before age 30 and is extremely unlikely to develop after age 40 [3]. As an addictive drug, cannabis has been historically surrounded by much controversy until a relatively recent discovery of the endocannabinoid signaling system (reviewed in [12, 13]) and a greater understanding of the neurochemical basis of cannabis' reinforcing effects on the brain [14]. Strong evidence from preclinical, clinical, and epidemiological studies support the development of cannabis tolerance and withdrawal, which indicate neurological adaptation to the drug, with prolonged exposure to cannabis [4, 15–20]. Tolerance may be subjectively experienced as a feeling that the same dose of cannabis is less efficacious, whereas withdrawal occurs when a drug is abruptly discontinued following prolonged exposure. Pharmacological tolerance for cannabinoids is caused by pharmacodynamic events such as downregulation of cannabinoid receptors [21, 22].

Empirical evidence for clinical withdrawal syndrome among heavy chronic cannabis users led to its inclusion in the current version of the DSM-5. Symptoms of cannabis withdrawal commonly appear after 24 hours of abstinence, reach their peak around two to six days, and remit within two weeks, although impaired sleep patterns may persist for longer periods [23]. According to DSM-5, withdrawal is diagnosed if at least three of the following symptoms develop within a week of abstinence: irritability, anger, or aggression; nervousness or anxiety; sleep difficulty (insomnia, disturbing dreams); decreased appetite or weight loss; restlessness; depressed mood; and at least one of the following physical discomforts: abdominal pain, shakiness/tremors, fever, chills, or headache. Additionally, the following symptoms may be observed a week post-abstinence: fatigue, yawning, difficulty in concentration, and rebound periods of increased appetite and hypersomnia following initial bouts of appetite loss and insomnia [8]. Cannabis withdrawal symptoms may cause significant distress, and most likely contribute to relapse among those seeking treatment for cannabis use [24]. Therefore, much of the focus of pharmacotherapy development for CUD has been on alleviating symptoms of withdrawal [25].

A major contributor to CUD is the development of craving such that individuals with a history of cannabis use are vulnerable to strong desire for cannabis in the presence of cues associated with the substance [26, 27]. As with other drugs of abuse [28], cannabis users learn to selectively process cannabis-related stimuli over other environmental stimuli. Craving can be elicited both due to withdrawal symptoms as well as by substance-related cues in the drug user's environment when not abstaining. Craving is particularly relevant to the neurobiology of drug dependence, namely to neural circuitry involved in pleasure, incentive motivation [29], and in mood regulation [30]. With more clear evidence of addiction potential of cannabis [17] and significance of cannabis withdrawal syndrome [31], emerging cannabis cue-reactivity research [32–38] may play an important role in cannabis treatment, in cannabis relapse prevention, and specifically in the development of pharmacotherapy for cannabis use disorders [34].

Evidence-Based Psychological Interventions

Although most individuals with CUD do not seek treatment [11], there is a substantial proportion of heavy users who are in need of services. The US demand for treatment of CUD has increased by 72% during the 10-year period spanning 1999–2009 [39]. Among individuals receiving substance use treatment services, 17.5% sought treatment primarily for cannabis abuse, exceeded only by alcohol and all forms of opiates as primary substances [40]. For adolescents in drug treatment, CUD was secondary only to alcohol use disorders [40]. Adults who seek treatment for CUD average more than 10 years of near-daily use, make more than six serious attempts at quitting, and most perceive themselves as unable to stop [41].

Behavioral therapies (BTs) for CUD including motivational enhancement therapy (MET), cognitive behavioral therapy (CBT), and abstinence-based contingency management (CM) are efficacious psychotherapeutic approaches with outcomes comparable to treatments for other substance use disorders [41, 42]. MET addresses ambivalence and seeks to improve motivation to make changes in substance use or other problem behaviors [43]. Most METs incorporate personalized feedback on an individual's cannabis use delivered in a nonconfrontational manner, typically in two individual sessions of 50 minutes [44]. CBT views substance dependence as learned behavior that is used to cope with problems or to meet needs, and therefore considers the acquisition of coping skills as essential [45]. *Contingency management* is based on frequent monitoring of the target behavior (e.g., abstinence) and the provision of tangible incentives (e.g., prizes or cash vouchers) when the target behavior occurs [18, 46].

An online MET-CBT manual *Brief Counseling for Marijuana Dependence* [47], developed as part of the Marijuana Treatment Project [48] study on efficacy of cannabis dependence treatments in adults, is available from SAMHSA. A series of online treatment manuals for adolescent cannabis users from the Cannabis Youth Treatment Study [49] are also available from SAMHSA. These manuals were developed by the Center for Substance Abuse Treatment's (CSAT) Cannabis Youth Treatment (CYT) Project, which tested efficacy of five interventions for cannabis dependence, including those based on the MET-CBT treatment model [50, 51], family therapy with case management [52], community reinforcement approach [53], and multidimensional family therapy [54].

The effectiveness of BTs for treatment-seeking cannabis users was recently examined in a meta-analysis of 10 randomized controlled trials (RCTs) [55]. The aggregated treatment effect of behavioral therapies (CM, relapse prevention, MET, and combination of these strategies with CBT) across outcomes and time points (up to 12 months follow-up) was such that the average individual undergoing any active behavioral treatment fared better than 66% of those in control conditions (Hedges' $g = 0.44$). Effects were larger for studies with a waitlist control condition versus active control comparisons (e.g., treatment as usual). Few studies that compared BTs with non-waitlist controls (treatment as usual, psychological placebo) found comparable results in both conditions [56–58]. Combined MET/CBT treatment was also shown to be effective and cost-effective in RCTs for adolescents with CUD [49].

A combination of MET, CBT, and/or abstinence-based CM appears to be the most potent behavioral intervention for adults and adolescents with CUD. Five randomized controlled trials (RCTs utilizing a combination of manualized MET/CBT (9–14 weekly individual sessions)) and weekly CM monetary-based reinforcement of cannabis-negative urine specimens have demonstrated increased abstinence at end of treatment and up to 12 months in follow-ups [18, 56, 57, 59, 60]. As a stand-alone treatment, CM produces equivalent outcomes to MET/CBT/CM during treatment and comparable outcomes to CBT at follow-up but appears to be less efficacious than the combined CBT+CM intervention post-treatment with respect to cannabis abstinence. Indeed, MET/CBT appears to enhance maintenance of the CM effect [18, 56]. Other non-abstinence outcomes such as reductions in self-reported cannabis use days and cannabis-related problems, as well as psychosocial functioning, appear to be comparable across the various behavioral treatment conditions [18]. Given practical issues related to implementation and cost-effectiveness of treatment programs such as CM, this finding is an important point of consideration for treatments that target reductions in use versus abstinence goals.

The use of multicomponent treatments for CUD (e.g., MET/CBT/CM), though advantageous, is not without limitations. These include insufficient resources and high costs associated with treatment-provider training and treatment implementation [61], limited availability of treatment programs that provide MET/CBT or CM [62], practitioners' concerns about use of manual-based psychotherapies in outpatient clinical settings [63], and logistic barriers to disseminating efficacious treatments (e.g., rural areas). Many of these barriers to successful CUD treatment implementation and dissemination may be addressed with technology-delivered interventions [64].

Technology-based interventions have been developed to treat a number of mental health problems, including substance use. Improvement in cannabis outcomes has been demonstrated with MET/CBT interventions delivered by telephone [65], the Internet [66], computer-assisted programs [67], and with computer-based MET/CBT/CM interventions [68, 69]. A randomized trial comparing nine sessions of computer-delivered MET/CBT/CM, therapist-delivered MET/CBT/CM, and brief MET (two sessions) only conditions demonstrated comparable cannabis abstinence and reduction in days of use outcomes for computer- and therapist-delivered treatments with longer duration of abstinence than in the brief MET condition. Furthermore, computer-delivered intervention was significantly more cost-effective than therapist-delivered intervention. Additional RCTs are needed to replicate these promising findings and to test implementation and dissemination of technology-based CUD treatments across diverse treatment settings.

MET-based brief interventions (BMIs) are also specifically indicated for youth who may not be committed to engaging in treatment or even considering making changes in their cannabis use and who would not otherwise receive treatment [70]. BMIs show efficacy in reducing cannabis use and associated negative consequences in college cannabis users [71] and adolescents [72–76].

Parental involvement in BMIs for adolescent cannabis users increases effectiveness of the intervention, even among youth with cannabis dependence and conduct problems [77]. With some exceptions [78], findings from these clinical trials generally support the efficacy of a two-session MI-based protocol that includes structured assessment and feedback components (delivered in the context of a Cannabis Check-Up [75]). This intervention consisted of structured feedback and discussion of cannabis-related information based on personalized assessment of cannabis use and dependence symptoms, perceived pros and cons of continued use, cannabis outcome expectancies, perception of risk from cannabis use, and life goals. A particular emphasis in feedback delivery is placed on the participant's readiness to change (i.e., stage of change), and the ultimate choice for the goal of reducing or stopping cannabis use reserved for the participant. It is important to note that abstinence rates following brief interventions remain low [74], with reduced levels of substance use as a preferred treatment goal and more feasible outcome in the population of young substance users [79], and particularly with cannabis users [80].

Evidence-Based Pharmacological Interventions

Despite demonstrated demand for cannabis treatment among heavy cannabis users [41], there are no FDA-approved pharmacotherapies for CUD and no compelling clinical efficacy data to support any given pharmacological medication compound. As this area of investigation is still young, most of the current research is limited to small-scale laboratory models and small open-label trials. Existing studies on pharmacotherapeutic approaches focus on symptomatic treatment of cannabis withdrawal, on reduction of cannabis cravings, and on reduction of the reinforcing effects of cannabis. Medications investigated in the clinical laboratory setting include cannabinoid substitutes (partial agonists of the CB1 receptor), such as dronabinol (synthetic encapsulated delta-9-tetrahydrocannabinol, THC) and nabilone. Additionally, a small group of non-cannabinoid agents were tested due to past success in treating specific symptom clusters, blunting positive effects of cannabis or clinical evidence in treating opiate or tobacco use disorders. Most success has been obtained with cannabinoid substitutes as well as N-acetylcysteine, oxytocin, and gabapentin. The pharmacotherapy development literature related to CUD has been previously summarized in considerable detail [81–85]. Therefore, we focus on the most promising pharmacological targets.

Cannabinoid Targets

Most promising to date are the results of studies incorporating an agonist approach, assessing effects of treatment with dronabinol on withdrawal in heavy cannabis smokers. Human laboratory studies with dronabinol (50–60 mg/day) significantly decreased cravings, anxiety, chills, misery, troubled sleep, and decreased food intake, but did not affect self-administration [86, 87]. The findings of these studies were extended to an outpatient setting that showed that oral THC (10 or 30 mg, three times a day for 15 days) attenuated cannabis withdrawal symptoms such as aggression, craving, troubled sleep, and irritability

[88]. An RCT in 156 participants examining dronabinol (40 mg/day) [89] found that all participants reduced cannabis use over time irrespective of treatment, and there was no significant difference between treatment groups in the proportion of participants who achieved two weeks of abstinence at the end of the medication phase. However, the dronabinol group had higher treatment retention (77%) compared to placebo (61%), and, consistent with laboratory studies, withdrawal symptoms were significantly lower in the dronabinol group than placebo.

Nabilone, a cannabinoid agonist with better bioavailability, less individual variability and a more reliable dose-response function than dronabinol, has also been evaluated [90]. Nabilone (6–8 mg/day, for eight days), significantly reversed withdrawal-induced irritability and disruptions in sleep and food intake, as well as cannabinoid self-administration [91]. These findings are the most promising human laboratory evidence to date, where a single medication improved both cannabis withdrawal symptoms and prevented relapse, and suggest that nabilone is a promising candidate for investigation in a clinical trial for cannabis treatment.

A recent RCT in 51 treatment-seeking cannabis users examined nabiximols (Sativex®; 1:1 ratio of THC [86.4 mg] and cannabidiol [80 mg]) as a therapy for attenuating cannabis withdrawal [92]. Nabiximols attenuated cannabis withdrawal symptoms and improved patient retention in treatment. However, placebo was as effective as nabiximols in promoting long-term reductions in cannabis use following medication cessation, suggesting that this combination is useful in treating cannabis withdrawal but not relapse.

An alternative approach to agonist medications is directly blocking the cannabinoid 1 receptor (CB1) to antagonize the subjective and reinforcing effects of cannabis. The CB1 receptor mediates the positive subjective and reinforcing effects of cannabis [93], and the subjective effects of cannabis are attenuated by the CB1 receptor antagonist, rimonabant [94, 95]. Further study of rimonabant has, however, been discontinued following evidence that its chronic administration produced side effects such as depression and anxiety [96].

Non-Cannabinoid Targets

Alternately, the endogenous opiate system is another potential candidate for investigation, with animal evidence indicating that opiate antagonists attenuate some behavioral effects of THC. A few laboratory studies have assessed the effects of acute doses of naltrexone, an opiate antagonist used to treat alcohol and opiate dependence, on responses to dronabinol and cannabis in humans with mixed results. However, in daily cannabis smokers, acute administration of a range of acute naltrexone doses (12–100 mg) enhanced the subjective and cardiovascular effects of cannabis (3.27% THC) compared to placebo capsules [97, 98]. Yet, repeated naltrexone administration (50 mg), for two weeks or longer, appears to blunt positive subjective and reinforcing effects of smoked cannabis [99]. Thus, repeated naltrexone administration shows promise in treating cannabis withdrawal and relapse, warranting further clinical evaluation.

Other individual laboratory studies have assessed the effects of various medications on responses to cannabis. α_2-adrenergic receptor agonists such as clonidine and lofexidine were evaluated based on evidence in treating opiate, nicotine, and alcohol withdrawal. Clonidine (0.1–0.4 mg) [100] blunted cardiovascular effects, and lofexidine (2.4 mg/day) [87] by itself had a sedating effect and worsened abstinence-related anorexia. Given the absence of any change in the mood effects of cannabis, neither clonidine nor lofexidine appear likely to be useful for treatment of CUD; no further research has been undertaken.

A number of antidepressants have been evaluated both in the clinic and in the laboratory. Bupropion maintenance (300 mg/day) reduced some subjective effects of cannabis, but also decreased social behavior after smoking cannabis [101, 102]. Repeated dosing of nefazodone (450–600 mg/day) [102, 103] and mirtazapine (30 mg/day) [104] did not alter the subjective effects of cannabis. Similarly, venlafaxine (375 mg/day) [105] and fluoxetine (10–20 mg/day) [106] alleviated depression, but not cannabis use, in depressed cannabis users. A study examining the anti-anxiety drug buspirone (60 mg/day) reported a high dropout rate (50%) and no direct effect of buspirone on self-reported anxiety, withdrawal symptoms, or craving in cannabis users [107]. Escitalopram (10 mg/day), a selective serotonin reuptake inhibitor, also failed to decrease depression or anxiety during cannabis withdrawal or increase rates of abstinence in a double-blind, placebo-controlled clinical study [108]. Existing data, therefore, do not support the likely utility of antidepressant or anti-anxiety medications in treating CUD.

Other types of medications evaluated include anti-psychotics, antiepileptics, and mood stabilizers. Divalproex maintenance (250–2,000 mg/day) decreased cannabis craving during abstinence, but was poorly tolerated, with increased side effects, including anxiety, irritability, fatigue, headaches, nausea, drowsiness, and poor compliance relative to placebo [86, 109]. Lithium (600–1,000 mg/day) reduced rates of withdrawal, and follow-up reports of abstinence were higher than in some previous studies [110, 111]. An inpatient laboratory study evaluating the effects of the antipsychotic quetiapine maintenance (200 mg/day) reported improved sleep quality, increased caloric intake, and decreased weight loss during cannabis withdrawal compared with placebo; however, quetiapine increased cannabis craving and self-administration [112]. On the other hand, a small open-label study in treatment seekers showed that quetiapine (25–600 mg/day) was well tolerated and associated with decreased cannabis use [113]. Overall, these classes of medications are poorly tolerated, which limits their clinical utility.

Chronic cannabis use is also associated with reduced levels of both GABA and glutamate throughout the cingulate cortex, suggesting these systems may provide potential pharmacological targets. Baclofen (60 mg), a $GABA_B$ agonist and muscle relaxant, produced mild effects in reducing cannabis' euphoric effects while the maintenance with the higher dose (90 mg) decreased ratings of both cannabis and cigarette craving [104]. The $GABA_A$ agonist, zolpidem, by contrast, attenuated sleep disruption during cannabis withdrawal, supporting further study of this medication as an adjunct medication for treating CUD [114]. A follow-up study, however, found a combination of zolpidem with nabilone to be no more effective than nabilone in reducing cannabis withdrawal and relapse [115].

Gabapentin, an antiepileptic and analgesic for neuropathic pain, is another promising drug. In a 12-week trial, gabapentin (1,200 mg/day) significantly attenuated withdrawal severity and reduced cannabis use as compared to placebo but the study had a high dropout rate (72%) [116]. Nonetheless, this proof of concept study supports continued research on gabapentin.

The clinical utility of atomoxetine (a norepinephrine reuptake inhibitor indicated for attention deficit hyperactivity disorder, ADHD) to treat cannabis withdrawal has also been investigated with negative results. A placebo-controlled trial evaluated the effects of atomoxetine on symptoms of ADHD and cannabis use in cannabis-dependent adults [117], and found that atomoxetine improved some ADHD symptoms but did not reduce cannabis use in this population.

The hormone oxytocin is another potential treatment approach, as it has been shown in several preclinical models to reduce drug reinforcement and anxiety-like behavior. A trial is currently underway examining the effects of intranasal oxytocin following preliminary laboratory findings that acute administration of oxytocin (40 IU) alleviated stress-induced reactivity and craving in eight cannabis users [118]. These data are supported by findings that oxytocin release mediates lithium's effects on reduction in cannabis withdrawal symptoms [119].

Recent studies tested the antioxidant N-acetylcysteine (NAC), shown in animal studies to reverse alterations to the glutamate system associated with repeated self-administration of a range of addictive drugs. NAC maintenance (2,400 mg/day) decreased cannabis craving and cannabis use, as evidenced by fewer cannabinoid-positive urine tests [120, 121]. Future studies need to further assess its mechanism of action and effectiveness in larger samples.

In summary, the most promising pharmacotherapy to date is the cannabinoid agent nabilone, which was shown in a human laboratory study to reduce a broad range of withdrawal symptoms associated with cannabis abstinence in daily users and in cannabis self-administration. Nabiximols has also shown promise in clinical trials in reducing cannabis withdrawal symptoms, but not in promoting long-term abstinence. In addition to cannabinoid substitutes, there are a number of possible directions that may yield effective treatments for CUD in the future. Despite overall disappointing results in clinical studies conducted to date, a few non-cannabinoid targets (e.g., oxytocin, gabapentin, the antioxidant NAC) have emerged as feasible candidates that warrant further evaluation. Naltrexone maintenance also appears to reduce cannabis withdrawal and relapse, suggesting that endogenous opioid systems may play a neuromodulatory role in mediating cannabis dependence. Other possible directions for the future include new CB1 antagonists currently in development. In addition, inhibition of endocannabinoid catabolic enzymes, fatty acid amide hydrolase (FAAH), and monoacylglycerol lipase (MAGL) reduces cannabinoid withdrawal in animal models of cannabinoid dependence by elevating levels of the endogenous cannabinoid agonists anandamide and 2-arachidonyl glycerol, respectively. Unlike exogenous cannabinoids, FAAH inhibitors do not appear to possess abuse liability. Clinical trials are currently underway measuring the efficacy of FAAH inhibitors in reducing withdrawal in individuals with CUD. Finally, there is increased enthusiasm in cannabidiol (CBD), a non-psychoactive component of THC (and also present in nabiximols) as a potential target for treating cannabis withdrawal.

Strategies and Considerations for Integrating Psychological and Pharmacological Strategies

Over the last two decades, there has been a steady increase in the development of behavioral treatments and pharmacotherapy for CUD. A select number of cannabinoid and non-cannabinoid agents have been tested and show promise as supportive adjunct treatment to behavioral therapy. Furthermore, in the few randomized studies of cannabis pharmacotherapy as an adjunct treatment to a behavioral intervention, adding a pharmacological agent did not significantly enhance cannabis use outcomes relative to a placebo control (dronabinol + MET-CBT [89]; divalproex + CBT [109]; nefazodone, bupropion-SR + CBT [102]; venlafaxine + CBT [105]) or was associated with high study attrition and multiple side effects (buspirone + MET [107]). Adjunct pharmacotherapy in combination with evidence-based psychotherapy has been shown to maximize treatment outcome for other substance use disorders. Combined treatment with both psychosocial therapy and pharmacotherapy may also significantly improve recovery from CUD. As a number of pharmacotherapy development and evaluation studies are currently underway, such efforts are likely to result in the identification of effective pharmacological agents for treatment of CUD. Concurrent improvements in behavioral intervention approaches will set the stage for the ultimate combination of integrated psychological and pharmacological strategies that should improve outcomes for individuals with CUD.

Important Comorbidities and Other Pertinent Considerations

CUD is commonly associated with other substance use disorders and affective disorders [11, 122, 123]. National epidemiologic surveys find that individuals with a lifetime diagnosis of cannabis dependence are at increased risk for development of a comorbid alcohol use disorder (AUD; comorbidity of 86%) [11, 124, 125], and are twice as likely to have a current mood or anxiety disorder than those without CUD [126]. Similar to comorbidity profiles with other SUDs, co-occurrence of CUD and psychiatric disorders is associated with greater symptom severity, poorer CUD treatment outcomes, and greater health service use relative to patients without the comorbidity [127–131]. There is also evidence that concurrent cannabis use negatively affects individuals' response to AUD treatment, reducing sustained remission from alcohol and increased alcohol relapse risk [132, 133, 134].

Individuals with affective vulnerability are especially likely to use cannabis for coping reasons [135–137], as short-term relief of negative affect from cannabis [138] may be negatively reinforcing [139]. Without adaptive affect-modulating strategies, emotionally vulnerable cannabis users may rely on cannabis to decrease distress [140, 141], which may in turn promote problematic cannabis use and CUD [142–144]. The high prevalence of comorbid CUD and affective disorders calls for the development of integrated treatments that specifically focus on coping skills for mood and stress management [145], including increasing an individual's tolerance for emotional distress (particularly during cannabis withdrawal), increasing mindfulness [146, 147], and decreasing avoidance of distress via cannabis use.

Future Directions

Over the last two decades, there has been a steady increase in studies focusing on both psychosocial approaches and medication development for CUD. Behavioral treatment approaches have been consistently more effective than no intervention, but nonetheless produce low rates of long-term abstinence. Adjunct pharmacotherapy in combination with psychosocial approaches has been shown to maximize treatment outcome for other drugs of abuse, but lack of FDA-approved pharmacotherapy for CUD further limits treatment options for cannabis users. A select number of cannabinoid and non-cannabinoid agents show promise as supportive pharmacotherapy, but currently there are no conclusive data on the most efficacious combination of behavioral and pharmacotherapy treatment for CUD.

The use of multicomponent MET/CBT/CM behavioral treatment appears to be the most potent intervention for adults and adolescents with CUD to date. However, even with this best available treatment approach, only about 35% of cannabis users with CUD report abstinence at 12 months [18, 56]. Although relapse rates for cannabis are comparable to alcohol, tobacco [148], and other substances [149], more potent intervention strategies for CUD are clearly still needed. The legalization and increasingly positive attitudes, acceptability, and availability of marijuana have already resulted in doubling of the marijuana use and CUD prevalence rates over the past decade [2]. These growing trends will only serve to accelerate the incidence of CUD and increase demand for cost-effective and easily disseminated treatment. Specifically, future behavioral treatment studies should continue to test implementation and dissemination of technology-based CUD treatments across diverse treatment settings. Addressing specific mechanisms of action in these clinical trials by the inclusion of the moderators and intervention-specific mediators of treatment outcome will help us gain valuable knowledge in the specificity of empirically supported treatments for CUD [150].

An important consideration in the development and further augmentation of CUD treatments is focusing on developing strategies to help cannabis users, who are ambivalent about marijuana cessation, meet their treatment goal of reducing cannabis use and cannabis-related problems. Although better outcomes are observed among patients with abstinence versus moderation goals, reductions in use are also associated with reduced severity of cannabis-related problems and CUD symptoms [41]. As clinicians are commonly faced with cannabis users who are seeking help in reducing hazardous patterns of use, it may be helpful to examine strategies utilized by non-treatment-seeking cannabis users who have succeeded in making such changes. Consistent with natural recovery without treatment from other addictive disorders [151], a portion of cannabis users indeed make efforts and actually reduce or stop cannabis use on their own [152–156]. These studies find that cognitive (addressing expectancies and motives for use and non-use) [153] and behavioral (managing triggers and high-risk situations) strategies play a key role in both treatment-assisted and natural pathways to recovery [157]. Furthermore, a stepped care approach to recovery [152] from hazardous cannabis use may be implemented such that individuals at the lower end of the cannabis problem severity continuum may benefit from self-help materials and may succeed in achieving both moderation and abstinence recovery goals without formal treatment. On the other hand, cannabis users with higher CUD severity may need more intensive treatments, including treatments that specifically address co-occurring mental and substance use disorders [152].

Another consideration for cannabis users with higher CUD severity is based on the growing recognition of the long-term nature of drug addiction. Relapse rates for individuals with any substance use disorder are largely comparable to those for individuals with other chronic medical conditions, including diabetes, hypertension, or asthma [158]. Acute care models often fail to consider this chronic nature of addiction, where return to use likely indicates a need for re-engagement in treatment. Recovery management offers an alternative comprehensive approach to addiction treatment and recovery, with support services to enhance early pre-recovery engagement, recovery initiation, and long-term recovery maintenance [159].

Future directions in medication development for CUD may include the following considerations. First, as we have learned from other fields of medicine and from research on alcohol use disorders [160], we need to consider a personalized approach to pharmacological treatment of CUD, as there may be individual differences in response to different medications [161]. Pharmacogenetic and pharmacogenomic research offers promise in this respect [162]. Second, human laboratory studies are essential in understanding the mechanisms of drug treatment response [81, 163]. Further, validating laboratory findings with clinical data from cannabis users seeking treatment for CUD is the key next step in guiding the development of effective CUD treatments [164]. Preclinical research on new pharmacotherapy targets will continue to foster this growth. Because of the current federal scheduling regulations for cannabis, much of that research is limited to either synthetic cannabinoids or to government-grown cannabis in a limited range of strains (historically primarily THC) and restricted potency range. It is imperative for future research on cannabis to expand scientific investigations to major cannabinoids (THC and CBD) and to common strains of cannabis in order to build a solid evidence base for clinical and preclinical research [165].

Table 7.1 Summary table

KEY RESEARCH FINDINGS
1. Cannabis withdrawal is a major determinant of relapse among individuals seeking treatment for cannabis use disorder (CUD).
2. Demand for treatment of CUD has increased dramatically, with CUD comprising a significant proportion of all admissions to substance use treatment services, secondary only to alcohol and all forms of opiate use disorders.
3. A combination of MET, CBT, and abstinence-based CM is the most potent behavioral intervention for adults and adolescents with CUD.
4. Technology-based behavioral interventions show efficacy and cost-effectiveness and may increase successful implementation and dissemination of CUD treatments to diverse treatment settings.
5. There is no FDA-approved pharmacotherapy for CUD currently available. Cannabinoid receptor agonists nabilone and nabiximols are most effective in reducing cannabis withdrawal and relapse in laboratory models and may be promising targets for clinical trials. Preliminary results from clinical trials and laboratory support further research on naltrexone, gabapentin, and acetylcysteine (NAC).
RECOMMENDATIONS FOR EVIDENCE-BASED PRACTICE
1. Inclusion of CM with MET-CBT behavioral treatments for CUD will help enhance long-term abstinence outcomes.
2. Long-term recovery maintenance (recovery management treatment model) may be needed for cannabis users with more severe CUD.
3. Incorporate adjunct pharmacotherapy deemed effective in clinical trials with behavioral interventions for CUD, particularly in initial stages of treatment to alleviate withdrawal symptoms.
RECOMMENDATIONS FOR FUTURE RESEARCH
1. Addressing specific mechanisms of action of CUD treatment in clinical trials will add knowledge in the specificity of empirically supported treatments for CUD and ultimately improve treatment outcomes.
2. Developing integrated treatments for comorbid CUD and affective disorders, with the specific focus on coping skills for mood and stress management.
3. Future research and clinical trials with FAAH and MAGL inhibitors, and formulations containig cannabidiol, offer promise.
4. Consider a personalized approach to pharmacological treatment of CUD, as there may be individual differences in response to different medications.

References

1. SAMHSA. *Results from the 2013 National Survey on Drug Use and Health: summary of national findings*. Rockville (MD): Substance Abuse and Mental Health Services Administration, Quality CfBHSa; 2014 Contract No.: HHS Publication No. (SMA) 14-4863.
2. Hasin DS, Saha TD, Kerridge BT, Goldstein RB, Chou SP, Zhang H, et al. Prevalence of marijuana use disorders in the United States between 2001–2002 and 2012–2013. *JAMA Psychiatry*. 2015;72(12):1235–1242.
3. Anthony JC. The epidemiology of cannabis dependence. In: Roffman RA, Stephens RS, editors. *Cannabis dependence*. Cambridge: Cambridge University Press; 2006:58–105.
4. Hasin DS, Keyes KM, Alderson D, Wang S, Aharonovich E, Grant BF. Cannabis withdrawal in the United States: results from NESARC. *The Journal of Clinical Psychiatry*. 2008;69(9):1354–1363.
5. American Psychiatric Association. *Diagnostic and statistical manual of mental disorders (DSM-IV)*. Washington (DC): American Psychiatric Association Publishing; 1994.
6. First MB, Spitzer RL, Gibbon M, Williams JBW. *Structured clinical interview for DSM-IV axis I disorders*. New York: New York State Psychiatric Institute; 1995.
7. American Psychiatric Association. *Diagnostic and statistical manual of mental disorders*. 5th ed. Arlington (VA): American Psychiatric Publishing; 2013.
8. APA. American Psychiatric Association. *Diagnostic and statistical manual of mental disorders*. 5th ed. Arlington (VA): American Psychiatric Association; 2013.
9. Agrawal A, Lynskey MT, Bucholz KK, Kapoor M, Almasy L, Dick DM, et al. DSM-5 cannabis use disorder: a phenotypic and genomic perspective. *Drug Alcohol Depend*. 2014;134:362–369.
10. Mewton L, Slade T, Teesson M. An evaluation of the proposed DSM-5 cannabis use disorder criteria using Australian national survey data. *J Stud Alcohol Drugs*. 2013;74(4):614–621.
11. Stinson FS, Ruan WJ, Pickering R, Grant BF. Cannabis use disorders in the USA: prevalence, correlates and co-morbidity. *Psychological Medicine*. 2006;36(10):1447–1460.
12. Piomelli D. The endogenous cannabinoid system and the treatment of marijuana dependence. *Neuropharmacology*. 2004;47(Suppl 1):359–367.
13. Pacher P, Batkai S, Kunos G. The endocannabinoid system as an emerging target of pharmacotherapy. *Pharmacol Rev*. 2006;58(3):389–462.
14. Babor T. The diagnosis of cannabis dependence. In: Roffman RA, Stephens RS, editors. *Cannabis dependence: its nature, consequences and treatment*. New York: Cambridge University Press; 2006:21–36.
15. Agrawal A, Pergadia ML, Saccone SF, Lynskey MT, Wang JC, Martin NG, et al. An autosomal linkage scan for cannabis use disorders in the nicotine addiction genetics project. *Arch Gen Psychiatry*. 2008;65(6):713–721.
16. Compton WM, Saha TD, Conway KP, Grant BF. The role of cannabis use within a dimensional approach to cannabis use disorders. *Drug Alcohol Depend*. 2009;100(3):221–227.
17. Budney AJ. Are specific dependence criteria necessary for different substances: how can research on cannabis inform this issue? *Addiction*. 2006;101:125–133.

18. Budney AJ, Moore BA, Rocha HL, Higgins ST. Clinical trial of abstinence-based vouchers and cognitive-behavioral therapy for cannabis dependence. *Journal of Consulting and Clinical Psychology*. 2006;74(2):307–316.
19. Haney M, Spealman R. Controversies in translational research: drug self-administration. *Psychopharmacology*. 2008;199(3):403–419.
20. Lynskey MT, Agrawal A. Psychometric properties of DSM assessments of illicit drug abuse and dependence: results from the National Epidemiologic Survey on Alcohol and Related Conditions (NESARC). *Psychological Medicine*. 2007;37(9):1345–1355.
21. Gonzalez S, Cebeira M, Fernandez-Ruiz J. Cannabinoid tolerance and dependence: a review of studies in laboratory animals. *Pharmacology, Biochemistry, and Behavior*. 2005;81(2):300–318.
22. Onaivi ES, Chakrabarti A, Gwebu ET, Chaudhuri G. Neurobehavioral effects of delta 9-THC and cannabinoid (CB1) receptor gene expression in mice. *Behav Brain Res*. 1995;72(1–2):115–125.
23. Budney AJ, Hughes JR, Moore BA, Vandrey R. Review of the validity and significance of cannabis withdrawal syndrome. *Am J Psychiatry*. 2004;161(11):1967–1977.
24. Haney M, Bedi G, Cooper ZD, Glass A, Vosburg SK, Comer SD, et al. Predictors of marijuana relapse in the human laboratory: robust impact of tobacco cigarette smoking status. *Biological Psychiatry*. 2013;73(3):242–248.
25. Hart CL. Increasing treatment options for cannabis dependence: a review of potential pharmacotherapies. *Drug & Alcohol Dependence*. 2005;80:147–159.
26. Carter BL, Tiffany ST. Cue-reactivity and the future of addiction research. *Addiction*. 1999;94(3):349–351.
27. Niaura RS, Rohsenow DJ, Binkoff JA, Monti PM, Pedraza M, Abrams DB. Relevance of cue reactivity to understanding alcohol and smoking relapse. *Journal of Abnormal Psychology*. 1988;97(2):133–152.
28. Robinson TE, Berridge KC. The neural basis of drug craving: an incentive-sensitization theory of addiction. *Brain Research Reviews*. 1993;18(3):247–291.
29. Robinson TE, Berridge KC. Addiction. *Annu Rev Psychol*. 2003;54:25–53.
30. Witkin JM, Tzavara ET, Nomikos GG. A role for cannabinoid CB1 receptors in mood and anxiety disorders. *Behavioural Pharmacology*. 2005;16(5–6):315–331.
31. Budney AJ, Moore BA, Vandrey RG, Hughes JR. The time course and significance of cannabis withdrawal. *J Abnorm Psychol*. 2003;112(3):393–402.
32. Lundahl LH, Johanson CE. Cue-induced craving for marijuana in cannabis-dependent adults. *Exp Clin Psychopharmacol*. 2011;19(3):224–230.
33. Nickerson LD, Ravichandran C, Lundahl LH, Rodolico J, Dunlap S, Trksak GH, et al. Cue reactivity in cannabis-dependent adolescents. *Psychol Addict Behav*. 2011;25(1):168–173.
34. Lundahl LH, Greenwald MK. Effect of oral THC pretreatment on marijuana cue-induced responses in cannabis dependent volunteers. *Drug Alcohol Depend*. 2015;149:187–193.
35. Filbey FM, Schacht JP, Myers US, Chavez RS, Hutchison KE. Marijuana craving in the brain. *Proceedings of the National Academy of Sciences of the United States of America*. 2009;106(31):13016–13021.
36. Haughey HM, Marshall E, Schacht JP, Louis A, Hutchison KE. Marijuana withdrawal and craving: influence of the cannabinoid receptor 1 (CNR1) and fatty acid amide hydrolase (FAAH) genes. *Addiction*. 2008;103(10):1678–1686.

37. Schacht JP, Selling RE, Hutchison KE. Intermediate cannabis dependence phenotypes and the FAAH C385A variant: an exploratory analysis. *Psychopharmacology*. 2009;203(3):511–517.
38. Metrik J, Aston E, Kahler C, Rohsenow D, McGeary J, Knopik V, et al. Multidimensional assessment of cue-elicited increases in incentive salience for marijuana. *Drug Alcohol Depend*. 2016;167:82–88.
39. SAMHSA. *Results from the 2009 National Survey on Drug Use and Health: volume I. Summary of national findings*. Rockville (MD): Office of Applied Studies, NSDUH; 2010.
40. SAMHSA. *Treatment Episode Data Set (TEDS): 2002–2012. National admissions to substance abuse treatment services*. Rockville (MD): Substance Abuse and Mental Health Services Administration, Quality CfBHSa; 2014. Contract No.: HHS Publication No. (SMA) 14-4850.
41. Budney AJ, Roffman R, Stephens RS, Walker D. Marijuana dependence and its treatment. *Addict Sci Clin Pract*. 2007;4(1):4–16.
42. Dutra L, Stathopoulou G, Basden SL, Leyro TM, Powers MB, Otto MW. A meta-analytic review of psychosocial interventions for substance use disorders. *Am J Psychiatry*. 2008;165(2):179–187.
43. Miller WR, Rollnick S. *Motivational interviewing: preparing people for change*. 2nd ed. New York: Guilford Press; 2002.
44. Carey KB, Henson JM, Carey MP, Maisto SA. Which heavy drinking college students benefit from a brief motivational intervention? *Journal of Consulting and Clinical Psychology*. 2007;75:663–669.
45. Monti PM, Colby SM, O'Leary TA. Adolescents, alcohol, and substance abuse: reaching teens through brief interventions. *Am J Psychiatry*. 2002;159(11):1958.
46. Prendergast M, Podus D, Finney J, Greenwell L, Roll J. Contingency management for treatment of substance use disorders: a meta-analysis. *Addiction*. 2006;101(11):1546–1560.
47. Steinberg KL, Roffman RA, Carroll KM, McRee B, Babor TF, Miller M, et al. *Brief counseling for marijuana dependence: a manual for treating adults*. Rockville (MD): Center for Substance Abuse Treatment, Substance Abuse and Mental Health Services Administration; 2005.
48. MTPRG. Brief treatments for cannabis dependence: findings from a randomized multisite trial. *Journal of Consulting and Clinical Psychology*. 2004;72(3):455–466.
49. Dennis M, Godley SH, Diamond G, Tims FM, Babor T, Donaldson J, et al. The Cannabis Youth Treatment (CYT) study: main findings from two randomized trials. *Journal of Substance Abuse Treatment*. 2004;27(3):197–213.
50. Sampl S, Kadden R. *Motivational enhancement therapy and cognitive behavioral therapy for adolescent cannabis users: 5 Sessions*. Rockville (MD): Center for Substance Abuse Treatment, Substance Abuse and Mental Health Services Administration; 2001.
51. Webb C, Scudder M, Kaminer Y, Kadden R. *The motivational enhancement therapy and cognitive behavioral therapy supplement: 7 sessions of cognitive behavioral therapy for adolescent cannabis users*. Rockville (MD): Center for Substance Abuse Treatment, Substance Abuse and Mental Health Services Administration; 2001.
52. Hamilton NL, Brantley LB, Tims FM, Angelovich N, McDougall B. *Family support network for adolescent cannabis users, Cannabis Youth Treatment (CYT) series*. Rockville (MD): Center for Substance Abuse Treatment, Substance Abuse and Mental Health Services Administration; 2001.

53. Godley SH, Meyers RJ, Smith JE, Karvinen T, Titus JC, Godley MD, et al. *The adolescent community reinforcement approach for adolescent cannabis users.* Rockville (MD): Center for Substance Abuse Treatment, Substance Abuse and Mental Health Services Administration; 2001.
54. Liddle HA. *Multidimensional family therapy for adolescent cannabis users.* Rockville (MD): Center for Substance Abuse Treatment, Substance Abuse and Mental Health Services Administration; 2001.
55. Davis ML, Powers MB, Handelsman P, Medina JL, Zvolensky M, Smits JA. Behavioral therapies for treatment-seeking cannabis users: a meta-analysis of randomized controlled trials. *Eval Health Prof.* 2015;38(1):94–114.
56. Kadden RM, Litt MD, Kabela-Cormier E, Petry NM. Abstinence rates following behavioral treatments for marijuana dependence. *Addictive Behaviors.* 2007;32(6): 1220–1236.
57. Carroll KM, Easton CJ, Nich C, Hunkele KA, Neavins TM, Sinha R, et al. The use of contingency management and motivational/skills-building therapy to treat young adults with marijuana dependence. *Journal of Consulting and Clinical Psychology.* 2006;74(5):955–966.
58. Stephens RS, Roffman RA, Simpson EE. Treating adult marijuana dependence: a test of the relapse prevention model. *Journal of Consulting and Clinical Psychology.* 1994;62:92–99.
59. Budney AJ, Higgins ST, Radonovich KJ, Novy PL. Adding voucher-based incentives to coping skills and motivational enhancement improves outcomes during treatment for marijuana dependence. *Journal of Consulting and Clinical Psychology.* 2000;68(6):1051–1061.
60. Stanger C, Budney AJ, Kamon JL, Thostensen J. A randomized trial of contingency management for adolescent marijuana abuse and dependence. *Drug Alcohol Depend.* 2009;105(3):240–247.
61. Kirby KC, Benishek LA, Dugosh KL, Kerwin ME. Substance abuse treatment providers' beliefs and objections regarding contingency management: implications for dissemination. *Drug Alcohol Depend.* 2006;85(1):19–27.
62. Carroll KM. Lost in translation? Moving contingency management and cognitive behavioral therapy into clinical practice. *Annals of the New York Academy of Sciences.* 2014;1327:94–111.
63. Addis ME, Wade WA, Hatgis C. Barriers to dissemination of evidence-based practices: addressing practitioners' concerns about manual-based psychotherapies. *Clinical Psychology: Science and Practice.* 1999;6(4):430–441.
64. Marsch LA, Carroll KM, Kiluk BD. Technology-based interventions for the treatment and recovery management of substance use disorders: a JSAT special issue. *Journal of Substance Abuse Treatment.* 2014;46(1):1–4.
65. Gates PJ, Norberg MM, Copeland J, Digiusto E. Randomized controlled trial of a novel cannabis use intervention delivered by telephone. *Addiction.* 2012;107(12): 2149–2158.
66. Rooke S, Copeland J, Norberg M, Hine D, McCambridge J. Effectiveness of a self-guided Web-based cannabis treatment program: randomized controlled trial. *Journal of Medical Internet Research.* 2013;15(2):e26.
67. Kay-Lambkin FJ, Baker AL, Kelly B, Lewin TJ. Clinician-assisted computerised versus therapist-delivered treatment for depressive and addictive disorders: a randomised controlled trial. *The Medical Journal of Australia.* 2011;195(3): S44–50.

68. Budney AJ, Fearer S, Walker DD, Stanger C, Thostenson J, Grabinski M, et al. An initial trial of a computerized behavioral intervention for cannabis use disorder. *Drug Alcohol Depend.* 2011;115(1–2):74–79.
69. Budney AJ, Stanger C, Tilford JM, Scherer EB, Brown PC, Li Z, et al. Computer-assisted behavioral therapy and contingency management for cannabis use disorder. *Psychol Addict Behav.* 2015;29(3):501–511.
70. Stephens RS, Roffman RA, Fearer SA, Williams C, Picciano JF, Burke RS. The marijuana check-up: reaching users who are ambivalent about change. *Addiction.* 2004;99(10):1323–1332.
71. McCambridge J, Strang J. The efficacy of single-session motivational interviewing in reducing drug consumption and perceptions of drug-related risk and harm among young people: results from a multi-site cluster randomized trial. *Addiction.* 2004;99(1):39–52.
72. Winters KC, Lee S, Botzet A, Fahnhorst T, Nicholson A. One-year outcomes and mediators of a brief intervention for drug abusing adolescents. *Psychol Addict Behav.* 2014;28(2):464–474.
73. Winters KC, Fahnhorst T, Botzet A, Lee S, Lalone B. Brief intervention for drug-abusing adolescents in a school setting: outcomes and mediating factors. *Journal of Substance Abuse Treatment.* 2012;42(3):279–288.
74. Winters KC, Leitten W. Brief intervention for drug-abusing adolescents in a school setting. *Psychol Addict Behav.* 2007;21(2):249–254.
75. Berghuis J, Swift W, Roffman RA, Stephens RS, Copeland J. The teen cannabis check-up: exploring strategies for reaching young cannabis users' cannabis dependence. In: Roffman RA, Stephens RS, editors. *Cannabis dependence: its nature, consequences and treatment.* Cambridge: Cambridge University Press; 2006:275–296.
76. Martin G, Copeland J. The adolescent cannabis check-up: randomized trial of a brief intervention for young cannabis users. *Journal of Substance Abuse Treatment.* 2008;34(4):407–414.
77. Piehler TF, Winters KC. Parental involvement in brief interventions for adolescent marijuana use. *Psychol Addict Behav.* 2015;29(3):512–521.
78. Walker DD, Stephens R, Roffman R, Demarce J, Lozano B, Towe S, et al. Randomized controlled trial of motivational enhancement therapy with non-treatment-seeking adolescent cannabis users: a further test of the teen marijuana check-up. *Psychol Addict Behav.* 2011;25(3):474–484.
79. Tevyaw TO, Monti PM. Motivational enhancement and other brief interventions for adolescent substance abuse: foundations, applications and evaluations. *Addiction.* 2004;99(Suppl 2):63–75.
80. Sobell LC, Sobell MB, Wagner EF, Agrawal S, Ellingstad TP. Guided self-change: a brief motivational intervention for cannabis abuse. In: Roffman RA, Stephens RS, editors. *Cannabis dependence: its nature, consequences and treatment.* New York: Cambridge University Press; 2006:204–224.
81. Balter RE, Cooper ZD, Haney M. Novel pharmacologic approaches to treating cannabis use disorder. *Current Addiction Reports.* 2014;1(2):137–143.
82. Benyamina A, Lecacheux M, Blecha L, Reynaud M, Lukasiewcz M. Pharmacotherapy and psychotherapy in cannabis withdrawal and dependence. *Expert Review of Neurotherapeutics.* 2008;8(3):479–491.
83. Vandrey R, Haney M. Pharmacotherapy for cannabis dependence: how close are we? *CNS Drugs.* 2009;23(7):543–553.

84. Budney AJ, Vandrey RG, Stanger C. Intervenções farmacológica e psicossocial para os distúrbios por uso da cannabis. *Revista Brasileira de Psiquiatria.* 2010; 32:546–555.
85. Ramesh D, Haney M. Treatment of cannabis use disorders. In: el-Guebaly N, Carrà G, Galanter M, editors. *Textbook of addiction treatment: international perspectives.* Milan: Springer; 2014:367–380.
86. Haney M, Hart CL, Vosburg SK, Nasser J, Bennett A, Zubaran C, et al. Marijuana withdrawal in humans: effects of oral THC or divalproex. *Neuropsychopharmacology.* 2004;29(1):158–170.
87. Haney M, Hart CL, Vosburg SK, Comer SD, Reed SC, Foltin RW. Effects of THC and lofexidine in a human laboratory model of marijuana withdrawal and relapse. *Psychopharmacology.* 2008;197(1):157–168.
88. Budney AJ, Vandrey RG, Hughes JR, Moore BA, Bahrenburg B. Oral delta-9-tetrahydrocannabinol suppresses cannabis withdrawal symptoms. *Drug Alcohol Depend.* 2007;86(1):22–29.
89. Levin FR, Mariani JJ, Brooks DJ, Pavlicova M, Cheng W, Nunes EV. Dronabinol for the treatment of cannabis dependence: a randomized, double-blind, placebo-controlled trial. *Drug Alcohol Depend.* 2011;116(1–3):142–150.
90. Bedi G, Cooper ZD, Haney M. Subjective, cognitive and cardiovascular dose-effect profile of nabilone and dronabinol in marijuana smokers. *Addict Biol.* 2013;18(5):872–881.
91. Haney M, Cooper ZD, Bedi G, Vosburg SK, Comer SD, Foltin RW. Nabilone decreases marijuana withdrawal and a laboratory measure of marijuana relapse. *Neuropsychopharmacology.* 2013;38(8):1557–1565. doi:10.1038/npp.2013.54.
92. Allsop DJ, Copeland J, Lintzeris N, et al. Nabiximols as an agonist replacement therapy during cannabis withdrawal: a randomized clinical trial. *JAMA Psychiatry.* 2014;71(3):281–291.
93. Cooper ZD, Haney M. Cannabis reinforcement and dependence: role of the cannabinoid CB1 receptor. *Addict Biol.* 2008;13(2):188–195.
94. Huestis MA, Gorelick DA, Heishman SJ, Preston KL, Nelson RA, Moolchan ET, et al. Blockade of effects of smoked marijuana by the CB1-selective cannabinoid receptor antagonist SR141716. *Arch Gen Psychiatry.* 2001;58(4):322–328.
95. Huestis MA, Boyd SJ, Heishman SJ, Preston KL, Bonnet D, Le Fur G, et al. Single and multiple doses of rimonabant antagonize acute effects of smoked cannabis in male cannabis users. *Psychopharmacology.* 2007;194(4):505–515.
96. Taylor D. Withdrawal of Rimonabant: walking the tightrope of 21st century pharmaceutical regulation? *Current Drug Safety.* 2009;4(1):2–4.
97. Cooper ZD, Haney M. Opioid antagonism enhances marijuana's effects in heavy marijuana smokers. *Psychopharmacology.* 2010;211(2):141–148.
98. Haney M, Bisaga A, Foltin RW. Interaction between naltrexone and oral THC in heavy marijuana smokers. *Psychopharmacology.* 2003;166(1):77–85.
99. Haney M, Ramesh D, Glass A, Pavlicova M, Bedi G, Cooper ZD. Naltrexone maintenance decreases cannabis self administration and subjective effects in daily cannabis smokers. *Neuropsychopharmacology.* 2015;40(11):2489–2498. doi:10.1038/npp.2015.108.
100. Cone EJ, Welch P, Lange WR. Clonidine partially blocks the physiologic effects but not the subjective effects produced by smoking marijuana in male human subjects. *Pharmacology, Biochemistry, and Behavior.* 1988;29(3):649–652.

101. Haney M, Ward AS, Comer SD, Hart CL, Foltin RW, Fischman MW. Bupropion SR worsens mood during marijuana withdrawal in humans. *Psychopharmacology*. 2001;155(2):171–179.
102. Carpenter KM, McDowell D, Brooks DJ, Cheng WY, Levin FR. A preliminary trial: double-blind comparison of nefazodone, bupropion-SR, and placebo in the treatment of cannabis dependence. *Am J Addict*. 2009;18(1):53–64.
103. Haney M, Hart CL, Ward AS, Foltin RW. Nefazodone decreases anxiety during marijuana withdrawal in humans. *Psychopharmacology*. 2003;165(2):157–165.
104. Haney M, Hart CL, Vosburg SK, Comer SD, Reed SC, Cooper ZD, et al. Effects of baclofen and mirtazapine on a laboratory model of marijuana withdrawal and relapse. *Psychopharmacology*. 2010;211(2):233–244.
105. Levin FR, Mariani J, Brooks DJ, Pavlicova M, Nunes EV, Agosti V, et al. A randomized double-blind, placebo-controlled trial of venlafaxine-extended release for co-occurring cannabis dependence and depressive disorders. *Addiction*. 2013;108(6):1084–1094.
106. Cornelius JR, Bukstein OG, Douaihy AB, Clark DB, Chung TA, Daley DC, et al. Double-blind fluoxetine trial in comorbid MDD-CUD youth and young adults. *Drug Alcohol Depend*. 2010;112(1–2):39–45.
107. McRae-Clark AL, Carter RE, Killeen TK, Carpenter MJ, Wahlquist AE, Simpson SA, et al. A placebo-controlled trial of buspirone for the treatment of marijuana dependence. *Drug Alcohol Depend*. 2009;105(1–2):132–138.
108. Weinstein AM, Miller H, Bluvstein I, Rapoport E, Schreiber S, Bar-Hamburger R, et al. Treatment of cannabis dependence using escitalopram in combination with cognitive-behavior therapy: a double-blind placebo-controlled study. *The American Journal of Drug and Alcohol Abuse*. 2014;40(1):16–22.
109. Levin FR, McDowell D, Evans SM, Nunes E, Akerele E, Donovan S, et al. Pharmacotherapy for marijuana dependence: a double-blind, placebo-controlled pilot study of divalproex sodium. *Am J Addict*. 2004;13(1):21–32.
110. Bowen R, McIlwrick J, Baetz M, Zhang X. Lithium and marijuana withdrawal. *Can J Psychiatry*. 2005;50(4):240–241.
111. Winstock AR, Lea T, Copeland J. Lithium carbonate in the management of cannabis withdrawal in humans: an open-label study. *J Psychopharmacol*. 2009;23(1):84–93.
112. Cooper ZD, Foltin RW, Hart CL, Vosburg SK, Comer SD, Haney M. A human laboratory study investigating the effects of quetiapine on marijuana withdrawal and relapse in daily marijuana smokers. *Addict Biol*. 2013;18(6):993–1002. doi:10.1111/j.1369-1600.2012.00461.x.
113. Mariani JJ, Pavlicova M, Mamczur AK, Bisaga A, Nunes EV, Levin FR. Open-label pilot study of quetiapine treatment for cannabis dependence. *The American Journal of Drug and Alcohol Abuse*. 2014;40(4):280–284.
114. Vandrey R, Smith MT, McCann UD, Budney AJ, Curran EM. Sleep disturbance and the effects of extended-release zolpidem during cannabis withdrawal. *Drug Alcohol Depend*. 2011;117(1):38–44.
115. Herrmann ES, Cooper ZD, Bedi G, Ramesh D, Reed SC, Comer SD, et al. Effects of zolpidem alone and in combination with nabilone on cannabis withdrawal and a laboratory model of relapse in cannabis users. *Psychopharmacology*. 2016:1–10.
116. Mason BJ, Crean R, Goodell V, Light JM, Quello S, Shadan F, et al. A proof-of-concept randomized controlled study of gabapentin: effects on cannabis use,

withdrawal and executive function deficits in cannabis-dependent adults. *Neuropsychopharmacology.* 2012;37(7):1689–1698.
117. McRae-Clark AL, Carter RE, Killeen TK, Carpenter MJ, White KG, Brady KT. A placebo-controlled trial of atomoxetine in marijuana-dependent individuals with attention deficit hyperactivity disorder. *Am J Addict.* 2010;19(6):481–489.
118. McRae-Clark AL, Baker NL, Maria MM, Brady KT. Effect of oxytocin on craving and stress response in marijuana-dependent individuals: a pilot study. *Psychopharmacology.* 2013;228(4):623–631. doi:10.1007/s00213-013-3062-4.
119. Cui SS, Bowen RC, Gu GB, Hannesson DK, Yu PH, Zhang X. Prevention of cannabinoid withdrawal syndrome by lithium: involvement of oxytocinergic neuronal activation. *The Journal of Neuroscience.* 2001;21(24):9867–9876.
120. Gray KM, Carpenter MJ, Baker NL, DeSantis SM, Kryway E, Hartwell KJ, et al. A double-blind randomized controlled trial of N-acetylcysteine in cannabis-dependent adolescents. *Am J Psychiatry.* 2012;169(8):805–812.
121. Gray KM, Watson NL, Carpenter MJ, Larowe SD. N-acetylcysteine (NAC) in young marijuana users: an open-label pilot study. *Am J Addict.* 2010;19(2):187–189.
122. Conway KP, Compton W, Stinson FS, Grant BF. Lifetime comorbidity of DSM-IV mood and anxiety disorders and specific drug use disorders: results from the National Epidemiologic Survey on Alcohol and Related Conditions. *The Journal of Clinical Psychiatry.* 2006;67:247–257.
123. Kevorkian S, Bonn-Miller MO, Belendiuk K, Carney DM, Roberson-Nay R, Berenz EC. Associations among trauma, posttraumatic stress disorder, cannabis use, and cannabis use disorder in a nationally representative epidemiologic sample. *Psychol Addict Behav.* 2015;29(3):633–638.
124. Agrawal A, Lynskey MT, Madden PA, Bucholz KK, Heath AC. A latent class analysis of illicit drug abuse/dependence: results from the National Epidemiological Survey on Alcohol and Related Conditions. *Addiction.* 2007;102(1):94–104.
125. Midanik LT, Tam TW, Weisner C. Concurrent and simultaneous drug and alcohol use: results of the 2000 National Alcohol Survey. *Drug Alcohol Depend.* 2007;90(1):72–80.
126. Agosti V, Nunes E, Levin F. Rates of psychiatric comorbidity among U.S. residents with lifetime cannabis dependence. *The American Journal of Drug and Alcohol Abuse.* 2002;28:643–652.
127. Carey KB. Clinically useful assessments: substance use, and comorbid psychiatric disorders. *Behav Res Ther.* 2002;40:1345–1361.
128. Ouimette P, Finney JW, Moos RH. Two-year posttreatment functioning and coping of substance abuse patients with posttraumatic stress disorder. *Psychol Addict Behav.* 1999;13:105–114.
129. Saladin ME, Brady KT, Dansky BS, Kilpatrick DG. Understanding comorbidity between PTSD and substance use disorders: two preliminary investigations. *Addictive Behaviors.* 1995;20:643–655.
130. Tate SR, Brown SA, Unrod M, Ramo DE. Context of relapse for substance-dependent adults with and without comorbid psychiatric disorders. *Addictive Behaviors.* 2004;29:1707–1724.
131. Watkins KE, Burnam A, Kung FY, Paddock S. A national survey of care for persons with co-occurring mental and substance use disorders. *Psychiatr Serv.* 2001;52:1062–1068.
132. Aharonovich E, Liu X, Samet S, Nunes E, Waxman R, Hasin D. Postdischarge cannabis use and its relationship to cocaine, alcohol, and heroin use: a prospective study. *Am J Psychiatry.* 2005;162(8):1507–1514.

133. Mojarrad M, Samet JH, Cheng DM, Winter MR, Saitz R. Marijuana use and achievement of abstinence from alcohol and other drugs among people with substance dependence: a prospective cohort study. *Drug Alcohol Depend.* 2014;142:91–97.
134. Subbaraman, MS., Metrik, J., Patterson, D., & Swift, R. (2017). Cannabis use during alcohol treatment for alcohol use disorders predicts alcohol treatment outcomes. *Addiction*, 112, 685-694
135. Simons JS, Gaher RM, Correia CJ, Hansen CL, Christopher MS. An affective-motivational model of marijuana and alcohol problems among college students. *Psychol Addict Behav.* 2005;19:326–334.
136. Buckner JD, Zvolensky MJ. Cannabis and related impairment: the unique roles of cannabis use to cope with social anxiety and social avoidance. *Am J Addict.* 2014;23(6):598–603.
137. Johnson K, Mullin JL, Marshall EC, Bonn-Miller MO, Zvolensky M. Exploring the mediational role of coping motives for marijuana use in terms of the relation between anxiety sensitivity and marijuana dependence. *The American Journal on Addictions.* 2010;19(3):277–282.
138. Metrik J, Kahler CW, McGeary JE, Monti PM, Rohsenow DJ. Acute effects of marijuana smoking on negative and positive affect. *Journal of Cognitive Psychotherapy.* 2011;25:1–16.
139. Baker TB, Piper ME, McCarthy DE, Majeskie MR, Fiore MC. Addiction motivation reformulated: an affective processing model of negative reinforcement. *Psychol Rev.* 2004;111:33–51.
140. Bonn-Miller MO, Vujanovic AA, Twohig MP, Medina JL, Huggins JL. Post-traumatic stress symptom severity and marijuana use coping motives: a test of the mediating role of non-judgmental acceptance within a trauma-exposed community sample. *Mindfulness.* 2010;1(2):98–106.
141. Potter CM, Vujanovic AA, Marshall-Berenz EC, Bernstein A, Bonn-Miller MO. Posttraumatic stress and marijuana use coping motives: the mediating role of distress tolerance. *J Anxiety Disord.* 2011;25(3):437–443.
142. Farris SG, Metrik J, Bonn-Miller MO, Kahler CW, Zvolensky MJ. Associations between anxiety sensitivity and distress intolerance with cannabis problems and dependence symptoms: the mediating role of coping motives. *Journal of Studies on Alcohol and Drugs.* 2016;77(6):889–897.
143. Bonn-Miller MO, Zvolensky MJ. An evaluation of the nature of marijuana use and its motives among young adult active users. *Am J Addict.* 2009;18:409–416.
144. Metrik J, Jackson K, Bassett SS, Zvolensky MJ, Seal K, Borsari B. The mediating roles of coping, sleep, and anxiety motives in cannabis use and problems among returning veterans with PTSD and MDD. *Psychol Addict Behav.* 2016;30(7):743–754.
145. Buckner JD, Zvolensky MJ, Schmidt NB, Carroll KM, Schatschneider C, Crapanzano K. Integrated cognitive behavioral therapy for cannabis use and anxiety disorders: rationale and development. *Addictive Behaviors.* 2014;39(3):495–496.
146. Segal ZV, Teasdale JD, Williams JMG. Mindfulness-based cognitive therapy: theoretical rationale and empirical status. In: Hayes SC, Follette VM, Linehan MM, editors. *Mindfulness and acceptance: expanding the cognitive-behavioral tradition.* New York: Guilford Press; 2004:45–65.

147. Bonn-Miller M, Vujanovic A, Twohig M, Medina J, Huggins J. Posttraumatic stress symptom severity and marijuana use coping motives: a test of the mediating role of non-judgmental acceptance within a trauma-exposed community sample. *Mindfulness.* 2010;1(2):98–106.
148. Fiore MC, Jaén CR, Baker TB, et al. *Treating tobacco use and dependence: 2008 update.* Rockville (MD): US Department of Health and Human Services Public Health Service; May 2008.
149. McRae AL, Budney AJ, Brady KT. Treatment of marijuana dependence: a review of the literature. *Journal of Substance Abuse Treatment.* 2003;24(4):369–376.
150. Magill M, Longabaugh R. Efficacy combined with specified ingredients: a new direction for empirically supported addiction treatment. *Addiction.* 2013;108(5): 874–881.
151. Klingemann H, Sobell MB, Sobell LC. Continuities and changes in self-change research. *Addiction.* 2010;105(9):1510–1518.
152. Stea JN, Yakovenko I, Hodgins DC. Recovery from cannabis use disorders: abstinence versus moderation and treatment-assisted recovery versus natural recovery. *Psychol Addict Behav.* 2015;29(3):522–531.
153. Metrik, J., Farris, SG., Aston, ER., & Kahler, CW. (in press). Development and initial validation of a marijuana cessation expectancies questionnaire. *Drug and Alcohol Dependence.*
154. Copersino ML, Boyd SJ, Tashkin DP, Huestis MA, Heishman SJ, Dermand JC, et al. Quitting among non-treatment-seeking marijuana users: reasons and changes in other substance use. *The American Journal on Addictions.* 2006;15(4):297–302.
155. Ellingstad TP, Sobell LC, Sobell MB, Eickleberry L, Golden CJ. Self-change: a pathway to cannabis abuse resolution. *Addictive Behaviors.* 2006;31(3):519–530.
156. Price RK, Risk NK, Spitznagel EL. Remission from drug abuse over a 25-year period: patterns of remission and treatment use. *American Journal of Public Health.* 2001;91(7):1107–1113.
157. Sobell MB, Sobell LC. Stepped care as a heuristic approach to the treatment of alcohol problems. *Journal of Consulting and Clinical Psychology.* 2000;68(4):573–579.
158. McLellan AT, Lewis DC, O'Brien CP, Kleber HD. Drug dependence, a chronic medical illness: implications for treatment, insurance, and outcomes evaluation. *JAMA.* 2000;284(13):1689–1695.
159. Kelly JF, White WL. Addiction recovery management: theory, research and practice. *Current Clinical Psychiatry.* doi:10.1007/978-1-60327-960-4-2.
160. Lorenzo L, Giovanni A. Editorial. Pharmacotherapy of alcohol dependence: past, present and future research. *Current Pharmaceutical Design.* 2010;16(19):2074–2075.
161. Anton RF, Schacht JP, Book SW. Pharmacologic treatment of alcoholism. *Handbook of Clinical Neurology.* 2014;125:527–542.
162. Hutchison KE. Substance use disorders: realizing the promise of pharmacogenomics and personalized medicine. *Annu Rev Clin Psychol.* 2010;6(1):577–589.
163. Ray LA, Hutchison KE, Tartter M. Application of human laboratory models to pharmacotherapy development for alcohol dependence. *Curr Pharm Des.* 2010; 16(19):2149–2158.
164. Haney M. Self-administration of cocaine, cannabis and heroin in the human laboratory: benefits and pitfalls. *Addict Biol.* 2009;14(1):9–21.
165. Hagerty SL, Williams SL, Mittal VA, Hutchison KE. The cannabis conundrum: thinking outside the THC box. *Journal of Clinical Pharmacology.* 2015;55(8): 839–841.

Chapter 8

Stimulant Use Disorder

Allison M. Daurio and Mary R. Lee

Acknowledgments: This work was supported by intramural funding ZIA-AA000218, jointly supported by the National Institute on Alcohol Abuse and Alcoholism Division of Intramural Clinical and Biological Research, and the National Institute on Drug Abuse Intramural Research Program

Introduction

In the United States, lifetime prevalence of psychostimulant use for individuals ≥26 years of age is 17.1% for cocaine, 4.3% for crack cocaine, 5.7% for methamphetamine, and 9.2% for other psychostimulants [1]. In 2013, incidence of psychostimulant use was 1.2 million and prevalence of psychostimulant use disorder (PUD) was 1.3 million [2]. Despite the high incidence and prevalence of PUD, a minority of people who need treatment actually receives it [3]. Current treatment for PUD involves psychosocial and/or pharmacologic interventions. In this chapter, we review the current evidence-based psychosocial and pharmacologic treatments, as well as their combinations. We also review treatments that are the subject of research and present research on treating PUD that is comorbid with other psychiatric disorders. Finally, we present future directions for treatment of PUD.

Evidence-Based Psychological Interventions

Psychological interventions have been the primary method used to treat psychostimulant addiction, given the dearth of effective pharmacologic treatments for this disorder. Evidence-based interventions are contingency management (CM) and/or cognitive behavioral therapy (CBT). The effectiveness of these methods is based on outcome measures such as rates of: treatment retention, abstinence and drug use relapse. Of note, most of the data on drug use is collected only during treatment [4, 5], with few studies measuring drug use outcomes after the end of the research intervention. Drug use is assessed by self-report and/or by urine drug toxicology. Studies on psychosocial interventions are summarized in Table 8.1, and their combination with pharmacologic treatments is summarized in Table 8.3.

Contingency Management (CM)

Contingency management [6] uses operant conditioning to overcome the reinforcing effects of an individual's primary drug. In particular, CM rewards individuals affected by addiction with vouchers redeemable for goods, services, or cash when they abstain from their drug of choice (as measured by urine toxicology) or when they are compliant with their recovery program [7]. Vouchers are awarded on either a predetermined, fixed schedule or random schedule. When vouchers are awarded on a random schedule, an individual draws from a mix of possible awards, only some of which have material value (cf., 7).

CM may be most useful to attract individuals into treatment and to help patients achieve initial abstinence from their drug of choice. CM boosts retention rates in treatment by one to three additional weeks [7–10]. With CM, there are higher rates of continuous abstinence compared to those observed using methadone maintenance [11], group therapy [12], and CBT [13]. In all of these three studies, CM is also associated with, on average, four additional clean urine samples over 12 weeks. The efficacy of CM is proportional to the value of the reimbursement while it is being disbursed [14]. However, despite the positive outcomes achieved during treatment, these effects are not sustained beyond the end of CM delivery (e.g., [11, 13, 15]). Overall, the cost of CM and the lack of effect after the intervention ends calls into question the feasibility of CM beyond attracting and retaining individuals in treatment.

Cognitive Behavioral Therapy (Individual CBT)

Cognitive behavioral therapy, a 12-week manualized treatment, has been adapted from its use as a treatment for depression [16], by Carroll and colleagues [17]. This approach teaches patients how to recognize and change maladaptive thoughts and behaviors related to their substance use, identify triggers, and employ techniques to stem craving and relapse. Homework is assigned between sessions to increase self-awareness of triggers and practice strategies to reduce craving and drug use. CBT is delivered in 12 one-hour-long sessions in either inpatient or outpatient settings. The schedule is flexible with respect to the number of sessions delivered per week or the addition of sessions if needed to optimize outcomes. Each 60-minute therapy session is delivered via the "20/20/20 rule." The first 20 minutes focus on any current concerns, including experiences with using new coping skills and overall functioning. In the next 20 minutes, the therapist introduces the patient to a new skill set. The final 20 minutes are used to role-play the new skill set taught in the session. Retention rates for CBT were superior compared to interpersonal therapy: 67% versus 33%; abstinence rates were also superior for CBT compared to interpersonal therapy: 57% versus 19% [18]. These improvements in retention and abstinence rates are dose-dependent, with longer treatment showing stronger effects [19]. Of note, CBT for PUD has also been effective in improving depressive symptomology during treatment [20], indicating that CBT is beneficial for both PUD and cooccurring psychiatric symptomology.

Importantly, CBT can have a delayed effect on abstinence rates [21]. Carroll and colleagues [21] randomized patients with PUD to CBT or clinical

Table 8.1 Studies on psychosocial treatments

Tx	Length	Drug	Adjunctive Pharm. Tx	Control Group	Outcome Measure Tx	Outcome Measure Post-Tx	Main Result	Notes	Ref.
CBT	2 or 4 CBT sessions	Amphetamine users	No exclusion for pharm use of other disorders (e.g., methadone)	Self-help booklet alone	Subjective: Use	6 months Objective: Abstinence	CBT (all): Reduced use and increased abstinence at 5-wk but not 6mo. Follow up All showed reduction in use & abstinence	All groups given self-help booklet	Baker, et al. (2005)
CBT	5 sessions	Meth abuse	None	None	Subjective: Drug use control	None	CBT: Higher confidence in controlling situations with drug	All arrested for meth use	Ziedonis & Kosten (1991)
CBT	2 or 4 sessions	Amphetamine users	Not an exclusion	Self-help booklet alone	Subjective: Use	6 months Objective: Abstinence	CBT (all): No difference of abstinence at end of tx. 6-month follow-up reduced abstinence		Baker, et al. (2001)
CBT4CBT	8 weeks	Cocaine dependence	Methadone maintenance and group therapy	Methadone maintenance and group therapy	Subjective: Use Objective: Abstinence	1, 3, 6 months Subjective: Use Objective: Abstinence	CBT4CBT: more continuous weeks of abstinence, and greater reduction in cocaine use at follow-ups		Carroll, et al. (2014)
CBT4CBT	8 weeks	Any drug dependence	Drug Counseling	Drug Counseling	None	1, 3, 6 months Subjective: Use Objective: Abstinence	CBT4CBT: Less drug use, increased abstinence at all three follow-ups	59% of Sample cocaine Dependent, same sample as Carroll et al., (2008)	Carroll, et al. (2009)
CBT4CBT	8 weeks	Any drug dependence	Drug Counseling	Drug Counseling	Subjective: Use Objective: Abstinence, retention	None	CBT4CBT: increased abstinence, and sustained abstinence objectively, but not subjectively, increased retention	59% of Sample cocaine Dependent	Carroll, et al. (2008)
CM	24 weeks	Any drug dependence	None	HIV prevention program alone	Objective: Abstinence, retention, health promoting behav.	1, 3, 6 months Objective: Abstinence	CM: No difference in retention, more health promoting behavior, higher abstinence at end of tx They were 2x more likely to remain abstinent at 3 and 6 months	CM group in HIV prevention program, 63% meth dependent	Reback, et al. (2010)
CM	12 weeks	Cocaine dependence	Methadone Maintenance	TAU, vouchers for each UA given	Objective: Abstinence, retention	3 and 6 months Objective: Abstinence	CM: increased continued abstinence, retention related to abstinence (not in TAU), increased abstinence at follow ups		Petry, et al. (2005)
CM	12 weeks	Stimulants 73% dependence 5.1% abuse	None	Group therapy	Objective: Abstinence, retention, tx participation	None	CM: More likely to be retained after 2 tx visits, higher participation, more abstinence if missing UA counted as missing, but no difference if (-) or counted as missing data	Prize-based CM	Pilowsky, et al. (2011)

continued ...

Table 8.1 Continued

Tx	Length	Drug	Adjunctive Pharm. Tx	Control Group	Outcome Measure Tx	Outcome Measure Post-Tx	Main Result	Notes	Ref.
CM	12 Weeks	Meth abuse or dependence	None	TAU (either matrix model or CBT)	Objective: Abstinence, retention	3 and 6 months Objective: Abstinence	CM: Increased retention (non-significant), increased abstinence during treatment. Abstinence difference lost at follow ups	Prize-based CM	Roll, et al. (2006)
CM	12 weeks	Meth dependence	None	None	Objective: Abstinence, retention	None	CM: 30% retention rate, with an average of 15/36 meth free UA		Shoptaw, et al. (2006)
CM	12 weeks	Meth users	None	No CM	Objective: Abstinence	3 months Objective: Abstinence	CM: No difference from control during or post-treatment	CM for risky sex behaviours; therapy referrals given to all	Menza, et al. (2010)
CM	12 weeks	Stimulants abuse	Methadone maintenance	Methadone maintenance, group and individual therapy	Objective: Retention, tx participation, abstinence	1, 3, 6 months Objective: abstinence	CM: No difference in retention or study participation, increased abstinence during treatment but not post-treatment	Prize-based CM	Peirce, et al. (2006)
CM	12 weeks	Stimulants users	None	Positive reinforcement ("good job"), group therapy	Objective: Retention, abstinence, tx participation	None	CM: Increased retention, treatment participation, and abstinence (only when missing urines were counted as positive)	CM + TAU, family or individual therapy if needed	Petry, et al. (2005)
CM	12 weeks	Cocaine or Heroin abuse/ dependence	Not an exclusion	TAU - group therapy	Objective: Retention, use	6 and 9 months Objective: use	CM: increased abstinence and retention, no difference of abstinence at follow-ups	Prize-based CM	Petry, et al. (2006)
CM	12 weeks	Cocaine users – 85% dependent	None	TAU - group therapy	Objective: Abstinence, use Subjective: use	None	CM ($240) + TAU: Most continued abstinence, and overall abstinence CM ($80): No difference between CM ($240) or TAU only in abstinence No difference in treatment retention or ASI scores between groups.	3 groups: CM ($250 max) & TAU, CM ($80 max) & TAU, TAU	Petry, et al. (2006)
CM	16 weeks	Meth dependence	None	TAU (Matrix Model)	Objective: Abstinence, retention	2, 4, 6, 8 months Objective: abstinence	CM (4 months): Increased retention, and abstinence compared with all other groups, abstinence remained significantly different from TAU at follow-ups CM (1 and 2): didn't differ from each other, increased retention and UA compared to TAU	4 groups: TAU or TAU with 1, 2, or 4 months of CM	Roll, et al. (2013)
CM	12 weeks	Cocaine abuse	Methadone maintenance	Methadone maintenance	Objective: Abstinence, retention	9 months Objective: abstinence	CM: Increased retention, and abstinence, lost at follow-up		Petry, et al. (2012)
CM, CBT, CM + CBT	16 weeks	Stimulant dependence	None	None	Objective: abstinence	1, 10, 36 weeks Subjective: Use Objective: Abstinence	CM or CM + CBT: Increased overall and continued abstinence, and retention compared to only CBT CM + CBT: no additive effects Follow-ups found no difference between groups.	CBT was group CBT	Rawson, et al. (2006)

continued...

Table 8.1 Continued

Tx	Length	Drug	Adjunctive Pharm. Tx	Control Group	Outcome Measure Tx	Outcome Measure Post-Tx	Main Result	Notes	Ref.
CM, CBT, CM + CBT	16 weeks	Cocaine dependence	Methadone maintenance	Methadone Maintenance (TAU)	Objective: abstinence, retention	1, 10, 36 weeks Objective: use	CM or CM + CBT: increased abstinence compared to TAU, no difference in retention CBT: didn't differ in abstinence (in between CM groups and TAU), no difference in retention, increased abstinence compared to TAU at 10 and 36 week All: increased abstinence than TAU at 1 week		Rawson, et al. (2002)
CM, CBT, CM + CBT, GCBT	16 or 8 weeks	Meth abuse/ dependence	None	None	None	8, 16 and 26 weeks post-baseline visit Subjective: use Sex behavior Objective: abstinence	GCBT (16weeks): increased continuous abstinence, decreased use compared to CBT + CM (8 week) GCBT + CM (8weeks): lowered risk sex behavior and was retained at 26 weeks		Reback & Shoptaw, (2014)
CM, CM + CBT or GCBT	16 weeks	Meth dependence	None	Standard CBT only	Subjective: use, risky sex behavior. Objective: Abstinence, retention	6 and 12 months Subjective: risky sex behavior Objective: Abstinence	CM or CM + CBT: increased retention and abstinence CBT: lowest on treatment outcomes GCBT: reduced risky sexual behavior at follow-ups Follow-ups: No difference between groups on abstinence	Same sample as peck et al. (2007) and Jaffe et al., 2007	Shoptaw, et al. (2005)
CM, CM + CBT or GCBT	16 Weeks	Meth dependence	None	Standard CBT only	Subjective: use, risky sex behavior. depression	None	GCBT: more rapid decrease of meth use Reducing use was associated with depression and sexual risk-taking decreases	Same sample as Shoptaw et al. (2005); Peck et al. (2007)	Jaffe, et al. (2007)
CM, CM + CBT or GCBT	16 Weeks	Meth dependence	None	Standard CBT only	Subjective: depression	6 and 12 months Subjective: depression	Recent meth use related to higher depression, though there was no prediction of meth use from depression	Same sample as Shoptaw et al. (2005); Jaffe et al. (2007)	Peck, et al. (2005)
Matrix Model	16 weeks	Meth dependence	None	TAU - varied between sites	Objective: abstinence	6 and 12 months Objective: abstinence	Matrix Model: increased retention, tx completion, overall and continued abstinence, lost at follow-ups	Court-mandated tx didn't show effects	Rawson, et al. (2004)
Matrix Model	16 weeks on med, 26 in therapy	Cocaine or Meth abuse/ dependence	Desipramine or placebo in 2/3 of sample	Placebo	Objective: abstinence	6 months Objective: abstinence	Matrix Model: Increase overall and continued abstinence at follow-up Predictors of abstinence: tx retention and participation, abstinence at end of tx	Doesn't indicate drug dosage, or differences between the 3 groups	Shoptaw, et al. (1994)
Matrix Model	26 or 16 weeks	Cocaine or Meth abuse	None	NA	Objective: abstinence	None	Treatment retention and abstinence was not dependent on methamphetamine or cocaine dependence	1987-1990 26 weeks, 1991-to end of study 16 week tx	Huber, et al. (1997)

management. Although there was no group difference in abstinence rates at the end of 12 weeks' treatment, abstinence rates diverged 12 months post-treatment such that individuals who received CBT continued to reduce their drug use, while those who received clinical management did not [21]. The consolidation of response post-CBT was replicated in another study in heroin-dependent cocaine users [22]. Patients were randomized to receive CM, CBT, both, or neither, in addition to methadone maintenance and weekly individual counseling sessions. On follow-up, the group that received CBT, CM, and CBT + CM continued to reduce their drug use after treatment compared to methadone and drug counseling alone. In another study, CBT was associated with higher abstinence rates at six-month follow-up, as compared to a self-help booklet: 62.5% for one session, 85.7% for three to four sessions CBT versus 21.4% abstinence for the self-help booklet group [19].

Despite these encouraging research outcomes with CBT to treat stimulant addiction (compared to interpersonal therapy, clinical management, and self-help programs), CBT is not used regularly in community drug rehabilitation programs [23]. One reason is the lack of therapist training both during graduate education [24] and at the postgraduate level (i.e., with training delivered at the treatment centers themselves) [25].

In response to the barriers to CBT delivery and training, CBT has been modified so it can be integrated more easily into community rehabilitation programs, targeted to treat special populations, and combined with other common outpatient treatment modalities such as 12-step facilitation. In this next section, we discuss adaptations of CBT, including computer-based training for CBT, gay-specific CBT, and the matrix model.

Computer-Based Training for Cognitive Behavioral Therapy (CBT4CBT)

Computer-based training for CBT was designed to overcome the barriers to delivering manualized CBT as part of community drug rehabilitation treatment. It consists of six modules adapted from the CBT manual for substance use disorder treatment [26] and is delivered over eight weeks. These modules include: (1) changing and understanding patterns of substance use; (2) coping with craving; (3) refusing offers of substances; (4) problem-solving skills; (5) identifying and changing thoughts about substance; and (6) improving decision-making skills. Each module teaches skills by narrating multiple scenarios involving drug use and demonstrating different behaviors and their respective outcomes. These serve as examples for the patient to learn alternative behaviors in order to remain abstinent in high-risk situations. Skills are also reinforced with homework assignments. CBT4CBT showed 70–83% completion rates with an average of 70% of total therapy days attended [26, 27]. This is in contrast to prior research showing low retention rates for computerized treatment [28, 29]. CBT4CBT improved abstinence rates and reduced psychostimulant use compared to group and supportive counseling [26, 27]. These effects on stimulant abstinence were sustained at one-, three-, and six-month follow-up post-treatment [30]. CBT4CBT is accessible and is designed to accommodate individuals with limited computer skills. CBT4CBT has great potential to increase access to effective treatment, with the only limitation being access to computer services. When added to the standard treatment across three different outpatient clinics, CBT4CBT did not appreciably increase the cost of treatment [31]. Although not formally calculated, cost-effectiveness would be apparent when the improvement in societal outcomes (e.g., crime, spread of the disease) with CBT4CBT is taken into account. Overall, studies to date show that CBT4CBT is both a cost-effective and reliable treatment for individuals affected by PUD.

Gay-Specific Cognitive Behavioral Therapy (GCBT)

Men who have sex with men (MSM) have a higher prevalence of psychostimulant use than the general population [32]. This group also has an increased risk of transmission and higher rates of sexually transmitted diseases such as syphilis and human immunodeficiency virus (HIV) via unprotected anal sex and sharing needles for drug use. Due to these specific public health issues, researchers have worked to develop treatments targeting MSM who use psychostimulants. Specifically, GCBT targets both drug use and risky sexual behavior. In a study comparing GCBT to conventional CBT, CM, or CBT + CM, there were no differences in treatment response at 26 weeks' follow-up in terms of drug use. However, individuals in GCBT reduced their stimulant use faster than the comparative groups [33]. In another study comparing 16 weeks of GCBT to eight weeks of either CBT, CBT + CM, or GCBT, 16 weeks of GCBT showed the largest benefit in continued abstinence and total substance use with medium effect sizes [34]. In terms of reduced risky sexual behavior, GCBT helped reduce the occurrence of unprotected receptive anal intercourse within the first four weeks of treatment, as compared to CM, CM + CBT, or CBT [10]. GCBT has been shown to reduce oral sex by 25%, unprotected receptive anal sex by 23%, unprotected insertive anal sex by 20%, and the mean number of sexual partners from 8.6 to 2.9 individuals [35]. GCBT may not be specifically better in reducing stimulant use compared to other evidence-based treatments, but it shows equal efficacy. Further, it addresses risky sexual behavior as a preventative measure in the transmission of HIV. Therefore, it is an important form of treatment for this specific subpopulation of stimulant users.

Matrix Model

The primary goal of the matrix model is to build a more personalized treatment option for individuals affected by PUD that helps individuals stay abstinent, stay in long-term treatment, become more knowledgeable about addiction and relapse, provide support to families, connect with community resources, and have an ongoing measure of treatment efficacy [36]. The matrix model integrates CBT, family education, and the 12-step approach into a 16-week intensive outpatient treatment program. Like CBT and CM, the matrix model is effective in treating PUD by increasing treatment retention and abstinence rates compared to 12-step facilitation or clinical management [36]. It also improves treatment retention rates and psychosocial functioning compared to 12-step facilitation only [37, 38]. When compared to 12-step only, the matrix model showed threefold greater abstinence rates [36, 39]. In an open trial using the matrix model, 88% of the participants achieved abstinence by the end of treatment [39]. This model also focuses on reducing other substance use, such as alcohol and marijuana, since in the original pilot of the matrix model the use of non-stimulant substances was the strongest predictor of relapse to stimulant use [39]. As this approach requires individualized treatment in addition to multiple types of group therapy and frequent urine testing, it is costly. Furthermore, although it is a form of outpatient treatment, it requires a considerable time commitment.

Barriers to Delivering Evidence-Based Therapies (EBTs)

There are numerous evidence-based treatment options for stimulant users. In the studies reviewed here, CM, CBT, CBT4CBT, GCBT, and the matrix model, all increased treatment retention, reduced psychostimulant use, and increased abstinence rates when compared to standard treatment, usually group or supportive counseling (e.g., 12-step facilitation). Unlike CM, CBT is associated with sustained improvement in drug use outcomes, even after the treatment has ended. Although CM and/or CBT have been shown to be the most effective forms of treatment for stimulant addiction, there are few facilities that use these practices as their primary treatment approach [40]. Specifically, only 17% of treatment centers reported CBT as their primary treatment approach, and 40% indicated they were unfamiliar with CM [40]. There are many reasons evidence-based therapies (EBTs) are not widely used. First, there is poor training of EBTs in programs. Specifically, social work and PsyD programs, which have the largest number of students, require didactic and clinical supervision during training on EBTs only 10% of the time [24]. This study also found that MD and clinical psychology PhD programs only require didactic and clinical training 22% of the time in EBTs. Second, the majority of therapies taught in training programs have no scientific basis for their effects [24]. Third, there are system-wide failures existing in the addiction field. The majority of those treating substance users do not have adequate training, and there is a vulnerable infrastructure continuously undergoing leadership, workforce, and information system changes within treatment programs (for a review, see [41]). It is important that the research field continues to train and disseminate EBTs in order to make sure individuals obtain the best treatment available.

Evidence-Based Pharmacological Interventions

To date, there are no pharmacological interventions approved by the Food and Drug Administration (FDA) for treating PUD. Pharmacologic strategies for treatment are based on targeting neurotransmitters that are involved in the neuroadaptations that occur in the development of PUD. These include dopamine, glutamate, serotonin, and gamma-aminobutyric acid (GABA). Bupropion and modafinil have been investigated most extensively in clinical trials. Both bupropion and modafinil are not themselves reinforcing, making them attractive options for the treatment of PUD [42, 43]. In this next section, we review studies investigating pharmacotherapies for PUD. Studies on pharmacologic interventions are summarized in Table 8.2, and their combination with psychosocial treatments is summarized in Table 8.3.

Medications That Modulate Monoamine Neurotransmitters

Bupropion

Bupropion is an atypical antidepressant with stimulant properties that is approved for treatment of nicotine dependence. Bupropion inhibits dopamine reuptake and is thought to increase dopamine transmission in the prefrontal cortex and nucleus accumbens [44]. Use of bupropion might remediate the frontal hypodopaminergic state observed in individuals affected by chronic PUD [45]. Treatment trials with bupropion in cocaine dependence show mixed results. When given as an adjunct to CBT, it has no effect [46, 47]; however, bupropion improved the duration of abstinence when given with CM [48]. In another study, its effect to increase abstinence rates was limited to a subgroup of individuals with significant depressive symptoms [49]. It has been shown to reduce methamphetamine craving [50]. Bupropion has been effective in increasing abstinence with 1.27–1.39 higher odds of having an abstinent week compared to placebo in low using, albeit still dependent stimulant users [51]. In this same sample, bupropion showed overall efficacy when comparing individuals that had more than one week of abstinence and completed treatment [52]; however, these results were inconsistent in another study that found null results [46]. Bupropion is well tolerated and adherence is good.

Modafinil

Modafinil modulates dopamine by blocking the dopamine transporter (DAT) and increasing extracellular dopamine levels in humans and non-human primates [53–55]. This action of modafinil, therefore, might remediate the hypodopaminergic state observed in psychostimulant dependence. It also modulates other neurotransmitter systems such as glutamate, GABA, and norepinephrine [53, 54, 56]. In clinical studies, modafinil has shown good safety when administered

Table 8.2 Studies on pharmacological treatments

Intervention	Length	Drug	Adjunctive Psych Tx	Control	Outcome Measure Tx	Outcome Measure Post-Tx	Main Result	Notes	Reference
Amantadine (300mg) Desipramine (150mg)	12 weeks	Meth Dependence	Methadone + Relapse prevention	Placebo	Subjective: craving Objective: abstinence	None	No difference in abstinence. Desipramine + Amantadine: in depressed patients there was a decreased craving and abstinence compared to placebo, but not between medications	All opioid dependent (n=20 had depression)	Ziedonis & Kosten (1991)
Aripiprazole (15mg) or Methylphenidate (54 mg)	20 weeks	Amphetamine or Meth Dependence	CBT	Placebo	Objective: abstinence	None	Aripiprazole: increased use, terminated ½ through trial. Methylphenidate: increased abstinence		Tiihonen, et al. (2007)
Aripiprazole (20mg)	2 weeks	Meth Dependence	None	Placebo	Subjective: Craving, depression, psychiatric sx, desire, mood, drug effects	None	Aripiprazole: no difference in depression, mood, psychiatric symptom, increased positive effects of meth and desire in meth (both non-significant)	Phase 1 study	Newton, et al. (2008)
Baclofen (20 mg tid) or gabapentin (800 mg tid)	16 weeks	Meth Dependence	Matrix Model	Placebo	Subjective: depression, craving Objective: abstinence, retention	None	Baclofen and gabapentin: no difference in outcome measures. Baclofen: higher med adherence showed increased abstinence compared to placebo		Heinzerling, et al. (2006)
Baclofen (20 mg tid)	8 weeks	Cocaine Dependence	CBT	Placebo	Subjective: use Objective: abstinence, retention	None	Baclofen: no difference in retention, self-reported use, or proportion of days used	Multi-center trial	Kahn, et al. (2009)
Bupropion (150 mg bid.)	12 weeks	Meth Abuse or Dependence	None	Placebo	Objective: CV response after i.v. Meth	None	Bupropion: Minor AEs, no change in ECG or significant changes in lab values. Attenuated cardiovascular effects of meth. Meth metabolized slower w/drug	Safety study	Newton, et al. (2005)
Bupropion (150 mg bid.)	16 weeks	Cocaine Abuse or Dependence	Group therapy + CBT	Placebo	Subjective: Craving, use, depression, Objective: Retention	None	Bupropion: No differences in outcome measures	Excluded depressed patients	Shoptaw, et al. (2008)
Bupropion (150 mg BID)	12 weeks	Meth Dependence	CBT and CM	Placebo	Subjective: craving, depression Objective: abstinence, retention	None	Bupropion: No difference in outcome measures		Shoptaw, et al. (2008)

continued …

Table 8.2 Continued

Intervention	Length	Drug	Adjunctive Psych Tx	Control	Outcome Measure Tx	Post-Tx	Main Result	Notes	Reference
Bupropion (150 mg bid.)	12 weeks	Meth Dependence	CBT	Placebo	Objective: abstinence, retention	None	Bupropion: no difference in retention, increased abstinence in male ppts w/low baseline use and non-depressed ppts with low baseline meth use	Same sample as McCann et al., (2012)	Elkashef, et al. (2008)
Bupropion (150 mg bid.)	12 weeks	Meth Dependence	CBT	Placebo	Objective: abstinence	None	Bupropion: showed more beyond threshold abstinence weeks of success compared to placebo	Success defined as tx completion and number of abstinence weeks. Same sample as Elkashef et al. (2008)	McCann & Li (2012)
Bupropion (150 mg)	-	Meth Abuse or Dependence	None	Placebo	Subjective: craving, likelihood to use	None	Bupropion: reduced cue-induced craving, but not participants likelihood of using reports		Newton, et al. (2006)§
Bupropion (150 mg bid.)	12 weeks	Cocaine Dependence	Standard methadone tx	Placebo	Subjective: craving, depression, use Objective: retention	None	Bupropion: No difference in outcome measures overall, subgroup of depressed cocaine addicts decreased in cocaine use	All with opioid dependence	Margolin, et al. (1995).
Desipramine (300 mg max. does)	12 weeks	Cocaine Dependence	Relapse Prevention, case management	Placebo	Subjective: depression, use, craving Objective: abstinence, depression	None	Desipramine: No difference in retention, use decreased depression Individuals with improved depression lowered their use, amount of money spent on cocaine/day and craving	All comorbid with MDD or Dysthymia	McDowell, et al. (2005)
Dexamphetamine (60mg)	12 weeks	Meth Dependence	4 CBT sessions	Placebo	Subjective: severity of dependence Objective: Retention, use	2 months	Dexamphetamine: no difference in use, increased retention in lowered severity of dependence at 2 months follow-up.		Longo, et al. (2010).
Dexamphetamine (60mg)	8 weeks	Meth users	Motivational Enhancement Therapy	Placebo	Subjective: use, craving, objective: use, withdrawal, retention	None	Dexamphetamine: No difference in the use, or retention. Reduced withdrawal and craving		Galloway, et al. (2011).
Dexamphetamine (max 90mg)	NA	Amphetamine Dependence	Psychotherapy - doesn't specify	NA	Objective: Abstinence	None	Dexamphetamine: 59.5-64.1% of users stopped using drug by the end of treatment with majority of patients stopping by 2 months	Dosage was dependent on self-report use; retrospective case note study	White, (2000)*
Dexamphetamine (60 mg)	12 weeks	Amphetamine Dependence	TAU	TAU only	Objective: use, retention	None	Dexamphetamine: no difference in use, increased retention		Shearer, J. et al. (2001).
Dexamphetamine (Max 60mg)	NA	Amphetamine Users	TAU	TAU only	Subjective: use, intake of drug Objective: retention	None	Dexamphetamine: increased retention, decreased use and injection of drug	Control admitted to tx prior to admin dexamphetamine tx	McBride, Andrew J., et al (1997)*

continued ...

Table 8.2 Continued

Intervention	Length	Drug	Adjunctive Psych Tx	Control	Outcome Measure Tx	Outcome Measure Post-Tx	Main Result	Notes	Reference
Dextroamphetamine (30 or 60mg)	12 weeks	Cocaine Dependence	CBT	Placebo	Subjective: depression Objective: abstinence, retention	None	Dextroamphetamine (60mg): increased abstinence, decreased depression Dexamphetamine (30mg): Increased retention and depression		Grabowski, J., et al. (2001)
Dextroamphetamine (30 or 60mg) or Risperidone (2 or 4 mg)	24 weeks	Cocaine Dependence	Methadone + CBT	Placebo	Subjective: use Objective: use	None	No difference in retention Dextroamphetamine (60mg): reduced use. Risperidone: there was no in use	All heroin dependent 2 studies: 1) dextroamphetamine 2) risperidone	Grabowski, J., et al. (2004)
Dexamphet-amine (60 mg max)	14 weeks	Cocaine Dependence	None	Placebo	Subjective: craving, dependence severity, use Objective: abstinence	None	Dexamphetamine: There were no significant differences in retention or outcome measures Within group change from baseline in use, craving, severity of dependence (not occurring in placebo)		Shearer, et al. (2003)
Disulfiram (250mg)	12 weeks	Cocaine Dependence	Buprenorphine, group drug counseling	Placebo	Subjective: use Objective: abstinence	None	Disulfiram: reduced use, increased abstinence, and had more rapid decrease in use	All opioid dependent	George, et al. (2000)
Disulfiram (250mg)	12 weeks	Cocaine Dependence	Methadone Maintenance	Placebo	Subjective: use, craving Objective: abstinence	None	Disulfiram: only reduced self-reported use, no difference on craving or abstinence No difference in retention rates	All opioid dependent	Petrakis, et al. (2000)
Disulfiram (62.5, 125, 250mg)	14 weeks	Cocaine Dependence	Methadone Maintenance, CBT	Placebo	Subjective: use Objective: abstinence, retention	None	Disulfiram (62.5, 125 mg): increased drug use Disulfiram (250 mg): decreased use, increased abstinence over time but no changes compared to placebo	All opioid dependent	Oliveto, et al. (2015)
Gabapentin (600 or 1200 mg)	NA	Cocaine Dependence	None	Placebo	Subjective: drug effects Objective: self-administration	None	Gabapentin: did not influence cocaine self administration or subjective drug effects		Hart, et al. (2007)
Imipramine (150 mg/day)	6 months	Meth Dependence	Relapse HIV prevention group therapy	Imipramine (10 mg)	Subjective: Depression, craving, use Objective: abstinence	None	Imipramine: No difference in craving, depression symptoms, use, abstinence		Galloway, et al. (1996)
Imipramine (150 mg/day)	6 months	Cocaine or Meth Dependence	Relapse HIV prevention group therapy	Imipramine (10 mg)	Subjective: craving, use Objective: abstinence	None	Imipramine (150mg): increased retention, no difference in craving, use, or abstinence		Galloway, et al. (1994)
Methylphenidate (45 mg)	11 weeks	Cocaine Dependence	Individual therapy	Placebo	Subjective: Craving Objective: abstinence	None	Methylphenidate: No difference in outcome measures		Grabowski, et al. (1997)

continued ...

Table 8.2 Continued

Intervention	Length	Drug	Adjunctive Psych Tx	Control	Outcome Measure Tx	Outcome Measure Post-Tx	Main Result	Notes	Reference
Mirtazapine (30mg)	2 weeks	Amphetamine or Meth Dependence	Narrative therapy	Placebo	Objective: Withdrawal, sleep, retention	3 weeks Objective: Withdrawal, sleep, retention	Mirtazapine: no difference retention, withdrawal symptoms, sleep or rates of methamphetamine use.	Doesn't indicate psychosocial therapy type	Cruickshank, et al. (2008).
Modafinil (400mg)	8 weeks	Cocaine Dependence	CBT	Placebo	Subjective: Craving Objective: AE	None	Modafinil: Increased continued and overall abstinence, with no serious side effects		Dackis, et al (2005)
Modafinil (200 or 400 mg)	NA	Cocaine Dependence	None	Placebo	Subjective: Craving, drug effects Objective: CV	None	Modafinil: decreased cocaine's euphoric effects, with no difference on heart rate measure or craving	Took cocaine	Dackis, et al. (2003)
Modafinil (200 mg)	10 weeks	Meth Dependence	4 CBT sessions	Placebo	Objective: Retention, abstinence	12 weeks Objective: Retention, abstinence	Modafinil: No difference in retention, abstinence, or use at all time points		Shearer, et al (2009)
Modafinil (300mg)	8 weeks	Cocaine Dependence	Individual therapy	Placebo	Subjective: Craving, use Objective: abstinence	None	Modafinil: Increased abstinence, reduced use, and decreased craving		Kampman, et al (2015)
Modafinil (400 mg)	12 weeks	Meth Dependence	CBT + CM	Placebo	Subjective: Craving, depression Objective: Abstinence, Retention	None	Modafinil: No difference in use, retention, depressive symptoms, or cravings. If CBT attendance was low increased abstinence		Heinzerling, et al. (2010)
Modafinil (400 mg) or Mirtazapine (30mg)	10 days	Meth Dependence	None	Pericyazine (TAU)	Subjective: Sleep Objective: Withdrawal	None	Modafinil: No difference in sleep, reduced withdrawal followed by mirtazapine	Test for withdrawal sx not tx of disorder	McGregor, et al. (2008)
Modafinil (200 or 400mg)	12 weeks	Cocaine Dependence	CBT	Placebo	Subjective: use, craving	None	Modafinil: No difference in retention or percent of non-using days. Increased consecutive non-use days and 200mg-dosing reduced craving		Anderson, et al. (2009)
Modafinil (200 or 400mg)	12 weeks	Meth Dependence	CBT	Placebo	Subjective: use Objective: abstinence	None	Modafinil: No difference in retention, abstinence or use		Anderson, et al. (2012)
Modafinil (400 or 800 mg)	NA	Cocaine Dependence	None	Placebo	Subjective: Drug effects Objective: CV	None	Modafinil: No effects on cardiovascular or hemodynamic responses, reduced drug effect and worth	Interaction w/ cocaine study	Malcolm, et al. (2006)
Modafinil (200 or 400mg)	NA	Cocaine Dependence	None	Placebo	Subjective: Drug effects Objective: CV, self-administration	None	Modafinil: reductions in purchase and monetary value of cocaine during self-administration, attenuated cardiovascular effects		Hartet al. (2008)

continued ...

Table 8.2 Continued

Intervention	Length	Drug	Adjunctive Psych Tx	Control	Outcome Measure Tx	Outcome Measure Post-Tx	Main Result	Notes	Reference
Modafinil (200 mg)	NA	Meth Dependence	None	Placebo	Objective: CV self-administration	None	Modafinil: Reduced of cardiovascular effects and self-administrations (all non-significant)		De La Garza, et al. (2010)
Modafinil (200 mg)	16 weeks	Stimulant Abuse or Dependence	HIV meds + CBT	None	Subjective: depression, craving Objective: abstinence	None	Modafinil: Increased abstinence, retention Responders were more likely abusers rather than dependent and had decreased craving and had higher change in depression	Modafinil given for 12 weeks w/ 4 weeks of placebo	McElhiney, et al. (2009)
Modafinil (200 mg or 400 mg)	8 weeks	Cocaine Dependence	CBT	Placebo	Objective: abstinence, retention	None	Modafinil No difference in retention or overall abstinence. Males on 400 mg/day showed more abstinence than males on placebo.		Dackis, et al. (2012)
Nalmefene (18 mg as needed)	5 months	Cocaine Dependence	None	No	NA	None	No complaints of wakefulness or cognition, did not develop other side effects, reduced craving	Case study – to reduce craving	Grosshans, et al. (2015)
N-acetylcysteine (600mg bid)	3 days	Cocaine Dependence	None	Placebo	Subjective: Craving Objective: cue-viewing	None	N-acetylcysteine: Decreased desire to use, interest in drug, and spent less time observing drug cues	Double-blind cross over cue-reactivity	LaRowe, et al. (2007)
N-acetylcysteine (1200, 2400, or 3600mg)	4 weeks	Cocaine Dependence	None	None	Subjective: use, AE Objective: abstinence, retention	None	N-acetylcysteine (All): No significant AEs, 9 of 15 terminated drug use, reduced use N-acetylcysteine (2400, 3600 mg): Increased retention	Open-label	Mardikian, et al. (2007)
N-acetylcysteine (600 or 1200mg bid) Naltrexone (200mg)	8 weeks	Amphetamine Dependence	None	Placebo	Subjective: Craving Objective: abstinence	None	N-acetylcysteine + Naltrexone: No difference in craving or abstinence		Grant, et al. (2010)
N-acetylcysteine (600 or 1200mg bid)	8 weeks	Cocaine Dependence	CBT	Placebo	Subjective: use, craving Objective: abstinence	None	N-acetylcysteine: No difference in abstinence, craving, relapse rates		LaRowe, et al. (2013)
N-acetylcysteine (1200mg)	8 weeks	Meth Dependence	Matrix Model	Placebo	Subjective: Craving	None	N-acetylcysteine: reduced craving	Double-blind cross over	Mousavi, et al. (2015)
Ondansetron (.25mg, 1mg, 4 mg Bid)	8 weeks	Meth Dependence	CBT	Placebo	Subjective: use Objective: abstinence	None	Ondansetron: No difference in use, clinical severity, withdrawal, craving, or study retention between groups	Secondary outcomes: Withdrawal, craving, clinical severity & retention	Johnson, et al. (2006)
Risperidone (4 mg)	4 weeks	Meth Dependence	NA	NA	Subjective: use, symptoms Objective: motor function	None	Risperidone: Decrease use days, improved fine motor function, decline in symptom distress		Meredith, et al. (2007)

continued...

Table 8.2 Continued

Intervention	Length	Drug	Adjunctive Psych Tx	Control	Outcome Measure Tx	Outcome Measure Post-Tx	Main Result	Notes	Reference
Risperidone (long lasting 25 mg injects.)	8 weeks	Meth Dependence	Relapse Prevention	NA	Subjective: craving, drug effect Objective: abstinence	None	Risperidone: increase in abstinence, decrease craving and euphoria experienced while on meth	Max 4 injections received	Meredith, et al. (2009)
Sertraline (200 mg), Sertraline (200mg) + Gabapentin (1200mg)	12 weeks	Cocaine Dependence	CBT	Placebo	Subjective: depression, use Objective: abstinence	None	Sertraline: increased abstinence, and less number of relapses Sertraline + gabapentin: no difference in outcomes All decreased depression scores throughout treatment with no differences between groups	All had a score greater than 15 on HAM-D	Mancino, et al. (2014)
Topiramate (200mg)	13 weeks	Meth Dependence	Behavioral compliance enhancement	Placebo	Subjective: use, dependence severity Objective: abstinence	None	Topiramate: Reduced severity of dependence, use in those abstinent in the beginning of trial, no difference in abstinence		Elkashef, et al. (2012)
Topiramate (300mg)	12 weeks	Cocaine Dependence	CBT	Placebo	Subjective: craving, use, global functioning Objective: abstinence	None	Topiramate: Increased abstinence, global functioning, reduced craving and use		Johnson, et al. (2013)
Venlafaxine (300 mg target)	12 weeks	Cocaine Dependence	MI and weekly individual CBT	Placebo	Subjective: depression Objective: abstinence	None	Venlafaxine: no difference on abstinence, no antidepressant effect	All diagnosed with MDD or Dysthymia	Raby, et al. (2014)

Table 8.3 Studies on combined psychosocial and pharmacological treatments

Intervention	Length	Drug	Adjunct Psych/Pharm Tx	Control	Outcome Measure Tx	Outcome Measure Post-Tx	Main Result	Notes	Reference
Desipramine (50-300 mg) and CBT/Clinical Management	12 weeks	Cocaine Dependence	None	Clinical management plus placebo	Subjective: use Objective: Abstinence, retention	None	No difference in retention, or use CBT: increased continuous abstinence in high-users Clinical Management: increase abstinence in low users Desipramine: reduced use in 1st 6 weeks of tx	Average was 200 mg/day of drug; most comorbid w/ personality disorder DX	Carroll, et al (1994)
Disulfiram (250-500mg) and CBT/TSF/ Clinical management	12 weeks	Cocaine and Alcohol Dependence	None	Clinical management	Subjective: Use Objective: Abstinence Retention	None	Disulfiram: increased retention, increased continuous abstinence TSF, CBT: increased continuous abstinence	Can't tell if there's an additive effect	Carroll, et al. (1998)
Disulfiram (250 mg) and CBT	12 weeks	Cocaine Dependence	None	Interpersonal therapy and placebo	Subjective: Drug use Objective: abstinence	None	CBT: decreased use and abstinence Disulfiram: decreased use No additive effects of both CBT and Disulfiram,		Carroll, et al. (2004)
Disulfiram (250 mg) and CM	12 weeks	Cocaine Dependence	CBT	Placebo	Subjective: Use Objective: Abstinence	3,6,9,12 months Subjective: Use Objective: Abstinence	No difference of percent of self-reported abstinence or retention CM + placebo: greatest increase in abstinence and use Disulfiram + placebo or CM: increased abstinence and use compared to placebo + CBT group Results maintained at follow-ups	4 groups: CM + CBT + placebo, CM + CBT + Disulfiram, CBT + disulfiram, CBT + placebo	Carroll et al, (2016)
Methyl-phenidate (20-30mg) and CBT	12 weeks	Cocaine Dependence	Diacetyl-morphine for heroin	Treatment as Usual, placebo	Subjective: use Objective: Abstinence	None	Methylphenidate: no improvement on use. or abstinence CBT (group): no difference on outcome measures, least retained	Group CBT	Dursteler-MacFarland, et al. (2013)
Sertraline (50 mg) and CM	12 weeks	Meth Dependence	None	Matrix model, relapse prevention	Subjective: Craving, depression Objective: Abstinence	None	No difference in craving or depression CM groups: increased retention, overall and continuous abstinence Sertraline only: increased positive drug test, low retention, relapse counseling attendance	Four groups: Sertraline, placebo, Sertraline + CM, CM+ placebo	Shoptaw, et al. (2006)
Bupropion (300 mg) + CM	25 weeks	Cocaine User	Methadone maintenance	Placebo or Voucher-based control	Objective: Abstinence	None	CM + Bupropion: increased overall and continued abstinence Response order: CM + bupropion > CM + placebo > Voucher + Bupropion >both controls	Voucher-based control received $3 voucher for every UA turned in	Poling, et al. (2006)

with cocaine [57–59] or methamphetamine [60]. Further, in a pilot study, modafinil reduced the average amount of self-administered cocaine compared to placebo [58]. Double-blind randomized control trials have produced mixed results. In three trials, modafinil increased continued abstinence [61–63], while other trials have failed to show differences between modafinil and placebo in reducing stimulant use [64–67].

Psychostimulants

Use of psychostimulants such as dextroamphetamine or methylphenidate as a replacement therapy for PUD has been studied analogous to other replacement therapies for opioid (methadone and buprenorphine) or nicotine dependence (nicotine replacement therapy). Initial nonrandomized studies of dextroamphetamine as a replacement therapy for PUD were promising. Treatment with dextroamphetamine reduced stimulant use and stimulant injections by half [68, 69]. Further, randomized trials yielded mixed results. During the treatment period, several studies reported no difference between placebo and dextroamphetamine [70, 73]; and others found up to a 40% reduction in psychostimulant use [74]. In contrast, during post-treatmetn follow-up, one of these studies reported that dextroamphetamine was associated with a reduced severity of dependence [72]. Methylphenidate, another psychostimulant, failed to show significant differences in cocaine abstinence or craving compared to placebo [75, 76].

Antipsychotics

Aripiprazole acts primarily as a partial agonist at D2 receptors on dopamine [77, 78]. It is also a 5-hydroxytryptamine (5-HT)$_{1A}$ agonist and a 5-HT$_{2A}$ receptor antagonist. As a partial D2 agonist, aripiprazole should function as a replacement medication when dopamine levels are low, as in withdrawal, and as an antagonist when dopamine levels are high, as is the case during active use. However, results of randomized, placebo-controlled trials of aripiprazole in PUD did not show reduction in drug use, and a worsening in craving measures was reported [79, 80]. The trials were stopped early. A similar pattern of results was found for risperidone, an atypical antipsychotic. Open-label studies were positive with reduction in drug use from an average of 4.1 days of use per week to one day [81, 82]; however, one double-blind randomized trial found no effect on cocaine use or treatment retention [83].

Additional Antidepressants

Several antidepressants have been tested for PUD. Imipramine [84, 85], mirtazapine [86, 87], desipramine [4, 88], and venlafaxine [90] all failed to show significant decreases in stimulant use or abstinence compared to placebo. The effects of sertraline are mixed: one study found sertraline increased methamphetamine use [5]; another study found increased cocaine abstinence [91].

However, antidepressants may be beneficial in the treatment of PUD in the setting of comorbid depression. For example, desipramine compared to placebo was beneficial in treating methamphetamine use in a subgroup of patients with depression only [89]. Additionally, improvements in depressive mood were significantly correlated with reduced use and craving, as well as increased abstinence [88, 90].

GABA Agonists

Two GABAergic medications, gabapentin and baclofen, have been studied for the treatment of PUD. GABA agonists are thought to prevent the reinforcing effects of stimulants by inhibiting dopamine in the nucleus accumbens and ventral tegmental area [92]. Studies with gabapentin (whose mechanisms of action seem to involve not only GABA but also voltage-gated calcium channels) were negative in randomized, placebo-controlled treatment trials. These studies reported no effect on methamphetamine use, abstinence, craving, or depressive symptoms [91, 93]. In human laboratory cocaine self-administration studies, gabapentin failed to reduce drug intake or blunt cocaine-induced euphoria [94]. Similar results were found for baclofen. However, in individuals with good compliance for baclofen, there was an increase in abstinence from psychostimulants [93]. However, in a multicenter trial of severely cocaine-dependent individuals, baclofen showed no efficacy to reduce stimulant use or increase abstinence [95].

Other Pharmacotherapies

There has been recent interest in using 5-HT antagonists in PUD treatment. The reinforcing properties of psychostimulants are mediated in part by the modulation of dopamine in the cortico-mesolimbic pathway by serotonin [96]. Ondansetron, a 5-HT$_3$ antagonist approved for treatment of nausea in chemotherapy, has been investigated for its potential effects in methamphetamine abuse. In an initial study of healthy volunteers, ondansetron showed a reduction in d-amphetamine's euphoric response [97]. However, in a randomized double-blind placebo-controlled trial, there was no effect of ondansetron on methamphetamine use outcomes, including clinical severity, withdrawal, or craving [98].

N-acetylcysteine (NAC) is an amino acid recently studied for the possible treatment of PUD. NAC is thought to reduce craving of stimulants by restoring extracellular glutamate in the nucleus accumbens [99]. In open pilot studies, NAC reduces cue-induced cocaine craving [100] and cocaine use [101]. In double-blind crossover trials using the matrix model adjunctive with NAC or placebo, NAC reduced methamphetamine craving [102]. However, in double-blind, placebo-controlled studies, there were no differences in stimulant craving or abstinence [103, 104].

Another potential treatment for PUD is topiramate, a drug with multiple mechanisms of action, including (but not limited to) actions via GABA$_A$ and (AMPA)/kainate mediated glutamate receptors. Two double-blind randomized trials have been conducted with promising results. One study, with cocaine-dependent individuals, found topiramate reduced cocaine craving and use [105]. In the second study, with methamphetamine-dependent adults, topiramate reduced methamphetamine dependence severity and use only in patients who were abstinent at the beginning of the trial [106]. Of note, a secondary analysis of this sample showed topiramate modulates genetic expression of GABA and glutamate receptor signally underlying addictive behavior (see [107]). Though these studies are preliminary, topiramate shows promising potential in treating PUD.

Disulfiram is an FDA-approved treatment for alcohol dependence. Disulfiram was first used in PUD to reduce alcohol intake in individuals with PUD [108], and further studies investigated whether this would extend to reducing psychostimulant use as well [109]. Studies to date on this have yielded inconclusive results. One study [110] tested the effects of disulfiram given in combination with CBT, or 12-step facilitation, or clinical management versus CBT alone, or 12-step facilitation alone in patients with cocaine dependence and comorbid alcohol use disorder. In this study, disulfiram was associated with better retention in treatment, as well as longer duration of abstinence from cocaine and alcohol. Cocaine-dependent, methadone-maintained individuals treated with disulfiram reported on average three less stimulant-using days compared to placebo [111]. In another trial, in which everyone received individual CBT and either adjunctive disulfiram, CM, both, or placebo, disulfiram reduced stimulant use compared to the double placebo group [112]. In this study, disulfiram did not reduce stimulant use compared with individuals that received CM only, and there were no additive effects of disulfiram when it was used with CM. However, in two other randomized trials comparing disulfiram to placebo samples, there were no differences in stimulant abstinence or use [113, 114].

Strategies and Considerations for Integrating Psychological and Pharmacological Strategies

Screening in Emergency Departments (EDs) and Primary Care

Evidence indicates that screening for substance use disorders reduces mortality and medical comorbidities [115]. Although valid and reliable screening tools exist [116], screening for drug and alcohol use disorders is rarely done in primary care [23]. The Drug Abuse Warning Network (DAWN) currently estimates 2.5 million emergency department (ED) visits a year involve illicit drug use, of which stimulant use accounts for the largest number of visits (162/100,000 population). Drug screening during ED visits is an opportune time for physicians to disseminate information on effective treatment programs. Doing so might reduce the gap between individuals that need treatment and those that actually receive it.

Integration of Primary Care and Stimulant Treatment

There are both clinical and economic benefits associated with integrating primary care with PUD treatment. In a randomized trial, the integration of care increases abstinence by 13 days and doubles the likelihood of being abstinent compared to individuals that received primary care separate from drug treatment (TAU) [117]. Further, medical care costs decreased with integrated care [118]. However, only 54% of substance programs perform a physical at intake, and less than 15% of substance programs employ a nurse [41]. The health services community needs to work more closely together in order to ensure the best and most effective care is given to those that are seeking treatment for medical maladies and their stimulant use.

Integration of Mental Healthcare and Stimulant Addiction

The majority of individuals with PUD have more than one mental disorder, and individuals that have comorbid psychiatric disorders are more likely to experience more persistent and severe symptomology [119]. A rational approach to treating comorbid psychiatric and PUDs might be to use FDA-approved drugs for the psychiatric disorder (e.g., fluoxetine for individual's comorbid depression) and one of the evidence-based psychosocial treatments discussed in this chapter for their stimulant use. There may be an additive or synergistic effect for using this combination of modalities. Further research on treating this population should be done. By treating multiple disorders instead of singular disorders, individuals may experience a more rapid lowered symptomology. Overall, doctors and mental health services must start working together from the prevention level (i.e., screening during emergency room visits) to the treatment level to provide the most effective and well-rounded treatment for those individuals suffering from stimulant use disorder.

Important Comorbidities and Other Pertinent Considerations

Individuals with PUD have high rates of concurrent substance use disorders; specifically, one is seven times more likely to have another alcohol or drug use disorder [120] and 13.5 times more likely to have a comorbid personality disorder [121]. Respectively, 48.05% and 35.1% of individuals with PUD also meet criteria for a mood or anxiety disorder [122]. Collectively, individuals affected by PUD have a complex and widespread mental health profile that often is not addressed when these individuals seek treatment for their PUD. Medical illness complicates the picture with increased risk for cardiovascular events such as myocardial infraction or stroke [123]. Further, due to high-risk sexual behavior and intravenous drug use, individuals that use stimulants are at a higher risk for contracting and transmitting HIV and other sexually transmitted diseases [32, 124].

The use of stimulants while pregnant is related to premature delivery, low birth weight, neonatal abstinence syndrome, and the separation of the placenta from the uterus [125]. Education on the medical and psychiatric risks associated with PUD, as well as the integration of care for these disorders, may improve outcomes in this challenging patient population.

Conclusion

In this chapter, we reviewed the current treatment options for PUD. Currently, only psychosocial interventions have shown efficacy in reducing psychostimulant use. Specifically, CM improves treatment retention and abstinence rates for the duration of the intervention. CBT is an adaptable and effective treatment for PUD that has enduring effects to improve outcomes after treatment has ceased. With respect to pharmacotherapies, although most clinical trials have not produced robust results to reduce psychostimulant use, bupropion, risperidone, and topiramate show some promise [50, 81, 105]. We further emphasized the importance of integration of screening for substance use disorders into primary care, and integration of treatment for PUD with primary and psychiatric care. Next, we will discuss the future directions of the treatment of psychostimulant use disorder.

Future Directions

The Future Role of Medicine in PUD Treatment

There are several important future directions for treating PUD. First, a reversible competitive inhibitor of aldehyde dehydrogenase-2 (ALDH2), which reduces drug-stimulated dopamine release, may be a new pharmaceutical modality for treating PUD. ALDH2 inhibitors reduce drug-primed reinstatement of stimulant-seeking behavior in rats [126]. This ALDH2 inhibitor has not been tested in humans. Second, the current development of vaccines has yielded encouraging outcomes. Stimulant vaccines are designed to produce antibodies that would in turn bind to the ingested psychostimulant, reduce their metabolism, and render them unable to cross the blood–brain barrier. The current cocaine vaccine is effective in reducing cocaine use in individuals who mount an antibody response [127, 128]. Further, a vaccine for methamphetamine use has passed a phase 1 safety trial and will be moving forward to phase 2 trials to test its effectiveness in treating methamphetamine use disorder [129]. With continued development and understanding of immunology research, vaccines are a favorable step in combatting psychostimulant addiction.

The Future Role of Non-Pharmaceutical Interventions in PUD

Therapeutic alliance (TA) is one dimension of psychotherapy (not specific to any one psychotherapy technique) that has been shown to predict positive outcome across different therapies with different clinical populations [130]. TA refers not only to the bond between therapist and patient, but it also includes factors that reflect an alliance between patient and therapist regarding the work of therapy (i.e., an agreement on therapeutic goals and the tasks necessary to achieve them) [131]. In treatment for depression, a good TA has been a consistent predictor of symptom relief and adjustment during and post-therapy [132–134]. The role of TA in substance treatment is less clear.

In a review [135], early TA was found to predict retention in drug treatment and to influence early improvements during treatment, but not to predict post-treatment outcome. However, a study testing substance users' role expectations found that cognitive dissonance on the therapist role negatively affected TA [136]. This in turn was related to reduced therapy retention. Therapists in drug treatment programs often have the additional roles of enforcing rules, limiting access to the drug, and reporting to the criminal justice system. These additional roles, unique to drug treatment therapists, may put the TA at risk. If practitioners explicitly discuss with a patient in the beginning of therapy about the roles of both the therapist and client, then there may be improvements in treatment outcomes of therapy. Approaches that directly modulate TA may improve PUD therapy outcomes. For example, preliminary work suggests the potential therapeutic use of oxytocin in cocaine-dependent patients [137], and adjunctive medications that decrease anxiety or increase social approach such as oxytocin might yield improvements in TA. This in turn might improve psychosocial treatment outcomes.

Another potential approach to treating stimulant addiction is the use of noninvasive neuromodulation techniques such as repetitive transcranial magnetic stimulation (rTMS) or transcranial direct current stimulation (tDCS). RTMS uses a magnetic field that passes unimpeded through the skull and generates an electrical current in the brain via electromagnetic transduction, depolarizing the neurons in cortex underlying the coil. TDCS applies direct current stimulation to the scalp via an anode and cathode that are placed on the scalp, usually over the dorsolateral prefrontal cortex, right and left. A small amount of current passes through the skull, which then modulates brain activity by changing the resting membrane potential of neurons underlying the cathode and anode; synaptic activity at the neurons may also be changed [138]. In general, low-frequency rTMS is thought to inhibit neuronal activity, while high-frequency rTMS excites neuronal activity [139]. There are four small studies that tentatively suggest a role of rTMS in cocaine use disorder: high-frequency (10 Hz or 15 Hz) rTMS to the left [140, 141], right [142], or medial [143] prefrontal cortex reduces cocaine craving. However, low-frequency rTMS to the left dorsolateral prefrontal cortex was found to increase methamphetamine craving [144]. In two double-blind studies, tDCS (right anodal, left cathodal) to the dorsal lateral prefrontal cortex reduced stimulant craving [145, 146]. Given this trend in the research, high-frequency rTMS and tDCS may provide a useful technique in curbing stimulant use.

Table 8.4 Summary table

KEY RESEARCH FINDINGS
1. Contingency management is an efficacious approach for increasing engagement in treatment and reducing stimulant use, but its effects diminish when the incentive protocol terminates. 2. Cognitive behavioral therapy is efficacious for treating PUD, but is substantially underutilized by the clinical community. 3. Computer-based CBT (CBT4CBT) is an effective adaptation and is cost-effective. 4. Gay-specific CBT is equally effective to other treatments, but reduces HIV risk behaviors. 5. The matrix model is an efficacious multicomponent program, but is resource-intensive. 6. No medications have received FDA approval for the treatment of PUD.
RECOMMENDATIONS FOR EVIDENCE-BASED PRACTICE
1. Utilization of the empirically supported psychosocial treatments to the extent that resources permit. Contingency management, cognitive behavioral therapy, or the matrix model may be viable in well-resourced environments; CBT4CBT may be viable in low-resource environments. 2. Increase training in evidence-based treatments for clinicians and increase the utilization of these treatments in healthcare systems more broadly. 3. Increase screening for PUD in primary care clinics, emergency departments, and other nonspecialist clinical contexts.
RECOMMENDATIONS FOR FUTURE RESEARCH
1. Systematic strategies for treating concurrent PUD and other commonly comorbid psychiatric disorders should be investigated toward ultimately developing practice guidelines. 2. Although efficacious medications have not be identified to date, the search should remain a priority. 3. Further investigation of neuromodulatory interventions (e.g., rTMS, tDCS) is warranted.

References

1. National Institute on Drug Abuse. *National Survey of Drug Use and Health* [Webpage]. 2015. Available from: www.drugabuse.gov/national-survey-drug-use-health.
2. Substance Abuse and Mental Health Services Administration. *Results from the 2013 National Survey on Drug Use and Health: summary of national findings.* . Washington (DC): Substance Abuse and Mental Health Services Administration; 2014.

3. Substance Abuse and Mental Health Services Administration. *The NSDUH Report—alcohol treatment: need, utilization, and barriers*. Washington (DC): Substance Abuse and Mental Health Services Administration; 2009.
4. Carroll KM, Rounsaville BJ, Gordon LT, Nich C, Jatlow P, Bisighini RM, et al. Psychotherapy and pharmacotherapy for ambulatory cocaine abusers. *Archives of General Psychiatry*. 1994;51(3):177–187.
5. Shoptaw S, Huber A, Peck J, Yang X, Liu J, Jeff D, et al. Randomized, placebo-controlled trial of sertraline and contingency management for the treatment of methamphetamine dependence. *Drug Alcohol Depend*. 2006;85(1):12–18.
6. Budney A, Higgins S. *A community reinforcement plus vouchers approach: treating cocaine addiction* (NIDA Publication No. 98-4309 ed.). Rockville (MD): National Institute on Drug Abuse; 1994.
7. Petry NM, Peirce JM, Stitzer ML, Blaine J, Roll JM, Cohen A, et al. Effect of prize-based incentives on outcomes in stimulant abusers in outpatient psychosocial treatment programs: a national drug abuse treatment clinical trials network study. *Archives of General Psychiatry*. 2005;62(10):1148–1156.
8. Rawson RA, McCann MJ, Flammino F, Shoptaw S, Miotto K, Reiber C, et al. A comparison of contingency management and cognitive-behavioral approaches for stimulant-dependent individuals. *Addiction*. 2006;101(2):267–274. Available from: http://onlinelibrary.wiley.com/o/cochrane/clcentral/articles/342/CN-00562342/frame.html.
9. Roll JM, Chudzynski J, Cameron JM, Howell DN, McPherson S. Duration effects in contingency management treatment of methamphetamine disorders. *Addictive Behaviors*. 2013;38(9):2455–2462.
10. Shoptaw S, Reback CJ, Peck JA, Yang X, Rotheram-Fuller E, Larkins S, et al. Behavioral treatment approaches for methamphetamine dependence and HIV-related sexual risk behaviors among urban gay and bisexual men. *Drug Alcohol Depend*. 2005;78(2):125–134.
11. Petry NM, Alessi SM, Ledgerwood DM. A randomized trial of contingency management delivered by community therapists. *Journal of Consulting and Clinical Psychology*. 2012;80(2):286–298.
12. Reback CJ, Peck JA, Dierst-Davies R, Nuno M, Kamien JB, Amass L. Contingency management among homeless, out-of-treatment men who have sex with men. *Journal of Substance Abuse Treatment*. 2010;39(3):255–263.
13. Roll JM, Petry NM, Stitzer ML, Brecht ML, Peirce JM, McCann MJ, et al. Contingency management for the treatment of methamphetamine use disorders. *Am J Psychiatry*. 2006;163(11):1993–1999.
14. Petry NM, Tedford J, Austin M, Nich C, Carroll KM, Rounsaville BJ. Prize reinforcement contingency management for treating cocaine users: how low can we go, and with whom? *Addiction*. 2004;99(3):349–360.
15. Petry NM, Alessi SM, Carroll KM, Hanson T, MacKinnon S, Rounsaville B, et al. Contingency management treatments: reinforcing abstinence versus adherence with goal-related activities. *Journal of Consulting and Clinical Psychology*. 2006;74(3):592–601.
16. Muñoz RF, Miranda J. *Individual therapy manual for cognitive-behavioral treatment of depression*. Santa Monica (CA): RAND; 1996.
17. Carroll KM, Nich C, Rounsaville BJ. Utility of therapist session checklists to monitor delivery of coping skills treatment for cocaine abusers. *Psychotherapy Research*. 1998;8(3):307–320.

18. Carroll KM, Rounsaville BJ, Gawin FH. A comparative trial of psychotherapies for ambulatory cocaine abusers: relapse prevention and interpersonal psychotherapy. *The American Journal of Drug and Alcohol Abuse*. 1991;17(3):229–247.
19. Baker A, Boggs TG, Lewin TJ. Randomized controlled trial of brief cognitive-behavioural interventions among regular users of amphetamine. *Addiction*. 2001;96(9):1279–1287.
20. Baker A, Lee NK, Claire M, Lewin TJ, Grant T, Pohlman S, et al. Brief cognitive behavioural interventions for regular amphetamine users: a step in the right direction. *Addiction*. 2005;100(3):367–378.
21. Carroll KM, Rounsaville BJ, Nich C, Gordon LT, Wirtz PW, Gawin F. One-year follow-up of psychotherapy and pharmacotherapy for cocaine dependence: delayed emergence of psychotherapy effects. *Archives of General Psychiatry*. 1994;51(12):989–997.
22. Epstein DH, Hawkins WE, Covi L, Umbricht A, Preston KL. Cognitive-behavioral therapy plus contingency management for cocaine use: findings during treatment and across 12-month follow-up. *Psychol Addict Behav*. 2003;17(1):73–82.
23. Institute of Medicine Committee on Community-Based Drug Treatment. Lamb S, Greenlick MR, McCarty D, editors. *Bridging the gap between practice and research: forging partnerships with community-based drug and alcohol treatment*. Washington (DC): National Academies Press (US). Copyright 1998 by the National Academy of Sciences. All rights reserved; 1998.
24. Weissman MM, Verdeli H, Gameroff MJ, Bledsoe SE, Betts K, Mufson L, et al. National survey of psychotherapy training in psychiatry, psychology, and social work. *Archives of General Psychiatry*. 2006;63(8):925–934.
25. Olmstead TA, Abraham AJ, Martino S, Roman PM. Counselor training in several evidence-based psychosocial addiction treatments in private US substance abuse treatment centers. *Drug Alcohol Depend*. 2012;120(1–3):149–154.
26. Carroll KM, Ball SA, Martino S, Nich C, Babuscio TA, Nuro KF, et al. Computer-assisted delivery of cognitive-behavioral therapy for addiction: a randomized trial of CBT4CBT. *Am J Psychiatry*. 2008;165(7):881–888.
27. Carroll KM, Kiluk BD, Nich C, Gordon MA, Portnoy GA, Marino DR, et al. Computer-assisted delivery of cognitive-behavioral therapy: efficacy and durability of CBT4CBT among cocaine-dependent individuals maintained on methadone. *Am J Psychiatry*. 2014;171(4):436–444.
28. Kiluk BD, Sugarman DE, Nich C, Gibbons CJ, Martino S, Rounsaville BJ, et al. A methodological analysis of randomized clinical trials of computer-assisted therapies for psychiatric disorders: toward improved standards for an emerging field. *Am J Psychiatry*. 2011;168(8):790–799.
29. Andréasson S, Finn SW, Bakshi AS. Barriers to treatment for alcohol dependence: a qualitative study. *Addict Sci Clin Pract*. 2013;8(Suppl 1):A5.
30. Carroll KM, Ball SA, Martino S, Nich C, Babuscio TA, Rounsaville BJ. Enduring effects of a computer-assisted training program for cognitive behavioral therapy: a 6-month follow-up of CBT4CBT. *Drug Alcohol Depend*. 2009;100(1–2):178–181.
31. Olmstead TA, Ostrow CD, Carroll KM. Cost-effectiveness of computer-assisted training in cognitive-behavioral therapy as an adjunct to standard care for addiction. *Drug Alcohol Depend*. 2010;110(3):200–207.

32. Mattison AM, Ross MW, Wolfson T, Franklin D. Circuit party attendance, club drug use, and unsafe sex in gay men. *Journal of Substance Abuse*. 2001;13(1–2): 119–126.
33. Jaffe A, Shoptaw S, Stein J, Reback CJ, Rotheram-Fuller E. Depression ratings, reported sexual risk behaviors, and methamphetamine use: latent growth curve models of positive change among gay and bisexual men in an outpatient treatment program. *Experimental and Clinical Psychopharmacology*. 2007;15(3):301–307.
34. Reback CJ, Shoptaw S. Development of an evidence-based, gay-specific cognitive behavioral therapy intervention for methamphetamine-abusing gay and bisexual men. *Addictive Behaviors*. 2014;39(8):1286–1291.
35. Reback CJ, Larkins S, Shoptaw S. Changes in the meaning of sexual risk behaviors among gay and bisexual male methamphetamine abusers before and after drug treatment. *AIDS and Behavior*. 2004;8(1):87–98.
36. Rawson RA, Shoptaw SJ, Obert JL, McCann MJ, Hasson AL, Marinelli-Casey PJ, et al. An intensive outpatient approach for cocaine abuse treatment: the matrix model. *Journal of Substance Abuse Treatment*. 1995;12(2):117–127.
37. Shoptaw S, Rawson RA, McCann MJ, Obert JL. The matrix model of outpatient stimulant abuse treatment: evidence of efficacy. *Journal of Addictive Diseases*. 1994;13(4):129–141.
38. Rawson RA, Marinelli-Casey P, Anglin MD, Dickow A, Frazier Y, Gallagher C, et al. A multi-site comparison of psychosocial approaches for the treatment of methamphetamine dependence. *Addiction*. 2004;99(6):708–717.
39. Rawson RA, Obert JL, McCann MJ, Ling W. Psychological approaches for the treatment of cocaine dependence: a neurobehavioral approach. *Journal of Addictive Diseases*. 1991;11(2):97–119.
40. McGovern MP, Fox TS, Xie H, Drake RE. A survey of clinical practices and readiness to adopt evidence-based practices: dissemination research in an addiction treatment system. *Journal of Substance Abuse Treatment*. 2004;26(4):305–312.
41. McLellan AT, Meyers K. Contemporary addiction treatment: a review of systems problems for adults and adolescents. *Biological Psychiatry*. 2004;56(10): 764–770.
42. Nomikos GG, Damsma G, Wenkstern D, Fibiger HC. Acute effects of bupropion on extracellular dopamine concentrations in rat striatum and nucleus accumbens studied by in vivo microdialysis. *Neuropsychopharmacology*. 1989;2(4):273–279.
43. Malcolm R, Book SW, Moak D, DeVane L, Czepowicz V. Clinical applications of modafinil in stimulant abusers: low abuse potential. *The American Journal on Addictions*. 2002;11(3):247–249.
44. Stahl SM, Pradko JF, Haight BR, Modell JG, Rockett CB, Learned-Coughlin S. A review of the neuropharmacology of bupropion, a dual norepinephrine and dopamine reuptake inhibitor. *Primary Care Companion to the Journal of Clinical Psychiatry*. 2004;6(4):159–166.
45. Volkow ND, Chang L, Wang GJ, Fowler JS, Franceschi D, Sedler M, et al. Loss of dopamine transporters in methamphetamine abusers recovers with protracted abstinence. *The Journal of Neuroscience*. 2001;21(23):9414–9418.
46. Shoptaw S, Heinzerling KG, Rotheram-Fuller E, Steward T, Wang J, Swanson AN, et al. Randomized, placebo-controlled trial of bupropion for the treatment of methamphetamine dependence. *Drug Alcohol Depend*. 2008;96(3):222–232.
47. Shoptaw S, Heinzerling KG, Rotheram-Fuller E, Kao UH, Wang PC, Bholat MA, et al. Bupropion hydrochloride versus placebo, in combination with cognitive

behavioral therapy, for the treatment of cocaine abuse/dependence. *Journal of Addictive Diseases.* 2008;27(1):13–23.

48. Poling J, Oliveto A, Petry N, Sofuoglu M, Gonsai K, Gonzalez G, et al. Six-month trial of bupropion with contingency management for cocaine dependence in a methadone-maintained population. *Archives of General Psychiatry.* 2006; 63(2):219–228.

49. Margolin A, Kosten TR, Avants SK, Wilkins J, Ling W, Beckson M, et al. A multicenter trial of bupropion for cocaine dependence in methadone-maintained patients. *Drug Alcohol Depend.* 1995;40(2):125–131.

50. Newton TF, Roache JD, De La Garza R, Fong T, Wallace CL, Li SH, et al. Bupropion reduces methamphetamine-induced subjective effects and cue-induced craving. *Neuropsychopharmacology.* 2006;31(7):1537–1544.

51. Elkashef AM, Rawson RA, Anderson AL, Li SH, Holmes T, Smith EV, et al. Bupropion for the treatment of methamphetamine dependence. *Neuropsychopharmacology.* 2008;33(5):1162–1170.

52. McCann DJ, Li SH. A novel, nonbinary evaluation of success and failure reveals bupropion efficacy versus methamphetamine dependence: reanalysis of a multisite trial. *CNS Neuroscience & Therapeutics.* 2012;18(5):414–418.

53. Madras BK, Xie Z, Lin Z, Jassen A, Panas H, Lynch L, et al. Modafinil occupies dopamine and norepinephrine transporters in vivo and modulates the transporters and trace amine activity in vitro. *The Journal of Pharmacology and Experimental Therapeutics.* 2006;319(2):561–569.

54. Volkow ND, Fowler JS, Logan J, Alexoff D, Zhu W, Telang F, et al. Effects of modafinil on dopamine and dopamine transporters in the male human brain: clinical implications. *JAMA.* 2009;301(11):1148–1154.

55. Kim D. Practical use and risk of modafinil, a novel waking drug. *Environmental Health and Toxicology.* 2012;27:e2012007.

56. Ferraro L, Antonelli T, O'Connor WT, Tanganelli S, Rambert FA, Fuxe K. The effects of modafinil on striatal, pallidal and nigral GABA and glutamate release in the conscious rat: evidence for a preferential inhibition of striato-pallidal GABA transmission. *Neuroscience Letters.* 1998;253(2):135–138.

57. Dackis CA, Lynch KG, Yu E, Samaha FF, Kampman KM, Cornish JW, et al. Modafinil and cocaine: a double-blind, placebo-controlled drug interaction study. *Drug Alcohol Depend.* 2003;70(1):29–37.

58. Hart CL, Haney M, Vosburg SK, Rubin E, Foltin RW. Smoked cocaine self-administration is decreased by modafinil. *Neuropsychopharmacology.* 2008;33(4): 761–768.

59. Malcolm R, Swayngim K, Donovan JL, DeVane CL, Elkashef A, Chiang N, et al. Modafinil and cocaine interactions. *The American Journal of Drug and Alcohol Abuse.* 2006;32(4):577–587.

60. De La Garza R, Zorick T, London ED, Newton TF. Evaluation of modafinil effects on cardiovascular, subjective, and reinforcing effects of methamphetamine in methamphetamine-dependent volunteers. *Drug Alcohol Depend.* 2010;106(2–3): 173–180.

61. Dackis CA, Kampman KM, Lynch KG, Pettinati HM, O'Brien CP. A double-blind, placebo-controlled trial of modafinil for cocaine dependence. *Neuropsychopharmacology.* 2005;30(1):205–211.

62. Kampman KM, Lynch KG, Pettinati HM, Spratt K, Wierzbicki MR, Dackis C, et al. A double blind, placebo controlled trial of modafinil for the treatment of

cocaine dependence without co-morbid alcohol dependence. *Drug Alcohol Depend.* 2015;155:105–110.
63. Anderson AL, Li SH, Biswas K, McSherry F, Holmes T, Iturriaga E, et al. Modafinil for the treatment of methamphetamine dependence. *Drug Alcohol Depend.* 2012;120(1–3):135–141.
64. Lotfipour S, Cisneros V, Chakravarthy B, Barrios C, Anderson CL, Fox JC, et al. Assessment of readiness to change and relationship to AUDIT score in a trauma population utilizing computerized alcohol screening and brief intervention. *Substance Abuse.* 2012;33(4):378–386.
65. Heinzerling KG, Swanson AN, Kim S, Cederblom L, Moe A, Ling W, et al. Randomized, double-blind, placebo-controlled trial of modafinil for the treatment of methamphetamine dependence. *Drug Alcohol Depend.* 2010;109(1–3):20–29.
66. Shearer J, Darke S, Rodgers C, Slade T, van Beek I, Lewis J, et al. A double-blind, placebo-controlled trial of modafinil (200 mg/day) for methamphetamine dependence. *Addiction.* 2009;104(2):224–233.
67. Dackis CA, Kampman KM, Lynch KG, Plebani JG, Pettinati HM, Sparkman T, et al. A double-blind, placebo-controlled trial of modafinil for cocaine dependence. *Journal of Substance Abuse Treatment.* 2012;43(3):303–312.
68. McBride AJ, Sullivan G, Blewett AE, Morgan S. Amphetamine prescribing as a harm reduction measure: a preliminary study. *Addict Res.* 1997;5(2):95–112.
69. White R. Dexamphetamine substitution in the treatment of amphetamine abuse: an initial investigation. *Addiction.* 2000;95(2):229–238.
70. Galloway GP, Buscemi R, Coyle JR, Flower K, Siegrist JD, Fiske LA, et al. A randomized, placebo-controlled trial of sustained-release dextroamphetamine for treatment of methamphetamine addiction. *Clinical Pharmacology and Therapeutics.* 2011;89(2):276–282.
71. Grabowski J, Shearer J, Merrill J, Negus SS. Agonist-like, replacement pharmacotherapy for stimulant abuse and dependence. *Addictive Behaviors.* 2004;29(7):1439–1464.
72. Longo M, Wickes W, Smout M, Harrison S, Cahill S, White JM. Randomized controlled trial of dexamphetamine maintenance for the treatment of methamphetamine dependence. *Addiction.* 2010;105(1):146–154.
73. Shearer J, Wodak A, Mattick RP, Van Beek I, Lewis J, Hall W, et al. Pilot randomized controlled study of dexamphetamine substitution for amphetamine dependence. *Addiction.* 2001;96(9):1289–1296.
74. Shearer J, Wodak A, van Beek I, Mattick RP, Lewis J. Pilot randomized double blind placebo-controlled study of dexamphetamine for cocaine dependence. *Addiction.* 2003;98(8):1137–1141.
75. Dursteler-MacFarland KM, Farronato NS, Strasser J, Boss J, Kuntze MF, Petitjean SA, et al. A randomized, controlled, pilot trial of methylphenidate and cognitive-behavioral group therapy for cocaine dependence in heroin prescription. *Journal of Clinical Psychopharmacology.* 2013;33(1):104–108.
76. Grabowski J, Roache JD, Schmitz JM, Rhoades H, Creson D, Korszun A. Replacement medication for cocaine dependence: methylphenidate. *Journal of Clinical Psychopharmacology.* 1997;17(6):485–488.
77. Burris KD, Molski TF, Xu C, Ryan E, Tottori K, Kikuchi T, et al. Aripiprazole, a novel antipsychotic, is a high-affinity partial agonist at human dopamine D2 receptors. *The Journal of Pharmacology and Experimental Therapeutics.* 2002;302(1):381–389.

78. Shapiro DA, Renock S, Arrington E, Chiodo LA, Liu LX, Sibley DR, et al. Aripiprazole, a novel atypical antipsychotic drug with a unique and robust pharmacology. *Neuropsychopharmacology*. 2003;28(8):1400–1411.
79. Tiihonen J, Kuoppasalmi K, Fohr J, Tuomola P, Kuikanmaki O, Vorma H, et al. A comparison of aripiprazole, methylphenidate, and placebo for amphetamine dependence. *Am J Psychiatry*. 2007;164(1):160–162.
80. Newton TF, Reid MS, De La Garza R, Mahoney JJ, Abad A, Condos R, et al. Evaluation of subjective effects of aripiprazole and methamphetamine in methamphetamine-dependent volunteers. *The International Journal of Neuropsychopharmacology*. 2008;11(8):1037–1045.
81. Meredith CW, Jaffe C, Yanasak E, Cherrier M, Saxon AJ. An open-label pilot study of risperidone in the treatment of methamphetamine dependence. *J Psychoactive Drugs*. 2007;39(2):167–172.
82. Meredith CW, Jaffe C, Cherrier M, Robinson JP, Malte CA, Yanasak EV, et al. Open trial of injectable risperidone for methamphetamine dependence. *Journal of Addiction Medicine*. 2009;3(2):55–65.
83. Grabowski J, Rhoades H, Stotts A, Cowan K, Kopecky C, Dougherty A, et al. Agonist-like or antagonist-like treatment for cocaine dependence with methadone for heroin dependence: two double-blind randomized clinical trials. *Neuropsychopharmacology*. 2004;29(5):969–981.
84. Galloway GP, Newmeyer J, Knapp T, Stalcup SA, Smith D. Imipramine for the treatment of cocaine and methamphetamine dependence. *Journal of Addictive Diseases*. 1994;13(4):201–216.
85. Galloway GP, Newmeyer J, Knapp T, Stalcup SA, Smith D. A controlled trial of imipramine for the treatment of methamphetamine dependence. *Journal of Substance Abuse Treatment*. 1996;13(6):493–497.
86. Cruickshank CC, Montebello ME, Dyer KR, Quigley A, Blaszczyk J, Tomkins S, et al. A placebo-controlled trial of mirtazapine for the management of methamphetamine withdrawal. *Drug and Alcohol Review*. 2008;27(3):326–333.
87. McGregor C, Srisurapanont M, Mitchell A, Wickes W, White JM. Symptoms and sleep patterns during inpatient treatment of methamphetamine withdrawal: a comparison of mirtazapine and modafinil with treatment as usual. *Journal of Substance Abuse Treatment*. 2008;35(3):334–342.
88. McDowell D, Nunes EV, Seracini AM, Rothenberg J, Vosburg SK, Ma GJ, et al. Desipramine treatment of cocaine-dependent patients with depression: a placebo-controlled trial. *Drug Alcohol Depend*. 2005;80(2):209–221.
89. Ziedonis DM, Kosten TR. Pharmacotherapy improves treatment outcome in depressed cocaine addicts. *J Psychoactive Drugs*. 1991;23(4):417–425.
90. Raby WN, Rubin EA, Garawi F, Cheng W, Mason E, Sanfilippo L, et al. A randomized, double-blind, placebo-controlled trial of venlafaxine for the treatment of depressed cocaine-dependent patients. *The American Journal on Addictions*. 2014;23(1):68–75.
91. Mancino MJ, McGaugh J, Chopra MP, Guise JB, Cargile C, Williams DK, et al. Clinical efficacy of sertraline alone and augmented with gabapentin in recently abstinent cocaine-dependent patients with depressive symptoms. *Journal of Clinical Psychopharmacology*. 2014;34(2):234–239.
92. Cousins MS, Roberts DC, de Wit H. GABA(B) receptor agonists for the treatment of drug addiction: a review of recent findings. *Drug Alcohol Depend*. 2002;65(3):209–220.

93. Heinzerling KG, Shoptaw S, Peck JA, Yang X, Liu J, Roll J, et al. Randomized, placebo-controlled trial of baclofen and gabapentin for the treatment of methamphetamine dependence. *Drug Alcohol Depend.* 2006;85(3):177–184.
94. Hart CL, Haney M, Vosburg SK, Rubin E, Foltin RW. Gabapentin does not reduce smoked cocaine self-administration: employment of a novel self-administration procedure. *Behav Pharmacol.* 2007;18(1):71–75.
95. Kahn R, Biswas K, Childress AR, Shoptaw S, Fudala PJ, Gorgon L, et al. Multi-center trial of baclofen for abstinence initiation in severe cocaine-dependent individuals. *Drug Alcohol Depend.* 2009;103(1–2):59–64.
96. Howell LL, Cunningham KA. Serotonin 5-HT^2 receptor interactions with dopamine function: implications for therapeutics in cocaine use disorder. *Pharmacological Reviews.* 2015;67(1):176–197.
97. Grady TA, Broocks A, Canter SK, Pigott TA, Dubbert B, Hill JL, et al. Biological and behavioral responses to D-amphetamine, alone and in combination with the serotonin^3 receptor antagonist ondansetron, in healthy volunteers. *Psychiatry Res.* 1996;64(1):1–10.
98. Johnson BA, Ait-Daoud N, Elkashef AM, Smith EV, Kahn R, Vocci F, et al. A preliminary randomized, double-blind, placebo-controlled study of the safety and efficacy of ondansetron in the treatment of methamphetamine dependence. *The International Journal of Neuropsychopharmacology.* 2008;11(1):1–14.
99. McFarland K, Lapish CC, Kalivas PW. Prefrontal glutamate release into the core of the nucleus accumbens mediates cocaine-induced reinstatement of drug-seeking behavior. *The Journal of Neuroscience.* 2003;23(8):3531–3537.
100. LaRowe SD, Myrick H, Hedden S, Mardikian P, Saladin M, McRae A, et al. Is cocaine desire reduced by N-acetylcysteine? *Am J Psychiatry.* 2007;164(7):1115–1117.
101. Mardikian PN, LaRowe SD, Hedden S, Kalivas PW, Malcolm RJ. An open-label trial of N-acetylcysteine for the treatment of cocaine dependence: a pilot study. *Progress in Neuro-Psychopharmacology & Biological Psychiatry.* 2007;31(2):389–394.
102. Mousavi SG, Sharbafchi MR, Salehi M, Peykanpour M, Karimian Sichani N, Maracy M. The efficacy of N-acetylcysteine in the treatment of methamphetamine dependence: a double-blind controlled, crossover study. *Arch Iran Med.* 2015;18(1):28–33.
103. LaRowe SD, Kalivas PW, Nicholas JS, Randall PK, Mardikian PN, Malcolm RJ. A double-blind placebo-controlled trial of N-acetylcysteine in the treatment of cocaine dependence. *The American Journal on Addictions.* 2013;22(5):443–452.
104. Grant JE, Odlaug BL, Kim SW. A double-blind, placebo-controlled study of N-acetyl cysteine plus naltrexone for methamphetamine dependence. *Eur Neuropsychopharmacol.* 2010;20(11):823–828.
105. Johnson BA, Ait-Daoud N, Wang XQ, Penberthy JK, Javors MA, Seneviratne C, et al. Topiramate for the treatment of cocaine addiction: a randomized clinical trial. *JAMA Psychiatry.* 2013;70(12):1338–1346.
106. Elkashef A, Kahn R, Yu E, Iturriaga E, Li SH, Anderson A, et al. Topiramate for the treatment of methamphetamine addiction: a multi-center placebo-controlled trial. *Addiction.* 2012;107(7):1297–1306.
107. Li MD, Wang J, Niu T, Ma JZ, Seneviratne C, Ait-Daoud N, et al. Transcriptome profiling and pathway analysis of genes expressed differentially in participants with or without a positive response to topiramate treatment for methamphetamine addiction. *BMC Med Genomics.* 2014;7:65.

108. Higgins ST, Budney AJ, Bickel WK, Hughes JR, Foerg F. Disulfiram therapy in patients abusing cocaine and alcohol. *Am J Psychiatry*. 1993;150(4):675–676.
109. Higgins ST, Roll JM, Bickel WK. Alcohol pretreatment increases preference for cocaine over monetary reinforcement. *Psychopharmacology*. 1996;123(1):1–8.
110. Carroll KM, Nich C, Ball SA, McCance E, Rounsavile BJ. Treatment of cocaine and alcohol dependence with psychotherapy and disulfiram. *Addiction*. 1998;93(5): 713–727.
111. Petrakis IL, Carroll KM, Nich C, Gordon LT, McCance-Katz EF, Frankforter T, et al. Disulfiram treatment for cocaine dependence in methadone-maintained opioid addicts. *Addiction*. 2000;95(2):219–228.
112. Carroll KM, Nich C, Petry NM, Eagan DA, Shi JM, Ball SA. A randomized factorial trial of disulfiram and contingency management to enhance cognitive behavioral therapy for cocaine dependence. *Drug Alcohol Depend*. 2016;160: 135–142. doi:10.1016/j.drugalcdep.2015.12.036.
113. Carroll KM, Fenton LR, Ball SA, Nich C, Frankforter TL, Shi J, et al. Efficacy of disulfiram and cognitive behavior therapy in cocaine-dependent outpatients: a randomized placebo-controlled trial. *Archives of General Psychiatry*. 2004;61(3): 264–272.
114. Oliveto A, Poling J, Mancino MJ, Feldman Z, Cubells JF, Pruzinsky R, et al. Randomized, double blind, placebo-controlled trial of disulfiram for the treatment of cocaine dependence in methadone-stabilized patients. *Drug Alcohol Depend*. 2011;113(2–3):184–191.
115. Polen MR, Whitlock EP, Wisdom JP, Nygren P, Bougatsos C. *Screening in primary care settings for illicit drug use: staged systematic review for the United States Preventive Services Task Force*. Rockville (MD): Agency for Healthcare Research and Quality; 2008.
116. Lanier D, Ko S. *Screening in primary care settings for illicit drug use: assessment of screening instruments: a supplemental evidence update for the US Preventive Services Task Force*. Rockville (MD): Agency for Healthcare Research and Quality; 2008.
117. Weisner C, Mertens J, Parthasarathy S, Moore C, Lu Y. Integrating primary medical care with addiction treatment: a randomized controlled trial. *JAMA*. 2001;286(14):1715–1723.
118. Parthasarathy S, Mertens J, Moore C, Weisner C. Utilization and cost impact of integrating substance abuse treatment and primary care. *Medical Care*. 2003;41(3): 357–367.
119. National Institute on Drug Abuse. *Comorbidity: addiction and other mental illnesses*. Bethesda (MD): National Institute on Drug Abuse; 2008.
120. Regier DA, Farmer ME, Rae DS, Locke BZ, Keith SJ, Judd LL, et al. Comorbidity of mental disorders with alcohol and other drug abuse: results from the Epidemiologic Catchment Area (ECA) study. *JAMA*. 1990;264(19):2511–2518.
121. Grant BF, Stinson FS, Dawson DA, Chou SP, Ruan WJ, Pickering RP. Co-occurrence of 12-month alcohol and drug use disorders and personality disorders in the United States: results from the National Epidemiologic Survey on Alcohol and Related Conditions. *Archives of General Psychiatry*. 2004;61(4): 361–368.
122. Conway KP, Compton W, Stinson FS, Grant BF. Lifetime comorbidity of DSM-IV mood and anxiety disorders and specific drug use disorders: results from the national epidemiologic survey on alcohol and related conditions. *J Clin Psychiat*. 2006;67(2):247–257.

123. Ciccarone D. Stimulant abuse: pharmacology, cocaine, methamphetamine, treatment, attempts at pharmacotherapy. *Primary Care.* 2011;38(1):41–58, v–vi.
124. Edlin BR, Irwin KL, Faruque S, Mccoy CB, Word C, Serrano Y, et al. Intersecting epidemics: crack cocaine use and HIV-infection among inner-city young-adults. *New England Journal of Medicine.* 1994;331(21):1422–1427.
125. National Institute on Drug Abuse. *Commonly abused drugs charts 2016.* Available from: www.drugabuse.gov/drugs-abuse/commonly-abused-drugs-charts.
126. Diamond I, Yao L. From Ancient Chinese medicine to a novel approach to treat cocaine addiction. *CNS & Neurological Disorders Drug Targets.* 2015;14(6):716–726.
127. Brimijoin S, Shen X, Orson F, Kosten T. Prospects, promise and problems on the road to effective vaccines and related therapies for substance abuse. *Expert Review of Vaccines.* 2013;12(3):323–332.
128. Orson FM, Wang R, Brimijoin S, Kinsey BM, Singh RA, Ramakrishnan M, et al. The future potential for cocaine vaccines. *Expert Opinion on Biological Therapy.* 2014;14(9):1271–1283.
129. Peterson EC, Gentry WB, Owens SM. Customizing monoclonal antibodies for the treatment of methamphetamine abuse: current and future applications. *Advances in Pharmacology.* 2014;69:107–127.
130. Horvath AO, Luborsky L. The role of the therapeutic alliance in psychotherapy. *Journal of Consulting and Clinical Psychology.* 1993;61(4):561–573.
131. Bordin E, editor. *The working alliance: basis for a general theory of psychotherapy.* Washington (DC): Annual Meeting of the Society for Psychotherapy Research; 1975.
132. Klein DN, Schwartz JE, Santiago NJ, Vivian D, Vocisano C, Castonguay LG, et al. Therapeutic alliance in depression treatment: controlling for prior change and patient characteristics. *Journal of Consulting and Clinical Psychology.* 2003;71(6): 997–1006.
133. Krupnick JL, Sotsky SM, Simmens S, Moyer J, Elkin I, Watkins J, et al. The role of the therapeutic alliance in psychotherapy and pharmacotherapy outcome: findings in the National Institute of Mental Health Treatment of Depression Collaborative Research Program. *Journal of Consulting and Clinical Psychology.* 1996;64(3):532–539.
134. Zuroff DC, Blatt SJ. The therapeutic relationship in the brief treatment of depression: contributions to clinical improvement and enhanced adaptive capacities. *Journal of Consulting and Clinical Psychology.* 2006;74(1):130–140.
135. Meier PS, Barrowclough C, Donmall MC. The role of the therapeutic alliance in the treatment of substance misuse: a critical review of the literature. *Addiction.* 2005;100(3):304–316.
136. Frankl M, Philips B, Wennberg P. Psychotherapy role expectations and experiences: discrepancy and therapeutic alliance among patients with substance use disorders. *Psychol Psychother.* 2014;87(4):411–424.
137. Lee MR, Glassman M, King-Casas B, Kelly DL, Stein EA, Schroeder J, et al. Complexity of oxytocins effects in a chronic cocaine dependent population. *Eur Neuropsychopharmacol.* 2014;24(9):1483–1491.
138. Stagg CJ, Nitsche MA. Physiological basis of transcranial direct current stimulation. *Neuroscientist.* 2011;17(1):37–53.
139. Gorelick DA, Zangen A, George MS. Transcranial magnetic stimulation in the treatment of substance addiction. *Annals of the New York Academy of Sciences.* 2014;1327:79–93.

140. Camprodon JA, Martinez-Raga J, Alonso-Alonso M, Shih MC, Pascual-Leone A. One session of high frequency repetitive transcranial magnetic stimulation (rTMS) to the right prefrontal cortex transiently reduces cocaine craving. *Drug Alcohol Depend.* 2007;86(1):91–94.
141. Terraneo A, Leggio L, Saladini M, Ermani M, Bonci A, Gallimberti L. Transcranial magnetic stimulation of dorsolateral prefrontal cortex reduces cocaine use: a pilot study. *Eur Neuropsychopharmacol.* 2016;26(1):37–44.
142. Politi E, Fauci E, Santoro A, Smeraldi E. Daily sessions of transcranial magnetic stimulation to the left prefrontal cortex gradually reduce cocaine craving. *The American Journal on Addictions.* 2008;17(4):345–346.
143. Hanlon CA, Dowdle LT, Austelle CW, DeVries W, Mithoefer O, Badran BW, et al. What goes up, can come down: novel brain stimulation paradigms may attenuate craving and craving-related neural circuitry in substance dependent individuals. *Brain Research.* 2015;1628:199–209.
144. Li X, Malcolm RJ, Huebner K, Hanlon CA, Taylor JJ, Brady KT, et al. Low frequency repetitive transcranial magnetic stimulation of the left dorsolateral prefrontal cortex transiently increases cue-induced craving for methamphetamine: a preliminary study. *Drug Alcohol Depend.* 2013;133(2):641–646.
145. Batista EK, Klauss J, Fregni F, Nitsche MA, Nakamura-Palacios EM. A randomized placebo-controlled trial of targeted prefrontal cortex modulation with bilateral tDCS in patients with crack-cocaine dependence. *The International Journal of Neuropsychopharmacology/Official Scientific Journal of the Collegium Internationale Neuropsychopharmacologicum.* 2015;18(12).
146. Shahbabaie A, Golesorkhi M, Zamanian B, Ebrahimpoor M, Keshvari F, Nejati V, et al. State dependent effect of transcranial direct current stimulation (tDCS) on methamphetamine craving. *The International Journal of Neuropsychopharmacology/Official Scientific Journal of the Collegium Internationale Neuropsychopharmacologicum.* 2014;17(10):1591–1598.

Chapter 9

Gambling Disorder

Jon E. Grant and Samuel R. Chamberlain

Introduction

Gambling disorder is characterized by persistent and recurrent maladaptive patterns of gambling behavior, leading to impaired functioning. It is also associated with higher risk of bankruptcy, divorce, and incarceration, as well as reduced quality of life [1]. Gambling disorder typically begins in adolescence or early adulthood, with earlier onset in men [2–3]. Males are more likely to report strategic types of gambling, whereas females tend to undertake nonstrategic forms of gambling such as slot machines or bingo [4]. Across genders, advertisements represent a common trigger for gambling urges, while feeling bored or lonely is more likely to trigger gambling urges in women [5–6].

Gambling disorder is associated with marked functional impairment across several domains, including ability to function socially and in employment [1, 7]. Even when not undertaking gambling behaviors, urges and thoughts related to gambling occur, which can interfere with concentration and ability to engage on social, household, or occupational tasks [8]. Gambling disorder is often associated with marital disharmony, and diminished intimacy and trust [9]. Financial problems can include defaulting on credit cards and loans, mortgage foreclosures, and bankruptcy [7]. Some individuals with gambling disorder engage in illegal acts in order to fund their habit, such as stealing or financial fraud [7].

Diagnosis

The diagnosis of full gambling disorder requires endorsement of four or more of nine core symptoms during a given 12-month period. These symptoms are: being preoccupied with gambling; needing to increase the amount of money used to gamble in order to experience the same feeling of excitement; trying unsuccessfully to reduce or quit gambling; becoming restless when unable to gamble; gambling to escape an unpleasant feeling such as anxiety or depression; returning to gambling in an attempt to win money back ("chasing losses"); lying to people about the extent of the gambling; jeopardizing or losing a significant relationship or opportunity due to gambling; and relying on others to help with the financial problems caused by gambling [10]. The diagnosis of gambling disorder would not be made if the symptoms were more appropriately accounted for by manic symptoms.

Assessment

Comprehensive assessment of an individual with gambling disorder should focus on the gambling behaviors, related mental and physical issues, previous treatments received, what the person has tried on his or her own to control their gambling, and treatment expectations. Assessment for gambling disorder must include current gambling patterns, functional impact, reasons for seeking intervention, gambling-related cognitions (to aid psychotherapy), and whether they have strong gambling urges (which may assist with choice of pharmacological intervention).

The clinician should assess for comorbid psychiatric problems, including suicidal thoughts, mood disorders, and other addictive problems such as nicotine and alcohol use disorders [11]. Psychiatric factors contributing to ongoing gambling disorder should be identified (such as gambling due to mania, or gambling more when intoxicated). Identification of psychiatric comorbidities and their contributions to gambling is also important when considering treatment sequencing.

The clinician should record previous attempts to control the gambling, previous interventions (including self-exclusion programs at casinos, Gamblers Anonymous), and what the person hopes for in terms of treatment outcomes (e.g., controlled behavior or abstinence). Collateral information is often beneficial given that many individuals may minimize the extent of their problem.

Assessment Instruments

Various interview-based and self-report screening tools have been developed for the assessment of gambling disorder. The South Oaks Gambling Screen (SOGS) is widely used, available in several languages, and can be administered in either self-report or interview formats [12]. Another commonly used screening tool is the Problem Gambling Severity Index (PGSI). The PGSI assesses low-risk, moderate-risk, and problem gambling [12].

Symptom severity in gambling disorder can be assessed through a variety of instruments. The clinician-administered Yale-Brown Obsessive Compulsive Scale Modified for Pathological Gambling (PG-YBOCS) and the self-report Gambling Symptom Assessment Scale (GSAS) are good examples, covering both urges and behavior, and have shown excellent reliability and validity [12].

Etiological Theories

Repetitive engagement in gambling-related behaviors has been argued to be suggestive of underlying problems with cognitive functions that are dependent on the function of cortico-striatal brain circuitry. Consistent with this view, cognitive impairments have been identified in people with gambling disorder compared to healthy controls, including in the domains of planning, top-down control, working memory, cognitive flexibility, and temporal processing [13]. These deficits could occur in people "at risk" before symptoms develop, or arise because of the disorder itself. While there are few, if any, studies of cognitive functioning in unaffected close relatives of people with gambling disorder, studies show that people at risk of developing gambling disorder have decision-making deficits, compared to people who are not at risk [14].

Certain environmental factors may also contribute to the occurrence of gambling disorder. Environmental aspects germane to gambling (e.g., accessibility to gambling, nature of any prizes) may all play their part in the development and maintenance of underlying symptoms. Early negative childhood experiences (trauma, abuse) are higher in people with gambling disorder compared to recreational gamblers; furthermore, more severe childhood experiences can result in more severe gambling symptoms and earlier age of symptom onset [11]. Parental history of gambling problems can predispose offspring to having related difficulties [15].

Evidence-Based Psychological Interventions

Unfortunately, only a small proportion of individuals with gambling disorder seek treatment—as low as 6% of such individuals. There are likely to be several reasons for this, including lack of knowledge that gambling disorder is a recognizable and treatable psychiatric condition, shame, and avoidance. There is a historical literature of case reports in which psychodynamic psychotherapy and psychodynamic psychotherapy were used to treat gambling, but there are no controlled trials to support the use of these forms of treatment. Some evidence exists that Gamblers Anonymous and self-exclusion contracts may be beneficial for individuals with gambling disorder, but findings have been inconsistent in terms of whether longer-term benefits persist.

There are, however, several established psychological treatment options for gambling disorder, including brief interventions, group cognitive behavioral therapy, and individual cognitive behavioral therapy, which have all demonstrated benefit in the management of gambling disorder [1]. The most widely studied psychological treatment has been cognitive behavioral therapy (CBT). In a meta-analysis of 22 controlled trials, psychological treatments were more effective than no treatment with large effect sizes, even at 17-month follow-up [16]. Another meta-analysis of 25 studies reported positive study outcomes for different types of therapy and mechanisms of therapy delivery [17].

Cognitive aspects that are often included in CBT for gambling disorder include psychoeducation, awareness training, and cognitive restructuring. These treatments also often focus on identifying gambling-related triggers and encourage individuals to develop alternative non-gambling-related activities to compete with reinforcers that are associated with gambling.

Cognitive Therapy

In a study of 40 people, individual cognitive therapy plus relapse prevention was associated with reduced gambling frequency and better perceived self-control at 12 months compared to a waiting list control group [18]. Similar findings were identified in another study in 88 subjects [19]. Treatment discontinuation was high in both studies (35–50%), and there was no intent-to-treat analysis. The treatment was manualized, but therapist competence and adherence were not quantified.

Group cognitive therapy (session of two hours duration per week for 10 weeks) has also been evaluated in 71 subjects, again compared to a waiting list control group [20]. Some 88% of those in group CBT no longer met gambling disorder criteria, compared with 20% in the wait-list condition. These beneficial effects of treatment persisted at 24-month follow-up.

Cognitive Behavioral Therapy

In a randomized study of CBT in gambling disorder, comparison was made between individual stimulus control and exposure plus response prevention, group cognitive restructuring, or waiting list control [21]. At 12 months, individual treatment showed superiority over the other treatment arms.

One study examined whether CBT that included techniques designed to improve compliance was superior to standard CBT in 40 subjects with gambling disorder (eight sessions of manualized individual therapy). Some 65% of individuals in the CBT plus compliance techniques group completed the study, compared to 35% in the standard CBT group. At nine-month follow-up, there was no difference in outcomes between treatments, but both resulted in clinically significant change [22].

Melville and colleagues [23] reported two studies that used a system targeting three topics (problem-solving, relapse prevention, and understanding randomness) to improve treatment outcomes. In the first study, 13 subjects were assigned to either eight weeks of group CBT, the enhanced group CBT, or waiting list. In the second study, 19 subjects were assigned to a topic-enhanced group or a waiting list group for eight weeks. The enhanced CBT group showed significant treatment improvements that were maintained at six-month follow-up [23].

In a large study using eight-session manualized CBT, 231 subjects were randomized to receive weekly sessions with an individual counselor, therapy in the form of a workbook, or referral to Gamblers Anonymous [24]. The individual therapy and workbook treatments reduced gambling behaviors to a greater degree than referral to Gamblers Anonymous. This study used an intent-to-treat analysis.

One study examined cognitive-motivational behavior therapy (CMBT), which combines gambling-specific CBT with motivational interviewing, in order to help with treatment retention and compliance. Nine subjects received manualized treatment and were compared with a control group of 12 subjects receiving treatment as usual. One hundred percent of people in the CMBT group completed treatment, compared to 66.7% in the control group. Furthermore, significant improvements were observed at the 12-month follow-up in the CMBT group [25].

Cue Exposure

Cue exposure represents a well-validated form of CBT, which seeks to extinguish the feared or learned response. This is achieved through repeated exposure to a conditioned stimulus in the absence of the feared consequence. The first randomized study compared imaginal desensitization with traditional aversion therapy [26]. Superior improvements were observed in the imaginal desensitization group.

In a second study, 20 inpatient subjects were randomized to receive either imaginal desensitization or imaginal relaxation (14 sessions over a one-week period). Both groups improved following treatment, but the therapeutic gains were not maintained at one-year follow-up [27].

In a larger study, 120 subjects were randomly assigned to aversion therapy, imaginal desensitization, in-vivo desensitization, or imaginal relaxation. Superior improvements were observed at one-month and up to nine years later in the imaginal desensitization group [28]. Approximately half of subjects were lost to follow-up.

Grant and colleagues [29] conducted a randomized study in 68 subjects with gambling disorder using a manualized treatment of imaginal desensitization (including cue exposure plus negative mood induction) versus Gamblers Anonymous. The imaginal desensitization comprised six sessions. Individually tailored scripts were developed for each gambler, including gambling related cues with the intention of activating each gamblers urge via imagination. Of gamblers who received imaginal desensitization 64% were able to maintain abstinence for one month, as compared to only 17% in the control group (Gamblers Anonymous). In the former group, 77% maintained clinical response at six months [30].

Brief Interventions and Motivational Interviewing

Brief treatments are not necessarily regarded as treatment by individuals who access them [1], and therefore may be more appealing to gamblers with significant ambivalence about changing their behavior. Brief treatments can include single-session interventions, workbooks, or bibliotherapy. This approach often also includes motivational interviewing, an interactive approach to helping patients resolve ambivalence and change addictive behaviors.

Dickerson and colleagues randomly assigned 29 subjects to workbook or workbook plus a single in-depth interview [31]. The workbook included cognitive behavioral and motivational enhancement approaches. Both treatment groups experienced significant reductions in gambling symptoms at six months. In a separate study, people with gambling were assigned to a CBT workbook, a workbook plus a telephone motivational enhancement intervention, or waiting list. Frequency of gambling and amounts of money lost to gambling were lower in the workbook plus motivational enhancement group, though rates of abstinence did not differ between groups at six months [32]. Compared with the workbook alone, those gamblers assigned to the motivational intervention and workbook reduced gambling throughout a two-year follow-up period [33]. In a randomized study undertaken by Diskin and Hodgins [34], single-session treatment with motivational interviewing plus a self-help workbook was compared to speaking with an interviewer about gambling for 30 minutes. When subjects were followed up at 12 months, those who received the motivational interviewing plus self-help workbook gambled less and spent less money than the control group.

Motivational interviewing has been compared in individual versus group settings. Oei and colleagues [35] randomized 102 gamblers to six weeks of individual or group CBT with motivational interviewing. Following initial treatment, and at six-month follow-up, those who received individual CBT programs had superior outcomes than the group CBT and waiting list control group. It should be noted that the group CBT treatment nonetheless was superior to waiting list control conditions on some measures. In a study using short-term group-CBT (GCBT) in 14 subjects, 85.7% experienced symptom improvement compared to 42.9% in a waiting list control group [36]. A study focusing on relapse-prevention bibliotherapy randomized 169 subjects who had recently quit gambling to either a summary booklet or to the same booklet plus seven additional informational booklets mailed over the next 12 months (repeated mailing group) [37]. At the 12-month assessment, 24% of the repeated mailing group reported using the strategies regularly to prevent relapse versus 13% of the single mailing group.

Two self-directed motivational interventions were compared with a waiting list control and a workbook-only control in 314 gambling disorder patients, over six weeks. Brief motivational treatment involved a telephone motivational interview and a mailed self-help workbook. Brief motivational booster treatment involved a telephone motivational interview, a workbook, and six booster telephone calls over a nine-month period. Both active treatment groups experienced less gambling at study end than those assigned to the control groups [38]. A similar combination of motivation interviewing and CBT was adapted to a Web-based format [39]. Waiting list control was compared to eight-week Internet-based CBT. The Internet-based intervention resulted in favorable changes in gambling, anxiety, depression, and quality of life [39]. Similar findings were observed in another study, conducted in 284 subjects [40]. A total of 150 patients with gambling problems were randomized to four individual sessions of motivational interviewing, eight sessions of CBT group therapy, or waiting list control. Active treatment was associated with superior short-term outcomes on some measures, but no significant differences were found between motivational interviewing and group CBT [41]. In a randomized study of 117 college students with gambling problems, no significant differences on outcome measures were found as a result of a 10-minute behavioral advice session, one session of motivational enhancement therapy, or one session of motivational enhancement therapy plus three sessions of CBT [42]. Finally, the most recent treatment study recruited 99 problem gamblers, who were randomized to one of four treatments: six sessions of cognitive therapy, behavior therapy, and motivational therapy, or a single-session intervention. All four treatments were associated with similar symptom improvements [43]. Collectively, these findings suggest that a variety of combinations of brief interventions and motivational interviewing have positive effects on gambling disorder, although the optimal combinations are less clear.

Family Therapy

A self-help workbook of the Community Reinforcement and Family Therapy (CRAFT) model, adapted for gambling, was evaluated in two randomized controlled trials [44, 45]. Family members were trained to use behavioral principles to reinforce non-gambling behavior. Some positive effects for family members and their gambling relatives were found in both of the studies, but support from a therapist was needed to enable family members to implement the techniques successfully.

A coping skill-training program has also been studied. The program consisted of 10 weekly individual sessions to teach more effective coping skills. A small ($n = 23$) randomized controlled trial comparing the coping skills program to a delayed treatment condition showed that partners of gamblers improved their ability to manage feelings of depression and anxiety, but that gambling outcomes were similar in both treatments [46].

Evidence-Based Pharmacological Interventions

There are no pharmacological interventions that are currently approved by the Food and Drug Administration (FDA) for the treatment of gambling disorder. Several medications, however, have been investigated as candidate treatments for gambling disorder. These have included opioid antagonists, glutamatergic agents, selective serotonin reuptake inhibitors (SSRIs), atypical neuroleptics, and lithium. In open-label trials, multiple medications have been shown to be associated with symptom improvement in ~70% of cases, including citalopram, escitalopram, carbamazepine, nefazodone, bupropion, valproate, naltrexone, and tolcapone. It should be noted that these studies were generally of 8–14-week duration. Eighteen double-blind, placebo-controlled pharmacotherapy studies have also been undertaken, some with mixed results.

Opioid Antagonists

The opioid system is heavily involved in reward and influences dopamine release in the nucleus accumbens, suggesting that medications acting on this system could be useful for targeting addictive behaviors such as gambling. In a 12-week double-blind, placebo-controlled trial of naltrexone (45 patients), active treatment was superior to placebo in terms of reduction in gambling symptoms [47]. Naltrexone, at a mean dose of 188 mg/day, reduced the frequency and intensity of gambling urges, as well as gambling-related behavior. A separate analysis of those subjects with at least moderate urges to gamble revealed that naltrexone was more effective in those individuals with more severe urges. The clinical use of naltrexone, however, is limited by significant side effects, as well as the occurrence of liver enzyme elevations, especially in patients taking nonsteroidal anti-inflammatory drugs [48].

A second randomized, placebo-controlled naltrexone study was undertaken in 77 subjects [49]. Subjects assigned to naltrexone had significantly greater reductions in gambling urges and gambling behavior compared to subjects on placebo, along with improvement in everyday functioning. However, a study in 101 gamblers receiving either as-needed placebo or naltrexone (50 mg) and psychosocial support for 20 weeks found no significant treatment group differences [50].

Two multicenter studies have demonstrated the efficacy nalmefene in the treatment of gambling disorder. In a large, multicenter, double-blind, placebo-controlled trial, 207 subjects were assigned to receive 16 weeks of either nalmefene at varying doses (25 mg/day, 50 mg/day, or 100 mg/day) or placebo. Of those assigned to nalmefene 59% showed significant reductions in gambling urges, thoughts, and behavior, versus only 34% on placebo [51]. The study, however, experienced a relatively high rate of treatment discontinuation (63%). A second multicenter, randomized, placebo-controlled study was performed with 233 participants using nalmefene 20 or 40 mg [52]. Nalmefene failed to show statistically significant differences from placebo on primary and secondary outcomes. Post hoc analyses of only participants who received a full titration of the medication for at least one week, however, demonstrated that nalmefene 40 mg/day resulted in significantly greater reductions on the primary outcome measure.

Potential side effects of opioid antagonists include nausea, dizziness, insomnia, headaches, and loose stools. In addition, naltrexone, but not nalmefene, has been associated with hepatotoxicity, especially at higher doses.

Glutamatergic Agents

Because enhancing glutamatergic neurotransmission in the nucleus accumbens has been implicated in reducing the reward-seeking behavior in substance addictions [53], N-acetylcysteine (NAC), a glutamate modulating agent, represents a potential medication for use in gambling disorder. In one study, NAC was administered to 27 gambling disorder subjects over an eight-week period, with responders then being randomized to receive an additional six-week, double-blind, placebo-controlled trial. Of those in the open-label phase, 59% experienced significant reductions in gambling symptoms and were classified as responders. At the end of the double-blind phase, 83% of those assigned to receive NAC were still classified as responders, compared to only 28.6% of those assigned to placebo [54].

In a 12-week, double-blind, placebo-controlled study combining NAC with imaginal desensitization in 28 nicotine-dependent gambling disorder subjects, NAC provided significant benefit compared to placebo on nicotine dependence symptoms during treatment and on gambling symptoms three months after formal treatment ended [55].

Topiramate is a drug that is thought to influence mesolimbic dopamine transmission indirectly. In a 14-week, double-blind, placebo-controlled trial of topiramate ($n = 42$ subjects), there was no significant treatment benefit for topiramate, versus placebo, on the outcome measures of interest [56].

Selective Serotonin Reuptake Inhibitors (SSRIs)

Six double-blind placebo-controlled trials have examined SSRIs for the treatment of gambling symptoms. One study, in a single subject, reported benefits from clomipramine (125 mg/day) compared to placebo [58].

In a six-month, double-blind, placebo-controlled study using sertraline (mean dose 95 mg/day) in 60 people with gambling disorder, active treatment did not differentiate from placebo [57].

In a double-blind, 16-week crossover study of fluvoxamine in 15 subjects, significant benefits were seen in terms of gambling symptoms compared to placebo [58]. However, the medication did not separate from placebo during the first phase, but did in the second phase. Fluvoxamine did not differentiate from placebo in a six-month double-blind, placebo-controlled trial of fluvoxamine in 32 gamblers [59]. Treatment discontinuation was high.

Significant improvement was observed for paroxetine compared to placebo in an eight-week trial [60]. However, a larger multicenter, double-blind, placebo-controlled trial in gambling disorder had negative results [61].

Other Antidepressants

Although the randomized, placebo-controlled trials of antidepressants have focused on medications with primarily serotonergic properties, one other antidepressant with different mechanisms of action has been tested. Bupropion, a dopaminergic medication, was studied in 39 subjects during a 12-week period (mean dose = 324 mg/day) [62]. At the end of the study, 35.7% of the bupropion-treated group and 47.1% of the placebo-treated group were considered responders.

Lithium

There has been one double-blind, placebo-controlled study using lithium in gambling disorder subjects, albeit these subjects had bipolar spectrum disorders.

Forty subjects were randomized to sustained release lithium carbonate (mean lithium level 0.87 mEq/L). Superior outcomes were found for lithium compared to placebo on some measures, including reductions in gambling urges/thoughts/behaviors, and reductions in manic symptoms [63].

Atypical Neuroleptics

Two studies have examined the use of olanzapine in the treatment of gambling disorder. In a 12-week, double-blind, placebo-controlled trial of 42 subjects, olanzapine (mean dose 8.9 mg) did not differentiate from placebo [64]. Similar negative results were observed in another olanzapine study, in 23 subjects treated over seven weeks [65].

Strategies and Considerations for Integrating Psychological and Pharmacological Approaches

There has only been one published study examining the relative efficacy of combining drug treatment with psychological treatment in gambling disorder. The trial involved imaginal desensitization with motivational interviewing used in combination with N-acetyl cysteine (NAC) or placebo [55]. Due to the positive benefits of the therapy, there was no indication in the acute trial that the addition of NAC provided any additional benefit for gambling symptoms. At three-month follow-up, individuals who received NAC during earlier therapy continued to benefit more from the imaginal desensitization with motivational interviewing after it was discontinued compared to those taking placebo. Thus, the findings of this study suggest that NAC helped cement the benefits of CBT.

There is a paucity of published trials examining treatment-resistant gambling disorder. We recommend that the following steps be undertaken in such cases. First, the individual could be offered a course of medication (opioid antagonist, N-acetyl cysteine, or lithium) as part of their treatment. Second, for those who have not responded to standard individual CBT, the addition of imaginal desensitization, motivational interviewing, or group CBT may be beneficial. Finally, it is worth re-evaluating the person in case of misdiagnosis, or comorbid disorders being overlooked.

Important Comorbidities and Other Pertinent Considerations

Psychiatric comorbidity is common in individuals with gambling disorder, especially with substance use disorders (including nicotine consumption) [1]. Gambling disorder is also associated with poorer overall health [9] and obesity [66]. Suicidality is common in people with gambling disorder—up to 24% report having attempted suicide at some point in life [67]. Suicidal thoughts and acts can arise due to a variety of factors, including the overwhelming financial consequences of the condition, and comorbid overlap with depression.

Among individuals with gambling disorder plus a comorbidity, the onset of gambling disorder precedes the comorbid disorder in ~23.5% of cases, whereas gambling follows the comorbid disorder in ~74.3% of cases. Mood and anxiety disorders tend to predict the subsequent onset of gambling disorder, whereas substance use disorders tend to develop after the onset of gambling disorder [68].

Another important consideration in the treatment of gambling disorder, and in research, is that high rates of early placebo response are often found. For this reason, it is important to monitor symptom severity over time, rather than to conclude a given treatment has been successful based on short-term treatment response. Also, involving a family member or close friend in treatment efforts that can assist in monitoring treatment outcomes is recommended.

Future Directions

Several conclusions can be drawn from the gambling disorder treatment studies published to date, and these in turn provide direction for future research. First, many of the treatment studies lack a large enough sample for adequate statistical power. Larger, multicenter studies are necessary, especially for promising treatment options such as CBT and opiate antagonists. Second, although CBT has shown efficacy, no manualized CBT treatment has been examined in a confirmatory independent study. Third, comparator and combination treatment studies are lacking. Fourth, it may be that gambling disorder exists in subtypes that respond differentially to treatment options. Finally, CBT studies have shown that both brief interventions and longer-term therapy are potentially effective, but the optimal duration of therapy is unclear.

References

1. Hodgins DC, Stea JN, Grant JE. Gambling disorders. *Lancet.* 2011;378:1874–1884.
2. Ibanez A, Blanco C, Moreryra P, Saiz-Ruiz J. Gender differences in pathological gambling. *J Clin Psychiatry.* 2003;64:295–301.
3. Shaffer HJ, Hall MN, Vander Bilt J. Estimating the prevalence of disordered gambling behavior in the United States and Canada: a research synthesis. *Am J Public Health.* 1999;89(9):1369–1376.
4. Potenza MN, Steinberg MA, McLaughlin SD, Wu R, Rounsaville BJ, O'Malley SS. Gender-related differences in the characteristics of problem gamblers using a gambling helpline. *Am J Psychiatry.* 2001;158:1500–1505.
5. Afifi TO, Cox BJ, Martens PJ, Sareen J, Enns MW. Demographic and social variables associated with problem gambling among men and women in Canada. *Psychiatry Res.* 2010;178:395–400.
6. Echeburúa E, González-Ortega I, de Corral P, Polo-López R. Clinical gender differences among adult pathological gamblers seeking treatment. *J Gambl Stud.* 2011;27:215–227.
7. Grant JE, Kim SW. Demographic and clinical features of 131 adult pathological gamblers. *J Clin Psychiatry.* 2001;62:957–962.

Table 9.1 Summary table

KEY RESEARCH FINDINGS
1. Gambling disorder is prevalent and functionally impairing; suicidality is common.
2. A range of psychotherapy and pharmacotherapy approaches may benefit those with gambling disorder.
3. For medications, the best evidence so far is for N-acetyl cysteine or certain opioid antagonists.
4. For psychotherapy, a single session of CBT may be as beneficial as other longer forms of therapy.
RECOMMENDATIONS FOR EVIDENCE-BASED PRACTICE
1. Multiple types and intensities of psychotherapy may be helpful for gambling disorder.
2. Opioid antagonists are the pharmacological treatment of choice for gambling.
3. N-acetyl cysteine, a nutritional supplement, may benefit gambling disorder.
4. Brief interventions may be as beneficial as longer forms of therapy.
5. Those attending Gamblers Anonymous appear to do better if they also undergo individual psychotherapy.
RECOMMENDATIONS FOR FUTURE RESEARCH
1. Perform multicenter studies of CBT.
2. Determine optimal duration of CBT.
3. Perform comparison studies of medication and therapy; and between medications.
4. Research subtypes of gamblers who respond preferentially to various treatments, and identify potential predictors of treatment response.
5. Research which treatments are better for particular comorbidities.

8. Kushner MG, Abrams K, Donahue C, Thuras P, Frost R, Kim SW. Urge to gamble in problem gamblers exposed to a casino environment. *J Gambl Stud.* 2007;23:121–132.
9. Morasco BJ, Pietrzak RH, Blanco C, Grant BF, Hasin D, Petry NM. Health problems and medical utilization associated with gambling disorders: results from the National Epidemiologic Survey on Alcohol and Related Conditions. *Psychosom Med.* 2006;68:976–984.
10. American Psychiatric Association. *Diagnostic and statistical manual of mental disorders.* 5th ed. Washington (DC): American Psychiatric Press; 2013.
11. Petry NM, Stinson FS, Grant BF. Comorbidity of DSM-IV pathological gambling and other psychiatric disorders: results from the National Epidemiologic Survey on Alcohol and Related Conditions. *J Clin Psychiatry.* 2005;66:564–574.

12. Stinchfield R, Winters KC, Botzet A, Jerstad S, Breyer J. Development and psychometric evaluation of the gambling treatment outcome monitoring system (GAMTOMS). *Psychol Addict Behav.* 2007;21(2):174–184.
13. van Holst RJ, van den Brink W, Veltman DJ, Goudriaan AE. Why gamblers fail to win: a review of cognitive and neuroimaging findings in pathological gambling. *Neurosci Biobehav Rev.* 2010;34:87–107.
14. Grant JE, Chamberlain SR, Schreiber LR, Odlaug BL, Kim SW. Selective decision-making deficits in at-risk gamblers. *Psychiatry Res.* 2011;189(1):115–120.
15. Schreiber LR, Odlaug BL, Grant JE. Recreational gamblers with and without parental addiction. *Psychiatry Res.* 2012;196:290–295.
16. Pallesen S, Mitsem M, Kvale G, Johnsen BH, Molde H. Outcome of psychological treatments of pathological gambling: a review and meta-analysis. *Addiction.* 2005;100:1412–1422.
17. Gooding P, Tarrier N. A systematic review and meta-analysis of cognitive-behavioural interventions to reduce problem gambling: hedging our bets? *Behav Res Ther.* 2009;47:592–607.
18. Sylvain C, Ladouceur R, Boisvert JM. Cognitive and behavioral treatment of pathological gambling: a controlled study. *J Consult Clin Psychol.* 1997;65:727–732.
19. Ladouceur R, Sylvain C, Boutin C, Lachance S, Doucet C, Leblond J, et al. Cognitive treatment of pathological gambling. *J Nerv Ment Dis.* 2001;189:774–780.
20. Ladouceur R, Sylvain C, Boutin C, Lachance S, Doucet C, Leblond J. Group therapy for pathological gamblers: a cognitive approach. *Behav Res Ther.* 2003;41:587–596.
21. Echeburúa E, Baez C, Fernandez-Montalvo J. Comparative effectiveness of three therapeutic modalities in psychological treatment of pathological gambling: long-term outcome. *Behav Cog Psychother.* 1996;24:51–72.
22. Milton S, Crino R, Hunt C, Prosser E. The effect of compliance-improving interventions on the cognitive-behavioural treatment of pathological gambling. *J Gambl Stud.* 2002;18:207–229.
23. Melville CL, Davis CS, Matzenbacher DL, Clayborne J. Node-link-mapping-enhanced group treatment for pathological gambling. *Addict Behav.* 2004;29:73–87.
24. Petry, NM. *Pathological gambling: etiology, comorbidity, and treatment.* Washington (DC): American Psychological Association; 2005.
25. Wulfert E, Blanchard EB, Freidenberg BM. Retaining pathological gamblers in cognitive behavior therapy through motivational enhancement. *Behav Modif.* 2006;30:315–340.
26. McConaghy N, Armstrong MS, Blaszczynski A, Allcock C. Controlled comparison of aversive therapy and imaginal desensitization in compulsive gambling. *Br J Psychiatry.* 1983;142:366–372.
27. McConaghy N, Blaszczynski A. Imaginal desensitization: a cost-effective treatment in two shoplifters and a binge-eater resistant to previous therapy. *Austr NZ J Psychiatry.* 1988;22:78–82.
28. McConaghy N, Blaszczynski A, Frankova A. Comparison of imaginal desensitization with other behavioral treatments of pathological gambling: a two to nine year follow-up. *Br J Psychiatry.* 1991;159:390–393.
29. Grant JE, Donahue CB, Odlaug BL, Kim SW, Miller MJ, Petry NM. Imaginal desensitisation plus motivational interviewing for pathological gambling: randomised controlled trial. *Br J Psychiatry.* 2009;195:266–267.

30. Grant JE, Donahue CB, Odlaug BL, Kim SW. A 6-month follow-up of imaginal desensitization plus motivational interviewing in the treatment of pathological gambling. *Ann Clin Psychiatry.* 2011;23:3–10.
31. Dickerson M, Hinchy J, England LS. Minimal treatments and problem gamblers: a preliminary investigation. *J Gambl Stud.* 1991;6:87–102.
32. Hodgins DC, Currie SR, el-Guebaly N. Motivational enhancement and self-help treatments for problem gambling. *J Consult Clin Psychol.* 2001;69:50–57.
33. Hodgins DC, Currie SR, el-Guebaly N, Peden N. Brief motivational treatment for problem gambling: a 24-month follow-up. *Psychol Addict Behav.* 2004;18: 293–296.
34. Diskin KM, Hodgins DC. A randomized controlled trial of a single session motivational intervention for concerned gamblers. *Behav Res Ther.* 2009;47:382–388.
35. Oei TP, Raylu N, Casey LM. Effectiveness of group and individual formats of a combined motivational interviewing and cognitive behavioral treatment program for problem gambling: a randomized controlled trial. *Behav Cogn Psychother.* 2010; 38:233–238.
36. Myrseth H, Litlerè I, Støylen IJ, Pallesen S. A controlled study of the effect of cognitive-behavioural group therapy for pathological gamblers. *Nord J Psychiatry.* 2009;63:22–31.
37. Hodgins DC, Toneatto T, Makarchuk K, Skinner W, Vincent S. Minimal treatment approaches for concerned significant others of problem gamblers: a randomized controlled trial. *J Gambl Stud.* 2007;23:215–230.
38. Hodgins DC, Currie SR, Currie G, Fick GH. Randomized trial of brief motivational treatments for pathological gamblers: more is not necessarily better. *J Consult Clin Psychol.* 2009;77:950–960.
39. Carlbring P, Smit F. Randomized trial of internet-delivered self-help with telephone support for pathological gamblers. *J Consult Clin Psychol.* 2008;76: 1090–1094.
40. Carlbring P, Degerman N, Jonsson J, Andersson G. Internet-based treatment of pathological gambling with a three-year follow-up. *Cogn Behav Ther.* 2012;41: 321–324.
41. Carlbring P, Jonsson J, Josephson H, Forsberg L. Motivational interviewing versus cognitive behavioral group therapy in the treatment of problem and pathological gambling: a randomized controlled trial. *Cogn Behav Ther.* 2010;39:92–103.
42. Petry NM, Weinstock J, Morasco BJ, Ledgerwood DM. Brief motivational interventions for college student problem gamblers. *Addiction.* 2009;104:1569–1578.
43. Toneatto T. Single-session interventions for problem gambling may be as effective as longer treatments: results of a randomized control trial. *Addict Behav.* 2015; 52:58–65.
44. Makarchuk K, Hodgins DC, Peden N. Development of a brief intervention for concerned significant others of problem gamblers. *Addict Dis Their Treatment.* 2002;1:126–134.
45. Hodgins DC, Currie S, el-Guebaly N, Diskin KM. Does providing extended-release prevention bibliotherapy to problem gamblers improve outcome? *J Gambl Stud.* 2007; 23:41–54.
46. Rychtarik RG, McGillicuddy NB. Preliminary evaluation of a coping skills training program for those with a pathological-gambling partner. *J Gambl Stud.* 2006;22:165–178.

47. Kim SW, Grant JE, Adson DE, Shin YC. Double-blind naltrexone and placebo comparison study in the treatment of pathological gambling. *Biol Psychiatry.* 2001;49:914–921.
48. Kim SW, Grant JE, Adson DE, Remmel RP. A preliminary report on possible naltrexone and nonsteroidal analgesic interactions. *J Clin Psychopharmacol.* 2001;21:632–634.
49. Grant JE, Kim SW, Hartman BK. A double-blind, placebo-controlled study of the opiate antagonist, naltrexone, in the treatment of pathological gambling urges. *J Clin Psychiatry.* 2008;69:783–789.
50. Kovanen LI, Basnet S, Castrén S, Pankakoski M, Saarikoski ST, Partonen T, et al. Randomised, double-blind, placebo-controlled trial of as-needed naltrexone in the treatment of pathological gambling. *Eur Addict Res.* 2016;22(2):70–79.
51. Grant JE, Potenza MN, Hollander E, Cunningham-Williams R, Nurminen T, Smits G., et al. A multicenter investigation of the opioid antagonist nalmefene in the treatment of pathological gambling. *Am J Psychiatry.* 2006;163:303–312.
52. Grant JE, Odlaug BL, Potenza MN, Hollander E, Kim SW. Nalmefene in the treatment of pathological gambling: multi-centre, double-blind, placebo-controlled study. *Br J Psychiatry.* 2010;197:330–331.
53. Kalivas PW, Peters J, Knackstedt L. Animal models and brain circuits in drug addiction. *Molecular Interventions.* 2006;6:339–344.
54. Grant JE, Kim SW, Odlaug BL. N-acetyl cysteine, a glutamate-modulating agent, in the treatment of pathological gambling: a pilot study. *Biol Psychiatry.* 2007;62:652–657.
55. Grant JE, Odlaug BL, Chamberlain SR, Potenza MN, Schreiber LR, Donahue CB, et al. A randomized, placebo-controlled trial of N-acetylcysteine plus imaginal desensitization for nicotine-dependent pathological gamblers. *J Clin Psychiatry.* 2014;75:39–45.
56. Berlin HA, Braun A, Simeon D, Koran LM, Potenza MN, McElroy SL, et al. A double-blind, placebo-controlled trial of topiramate for pathological gambling. *World J Biol Psychiatry.* 2013;14:121–128.
57. Saiz-Ruiz J, Blanco C, Ibanez A, Masramon X, Gomez MM, Madrigal M, et al. Sertraline treatment of pathological gambling: a pilot study. *J Clin Psychiatry.* 2005;66:28–33.
58. Hollander E, DeCaria CM, Finkell JN, Begaz T, Wong CM, Cartwright C. A randomized double-blind fluvoxamine/placebo crossover trial in pathological gambling. *Biol Psychiatry.* 2000;47:813–817.
59. Blanco C, Petkova E, Ibanez A, Saiz-Ruiz J. A pilot placebo-controlled study of fluvoxamine for pathological gambling. *Ann Clin Psychiatry.* 2002;14:9–15.
60. Kim SW, Grant JE, Adson DE, Shin YC, Zaninelli RM. A double-blind placebo-controlled study of the efficacy and safety of paroxetine in the treatment of pathological gambling. *J Clin Psychiatry.* 2002;63:501–507.
61. Grant JE, Kim SW, Potenza MN, Blanco C, Ibanez A, Stevens LC, et al. Paroxetine treatment of pathological gambling: a multi-center randomized controlled trial. *Int Clin Psychopharmacol.* 2003;18:243–249.
62. Black DW, Arndt S, Coryell WH, Argo T, Forbush KT, Shaw MC, et al. Bupropion in the treatment of pathological gambling: a randomized, double-blind, placebo-controlled, flexible-dose study. *J Clin Psychopharmacol.* 2007;27:143–150.

63. Hollander E, Pallanti S, Allen A, Sood E, Baldini Rossi N. Does sustained-release lithium reduce impulsive gambling and affective instability versus placebo in pathological gamblers with bipolar spectrum disorders? *Am J Psychiatry.* 2005;162:137–145.
64. McElroy SL, Nelson EB, Welge JA, Kaehler L, Keck PE. Jr. Olanzapine in the treatment of pathological gambling: a negative randomized placebo-controlled trial. *J Clin Psychiatry.* 2008;69:433–440.
65. Fong T, Kalechstain A, Bernhard B, Rosenthal R, Rugle L. A double-blind, placebo-controlled trial of olanzapine for the treatment of video poker pathological gamblers. *Pharmacol Biochem Behav.* 2008;89:298–303.
66. Grant JE, Derbyshire K, Leppink E, Chamberlain SR. Obesity and gambling: neurocognitive and clinical associations. *Acta Psychiatr Scand.* 2015;131:379–386.
67. Ledgerwood DM, Petry NM. Gambling and suicidality in treatment-seeking pathological gamblers. *J Nerv Ment Dis.* 2004;192:711–714.
68. McCormick RA, Russo AM, Ramirez LF, Taber JI. Affective disorders among pathological gamblers seeking treatment. *Am J Psychiatry.* 1984;141:215–218.

Chapter 10

Addiction Treatment in Primary Care

Megan M. Yardley, Steven J. Shoptaw,
Keith G. Heinzerling, and Lara A. Ray

Funding sources: This work was supported by the following grants: R01 AA021744 (LAR), R21 AA022214 (LAR), R21 AA022752 (LAR), F32 AA023449 (MMY)

Overview

It is well established that substance use disorders (SUDs) represent chronic conditions comprised of biological and behavioral factors requiring screening, diagnosis, intervention, and medical management. To date, strategies used to manage and/or treat other chronic illnesses in primary care have not been widely adopted for the management and treatment of SUDs in the primary care setting [1]. In 2012, approximately 23 million people in the United States required treatment for an alcohol use disorder (AUD) or SUD, while only 11% actually received treatment [2]. The National Epidemiologic Survey on Alcohol and Related Conditions reports that only 26% of alcohol-dependent individuals ever sought treatment, including self-help groups (e.g., Alcoholics Anonymous), highlighting the underutilization of addiction treatment and support services [3]. And for those who do receive treatment for AUD, 40–60% are expected to relapse within one year [1]. Furthermore, one prospective cohort study found that only 63% of participants in an alcohol detoxification program ($n = 400$) accessed primary medical care [4]. Taken together, these statistics emphasize the need to boost the effectiveness of existing treatments for both AUD and SUD. One possible alternative to this complex issue of addiction services utilization that has garnered much attention in recent years consists of identifying a role for addiction medicine in a primary care setting.

This chapter provides a review of addiction medicine in primary care. First, we highlight the benefits of providing alcohol and substance use services in primary care. Second, we summarize results from several effectiveness trials that have been conducted assessing alcohol and substance use screening and brief intervention in primary care settings. Third, we provide a review and discussion of the proposed models to integrate the system of care. Finally, we present limitations to the integration of these services and discuss future directions to more effectively incorporate addiction medicine into the mainstream primary care setting.

Effectiveness Trials

While not standard practice, there is much theoretical support for the potential benefits of addressing substance use issues in primary care settings from the perspective of the patient, society, and providers [5]. Samet and colleagues argue that in linking primary care and substance use services, there is potential for improved overall medical care, primarily by increasing access to treatment for AUD/SUD, making it more available to patients and mitigating the risk of ineffective communication between providers. The authors argue that this linkage would encourage early identification of alcohol and other drug dependence (AOD), likely improving treatment outcomes for patients. Given that there are approximately 68 million people in the United States who use drugs and alcohol in an unhealthy fashion but do not meet the criteria for SUD, linking primary care, mental health, and AOD services could help reach some portion of this population that is not typically captured by specialty treatment settings [6].

In practice, what has been found to be most beneficial in primary care settings is a public health approach that involves screening, brief interventions, and referral to treatment (SBIRT) [7]. While SBIRT has been adapted to take many forms and to be implemented in various settings, its basic format is comprised of: (1) rapid assessment of alcohol and/or substance use; (2) if necessary, the brief intervention involves motivational interviewing by a physician; and (3) depending on the severity of the AUD/SUD, physicians will refer the patient to an alcohol/substance use treatment program. Fleming and colleagues conducted a study with problem drinkers comparing a treatment group who received two 10- to 15-minute counseling sessions with a primary care physician ($n = 392$) and a control group ($n = 382$) [8]. They found that at the 12-month follow-up, the physician intervention group reported decreased mean number of drinks in the past week, fewer binge drinking episodes, and lower frequency of excessive drinking from baseline compared with the control group. These findings highlight the benefits of physician intervention for alcohol use in a primary care setting and using an SBIRT model. Similarly, a meta-analysis of 22 randomized controlled studies evaluating the effectiveness of brief intervention in a primary care setting to reduce alcohol consumption found that brief intervention did result in lower alcohol consumption (g/week) after one-year follow-up with a mean difference of −38.42 [−54.16, −22.67] between brief intervention compared to control, suggesting a robust difference between the two groups [9]. As might be expected, recent studies suggest that while SBIRT may reduce unhealthy alcohol use, defined as risky use without significant psychosocial consequences, there is limited evidence suggesting that this approach is efficacious for individuals with alcohol dependence, a condition best addressed using formal treatment strategies [10].

Despite these mixed results, integrating SBIRT into a primary care setting offers an inexpensive option for early identification of hazardous use of substances, particularly alcohol [9, 11]. One study evaluating a large group of patients ($n = 19{,}372$) from 22 different primary care facilities reported that nearly one in five people in primary care settings are considered at-risk drinkers (i.e., >14 drinks/week for men; >7 drinks/week for women, or binge drinking). Given the staggering number of patients meeting the definition of at-risk drinking, early identification could promote early intervention, and in turn result in greater treatment success rates [12].

Not only can brief intervention be beneficial to the patient, but Fleming and colleagues report that brief intervention for problem drinkers is beneficial from an economical perspective as well [13]. The authors conducted a cost–benefit analysis of brief physician advice in primary care settings. Healthcare costs associated with brief intervention and economic costs (i.e., changes in healthcare utilization, legal costs, and vehicular accidents) were compared between the experimental (received physician-led brief intervention and health booklet; $n = 392$) and control (received health booklet only; $n = 382$) groups. The total benefit of the brief intervention was significant and estimated to be \$423,519 (\$1,515 per patient) as a result of lower hospitalizations, crime, and vehicle accidents. Given that the cost of the brief intervention was \$80,210 (\$205 per patient), the benefit–cost ratio was 5.6:1. In other words, the results from this study suggest that incorporating brief intervention into primary care settings for patients engaging in risky alcohol use may offer significant economic benefits to healthcare systems.

Given the benefits associated with using SBIRT for patients engaged in risky alcohol use in primary care settings discussed above, the use of SBIRT for illicit drug use has also been investigated. For example, the Addiction Health Evaluation and Disease management (AHEAD) study assessed the efficacy of chronic care management (CCM) to improve substance use outcomes in people ($n = 563$) with AOD compared to standard primary care [14]. Chronic care management included additional physician contact and support, including longitudinal care, motivational enhancement therapy, relapse prevention counseling, referrals, and on-site medical, mental health, substance use, and social work assistance. They found no difference between the two intervention groups over the 12-month follow-up period [14]. Moreover, there were no significant differences observed in secondary outcomes such as addiction severity, health-related quality of life, or drug problems.

Similarly, Saitz and colleagues conducted the Assessing Screening Plus Brief Intervention's Resulting Efficacy to Stop Drug Use (ASPIRE) study to compare the efficacy of three interventions in reducing unhealthy drug use in a primary care setting [15]. Subjects were primary care patients with an Alcohol, Smoking, and Substance (i.e., opioid, marijuana, and cocaine) Involvement Screening Test (ASSIST) substance-specific score ≥ 4 ($n = 528$) who were assigned one of three conditions: (1) brief negotiated interview (10- to 15-minute structured interview by health educators); (2) adaptation of motivational interviewing (30- to 40-minute motivational interviewing session in addition to a 20- to 30-minute booster by a Master's-level professional); and (3) no intervention. There was no effect of brief intervention or motivational interviewing on mean number of days of drug use in the past 30 days at the six-month follow-up compared to control, suggesting that while SBIRT has shown moderate efficacy for unhealthy alcohol use, there is little evidence to suggest that it is effective in SUD.

On the other hand, Weisner and colleagues suggest that patients with SUD in an integrated model of care experience significantly higher abstinent rates compared with patients who received medical and substance abuse care independently [16]. The Quit Using Drugs Intervention Trial (QUIT) project analyzed the effects of brief intervention in a primary care setting on risky psychoactive drug use. The treatment was comprised of a brief intervention (three to four minutes reviewing the hazards of the use of the specific substance followed by a "knock it off" message) by a physician and up to two 20- to 30-minute follow-up sessions. After three months, the intervention group used drugs, on average, 3.5 days less than a control group who received a brief health video and booklet [17]. In summary, while the literature is mixed, and some randomized controlled trials support the utility of a brief intervention in a primary care setting for SUD, the majority of literature shows no significant support for brief intervention for SUD in primary care settings, as opposed to fairly consistent support for SBIRT for heavy drinking, and some mixed effects for AUD-level drinking problems.

Proposed Models to Integrate the System of Care

From a societal perspective, implementing SBIRT for unhealthy alcohol and drug use in a primary care setting could reduce overall economic costs associated with substance use disorder, which is estimated to be over $700 billion, according to the National Institute of Drug Abuse [5, 18]. Moreover, it can be argued that by integrating heavy alcohol and substance use services into primary care treatment and employing strategies used to manage or treat other chronic illnesses, the stigma associated with substance use disorder will be lifted, thus promoting the utilization of these services by patients who need them [5].

In addition to the aforementioned benefits to patients and society, the linkage of services with primary care may provide physicians with benefits such as early identification, greater access to substance abuse medical training, increased appreciation of treatment and prevention of alcohol and substance use disorder among primary care physicians, and the opportunity to use these new-found tools to inform diagnoses and treatment of other behavior-related issues [5]. Furthermore, greater appreciation for identification of and referral to treatment for alcohol and drug use disorders at the general healthcare level, and related prevention and/or treatment strategies, may also affect reimbursement parity for these services in relation to other chronic illnesses.

Given that patients entering addiction treatment often do not receive primary care, there are three proposed models to facilitate the transition from addiction treatment to primary care, which include: (1) SBIRT; (2) facilitated referral to primary care; and (2) co-location/integration of substance use and primary care services [19]. Screening, brief intervention, and referral to treatment is discussed in detail above. One of the primary benefits to this model is the relative ease of implementation compared to the other two proposed models, as it requires relatively fewer resources and training. The second model is facilitated referral to primary care, requiring an additional staff member to facilitate a successful transition from substance use treatment service to off-site primary care services (and vice versa). Although this model was not found to be as effective as integrated care in a geriatric population [20], another study showed that individuals receiving enhanced specialty referrals and those receiving integrated care reduced average weekly drinking and binge drinking at the six-month follow-up at comparable levels [21]. Perceived advantages to the integrated care model over the facilitated referral include better communication between service providers, better coordination of care, and better management of substance use and comorbid conditions [19]. The most intensive of the three models, requiring the greatest financial and resource investment (i.e., staff, training, etc.) is the co-location and integration of substance use services and primary care. Co-location refers to specialty behavioral professionals, such as substance use counselors, providing their service in a primary care facility, whereas co-location refers to primary care services being offered by primary care physicians in a specialty behavioral health setting such as a substance use treatment facility [6].

A recent study that included patients at the UCLA Santa Monica Family Health Center assessed the effect of co-location of addiction and behavioral medicine services in a primary care setting on inpatient service utilization (Worley et al., *in preparation*). Cases were patients who had received treatment at the addiction or behavioral medicine clinic, and controls were patients who received healthcare services not including addiction or behavioral medicine at the facility. The authors found that in the group receiving treatment at the addiction medicine or behavioral medicine clinics, compared to 12 months prior to the qualifying visit, prevalence of inpatient service use decreased from 17.9% to 13.6% compared to a decrease from 8.7% to 8.3% in controls. These results suggest that co-location may be an effective mechanism to improve outcomes related to addiction treatment. Taken together, while it appears that combining primary medical care and substance use services may offer a range of benefits to the patient, society, and providers, the data presented above suggest that the proposed models of integration have not been sufficiently developed or tested to the point of offering feasible solutions to address AUD or SUD in a primary care setting. Nevertheless, this is an incipient field with the potential for substantive gains to patients and healthcare systems, should effective models be developed and implemented.

Limitations and Future Directions

While the linkage of substance use services and primary care appears promising, in theory, the integration of these services has not been widely implemented [6], and the effectiveness trials, discussed above, do not provide consistent support for the implementation of substance use services, in their current format, in a primary care setting, perhaps with the exception of SBIRT for heavy drinking. From a healthcare perspective, however, the efforts to integrate substance use services in primary care may be moving forward, despite the relatively low level of empirical support for the programs and models of integration reviewed above. For example, Padwa and colleagues conducted a survey for substance use disorder administrators ($n = 44$) regarding implemented integration services, and found that just over half ($n = 25$) of the administrators reported that integration efforts are ongoing while about 40% ($n = 18$) reported that integration of these services will be initiated within the year.

Thus, while the integration of services remains highly desirable to many healthcare systems, there are several obstacles that may impede its feasibility. Presently, primary care physicians receive little training in regard to substance use identification, screening, and treatment [5]. This is highlighted in a recent survey conducted by Urada and colleagues assessing the integration of substance use services and primary medical care, and identifying challenges related to linking these services [22]. They report that physicians found that substance use services, compared to mental health services, were less effective, and therefore tended to be less integrated in the primary care setting, primarily due to perceptions on lack of provider education in this area. In other words, when physicians are considered as "consumers" of the integration, questions about the effectiveness of the interventions, as well as the capabilities of the individual providers and systems, are consistently raised. Another major obstacle in the integration of substance use services and primary care is the availability of sufficient funding to maintain integrated care [6]. In the survey conducted by Padwa and colleagues [6], more than 92% reported funding as a barrier to the successful integration of these services. While relatively less challenging to overcome than systemic and funding issues, there are also regulatory barriers related to documentation that result from integrating substance use and primary care services [6]. Specifically, Federal Regulation 42 C.F.R. Part 2 prohibits the sharing of substance use disorder treatment with other health professionals or inclusion of these treatment records in open electronic medical records without patient written consent.

In summary, support for the integration of addiction services in primary care is currently limited by the lack of trials demonstrating the effectiveness for incorporating addiction medicine into the mainstream primary care setting, the monetary investment necessary to implement many of the strategies discussed herein, and the lack of compelling models for effective integration of care.

There is much that remains unclear in the evidence base that might guide the integration of addiction services in primary care. The current state of the field calls for well-designed research protocols that identify interventions with efficacy that can be effectively implemented in primary care settings. This includes specifying how long intervention effects can be observed and the mechanisms by which interventions produce their effects (e.g., the importance of the physician delivering the message, use of computer-assisted survey techniques that might reduce under-reporting biases). There also are questions of whether unique patient characteristics might moderate intervention efficacy, including groups of patients for whom health disparities have been documented.

The current chapter summarizes the observed benefits to the patient, provider, and healthcare systems of addressing heavy alcohol use through the implementation of brief intervention into primary care settings. While SBIRT has shown moderate efficacy in reducing unhealthy alcohol use, defined as risky use without significant psychosocial consequences, there is little evidence suggesting that it is efficacious among individuals with alcohol dependence [10] or among individuals with AOD [14, 15]. In addition, significant barriers have been identified, including lack of physician training, funding support, and efficient integration strategies. Future directions include increasing physician training in addiction medicine and implementation of these models of integrated care in settings where substance use is more prevalent (i.e., emergency care settings).

In conclusion, the interest in integrating addiction services in primary care remains high and the current state of the field calls for innovative approaches to the integration of addiction services in primary care, with new models that can effectively satisfy the needs of the multiple stakeholders in this complex system, namely providers, consumers, healthcare administrators, and funding sources.

Table 10.1 Summary table

KEY RESEARCH FINDINGS
1. Addictive disorders are highly prevalent, but the large majority of affected individuals are not identified by the medical established and are not engaged in any treatment.
2. Screening, brief intervention, and referral to treatment (SBIRT) has been shown to be efficacious for unhealthy alcohol use (excessive consumption without necessarily psychosocial impairment), but not alcohol dependence.
3. Results of SBIRT for other substance use disorders are mixed.
RECOMMENDATIONS FOR EVIDENCE-BASED PRACTICE
1. Given the high prevalence of addictive disorders, universal screening using brief validated measures is warranted in primary care.
2. SBIRT for alcohol is recommended as standard practice in primary care.
3. For individuals who require more than an SBIRT intervention, facilitated referral from primary care to specialty addiction treatment is appropriate. Co-location of primary care and some level of addiction services is ideal, but may be cost-prohibitive.
RECOMMENDATIONS FOR FUTURE RESEARCH
1. Further examination of co-location of primary care and addiction treatment via proof of concept and demonstration projects is warranted.
2. Strategies for systematically increasing primary care physician awareness and skills are a high priority.
3. Clarification of where the impact of primary care interventions is strongest and weakest (i.e., identification of patient types and treatment modalities that are most effective, and vice versa).

References

1. McLellan AT, et al. Drug dependence, a chronic medical illness: implications for treatment, insurance, and outcomes evaluation. *JAMA*. 2000;284(13):1689–1695.
2. O'Connor PG, Sokol RJ, D'Onofrio G. Addiction medicine: the birth of a new discipline. *JAMA Intern Med*. 2014;174(11):1717–1718.
3. Enoch M. Genetic influences on response to alcohol and response to pharmacotherapies for alcoholism. *Pharmacol Biochem Beh*. 2014:17–24.
4. Saitz R, et al. Linkage with primary medical care in a prospective cohort of adults with addictions in inpatient detoxification: room for improvement. *Health Services Research*. 2004;39(3):587–606.
5. Samet JH, Friedmann P, Saitz R. Benefits of linking primary medical care and substance abuse services: patient provider, and societal perspectives. *JAMA Intern Med*. 2001;161(1):86–91.
6. Padwa H, et al. Integrating substance use disorder services with primary care: the experience in California. *J Psychoactive Drugs*. 2012;44(4):299–306.
7. Agerwala SM, McCance-Katz EF. Integrating screening, brief intervention, and referral to treatment (SBIRT) into clinical practice settings: a brief review. *J Psychoactive Drugs*. 2012;44(4):307–317.
8. Fleming MF, et al. Brief physician advice for problem alcohol drinkers: a randomized controlled trial in community-based primary care practices. *JAMA*. 1997;277(13):1039–1045.
9. Kaner EF, et al. Effectiveness of brief alcohol interventons in primary care populations. *Cochrane Database Syst Rev*. 2007;18(2):CD004148.
10. Saitz R. Alcohol screening and brief intervention in primary care: absence of evidence for efficacy in people with dependence or very heavy drinking. *Drug Alcohol Rev*. 2010;29(6):631–640.
11. Merrill JO. Integrating medical care and addiction treatment. *J Gen Intern Med*. 2003;18(1):68–69.
12. Fleming MF, et al. At-risk drinking in an HMO primary care sample: prevalence and health policy implications. *Am J Public Health*. 1998;88(1):90–93.
13. Fleming MF, et al. Benefit-cost analysis of brief physician advice with problem drinkers in primary care settings. *Medical Care*. 2000;38(1):7–18.
14. Saitz R, et al. Chronic care managment for dependence on alcohol and other drugs: the AHEAD randomized trial. *JAMA*. 2013;310(11):1156–1167.
15. Saitz R, et al. Screening and brief intervention for drug use in primary care: the ASPIRE randomized clinical trial. *JAMA*. 2014;312(5):502–513.
16. Weisner C, et al. Integrating primary medical care with addiction treatment: a randomized controlled trial. *JAMA*. 2001;286(14):1715–1723.
17. Gelberg L, et al. Project QUIT (Quit Using Drugs Intervention Trial): a randomized controlled trial of a primary care-based multi-component brief intervention to reduce risky drug use. *Addiction*. 2015;110:1777–1790.
18. *Trends & statistics*; November 23, 2015. Available from: www.drugabuse.gov/related-topics/trends-statistics.
19. Cucciare MA, et al. Enhancing transitions from addiction treatment to primary care. *Journal of Addictive Diseases*. 2014;33:340–353.
20. Bartels SJ, et al. Improving access to geriatric mental health services: a randomized trial comparing treatment engagement with integrated versus enhanced referral care for depression, anxiety, and at-risk alcohol use. *Am J Psychiat*. 2004;161(8):1455–1462.

21. Oslin DW, et al. PRISM-E: comparison of integrated care and enhanced specialty referral in managing at-risk alcohol use. *Psychiatr Serv*. 2006;57(7):954–958.
22. Urada D, et al. Integration of substance use disorder services with primary care: health center surveys and qualitative interviews. *Substance Abuse Treatment, Prevention, and Policy*. 2014;9(15).

Index

acamprosate 89–90
acute drug effects 39
addiction: biological models of: genetic influences 36–37; neurobiological models 34–36; psychological models: acute drug effects 39; cognitive processes 39–41; developmental psychopathology 42–43; personality factors 41; reinforcement-based approach 38–39; social models: social influence and mechanisms 44–45; social networks 43–44; sociocultural influences 45; treatment, primary care: effectiveness trials 258–260; limitations 262–264; system of care 260–262
addictive behavior 3
addictive disorders 4; empirically supported therapies (ESTs) 67–69; evidence-based approaches 61–66; acceptable deviation 69–70; measurement-based practice 72–73; medical *vs.* contextual model 66–67; practice-based evidence 72–73; Quality Enhancement Research Initiative (QUERI) 70–72; research designs 57–61; research process 57–61; strength of evidence 57–61
alcohol dependence (AD) 5
alcohol use disorders (AUDs): alcohol consumption: burden of disease attributable to 8–9; health burden caused by 6–8; burden of disease attributable to 9–11; epidemiology of 5–6; evidence-based psychological interventions: brief interventions (BIs) 83–84; computer-based interventions 86; counseling 82–83; evidence-based pharmacological interventions 86; longer-term interventions 84–85; FDA-approved medications: acamprosate 89–90; disulfiram 86–87; naltrexone 87–89; naltrexone and acamprosate 90; important comorbidities and pertinent considerations 94–96; integrative treatment of 96–98; medication adherence 91–94; prevalence of 81–82; psychological and pharmacological therapies 91–94; risk factor 11
Alcoholics Anonymous 43
allostatic model of addiction 36
Amato, L. 133
Amrhein, P. 72
antipsychotics 218–219
AUDs. *See* alcohol use disorders (AUDs)

biological models, addiction: genetic influences 36–37; neurobiological models 34–36

Blanchard, K.A. 68
brief interventions (BIs): alcohol use disorders (AUDs) 83–84; gambling disorder 245–246
bupropion 111–112, 198, 218

cannabis use disorder (CUD): evidence-based pharmacological interventions: cannabinoid targets 163–164; non-cannabinoid targets 164–166; evidence-based psychological interventions 159–162; important comorbidities and pertinent considerations 167; psychological and pharmacological strategies 166–167
cardio-toxicity 12
Carroll, K.M. 194, 195
cellular learning model of addiction 35
Chambless, D.L. 62, 66
computer-based interventions 86
cytisine 112–113

Diagnostic and Statistical Manual of Mental Disorders (DSM-IV) 14
Diagnostic and Statistical Manual of Mental Disorders (DSM) 5, 4
Dickerson, M. 245
disability adjusted life years (DALYs) 4
Diskin, K.M. 245
disulfiram 86–87

Edwards, G. 5
egocentric 43
empirically supported therapies (ESTs) 67–69
evidence-based pharmacological interventions: alcohol use disorders (AUDs) 86; cannabis use disorder (CUD): cannabinoid targets 163–164; non-cannabinoid targets 164–166; gambling disorder: antidepressants 249; atypical neuroleptics 249; glutamatergic agents 248; lithium 249; opioid antagonists 247–248; psychological and pharmacological approaches 249–250; selective serotonin reuptake inhibitors (SSRIs) 248–249; opioid use disorder (OUD): combination buprenorphine/naloxone 137–139; heroin assisted therapy (HAT) 140; levo-α-acetylmethadol (LAAM) 140; methadone maintenance treatment 136–137; naltrexone 139–140; stimulant use disorder: additional antidepressants 219; antipsychotics 218–219; bupropion 198, 218; GABA agonists 219; modafinil 218; psychostimulants 218; tobacco-related disorders: bupropion 111–112; cytisine 112–113; nicotine replacement therapy (NRT) 108–110; psychological and pharmacological interventions 114–115; second-line and experimental medications 113–114; varenicline 110–111
evidence-based psychological interventions: alcohol use disorders (AUDs): brief interventions (BIs) 83–84; computer-based interventions 86; counseling 82–83; evidence-based pharmacological interventions 86; longer-term interventions 84–85; cannabis use disorder (CUD) 159–162; gambling disorder 242–243; brief interventions 245–246; cognitive behavioral therapy (CBT) 243–244; cognitive therapy 243; Cue exposure 244; family therapy 246; motivational interviewing 245–246; stimulant use disorder 181–193; tobacco-related disorders: formal treatment programs 106–108; minimal contact interventions (MCIs) 105–106

FDA-approved medications: acamprosate 89–90; disulfiram 86–87; naltrexone 87–89; naltrexone and acamprosate 90
Finney, J.W. 59, 71
Fleming, M.F. 258, 259

GABA agonists 219
gambling disorder: assessment 241; assessment instruments 241; diagnosis 240–241; etiological theories 242; evidence-based pharmacological interventions: antidepressants 249; atypical neuroleptics 249; glutamatergic agents 248; lithium 249; opioid antagonists 247–248; psychological and pharmacological approaches 249–250; selective serotonin reuptake inhibitors (SSRIs) 248–249; evidence-based psychological interventions 242–243; brief interventions 245–246; cognitive

behavioral therapy (CBT) 243–244; cognitive therapy 243; Cue exposure 244; family therapy 246; motivational interviewing 245–246; important comorbidities and pertinent considerations 250
Global Burden of Disease and Injury (GBD) study 4
Global Strategy to Reduce the Harmful Use of Alcohol 26
Grant, B.F. 244
Gross, M.M. 5

Hail. L. 72
Hayaki, J. 68
heroin assisted therapy (HAT) 140
Hill, A. 12
Hodgins, D.C. 245
Hollon, S.D. 62, 66

illicit drug use disorders: burdens of 22–25; epidemiology of 20–21
incentive sensitization theory 34
International Classification of Diseases (ICD) 4

Kuerbis, A. 72

Labouvie, E. 68
levo-α-acetylmethadol (LAAM) 140
Lynch, K. 72

Manuel, J.K. 65
McKay, J.R. 72
Melville, C.L. 243
methadone maintenance treatment 136–137
Miller, W.R. 65
modafinil 218
Morgan, T.J. 68
Morgenstern, J. 68, 72

naltrexone 87–89, 139–140
naltrexone and acamprosate 90
nicotine replacement therapy (NRT) 108–110

Oei, T.P. 245
opioid use disorder (OUD): evidence-based pharmacological interventions: combination buprenorphine/naloxone 137–139; heroin assisted therapy (HAT) 140; levo-α-acetylmethadol (LAAM) 140; methadone maintenance treatment 136–137; naltrexone 139–140; evidence-based psychosocial interventions: cognitive behavioral therapy (CBT) 131–133; family/couples therapy 135; motivational interventions 134–135; reinforcement-based treatment 133–134; important comorbidities and pertinent considerations: chronic pain 142; infectious disease 142; polysubstance use 143; psychiatric comorbidities 142–143; sex and gender differences 144; integrating psychological and pharmacological treatments 141

Padwa, H. 262
psychological models, addiction: acute drug effects 39; cognitive processes 39–41; developmental psychopathology 42–43; personality factors 41; reinforcement-based approach 38–39
psychostimulant theory of addiction 34
psychostimulants 218

Quality Enhancement Research Initiative (QUERI) 70–72

reinforcement-based approach 38–39
Rottmann 12

Saitz, R. 259
Samet, J.H. 258
selective serotonin reuptake inhibitors (SSRIs) 248–249
smoking-related diseases 37. *See also* tobacco-related disorders
social models, addiction: social influence and mechanisms 44–45; social networks 43–44; sociocultural influences 45
social network analysis (SNA) 43
social networks 43–44
sociocentric 43
sociocultural influences 45
stimulant use disorder: cognitive behavioral therapy (CBT) 194–197; contingency management (CM) 194; evidence-based pharmacological interventions: additional antidepressants 219; antipsychotics

218–219; bupropion 198, 218; combined psychosocial and pharmacological treatments 220–223; GABA agonists 219; modafinil 218; pharmacological treatments 199–217; psychosocial treatments 182–193; psychostimulants 218; evidence-based psychological interventions 181–193; evidence-based therapies (EBTs) 197–198; important comorbidities and pertinent considerations 226; non-pharmaceutical interventions 227–229; psychological and pharmacological strategies: emergency departments (EDs) 225; mental healthcare 225–226; primary care 225; stimulant addiction 225–226; stimulant treatment 225

Suchman, E.A. 71

Tobacco Framework Convention 26
tobacco-related disorders: burden of 15–19; definition of 13; epidemiology of 13–15; evidence-based pharmacological interventions: bupropion 111–112; cytisine 112–113; nicotine replacement therapy (NRT) 108–110; psychological and pharmacological interventions 114–115; second-line and experimental medications 113–114; varenicline 110–111; evidence-based psychological interventions: formal treatment programs 106–108; minimal contact interventions (MCIs) 105–106; important comorbidities 115–118

Urada, D. 262

varenicline 110–111
ventral-to-dorsal striatum account 35

Weisner, C. 260
World Drug Reports 4
World Health Organization (WHO) 5, 12

years of life lost (YLL) 4
years of life lost to disability (YLD) 4

Taylor & Francis eBooks

Helping you to choose the right eBooks for your Library

Add Routledge titles to your library's digital collection today. Taylor and Francis ebooks contains over 50,000 titles in the Humanities, Social Sciences, Behavioural Sciences, Built Environment and Law.

Choose from a range of subject packages or create your own!

Benefits for you
- Free MARC records
- COUNTER-compliant usage statistics
- Flexible purchase and pricing options
- All titles DRM-free.

Benefits for your user
- Off-site, anytime access via Athens or referring URL
- Print or copy pages or chapters
- Full content search
- Bookmark, highlight and annotate text
- Access to thousands of pages of quality research at the click of a button.

REQUEST YOUR FREE INSTITUTIONAL TRIAL TODAY

Free Trials Available
We offer free trials to qualifying academic, corporate and government customers.

eCollections – Choose from over 30 subject eCollections, including:

Archaeology	Language Learning
Architecture	Law
Asian Studies	Literature
Business & Management	Media & Communication
Classical Studies	Middle East Studies
Construction	Music
Creative & Media Arts	Philosophy
Criminology & Criminal Justice	Planning
Economics	Politics
Education	Psychology & Mental Health
Energy	Religion
Engineering	Security
English Language & Linguistics	Social Work
Environment & Sustainability	Sociology
Geography	Sport
Health Studies	Theatre & Performance
History	Tourism, Hospitality & Events

For more information, pricing enquiries or to order a free trial, please contact your local sales team:
www.tandfebooks.com/page/sales

The home of Routledge books

www.tandfebooks.com